UNEQUAL PROTECTION

UNEQUAL PROTECTION

THE RISE OF CORPORATE DOMINANCE AND THE THEFT OF HUMAN RIGHTS

THOM HARTMANN

BK

Berrett–Koehler Publishers, Inc.
San Francisco
a BK Currents book

First published 2002. First published in paperback 2004. Reissued by Berrett-Koehler Publishers 2009.

Berrett-Koehler Publishers, Inc.
235 Montgomery Street, Suite 650, San Francisco, CA 94104-2916
Tel: (415) 288-0260 Fax: (415) 362-2512 www.bkconnection.com

Ordering Information
Quantity sales. Special discounts are available on quantity purchases by corporations, associations, and others. For details, contact the "Special Sales Department" at the Berrett-Koehler address above.
Individual sales. Berrett-Koehler publications are available through most bookstores. They can also be ordered directly from Berrett-Koehler: Tel: (800) 929-2929; Fax: (802) 864-7626; www.bkconnection.com.
Orders for college textbook/course adoption use. Please contact Berrett-Koehler: Tel: (800) 929-2929; Fax: (802) 864-7626.
Orders by U.S. trade bookstores and wholesalers. Please contact Ingram Publisher Services, Tel: (800) 509-4887; Fax: (800) 838-1149; E-mail: customer.service@ingrampublisherservices.com; or visit www.ingrampublisherservices.com/Ordering for details about electronic ordering.

Printed in the United States of America

ISBN 978-1-60509-571-4

Originally published by Rodale Inc. as ISBN 978-1-57954-627-4 (hardcover) and ISBN 978-1-57954-955-1 (paperback)

2009-1 dig

Internet addresses and telephone numbers given in this book were accurate at the time the book went to press.

Cover and Interior Designer: Christopher Rhoads

Dedicated to Jack and Norma Vance

CONTENTS

INTRODUCTION

It's really a wonder that I haven't dropped all my ideals, because they seem so absurd and impossible to carry out. Yet I keep them, because in spite of everything I still believe people are really good at heart.

—ANNE FRANK, FROM HER DIARY, JULY 15, 1944

This book is about the difference between humans and the corporations we humans have created. The story goes back to the birth of the United States, even to the birth of the Revolution. It continues through the writing of the Constitution and Bill of Rights in the 1780s and reaches its first climactic moment just under 100 years later, after the Civil War. The changes that ensued from that moment continue to unfold into the 21st century. And very few citizens of the world are unaffected.

In another sense, this book is about values and beliefs: how our values are reflected in the society we create, and how a society itself can work, or not work, to reflect those values.

INTENTIONS AND CULTURE

A culture is a collection of shared beliefs about how things are. These beliefs are associated with myths and histories that form a self-reinforcing loop, and the collection of these beliefs and histories form the stories that define a culture. Usually unnoticed, like the air we breathe, these stories are rarely questioned. Yet their impact can be enormous.

For example, for 6,000 to 7,000 years, since the earliest founding of what we call modern culture, there were the stories that "it's okay to own slaves, particularly if they are of a different race or tribe," and "women should be the property of, and subservient to, men."

But as time goes on, circumstances and cultures change: Beliefs that are questioned and aren't useful begin to fall away. This book will raise questions about some of our shared beliefs, asking, as many cultures have asked throughout history, "Do we want to keep this belief, or change to something that works better for us?"

THE STORY OF CORPORATE PERSONHOOD

Here we find the nub of this book, continuing a theme in my earlier writings. In *The Last Hours of Ancient Sunlight*, I identified those stories (among others) and suggested that true cultural change comes about when we first wake up to our own self-defeating beliefs . . . and then go about changing them. I also pointed out that the story that "we are separate and different from the natural world" is a toxic one, brought to us by Gilgamesh, then Aristotle, then Descartes, and it no longer serves us well.

In *The Prophet's Way*, I detailed how the story that "we are separate from divinity or consciousness" can perpetuate a helplessness and a form of spiritual slavery that are not useful for many individual humans or the planet as a whole. Mystics through the ages tell us a different story—the possibility of being personally connected to divinity. I suggested that, for many people, the mystic's story could be far more empowering and personally useful.

And in my books on Attention Deficit Disorder (ADD/ADHD), I suggested that neurologically different children are actually a useful asset to our culture (using Edison, Franklin, and Churchill as classic examples), and that we do ourselves a disservice—and we wound our children in the process—by telling them they have a brain disorder and tossing them into the educational equivalent of the trash basket. (And the most recent studies sponsored by the National Institutes of Mental Health are explicitly backing up my position.)

In *Unequal Protection*, I'm visiting the stories of democracy and corporate personhood—ones whose histories I only learned in detail while researching this book. (It's amazing what we *don't* learn in school!) Corporate personhood is the story that a group of people can get together and organize a legal fiction (that's the actual legal term for it) called a corporation—and that agreement could then have the rights and powers given to living, breathing humans by modern democratic governments. Democracy is the story of government of, by, and for the people; something, it turns out, that is very difficult to have function well in the same realm as corporate personhood.

A NEW BUT HIGHLY CONTAGIOUS STORY

Unlike the cultural stories I wrote about earlier, this last story is more recent. Corporate personhood tracks back in small form to Roman times when groups of people authorized by the Caesars organized to engage in trade. It took a leap around the year 1500 with the development of the first Dutch and then other European trading corporations, and then underwent a series of transformations in the United States of America in the 19th century, whose implications were every bit as world-changing as the institutionalization of slavery and the oppression of women in the holy books had been thousands of years earlier.

And in a similar fashion to the Biblical endorsement of slavery and oppression of women, this story of corporate personhood—which only came fully alive in the 1800s—was highly contagious: It has spread across most of the world in just the past half-century. It has—literally—caused some sovereign nations to rewrite their constitutions, and led others to sign treaties overriding previous constitutional protections of their human citizens.

GIVING BIRTH TO A NEW "PERSON"

Imagine: In today's America and most other democracies, when a new human is born, she is given a Social Security number (or its equivalent) and instantly, from the moment of birth, is protected by the full weight and power of the U. S. Constitution and the Bill of Rights (or their equivalent). Those rights, which have been fought for and paid for with the blood of our young men and women in uniform, fall fully upon her at the moment of birth.

This is the way we designed it; it's how we all agreed it should be. Humans get human rights. They're protected. We are, after all, fragile living things that can be suppressed and abused by the powerful, if not protected. And in American democracy, like most modern democracies, our system is set up so that it takes a lot of work to change the Constitution, making it very difficult to deny its protections to the humans it first protected against King George III and against numerous threats—internal and external—since then.

Similarly, when papers called articles of incorporation are submitted to governments in America (and most other nations of the world), another type of new "person" is brought forth into the nation (and most countries of the world). Just like a human, that new person gets a government-assigned number. (In the United States, instead of a Social Security number, it's called a Federal Employer Identification Number, or EIN.)

Under our current agreements, the new corporate person is instantly endowed with many of the rights and protections of personhood. It's neither male nor female, doesn't breathe or eat, can't be enslaved, can't give birth, can live forever, doesn't fear prison, and can't be executed if found guilty of misdoings. It can cut off parts of itself and turn them into new "persons," can change its identity in a day, and can have simultaneous residence in many different nations. It is not a human but a creation of humans. Nonetheless, the new corporation gets many of the constitutional protections America's Founders gave humans in the Bill of Rights to protect them against governments or other potential oppressors:

- Free speech, including freedom to influence legislation
- Protection from searches, as if their belongings were intensely personal
- Fifth Amendment protections against double jeopardy and self-incrimination, even when a clear crime has been committed
- The shield of the nation's due process and anti-discrimination laws
- The benefit of the constitutional amendments that freed the slaves and gave them equal protection under the law

Even more, although they now have many of the same "rights" as you and I—and a few more—they don't have the same fragilities or responsibilities, either under the law or under the realities of biology.

What most people don't realize is that this is a fairly recent agreement, a new cultural story, and *it hasn't always been this way*:

- Traditional English, Dutch, French, and Spanish law didn't say that corporations are people.
- The U. S. Constitution wasn't written with that idea; corporations aren't even mentioned.
- For America's first century, courts all the way up to the Supreme Court repeatedly said, "No, corporations do not have the same rights as humans."
- It's only since 1886 that the Bill of Rights and the Equal Protection Amendment have been explicitly applied to corporations.

Even more, corporate personhood was never formally enacted by any branch of the U. S. government:

- It was never voted by the public.
- It was never enacted by law.
- It was never even stated by a decision after arguments before the Supreme Court.

This last point will raise some eyebrows because for 100 years people have believed that the 1886 case *Santa Clara County v. Southern Pacific Railroad* did in fact include the statement "Corporations are persons." But this book will show that this was never stated by the Court: It was added by the court reporter who wrote the introduction to the decision, called headnotes. And as any law student knows, headnotes have no legal standing.

This book is about how that happened and what it has meant as events have unfolded. And, like most things that are bent from their original intentions, there have been many far-reaching consequences that were never intended. Constitutional mechanisms that were designed to protect humans got turned inside out, so today they do a much better job of protecting corporations, even when the result is *harm* to humans and other forms of life.

SHOULD WE KEEP THE STORY OF CORPORATE PERSONHOOD OR THE STORY OF DEMOCRACY?

The real issue, rarely discussed but always present, is whether corporations truly are *persons* in a democracy. Should they stand shoulder to shoulder with you and me in the arena of rights, responsibilities, and the unique powers and equal protections conferred upon humans by the founders and framers of the United States Constitution and other democracies around the world that have used the United States as a model? And is it possible to have a viable and thriving democracy if we keep the story of corporate personhood, or have we already lost much of our democracy as a result of it?

In researching this book, I was amazed to learn that America's Founders and early Presidents specifically warned that *the safety of the new republic depended on keeping corporations on a tight leash*—not abolishing them, but keeping them in check. When I showed early drafts of this book to different people, most of them were surprised to see how prophetic those early presidential warnings had been.

The essence of this book is the history of the corporation in America, its conflicts with democracy, and how corporate values and powers have come to dominate our world, for better or worse. Along the way over the past 2 centuries, those playing the corporate game at the very highest levels seem to have won a victory for themselves—a victory that is turning bitter in the mouths of many of the 6 billion humans on planet Earth. It's even turning bitter, in unexpected ways, for those who won it, as they find their own lives and families touched by an increasingly toxic environment, a fragile and top-heavy economy, and a hollow culture—all traceable back to the frenetic systems of big business that resulted from the doctrine that corporations are persons.

Corporations do much good in the world, and in my lifetime, I've started more than a dozen corporations, both for-profit and nonprofit. So it's important to say right up front that I'm not advocating dismantling the modern business corporation. It's a societal and business organizing system that has, in many ways, served us well, and has the potential to do much good in the future.

What I am suggesting, however, is that we should put corporations into their rightful context and place, as they had largely been until 1886. They are not human, even though they are owned and managed by humans. They are an agreement, not a living being. Corporations are just one of many methods humans can use to exchange goods, earn wealth, and create innovation; it's simply not appropriate that this single form should be granted "personhood" at a similar level to humans under the United States Constitution or that of any other nation that aspires to democracy.

It's my contention that corporations are not legally the same as natural persons, and that the 1886 Supreme Court reporter's comment in the *Santa Clara v. Southern Pacific Railroad* case was both in error and revealed a weakness in the Fourteenth Amendment that needs to be fixed by democratic citizen involvement today, if that is still possible.

As always, it's up to us to change the beliefs that no longer serve us. Indeed, in California and Pennsylvania, citizens have recently stood up and, through their local governments, begun to pass ordinances, laws, and resolutions that deny corporations the status of personhood. They don't ban corporations; they just say, "Corporations are not persons."

Why would this be such an issue? Why all the attention and effort?

If I've done my job well, by the end of this book your questions will be answered in full, and some positive, useful, forward-looking action steps will be well-heard, clearly visible, and in hand. And, perhaps, the world will have one less toxic story in circulation, as people wake up and take action to undo its consequences.

—Montpelier, Vermont

PROLOGUE

There's a new revolution happening in the United States, mirrored in communities all over the world, which has the potential to reshape the face of the planet.

It could make the world less toxic, people more free, children less anxious, and open literally millions of doors of opportunity for entrepreneurs, small-businesspeople, and medium-size companies.

"Nine states—most recently South Dakota and Nebraska—have adopted referenda prohibiting non-family-owned corporations from engaging in farming," says attorney Thomas Linzey of Chambersburg, Pennsylvania. His organization, the Community Environmental Legal Defense Fund, has helped eight township governments in Pennsylvania pass laws to keep out corporate factory farms.

But the revolution is not just about farming. "It's increasingly clear," Linzey says, "that the real issue is who, in a democracy, is supposed to make the basic decisions about community values, food production, and public health."

And who, in a democracy, should make such decisions? Who should have the right to vote and to influence the laws under which humans live? America's Declaration of Independence put it this way:

"We hold these Truths to be self-evident, that all Men are created equal, that they are endowed by their Creator with certain unalienable Rights, that among these are Life, Liberty, and the pursuit of Happiness—That to secure these rights, Governments are instituted among Men, deriving their just Powers from the Consent of the Governed . . ."

"Corporate governance is incompatible with people's ability to create sustainable democratic communities," according to Linzey. He and others in this growing worldwide movement argue that governments should be of, by, and for human people—not of, by, and for corporations.

But more than a century ago, something happened that gave corporations human rights. That's what people are working today to undo.

In Pennsylvania's Thompson Township, the Chairman of the elected Township Supervisors, Bruce Bivens said, "A person is a living thing and a corporation is not."

These are the first shots in a new American Revolution, one that will be fought with petitions and votes instead of guns and troops. It's a revolution to win back democracy.

PART 1
THE NATURE OF COMMUNITY, VALUES, AND GOVERNMENT

History has informed us that bodies of men, as well as individuals, are susceptible of the spirit of tyranny.

–THOMAS JEFFERSON, *A SUMMARY VIEW OF THE RIGHTS OF BRITISH AMERICA*, 1774

1

THE VALUES WE CHOOSE TO LIVE BY

All honor to Jefferson, to the man who in the concrete pressure of a struggle for national independence by a single people, had the coolness, forecast, and capacity to introduce into a merely revolutionary document, an abstract truth, and so to embolden it there, that today and in all coming days, it shall be a rebuke and a stumbling block to the very harbingers of reappearing tyranny and oppression.

—ABRAHAM LINCOLN, LETTER TO H. L. PIERCE, 1859, REFERRING TO JEFFERSON'S "DEVOTION TO THE PERSONAL RIGHTS OF MEN, HOLDING THE RIGHTS OF PROPERTY TO BE SECONDARY"

What's going on?

I love to walk, and I love rivers. Just in the past 8 months, I've walked over or along rivers in two cities in Australia, in England, in central Germany, boated around the canals of Amsterdam, visited a river near Vancouver, and briefly visited the Grand River in Michigan that my wife and I used to canoe 30 years ago when we were first married.

On most days, I take an afternoon walk into downtown Montpelier in central Vermont. On the way, I cross a bridge over the Winooski River, one of the larger rivers in the state, which flows to Lake Champlain and then through the St. Lawrence Seaway and out to the Atlantic.

All of these rivers, like most in the world, once teemed with fish and other wildlife. Early European visitors to North America reported that rivers from coast to coast were filled with fish; the plains thundered with the sound of buffalo, elk, and deer; the air was thick with birds and butterflies.

"The number of dead Salmon on the Shores & floating in the river is incredible to say," wrote William Clark in his journal on October 17, 1805, as he and Meriwether Lewis came upon an Indian tribe in the midst of a fishing expedition in the northwest. "And they have only to collect the fish, Split them open, and dry them on their Scaffolds on which they have great numbers. . . . The water of this river is clear, and a Salmon may be seen at the depth of 15 or 20 feet."

In visiting all the rivers I mentioned, though, I've never seen a salmon. And only rarely any other type of fish, for that matter. Because so many salmon rivers have crashed, over half the world's salmon now come from giant factory-farm fisheries where the fish are fed the dye astaxanthin to make their flesh pink and the sulfa and oxytetracycline antibiotics to increase yield.

For the few remaining wild fish, storm water runoff brings to the rivers of the modern world what Ben Davis of the Vermont Public Interest Research Group calls "a witches' brew of heavy metals, pesticides, herbicides, auto emissions, gasoline, and polyaromatic hydrocarbons."

Silt from upstream erosion wipes out fish breeding areas. Agricultural wastes, including liquefied manure and pesticides, find their way into the river. Drugs—from hormones to antibiotics to chemotherapy agents—pass through human and livestock kidneys intact, then through wastewater treatment facilities and into the river, where they make an impact on reproductive cycles and metabolic processes in aquatic wildlife.

Mercury and arsenic rain from skies contaminated by oil- and coal-burning power plants and toxic waste incinerators across the world. And as rainwater crosses dark asphalt parking lots and roads, it warms in the sun before passing into the rivers, raising their temperatures to the point where, as Davis points out, "stock fish often die within hours of being put into rivers."

At Lake Champlain, phosphorus from industrial and domestic wastewater promotes algal growth, sucking oxygen out of the waters and creating a few small "dead zones," and two-stroke engines from boats and jet skis dump over a half-million gallons of raw gasoline and oil every year.

And Vermont's rivers and lakes are among the cleanest and most beautiful in America, rich with wildlife compared with many in other states. As the World Water Council's vice president, William Cosgrove, told Reuters, "There is not a lake left on the planet that is not already being affected by human activities."

While government-mandated waterway cleanup in the developed world has made dramatic gains in the past 4 decades, the pressures of development and growth continue to threaten the world's rivers and lakes, producing, for example, a 7,000–square mile dead zone where the Mississippi River empties into the Gulf of Mexico. It's only one of many worldwide.

OTHER ECOSYSTEMS CRASH

In November 2001, the Associated Press reported that marine animal populations around the world are crashing. Worldwide fish catches declined by 26.5 percent between 1988 and 2001, and biologists with the U. S. Fish and Wildlife Service reported that "sea otters in the 1,000-mile long chain of islands known as the Aleutian chain that extends from the Alaska Peninsula had declined by about 70 percent since 1992." (Alaska's coastal waters are home to about 90 percent of the world's sea otters.)

Rainforests covered 15 percent of the Earth's surface in 1950. Today, it's less than half that, as more than 200,000 acres are cut or burned every single day. Yet the biodiversity of our rainforests is astounding. More different species of fish than exist in all of Europe's rivers can be found in a single pond in Brazil. There are more species of birds in one rainforest preserve in Peru than in the entire United States. While all of North America has about 700 species of trees, an equal number of different tree species can be found in just 25 acres of Borneo rainforest.

Half the world's plant and animal species live in endangered rainforests that now cover only 6 percent of the world's land surface, and the vast majority of these species have not yet been even cataloged or analyzed.

As the Pulitizer Prize–winning biologist E. O. Wilson of Harvard wrote 2 decades ago, "The one process ongoing in the 1980s that will take millions of years to correct is the loss of genetic and species diversity by the destruction of natural habitats. This is the folly that our descendants are least likely to forgive us for."

At current rates of destruction, the world's rainforests—with all their plants and animals and planetwide weather-controlling canopies of trees—are expected to be more than 90 percent wiped out by the year 2030.

Human assault of the forests began millennia ago, and is first chronicled in the oldest known written story, *The Epic of Gilgamesh*, when the first king of the first city-state—Gilgamesh of Sumeria about 6,000 years ago—cut down the forests of Lebanon and destroyed his own people by the desertification that followed that act.

Delphin M. Delmas, a California attorney you'll meet again in this book, described his first encounter with a redwood forest in the 1800s. "Your first feeling is one of awe. Your very breath seems hushed by the solemn stillness of the place. Here the winds are mute. Their distant murmurings are unheard within the depths of the shaded solitude. Your step falls noiseless upon the thick carpet of marl—the cast off vesture of countless seasons—upon which you tread. The crackling of a twig under your foot or the startled cry of a frightened bird but intensifies the silence which enfolds you like a shroud . . .

"A sense of humility overwhelms you as you gaze upon these massy pillars of Nature's temple, whose tops, lost amid the clouds, seem to support the vault of the blue empyrean. The spell, which the mystic light of some venerable cathedral may at times have thrown upon your soul, is tame compared to that which binds you here. That was man's place of worship; this is God's.

"In the presence of these Titanic offsprings of Nature, standing before you in the hoar austerity of centuries, how dwarfed seems your being, how fleeting your existence! They were here before you were born; and though you allow you thoughts to go back on the wings of imagination to your remotest ancestry, you realize that they were here when your first forefather had his being.

"All human work which you have seen or conceived of is recent in comparison. Time has not changed them since Columbus first erected an altar upon this continent, nor since Titus builded the walls of the Flavian amphitheater, nor since Solomon laid the foundations of the temple at Jerusalem. They were old when Moses led the children of Israel to the Promised Land, or when Egyptian monarchs piled up the pyramids and bade the Sphinx gaze with eyes of perpetual sadness over the desert sands of the Valley of the Nile.

"And if their great mother, Nature, is permitted still to protect them, here they will stand defying time when not a stone of this Capitol is left to mark the spot on which it now stands, and its very existence may have faded into the mists of tradition."

In the United States, forest cutting reached a fevered pitch in the late 19th and early 20th centuries, just before oil came to fully replace wood as a primary energy source. And even at that time, the redwoods were being cut for building materials at a rapid rate. As Delmas said, "You experience a feeling of profound sadness as you conjure up the picture of these venerable trees hacked and shivered, to become the commonplace materials of barter and trade. As you behold their lofty foliage stirred by the ocean breeze, you seem to hear them murmur a prayer to be saved from such desecration."

Delmas was so outraged by the clear-cutting of California's 2,000-year-old redwoods that he took on the case, pro bono, of fighting the loggers in the courts while working to pass laws to protect the ancient trees.

His speech to the California legislature, which resulted in the 1901 law preserving the remaining redwood forests, ended with an impassioned plea: "The slopes which surround this forest are already denuded. The work of devastation has reached the very edge of these woods.

"There, even while I speak, the axman stands ready to strike. If he pauses, it is only to await your decision. Two years from now his work will be done, and the last remaining fragment of the primeval trees, which clothe the mountains rising up at the very threshold of our metropolis, will have vanished. Vain, then, will be our regrets, and all attempts to repair the evil, vain. . . .

"Man's work, if destroyed, man may again replace. God's work God alone can re-create. Accede, then, to the prayers of the people. Save this forest. Save it now. The present generation approves the act; generations yet unborn, in grateful appreciation of your labors, will rise up to consecrate its consummation."

Delmas saved the last of the redwoods . . . until just a few decades ago, when cutting began anew.

HOW IS IT HAPPENING?

Given that poisoned waterways, clear-cut rainforests and redwoods, and dying oceans aren't healthy or aesthetic for humans (much less any other life form), why are they happening? Why are our air, food, and water so toxic that about a third of Americans will develop cancer in their lifetimes? Why are Third World nations being turned into toxic wastelands around industrial sites too dirty to exist in developed nations?

It's not just a problem of population or too many humans. It is, instead, a problem of values and law, a recent story in our culture.

Some among we humans have organized themselves together and formed a relatively new entity—the corporation—as a vehicle to accumulate wealth while minimizing risks and responsibilities. And a tiny percentage of these corporations have become so big and gained so much influence that they've effectively taken control of the governments the humans set up to *protect* themselves from tyranny—from forces that were too big for individuals to resist on their own.

Hiding behind the legal shield of government regulations that this elite corps themselves often helped write or lobbied to put in place, they have embarked on courses of action that are now collectively wiping out life forms across the planet even as they imperil the humans who created them. This book will explain how this came to be, will document some of the human harm that has resulted, and will lay out a plan for returning to our Founders' values.

It's not that this is the only way companies can "give people what they want." Technology is now so well advanced that virtually every area of industrial production and urban management can be done in far less toxic ways than we are currently following.

And it's important to note that the term *wealth*, which is what corporations are established to aggregate, comes from the Middle English term *welthe*, itself derived from the Old English *weal*, which was used to refer to one's state of well-being or the well-being of the commons (thus the *Commonwealth of Massachusetts*, for example).

It almost seems as if the world had been taken over by nonliving entities in a science fiction story—beings that look at everything as a resource to be tapped until it's used up, without consideration for how it affects any other living thing. Indeed, some time ago I suggested that the new and ascendant values of the world seemed like those of emotionless robots.

But a friend pointed out that when science fiction legend Isaac Asimov wrote his Three Laws of Robotics in 1950, the First Law said that robots must never harm human beings. Asimov later extended his model, adding a "Zeroth Law" that was even more important: Above all else, robots must not injure *humanity*. So the results we have today wouldn't even be consistent with the values given to Asimov's robots!

So again we ask, what values *do* allow this? What rules are we living by?

CORPORATE VALUES VERSUS HUMAN VALUES

"It's the hardest thing that I've ever dealt with in my life," B. J. Kincade told me from her home in Tulsa, Oklahoma. Her Web site, www.nocrashnoburn.com, tells what happened in her own words.

"The story began for my family on April 10, 1989. It was one of those unforgettably beautiful Oklahoma spring days: warm, calm, beautiful, sun shining, with the after-winter promise of many fair days soon to come. My son, Jim, had a side-impact collision in his 1984 . . . pickup with the now-infamous sidesaddle gas tanks. The collision exploded the unprotected gas tank on impact. His truck went up in a ball of flame and he had no chance to get out."

"He survived the accident?" I said.

"And he died in the fire," she said. Jim Kincade was one of over 1,800 Americans who died in such automotive fires because one of America's largest automakers chose to ignore the advice of their engineers and listened instead to their marketing department. To produce a truck that would hold 40 gallons of gasoline—thus having twice the gas capacity and range of their competitors—that company mounted the gas tanks in pickup trucks on the sides of the vehicle, outside the heavy steel frame that protects the rest of the interior of the vehicle.

The other two large American auto manufacturers turned down the idea because it could turn a truck into a rolling firebomb in a side-impact collision. An internal engineering report from one of the companies that chose not to use sidesaddle gas tanks said, "A frame-mounted fuel tank mounted on the outside of the frame rail is not acceptable. . . . Any side impact would automatically encroach on this area and the probability of tank leakage would be extremely high."

The corporation that made B. J. Kincade's son's pickup, however, had commissioned an analysis of the cost of making the fuel tanks safe. It would have cost the company $2.20 per truck to make safer gas tanks, according to one of their chief engineers. Given the millions of additional trucks they would sell to capitalize on this market, however, it would be cheaper to pay death benefits than to build a safe pickup.

The story came out in documents pried out of the company with a lawsuit initiated by Kincade and supported by Ralph Nader's Center for Auto Safety, although to this day the automaker has succeeded in keeping from Kincade the identity of the person or persons who made that fateful decision. "I wish I knew," she said, but odds are she'll never find out.

Thinking of the 1,800 fiery deaths that resulted from this decision, deaths that company anticipated and accepted, one is forced to ask: How is it that a decision like this could be made by one of the most impressive human enterprises in the world? What value system drives humans to such inhuman decisions?

To a large extent, today's legal foundation for the problem started in America in the 1800s. But in no way is it limited to America. We no longer live in a world where local actions—even a Supreme Court decision—produce solely local results.

CORPORATIONS PURSUING THEIR VALUES ACROSS THE WORLD

It's beyond the scope of this book to review the many well-documented cases of what happens when indigenous peoples seek to keep their land in the face of encroaching multinational oil, gold, uranium, logging, and mining corporations. Suffice it to say that the stories have much in common with the history of Native Americans, except that the language has been updated. Today, when people rise up and protest exploitation of themselves or the natural resources of their lands—even local and peaceful protests—they can be branded terrorists and the full weight of police, prisons, and armies is used against them.

This book isn't about those stories, it's about the underlying legal issues. But two contemporary stories illustrate the situation the world is in, broadening the case for action.

I personally experienced how angry these "invasions" can make the people whose lands and lives are affected.

We'd spent the day walking through the refugee camps of Uganda in East Africa, watching people die of malnutrition, malaria, and a dozen other diseases associated with the consequences of war and famine.

It was 1981, and Dick Gregory, the comedian and activist, had accompanied me to Uganda to view the devastation left in the wake of the Tanzanian invasion that expelled Idi Amin. I was working as a volunteer with the international Salem Children's Trust relief organization, and Dick was on our advisory board. I'd been in Uganda a year earlier, and had returned with Dick to see how our new famine-relief station in Mbale was doing, and to enlist Dick's help in our fund-raising efforts for the orphans of the war.

We were staying in Kampala, which was, at the time, a city slowly recovering from the ravages of both Amin and the recent war. There had been no consistent running water in 2 years, and electricity was sporadic. The sun sets quickly on the equator, the transition from daylight to night being so abrupt as to catch a person unawares, and after night fell, bands of teenage

Tanzanian soldiers and a newly forming Ugandan army, often dressed in rags and carrying Soviet-made AK-47 assault rifles, enforced a rigid curfew by gleefully shooting at anything or anybody who moved. The nights were sometimes punctuated by rapid-fire rifle shots and occasional screams. In the mornings, during my two visits to Uganda, we sometimes stepped over bodies on the Kampala sidewalks before going up north to the camps where the refugee situation was the worst.

Our second day in Kampala, Dick remembered that he had a relative who knew a former Ugandan diplomat. We made inquiries through our host, the Minister of Rehabilitation, and got the diplomat's address. He lived about a block from our hotel, and when we stopped at his house we learned he was out but would be back that night.

It was the end of the day, just after sunset, and we were safely back in our bulletproof cinder block hotel. In a characteristic burst of enthusiasm, Dick said, "Let's go visit that guy!"

"We'll get shot trying to run through the streets!" I said.

He grinned at me with a twinkle in his eye. "We're faster than them. I got a scholarship to Southern Illinois University as a runner! Can you keep up with me?"

I didn't answer because he was already halfway out the door.

Out of breath but still alive, we arrived at the home of the diplomat. He was a gentle man in his mid-sixties, and lived in a home that had once been elegant but had, during the war, been robbed of many of its furnishings. Our host's skin was the beautiful deep chocolate color of so many Ugandans, his hair graying, his carriage erect although he was thin and frail. After some small talk about Dick's relation, the discussion turned to the current government of Milton Obote, and then to Idi Amin, who had converted to Islam and therefore was then (and is now) living in a palace in Saudi Arabia.

I made a comment about Amin's brutality, and this very gentle man turned fierce. "You have no right to speak of Amin," he said, his voice thick with anger, his finger in my face. "It was your companies who kept him in power, who helped cover up his crimes, who flew in supplies for his cronies, and who paid for his torture chambers. He murdered over 100,000 of my countrymen, some of them my relatives. Long after it was obvious to us and to the world what kind of a monster he was, your companies—which had the power at any time to dispose of him by simply stopping their trade with him—helped him keep our people in terror and slavery."

It was a searing indictment, and I sat back in the old sofa, shocked. "I didn't have anything to do with that," I said lamely.

"You drank coffee and ate sugar," he said, trembling. "You had complicity even if you didn't know it. You could have found out. You could have stopped him."

"I'm sorry," I said, looking at the stained old Persian rug on the floor.

Dick moved the discussion in another direction and the evening became pleasant, as if the old man had relieved himself of some deep burden. After a few hours talk, we said our goodbyes and ran like madmen to make it back to our hotel without getting shot.

It was that evening that I realized how fully, in many regards, multinational corporations have become the tail that wags the dogs of the governments of the world.

FROM UGANDA TO NIGERIA

It's not just American companies who are playing this role around the world. In Nigeria, a European corporation pumps crude oil that provides much of the revenues that supported a corrupt and brutal military regime, not unlike the situation I saw in Uganda. When the people of the Ogoni tribe rose up to oppose the despoiling of their lands, their leaders were arrested and tried—by a military tribunal. Nigerian author Ken Saro-Wiwa, said in his closing statement of his trial:

"We all stand before history. I am a man of peace, of ideas. Appalled by the denigrating poverty of my people who live on a richly endowed land, distressed by their political marginalization and economic strangulation, angered by the devastation of their land, their ultimate heritage, anxious to preserve their right to life and to a decent living, and determined to usher to this country as a whole a fair and just democratic system which protects everyone and every ethnic group and gives us all a valid claim to human civilization, I have devoted my intellectual and material resources, my very life, to a cause in which I have total belief and from which I cannot be blackmailed or intimidated. . . .

"On trial also is the Nigerian nation, its present rulers and those who assist them. Any nation which can do to the weak and disadvantaged what the Nigerian nation has done to the Ogoni, loses a claim to independence and to freedom from outside influence. I am not one of those who shy away from protesting injustice and oppression, arguing that they are expected in a military regime. The military do not act alone. They are supported by a gaggle of politicians, lawyers, judges, academics and businessmen, all of them hiding under the claim that they are only doing their duty, men and women too afraid to wash their pants of urine. We all stand on trial, my lord, for by our actions we have denigrated our Country and jeopardized the future of our children. As we subscribe to the sub-normal and accept double standards, as we lie and cheat openly, as we protect injustice and oppression, we empty our classrooms, denigrate our hospitals, fill our stomachs with hunger and elect to make ourselves the slaves of those who ascribe to higher standards, pursue the truth, and honor justice, freedom, and hard work.

"I predict that the scene here will be played and replayed by generations yet unborn. Some have already cast themselves in the role of villains, some are tragic victims, some still have a chance to redeem themselves. The choice is for each individual."

On November 10, 1995, after 17 months in prison, and despite the protests of Nelson Mandela and governments and civil rights groups around the world, the Nigerian military government executed Ken Saro-Wiwa and eight other Ogoni activists. Ken's last words were "Lord take my soul, but the struggle continues."

What does the oil company say of this? Its Web site says (as of this writing) they "can not interfere in domestic politics," although they do note that as a company they had said Ken had a right to freely hold and air his views, that the company publicly supported a fair legal process for him, and that the former chairman of the company had sent a letter to the Nigerian Head of State appealing for clemency for Ken on humanitarian grounds after the trial.

It must be noted that this oil company has done better than any of the others in the region—after the executions, human rights group Amnesty International said this was the *only* company in Nigeria that has acknowledged *any* corporate responsibility for upholding human rights. Yet as of this writing, 7 years after the executions, they continue to pump oil in Nigeria, while the government of Nigeria continues to perpetrate human rights abuses.

But the oil company is simply doing what it was chartered to do—earn a profit extracting oil, wherever it can be found. There's no mystery; that's what the owners (the shareholders) hire executives to do, through the board of directors.

A HUNT FOR UNDERSTANDING, NOT VILLAINS

Before we pursue this question further, I need to make an important point: My purpose in this book is not to identify "culprits"—it's to point out a flaw in our social system, and propose a solution. There are no villains here.

During the Victorian era, a four-part story structure became popular; it was called the villain story. The model was that a social ill was identified, then a villain was identified who was responsible for it. In part three, the villain would be destroyed or have a change of heart, so that in the end, the social ill was eliminated. A good example is Charles Dickens' Victorian-era story of Ebenezer Scrooge, *A Christmas Carol.*

Victorian-era villain stories implicitly assumed that specific humans are to blame for societal problems. Part of the social shortsightedness of the era (perhaps of every era) was that nobody thought to examine the structure of the era's *institutions* as a source of problems. Instead, the cause was laid at the feet of individual people.

Similarly today, there are those who suggest that corporations that are convicted of crimes or misdoings (and some of the largest corporations in the world have been convicted of substantial crimes) committed their wrongs because of rogue humans. "If only ethical people ran the company," the refrain goes, "then the problems would be solved."

But there is no use trying to find villains, because the problem is in the structure of the situation.

Executives of some corporations today make decisions and issue orders that degrade our environment, infiltrate and manipulate cultural institutions (government, universities, even charities) for their own benefit, and abuse workforces, even children, in Third World factories that rival the abuses written about by Dickens. But the problem, at its deepest level, is not one of human nature or of human villains.

Instead, as we will see, when these abuses happen, the human harm that results—whether it affects the citizens of Vermont or B. J. Kincade's son or children in Indonesian sweatshops—arises from a combination of two factors.

First is the nature and structure of corporate charters and the growing reality that corporate purpose in today's world is increasingly singularly focused on seeking profits and shareholder dividends, without attaching any measurable value to other considerations.

But this in and of itself isn't the heart of the problem—that same structure embraces millions of small, ethically profitable companies. Running a for-profit company that's beneficial to humans and the community is not just possible: *it's normal*. Entrepreneurs and small companies have historically been the engines that have fueled the great majority of new jobs, new economic opportunity, and innovation.

THE UNINTENDED OUTCOME

The problem comes when this singular purpose of profits is combined with rights, personhood, and massive size, so that an imbalance results—an imbalance that was never intended by those who wrote the laws that authorize the existence of corporations.

This combination, warned about by U. S. presidents from Jefferson to Eisenhower, places the corporation in a position of unbalanced power over human citizens and allows it to manipulate governments, which then lose their connections to their own citizens and instead become instruments to further the corporate agenda of accumulating wealth.

Much of this happens where we don't see it. Many large American corporations have set up the environmentally dirty or labor-intensive parts of their operations just over the border in Mexico, or in South America or Asia, while keeping their corporate headquarters in relatively pristine U. S. suburban areas. The poor people who do the labor aren't stockholders, so their concern over their local environment, or their protests over wages that often top out at a dollar an hour, are invisible to the U. S. stockholders.

The market even rewards such corporate actions: When companies export jobs to the developing world, their stock often goes up. Within the context of a cultural story of *profit as the prime objective*, such companies are not acting immorally or improperly. In many cases, humans and other life forms only figure into the equation when the company is penalized, and then only as items on the balance sheet or profit-and-loss statement.

Increasingly, today, the bottom-line question for the world's democracies is, "Whose values will determine the future of the planet and her occupants—people or corporations?

First, let's examine where government comes from. After all, once upon a time there was no government—only people. What happened? What is the role of government?

2

BANDING TOGETHER FOR THE COMMON GOOD: CORPORATIONS, GOVERNMENT, AND "THE COMMONS"

A corporation has no rights except those given it by law. It can exercise no power except that conferred upon it by the people through legislation, and the people should be as free to withhold as to give, public interest and not private advantage being the end in view.

—WILLIAM JENNINGS BRYAN

In the beginning, there were *people*.

For thousands of years, it was popular among philosophers, theologians, and social commentators to suggest that the first humans lived as disorganized, disheveled, terrified, cold, hungry, and brutal lone-wolf beasts. But both the anthropological and archeological records prove it a lie.

Even our cousins the apes live in organized societies, and evidence of cooperative and social living is as ancient as the oldest hominid remains. For 100,000 years or more, even before the origin of Homo sapiens, around the world we primates have organized ourselves into various social forms, ranging from families to clans to tribes to nations and empires.

As psychologist Abraham Maslow and others have pointed out, the value system of humans is first based on survival. Humans must breathe air, eat food, drink water, make ourselves warm, and sleep safely. Once the basic survival and safety needs are accounted for, we turn to our social needs—family, companionship, love, and intellectual stimulation. And when those are covered, we work to fulfill our spiritual or personal needs for growth.

Our institutions reflect this hierarchy of needs. Families, be they tribal nomads or suburban yuppies, first attend to food, water, clothing and shelter needs. Then they consider transportation, social interaction, and livelihood. And when those basics are covered, our families turn to our intellectual and spiritual needs.

THE THREE LEGAL ENTITIES

As populations grew, particularly in agriculture-based societies, humans recognized that some form of centralized coordination was needed to keep societies organized, defended, and provided for. Thus government was born.

The value system of governments is always rooted in the survival and well-being of humans (or, at the very least, the survival and well-being of those who control the government). If big projects needed to be done, from building aqueducts to raising pyramids to conquering foreign lands, either the government undertook the task or it was financed and organized by wealthy individuals or churches made up of congregations of people functioning as a form of government. This was pretty much the way the world worked until the mid-1800s, with only a few exceptions.

Thus, there were historically two distinctly different legal entities: *humans and families*, and the *governments* they created. (Religious institutions, until the last 4 centuries or so, operated either as governments or as families/clans. King David ruled a theocratic kingdom, and the popes and mullahs and gurus exercised political authority over their followers. Those that didn't rise to such power worked as a social collection of humans that was functionally an extended family or tribe.)

Some of our governments have been pretty tyrannical, but even they rarely behaved in ways that were openly and directly toxic to the survival of all humans. Even the most brutal, despotic regimes operated in a way to ensure that water supplies were intact, food continued to flow, and those in power had a place to sleep. There were often huge disparities in the quality of these commodities between the least and most powerful in the society, but at least the humans who controlled them kept in mind the full spectrum of human needs. When they failed to, they either collapsed or were overthrown, as we see in a long line of civilizations that have risen and then collapsed.

It's instructive to consider how various governments have come to power. For about the last 6,000 years, it's happened in one of two ways. Either someone claimed divine authority from the god or gods of those people, or a warlord seized power with brute force.

RULED BY THE GODS

A good example of leadership by divine appointment is the Japanese empire. The oldest Japanese history books, the *Kojiki* and *Nihon Shoki*, explicitly say that the first emperor was crowned at least 2,660 years ago because he was a descendant of the Sun Goddess, Amaterasu Omikami, the greatest of the goddesses in the Japanese Shinto religion. The lineage from that first emperor to today's Japanese emperor is believed to be unbroken, although during the intervening millennia the emperors have often shared power with warlords or Shoguns.

Similarly, the Inca ruler Pachacuti organized the Inca into a huge empire in the early 15th century after claiming that he was a direct descendant of the Sun God, Inti.

While the Catholic line of popes couldn't claim a birth-lineage back to the first person they recognized as a human descendant of God, they do claim direct lineage by appointment and blessing. Like the Japanese and Incan emperors, the popes used the powers that come with divine claims to rule much of Europe for millennia. Claiming divine inspiration, they started numerous wars and repeatedly mustered military forces and policelike agencies.

Similar scenarios have played out in nearly every part of the world where agriculture-based cultures have risen to power.

RULED BY WARLORDS

Taking power by military conquest is such a familiar story that it hardly seems necessary to recount it. But it's interesting to personally witness artifacts of the warlord days, before there were war machines and weapons of mass destruction. It makes real the fact that long ago, people came to power by expanding the area they controlled.

When my family and I lived in rural Germany in 1986 and 1987, a pleasant weekend walk through the forest took us to the ruins of an ancient castle called Nordeck. It's been a ruin for nearly 1,000 years, surrounded now by a deep forest, on a steep hillside overlooking the Steinach River. But back in the 10th century, local warlords controlled commerce in that region of the Frankenwald by their control of the river.

From small starts like this, early in the history of modern Europe, local warlords took over increasingly large areas of land, building larger and larger armies and castles, conquering first villages and then states and then entire nations.

Similar scenarios played out in Asia as the Chinese emperors rose to power, and then the Huns attacked and were turned back by them. The Huns headed west to Europe and aided the Goths in defeating the Roman army, led by Emperor Valens, at Adrianople in 378 A.D. Warlords were on the march.

RULED BY WARLORDS *FROM* THE GODS

Often when warlords took over an area, they would claim that their victory was the will of the local god and/or goddess. A few years ago, my wife, Louise, and I saw an ancient sign of this when we were walking through the temples at Luxor in Egypt, and came across a set of hieroglyphic inscriptions on one wall that were clearly of a different style and period than those surrounding them. We asked an archeologist friend, Ahmed Abdelmawgood Fayed, what the hieroglyphs meant, and he said that the Greek-born Alexander the Great had them carved into the wall after his conquest of the region.

"The hieroglyphics say that he was descended from the Egyptian god Amun, the greatest of the gods," Ahmed said. Claiming lineage from Amun was Alexander's way of consolidating his local power among the Amun-worshiping Egyptians.

The warlord-blessed-by-divinity strategy played out in much of the world. To this day, on British coins you will find the inscription D.G. REG. F.D. The D.G. stands for *Dei Gratia*, Latin for "by the grace of God;" REG is short for *Regina*, or "Queen" in Latin; and the F.D. represents *Fidei Defensor*, "defender of the faith."

As British attorney and author L. L. Blake notes in defense of the British system, "That is a good description of the natural order: First of all, there is

God, and it is by His Grace that we have our system of Government; then there is the Queen, whose rule is utter service to the goodness which exists in men; finally there is the faith of the people, which needs to be maintained and defended."

DEMOCRATIC GOVERNMENTS AND REPUBLICS

The first documented rise of democracy came in response to a warlord-governor, Peisistratus, who seized power in Athens three different times during the 6th century BCE (which stands for "Before the Common Era," a term equivalent to BC that is increasingly preferred by historians). A hundred years after the Greek poet and statesman Solon suggested a constitutional reform package with democratic aspects, in 508 BCE the Greek politician Cleisthenes successfully led a radical reform movement that brought about the first democratic constitution in Athens the next year.

Over the next 50 years, Ephialtes and Pericles presided over an increasingly democratic form of government that finally—for the first time in the history of what we call civilization—brought to power people from the poorest parts of Athenian society.

Most people today don't realize how brief that democratic experiment in Athens was. It came to an end in 322 BCE, when the warlord Alexander the Great conquered the nation. Later, it fell under the rule of Rome.

THE AMERICAN MODEL

Democracy wouldn't return to Greece for over 2,000 years, in the Greek Revolution of 1821, which was largely inspired by and patterned after the American and French Revolutions.

Those revolutions brought forth the idea that governments should overtly and explicitly be controlled by and operate to the benefit of their citizens. When the Declaration of Independence said, "Governments are instituted among Men, deriving their just Powers from the Consent of the Governed," it was quite a departure from the governments that maintained authority through raw power or "divine right" (backed up by force). The new model was what Abraham Lincoln described in his Gettysburg Address as "government of the people, by the people, for the people."

It's important to understand how different this was from all previous governments because it illustrates the priorities of the people who framed American government and set in place the beginnings of modern democracies worldwide.

Being learned men, they knew well the long history of popes, czars, kaisers, and kings who had claimed the divine right of rule, usually with one official state religion, and they were determined that such a thing would never arise in their part of North America. When the Bill of Rights was framed, the very first amendment guaranteed that individuals are free to practice the religion of their choice. And it doesn't stop there—it explicitly keeps government *out* of the religion business by declaring, "Congress shall make no law respecting an establishment of religion."

Clearly, the founders were focused on protecting the freedom, rights, and liberty of the individual, in the model of Ephialtes and Pericles—the last elected officials to have explicitly governed in such a fashion.

THE THIRD ENTITY ARISES: CORPORATIONS

Meanwhile, back in the 1500s, European kingdoms had concluded that there were some human enterprises that were beyond the scope of government. This included organized religions, charities, international trade, and projects like discovering and administering distant lands.

The need for this started with problems like the ownership of land and other large assets including buildings or ships. Governments could own things, and people could own things, but if a church or a business wanted land and buildings, historically it had been the property of either a local government (usually a town) or a family. This brought up problems of government involvement in religion and trade, and issues of who in a family would inherit what.

A third type of entity was necessary to enable owning property independent of either the government or any one particular person or family. It was called the *corporation*, and is today the third legal entity in the triad that begins with humans and then continues with their two subordinate agents: governments and corporations. This new corporate entity was, of course, not something that was physically real; it was an agreement, a so-called legal fiction authorized by a government.

The first corporations were the Dutch trading companies, chartered in the 1500s. They came into being by declaration of the government, but were owned and operated by wealthy and powerful individuals. The corporation had a status that allowed it to own land, to participate in the legal process, and to hold assets such as bank accounts. It could buy and sell things.

But while even 16th-century European kingdoms were acknowledging that humans had at least some "natural rights," corporations were explicitly limited to those rights *granted* them by the governments that authorized them. In the early days, everybody knew that corporations weren't governments or humans. They were few and far between until the Industrial Revolution.

The United States Constitution doesn't mention the word "corporation," leaving the power to authorize the creation of corporations to the states. The Founders were far more worried about governments usurping human rights and privileges than they were worried about corporations taking over. They had put the East India Company in its place with the Boston Tea Party, and that, they thought, was the end of that.

American revolutionaries Thomas Paine and Thomas Jefferson, and decades later even the French observer Alexis de Tocqueville, fretted about a return of despotic government to America, running roughshod over the rights of citizens. Few, however, seriously considered the possibility of corporations rising up to take over the people of the world and then to take control of the people's governments. It was only after he had left the presidency that Thomas Jefferson wrote in 1816 about the rise of power of the "moneyed corporations."

"THE COMMONS" AS A LIMITED RESOURCE

In colonial times and before, a piece of land that was subject to common use was called a commons. The famous Boston Common is one example: It was originally the common grazing ground for the townspeople's cattle. The peculiar twisting streets of old Boston reflect the cow paths that were used as people walked their cattle to and from the Common.

The metaphor of the commons has been extended over the years to embrace all sorts of shared resources (as listed at the end of this chapter). The nature of a commons and how it's been considered at different times in history is central to the issue of why we have government in the first place, for the common welfare.

In 1883, William Forster Lloyd published an essay titled "The Tragedy of the Commons." It was, in part, a response to the Darwinist theory of economics that was then popular in England, which suggested that if the rich were unconstrained in their activities, the result would be a social benefit because the strong would survive and social benefits would trickle down.

Lloyd, writing 100 years after Adam Smith, said it wasn't so; people acting in their self-interest would deplete the commons. He wrote, "Suppose two persons to have a common purse, to which each may freely resort" (in other words, from which each may take as much as he wants).

With this limited common bag of money, Lloyd said, neither man has an incentive to keep adding to it. The result would be predatory behavior—whoever took the most coins out of the bag the fastest would end up the richest—and, as Lloyd said, "the motive for economy entirely vanishes."

Author Garret Hardin, in his 1968 essay of the same title, revived Lloyd's work for a worldwide public. He pointed out how Lloyd had used the example of a pastureland used in common by several shepherds. So long as the shepherds and their sheep are few in number, the pastureland is easily shared and rejuvenated. If one of the shepherds, however, were to dramatically increase the size of his flock, it could cause the pastureland to be wiped out, both for him and for the other shepherds.

Even decisions made on a much smaller scale—each person adding one animal at a time—would result in depletion, Hardin said, because for each farmer, buying another animal *seems* to benefit each one of them . . . until the commons is wiped out by overgrazing. Notice that this argument rests on two assumptions, neither of which was widely held in 18th-century America.

The first is that the commons are limited, so it would be possible for humans to use up so much of the available resources that the commons could collapse. This might be true in a single town, with a single grazing ground, but in those days the world as a whole seemed so vast that it was ludicrous to imagine running out.

The second assumption was that people will always operate in their own self-interest, even when it means they violate the interests of others or the interests of the community as a whole.

It's easy to see the importance of these assumptions in understanding the roles of governments and individuals regarding the commons. It speaks directly to the issue of our spoiled waterways, our spoiled air, and even the impact of business decisions on local communities in the sweatshop countries.

THE LIMITLESS COMMONS

In 1776, humans had been around for at least 100,000 years, but the population of the world was less than a billion. North America was so vast as to be almost unimaginable to the European mind. (Imagine if we today discovered a new planet we could live on, several times bigger than our own—we would think all our problems were solved.)

It was so vast that most of it had never even been surveyed or mapped by Europeans. The rivers teemed with fish, the forests were full of game, the prairies were thick with buffalo and elk. When human waste was dumped into rivers, it seemed to have no appreciable effect; it simply vanished. The smokestacks of the Industrial Revolution had not yet begun to foul America's air.

This was a starkly different view from what Lloyd and Hardin said later: In 1776, the American commons seemed limitless. It was on this assumption that Jefferson and Madison fought so hard to keep government small, limited, and uninvolved even in matters of commerce.

But as humans began to use coal and oil to aggressively convert the commons of the world to cropland, and the bountiful food supply fed an explosion of human populations, things changed. It's estimated that the world hit its first billion people in 1800, just as industry was beginning to take hold in America. The planet had 2 billion humans in 1930, doubling its population in just 130 years. The third billion humans took only 30 years to add, by 1960. The fourth billion came in 14 years (1974), and the fifth billion in just 13 years (1987). In the 13 years between 1987 and 1999, we added fully another billion humans to reach 6 billion as the century and the millennium turned.

The first 2 billion people took 100,000 years. The next 2 billion took 44 years. The next 2 billion took 27. The human "flock" has increased beyond the ability of the "pasture" to easily support it. The proof of this is that over 2 billion people (twice the population of the entire planet in Jefferson's day) will go to sleep tonight malnourished, knowing that tomorrow and most likely for the rest of their lives they will have no access to safe water or sanitation.

Many of our Founders believed that the limited commons was not a valid assumption, and the discovery of North America had turned Lloyd's argument on its side. Today, with six times as many people on the same planet, no matter how much we may love our Founders' ideals and rhetoric, in this arena the standards they defined for management of the "commons" no longer apply.

ENLIGHTENED SELF-INTEREST

The other idea popular among America's Founders was that a wise and informed electorate, and the politicians they elect, would reliably behave with "enlightened self-interest" or, as Alexis de Tocqueville wrote in 1840, "self-interest rightly understood." This was the opposite of Lloyd and Hardin's assumption that people will ultimately act as selfish individuals once population becomes great enough to strain a commons.

The core of the early American ideal was that every individual would see themselves as part of a larger community, and so would make decisions in the best interest of the entire community. The community serves the individual needs, while the individual serves the community needs. (It was an early form of a principle Karl Marx would later state as "From each according to his abilities, to each according to his needs.")

Such sentiments have been echoed in writings ranging from Thomas Jefferson to Ayn Rand to contemporary conservative pundits. They're at the core of Libertarian philosophy as preached by Rand.

And, in small communities, they work. There's some fascinating math that may underlie this, something that's suggestive of a key factor that's shifted as our population has grown.

WHO KNOWS YOU IN YOUR COMMUNITY?

Dr. Robin Dunbar of the University of Liverpool studied two dozen species of primates and found that for each, there was a specific average group or community size. This size was a function of what he called the neocortex ratio, a measurement of the brain's physical size. He found that as the ratio increases, community sizes grow.

Analyzing the size of human brains, and extrapolating from the two dozen primates he studied, Dr. Dunbar concluded that the largest community or group within which a human should be able to maintain consistent relationships was 150 people. Indeed, looking out at the world of human interactions, he found that number over and over again as typical clan sizes—from Australian Aborigines to Native Americans. Even Brigham Young, when he was organizing the first Mormon communities in Utah, "divided [his early Mormon followers] into smaller groups that could operate independently of each other and co-ordinate the activities of their members with maximum efficiency." The group size Young chose was 150 people.

This is also consistent with the observation that communism (with a small "c") works well on an Israeli kibbutz with 100 residents, but failed in the Soviet Union with 262 million people. And, as a foreshadowing of topics we'll visit later, in America, tens of thousands of small companies rarely behave in environmentally destructive or criminal ways, while virtually all of the serious corporate crime convictions of the past century have occurred among companies that are large enough for people to behave with some anonymity.

Dr. Dunbar's research suggests that we have the ability to know and maintain relationships with up to 150 people, but our brains can't handle more than that.

I'm going to go out on a limb for a moment and speculate that in a world where the community of leaders was less than 150—like colonial America—those leaders might well make choices that support the common good. Everybody knew everybody else, and there was social accountability. It wasn't possible to "perpetrate and hide"—you were known.

Keep in mind that 56 people signed the Declaration of Independence (which was written by one person and edited by three), and the Constitutional Congress that wrote the United States Constitution had only 55 attendees, 39 of whom signed it. Among such manageable numbers, I find it entirely credible that individuals might think they could manage the common resources of this newly conquered land in a way that would benefit all. Little to no government intervention would be necessary: There was easily enough to go around, and in those areas where things got tight, communities were small enough that everybody pulled together.

But today we live in a different time and a different world. There are both individuals and corporations who work avidly to grab from the common purse, or to do whatever they want with the common resources of the world for their own benefit—just as was predicted by Lloyd and Hardin. When laws stand in the way of taking from those resources, they work to change those laws to suit their own desires, and if their influence in government increases, they frequently win.

We have also learned that as our towns and schools increase in size, it becomes easier for people to vanish within their little group of 150-or-fewer friends—and thus behave in any way they want toward others, without getting caught at it in the larger community. This is the second time the issue of accountability has arisen. It's not the last.

ANONYMOUS PLUNDERING OF THE COMMONS

A few years ago, Louise and I owned a small piece of undeveloped land in central Vermont. In the cool crispness of late October, we were walking the land under a bright blue afternoon sky. Deep in the forest, partway to the river, we found the carcass of a small deer. She had been shot out of season and the poacher had field-dressed her, leaving behind only the bones, viscera, and parts of her hide as he carried away the meat.

We stood there for a long, shocked moment, confronted with the bloody remains of this sudden and methodical violence. A light wind rustled the brown leaves on the forest floor, and a nearby chipmunk made angry, insistent chirping noises, perhaps upset that humans were again invading his territory.

"Probably somebody from one of the poorer families down the road," I finally said. "Meat for the long winter."

Louise nodded and sighed, and after a brief ceremony, we continued our walk.

The story of the deer illustrates the reality behind one of the fables of our culture: that the commons will provide whatever we need, and will dispose of our waste, without limit.

The person who shot and field-dressed that doe probably didn't think they were stealing or doing anything similarly unethical. It's unlikely they thought of poaching as anything other than bending or breaking relatively small rules. After all, deer roam freely all over the northeastern United States and Canada, and there are plenty of them.

Instead, if he considered it, he probably thought he was taking from the commons—the millions of acres of woodland and hundreds of thousands of deer that are considered the joint property of individuals, corporations, and governments. "Nobody will notice one missing deer," he probably thought, "and it'll provide a few weeks' food for my family."

And as for leaving the waste behind, there's a good chance he left as quickly as he could—to escape accountability.

GOVERNMENT AND THE COMMONS

As human populations increased and the pressure on the commons grew, people authorized their governments to administer the commons "to promote the general welfare." One of the reasons so many of the early American writers and philosophers were disdainful of government was that the commons seemed limitless: There was no need to administer it.

Today, there is a general consensus among most humans that the commons are endangered and need to be managed. We pay more for a gallon of drinking water than we do for gasoline. Homes have air filters and ionizers, and cars have "recirculate" buttons, partially so that in downtown areas we don't have to breathe the exhaust of other automobiles. Our shared transportation systems (at least the roads and airports) get huge amounts of government funding, and we task our government with carefully monitoring and inspecting our common food supply. Education and health care are major concerns to most people, and thus considered part of the commons in most nations.

These are the commons that determine our quality of life and even our ability to live. They are rightfully the concern of humans and the governments that humans create to look after their interests. They're even the concern of the 27 million small and medium-size American companies where owners and managers interact daily with employees . . . where everybody knows each other.

ENTER THE BEHEMOTHS

The principle of the commons is founded on the idea of equal participation. Thus, one final consideration regarding the use of the commons is that our biggest corporations are very, very far from having a position of equal participation when they delve into the commons. In a planet of 6 billion humans, with 27 million companies in America, there is an enormous concentration of wealth at the top:

- 99.6 percent of American corporations have less than $10 million in capitalization.
- Only 2,500 American companies exceed $500 million.
- The Fortune 1,000 companies control about 70 percent of the American economy.
- In the entire world, fewer than 500 corporations have a net value exceeding $12 billion.
- Just 200 corporations conduct almost a third of the entire planet's economic activity and employ less than one-quarter of one percent of the world's workforce.
- Among the 100 largest "economies" in the world today, over half are corporations, not countries.

This situation must have been unimaginable when our country was founded. This is a dramatic concentration of power among companies far too big for everyone to know each other and thus exercise the sort of social pressure–based control that would protect the commons.

IS THERE A PROBLEM?

My point here is not that size is inherently bad. Some very large corporations have outstanding records of treating their people well and being assets to the local human community (and that's not to mention the innovations they've brought to the economy and its citizens). Rather, my point is that the situation today is very different from the assumptions that were considered valid when the Constitution was framed. There is clear evidence that the commons is being depleted, and rapidly.

One issue addressed in this book is the abundant evidence that many corporations use government influence to take advantage of the commons for their self-interest, not the public interest. For instance, through lobbying and campaign contributions, mining and drilling corporations get the federal government to give them free or inexpensive access to government-owned lands—commons held in trust for you and me and all U. S. citizens—to extract gold, uranium, lead, tin, oil, coal, gas, and other public resources, which they sell.

We'll see that corporations, asserting their due process rights as "persons," commonly insert themselves into the regulatory process to influence government control of how they can take advantage of the commons, which has the effect of legalizing their actions.

HIDE IT WHERE NOBODY CAN SEE IT

Consider injection wells. These wells are the reverse of the traditional concept of a well (something from which water or oil is drawn). Instead, an injection well exists to insert untreated toxic wastes into the earth below ground, where they're not visible.

On the Environmental Protection Agency's Web site, there is information about the Underground Injection Control (IUC) program. Through this program, the EPA says: The UIC Program works with state and local governments to oversee underground injection of waste in order to prevent contamination of drinking water resources. Some of the wastes the UIC program regulates include:

- Over 9 billion gallons of hazardous waste every year
- Over 2 billion gallons of brine from oil and gas operations every day
- Automotive, industrial, sanitary, and other wastes that are injected into shallow aquifers

In nearly every case, the wastes could be treated and rendered nonhazardous by conventional technologies. But the oil industry, the chemical industry, and the nation's biggest agricultural corporations don't want to pay the cost. The EPA even says so, on its page touting the UIC program: "Facilities across the United States and in Indian Country discharge a variety of hazardous and nonhazardous fluids into more than 400,000 injection wells. While treatment technologies exist, it would be very costly to treat and release to surface waters the billions and trillions of gallons of wastes that industries produce each year. Agribusiness and the chemical and petroleum industries all make use of underground injection for waste disposal."

So what do the companies do? Rather than bearing responsibility for the cost of processing their wastes, the industries have gotten government permission to just put them underground, thus legalizing potentially destructive behavior. (Note the familiar underlying assumption that there will be no long-term consequences; the commons will be able to handle it.)

If our economy were structured in such a way that the cost of restoring the commons was built into their industry and products, the waste produced while doing business would be a self-correcting issue—the people who generate the waste would also clean it up. But that's not how the system operates, by and large, and big business argues that if they have to pay to clean up their own waste it may even produce a reduction in overall economic activity because of increased prices.

Others point out that consumers are already paying the price in the form of treatment for cancers, asthma, and other diseases that are by-products of industrial pollution. And these are driving the economy as well, although by the corporate value of profit and cash flow instead of human values.

In March of 1968, Robert F. Kennedy raised this issue, challenging the dearly held concept that pure economic activity in and of itself—usually measured as gross national product (GNP)—is a truly useful and honest way to measure the impact of corporate activity on the human community and the life of the planet.

"Our gross national product now is over 800 billion dollars a year," Kennedy said, "but that gross national product, if we judge the United States of America by that, counts air pollution, and cigarette advertising, and ambulances to clear our highways of carnage. It counts special locks for our doors and the jails for the people who break them. It counts the destruction of the redwoods and the loss of our natural wonder in chaotic squall. It counts napalm, and it counts nuclear warheads, and armored cars for the police to fight the riots in our cities. It counts Whitman's rifles and Speck's knives and the television programs which glorify violence in order to sell toys to our children."

There are also important things that only measuring the flow of cash misses, Kennedy said. "Yet, the gross national product does not allow for the health of our children, the quality of their education, or the joy of their play. It does not include the beauty of our poetry or the strength of our marriages, the intelligence of our public debate or the integrity of our public officials. It measures neither our wit nor our courage, neither our wisdom nor our learning, neither our compassion nor our devotion to our country. It measures everything in short, except that which makes life worthwhile."

And the quality of the commons is not generally part of the equation used to calculate GNP (now more commonly called GDP, or gross domestic product).

WHAT ARE THE COMMONS TODAY?

Where do the commons begin and end? What are the things on which our quality of life depends and that we humans share in common? Different people have answered this question in different ways repeatedly over the years.

- At one time, telephone service was considered the commons, and telephone companies were both subsidized in bringing phone service to remote areas and regulated in what they could charge.
- During the Civil War era, the nation's railroad tracks were considered part of the commons.
- Today, the nation's transportation airspace is considered the commons, as government pays most of the cost of managing it and local communities pay the cost of building airports.
- Our water supplies and septic disposal infrastructure are considered part of the commons, as are our police, fire, and prisons.
- Education is in the realm of the commons right now, as is health care in most of the developed world, with the exception of the United States.
- National parks and vast tracts of forestland, pastureland, and other government-owned lands are part of the commons.
- Our banking system was often considered part of the commons: The privatizing of it was a huge and running battle in the United States throughout the first half of the 19th century. Since 1913, the 12 Federal Reserve Banks that handle the nation's money supply have been owned by commercial corporations (the member banks), as are all other U. S. banks, and the Federal Open Market Committee—which sets the nation's interest rates—does not allow the public into its meetings, does not publish transcripts of its meetings, and is responsible only to itself for its own budget.
- In some communities, electricity is part of the commons, although in most it has been taken over by for-profit corporations. But the electric utilities still have the right of eminent domain to take private land for power transmission lines, as if that land were still part of the commons. In the mid-1930s, for-profit corporations were not providing electricity to rural Americans, so in 1934 Franklin Delano Roosevelt passed the Rural Electrification Act (REA) which got electricity to

rural America. The situation repeated itself with regard to telephony, requiring Harry Truman to extend the REA to telephone service.

- The nation's radio and television airwaves were considered part of the commons until they were sold at auction during the Reagan era to help finance other priorities.
- The nation's system of highways and public streets are part of the commons, as is our public library system and post office (both created by Ben Franklin, a booster of the commons).
- The beaches, sky, waterways, oceans, and land held by government are part of the commons.

Because the commons is so close to home—it being those things that we rely on for our health, safety, and "pursuit of happiness"—it has incredible profit potential: Everyone needs it.

Right now, water is the hottest part of the commons, with some of the world's largest corporations pushing hard for water to be internationally defined as a marketable commodity, and for local water supplies to be turned over to them. During hard times, people may put off buying a new car or new clothes, but they must have water each and every day. No matter how poor or how frugal a person may be, they have no choice but to drink, and the battle for the commons of water is becoming global.

Because corporate behavior is rewarded only when it increases present value (the value of the assets held now by a corporation, its profitability, and/or its stock price), decision making in corporations works to extract future values and make them present values. For example, consider a corporation that makes money in a manufacturing process that produces toxic by-products. It's in their best interests in terms of present values to either lobby to allow those toxins to be released into the environment, or move their manufacturing process to a nation that allows that, instead of cleaning it up as they go along. Thus, somebody else in the future will have to deal with the toxins (in the United States, it's taxpayers paying for Superfund sites), and deal with the side effects of the toxins, such as cancer, neurological problems, and environmental damage, while the company's managers and directors direct profits to themselves in the present.

The core concept here is that the commons are something we all share, and therefore something that should be in the hands of "we, the people" to ensure its viability, rather than in the hands of private parties whose first goal is to milk the commons for profits. Once the latter happens, democracies weaken and plutocracies arise—a form of creeping feudalism that threatens peace, prosperity, and, perhaps most important, the future.

The stage is now set. We have looked at the nature of the problem—activities conducted by a small number of parties that are harmful to many. These activities are often a natural consequence of the way corporations are chartered—to make a profit. We have looked at the nature of government, particularly governments designed to serve the people, including managing the commons—the shared resources used by everyone in the community.

We have said that when the people within a company make a decision that harms the common welfare, they are often not held accountable for their actions because they claim "it was the corporation that did it." Yet we have also seen that these same parties have claimed, and won, constitutional protections for the legal fiction that we call corporations, protections that were originally designed to protect *people* from the dangers of despotic governments.

Let's now review the formative years of American government and worldwide modern democracies. In researching this book, I've discovered some rare manuscripts from those days that shed new light on the thinking of our Founders, as we lead up to the *Santa Clara* case in 1886 and then to today.

PART 2

FROM THE BIRTH OF AMERICAN DEMOCRACY THROUGH THE BIRTH OF CORPORATE PERSONHOOD

I shall therefore conclude with a proposal that your watchmen be instructed, as they go on their rounds, to call out every night, half-past twelve, "Beware of the East India Company."

—PAMPHLET SIGNED BY "RUSTICUS," 1773

3

THE BOSTON TEA PARTY REVEALED

They [those who wrote and signed the Declaration of Independence] meant to set up a standard maxim for free society, which would be familiar to all, and revered by all; constantly looked to, constantly labored for, and even though never perfectly attained, constantly approximated, and thereby constantly spreading and deepening the influence and augmenting the happiness and value of life to all people of all colors everywhere. The assertion that "all men are created equal" was of no practical use in effecting our separation from Great Britain; and it was placed in the Declaration not for that, but for future use. Its authors meant it to be—as, thank God, it is now providing itself—a stumbling block to all those who in after times might seek to turn a free people back into the hateful paths of despotism.

—ABRAHAM LINCOLN SPEECH IN SPRINGFIELD, JUNE 26, 1857, COMMENTING ON THE *DRED SCOTT* DECISION OF THE U. S. SUPREME COURT

As Abraham Lincoln biographer Albert J. Beveridge noted in 1928, "Facts when justly arranged interpret themselves. They tell the story. For this purpose a little fact is as important as what is called a big fact. The picture may be well-nigh finished, but it remains vague for want of one more fact. When that missing fact is discovered all others become clear and distinct; it is like turning a light, properly shaded, upon a painting which but a moment before was a blur in the dimness."

History, it turns out, has a few startling examples of people revolting against unrestrained corporate power. Consider, for example, the events that led to the American Revolution. Examining documents from the 1700s and 1800s, we discover a flash of light that gives us a fascinating view of American history.

For example, the Pilgrims were early arrivers to America, and their deeds and experiences make outstanding folklore, but they weren't the founders of America. This country was formally settled 19 years before their arrival, when land from the Atlantic to the Mississippi was staked out by what was then the world's largest transnational corporation. The Pilgrims arrived in America in 1620 aboard a boat they chartered from that corporation. That boat, the *Mayflower*, had already made three trips to North America from England on behalf of the East India Company, the corporation that owned it.

By the time of the early-1600s colonization of North America, the British Empire was just starting to become a world empire.

A century or so before that, as western European nations extended their reach and rule across the world in the 1400s and 1500s, England was far from being a world power. Following a series of internal battles and wars with Scotland and Ireland, and power struggles within the royal family and with the Catholic Church, England at that time was considered by the Spanish, French, and Dutch to be an uncultured tribe of barbarians ruled by sadistic warlords. Although Sir Francis Drake is touted in British history as a heroic explorer and battler of the Spanish Armada, in reality he was "a licensed pirate" (quoting from the modern East India Company's Web site), and even in the late 1500s England lacked a coherent naval strategy or vision.

The British first got the idea about the importance of becoming a world power in the late 1400s when they observed the result of Columbus's voyage to America, bringing back slaves, gold, and other treasures. That got Europe's attention, and threw Spain full-bore into a time of explosive boom. Then in 1522, when Magellan sailed all the way around the world, he proved that the planet was a closed system, raising the possibility of tremendous financial opportunity for whatever company could seize control of international trade.

In many of the European countries, particularly Holland and France, consortiums were put together to finance ships to sail the seas.

England got into the act a bit late, in 1580, with Queen Elizabeth I becoming the largest shareholder in *The Golden Hind*, a ship owned by Sir Francis Drake. She granted him "legal freedom from liability," an early archetype for modern corporations.

The investment worked out very well for Queen Elizabeth. There's no record of exactly how much she made when Drake paid her her share of the *Hind's* dividends, but it was undoubtedly vast, since Drake himself and the other minor shareholders all received a 5,000-percent return on their investment. Plus, the queen's placing a maximum loss to the initial investors of their investment amount only made it a low-risk investment to begin with. She also was endorsing an investment model that led to the modern limited liability corporation.

The queen also often granted monopoly rights over particular industries or businesses in exchange for a fee. The 1624 Statute of Monopolies did away with this ability of the Crown, although in the years thereafter the British government used tax laws to produce a similar result for the corporations favored by Parliament or the royal family.

LIMITING RISK BY INCORPORATING

A business can operate at a profit, a break-even, or a loss. If the business is a sole proprietorship or partnership (owned by one or a few people), and it loses more money than its assets are worth, the owners and investors are personally responsible for the debts, which may exceed the amount they originally invested. A small business owner could put up $10,000 of her own money to start a company, have it fail with $50,000 in debts, and be personally responsible for paying off that debt out of her own pocket.

But let's say you invest $10,000 in a limited liability corporation, and the corporation runs up $50,000 in debts, and defaults on those debts. You would lose only your initial $10,000 investment. The remaining $40,000 wouldn't be your concern because the amount of your investment is the "limit of your liability," even if the corporation goes bankrupt or defaults in any other way.

Who foots the bill? The creditors—the people to whom the corporation owes money. The company took the goods or services from them, didn't pay, and leaves them with the bill, exactly as if you had put in a week's work and not gotten paid for it.

And if the corporation declares bankruptcy and dissolves itself, there is nobody the creditors can go after. That's the main thing that makes a corporation a corporation, and it's why in England the abbreviation for a corporation isn't "Inc." as in the United States. It's "Ltd.," which stands for *limited liability corporation*. (also used in the United States and other nations.)

If you were a stockholder in a corporation that went under, it wouldn't even be reflected on your personal credit rating (unless you had volunteered to personally guarantee the corporation's debt). Your liability is limited to however much you invested.

Moreover, a corporation can outlast its founders. If you started a one-man glassblowing business, for example, when you die or can't work any more, the income stops. But a glassblowing corporation is an entity unto itself, and can continue on with new glassblowers and managers after the founders move on. The implication, of course, is that a corporation can pay profits as a dividend to its shareholders for centuries, theoretically forever.

This is what Queen Elizabeth had in mind. Incorporating *The Golden Hind* would limit her liability and that of the other noble and lesser noble investors, and maximize their potential for profit. So after the big bucks she made on Drake's expeditions on *The Golden Hind*, she started thinking about what could be done about the small role England played in world trade relative to Holland, France, Spain, and Portugal.

In part to remedy this situation, and in part to exploit a relative vacuum of power, she authorized a group of 218 London merchants and nobleman to form a corporation that would take on the mostly Dutch control of the worldwide spice trade. They formed what came to be the largest of England's corporations during that and the next century, the East India Company. Queen Elizabeth granted the company's corporate charter on December 31, 1600.

THE EAST INDIA COMPANY BUILDS ENGLAND . . . AND AMERICA

It went slowly at first. For several decades, the East India Company struggled to establish a commercial beachhead among the many Spice Islands and distant lands where there were potential products, raw materials, or markets.

The Dutch had so sewn up the world at this point in the early 1600s, however, that the only island the company was able to secure on behalf of England was the island of Puloroon (leading King James I, who commissioned the translation of the Bible into English, to declare himself "King of England, Scotland, Ireland, France, and Puloroon"). In addition, the company's hard-drinking Captain William Hawkins managed to befriend the alcoholic ruler of India, the Mogul Emperor Jehangir, building a powerful presence for the company on the Indian subcontinent (which the company would take over and rule as a corporate-run state within 2 centuries).

During this time, England had exported colonists to the Americas in large numbers, including many as prisoners (a practice they later moved to Australia when it was no longer practical to send them to North America). There was also a steady and growing exodus from England of various types of malcontents who, on arrival in America, redefined themselves as explorers and pioneers, or set up theocratic communities.

Much of this transportation was provided at a profitable price by the East India Company, which laid claim to parts of North America and created the first official colony in North America on company-owned land, deeded to the Virginia Company in 1606. (The companies had interlocking boards, as Sir Thomas Smythe administered the American operations of both from his house. Smythe was also the first North American governor of both the East India Company and the Virginia Company.) The company called it Jamestown, after company patron and stockholder King James I (who took the throne and the royal share of the company's stock when Queen Elizabeth died in 1603), and placed Jamestown on the Chesapeake Bay in the company-owned Commonwealth of Virginia, named after the now-deceased "Virgin Queen," Elizabeth I, who had granted the company its original charter. On the maps from that time, the two companies' claim of Virginia extended from the Atlantic Ocean all the way to the Mississippi River.

America was one of the East India Company's major international bases of operations, and once they figured out how to make a colony work, they grew rapidly. Through the 1600s and early 1700s, the company and its affiliates largely took control of North America, but also sent Captain Cook on his explorations of Australia, Hawaii, and other Pacific islands. He died in Hawaii while on a company mission of exploration.

The company's influence was pervasive wherever it went. For example, 100 years or more before Betsy Ross was born, the flag of the East India Company was made up of 13 horizontal red and white alternating bars, with a blue field in the upper left-hand corner with the Union Jack in it. Although, according to the well-known legend, Ross reversed the order of the red and white bars, the American flag is startling similar to that of the East India Company.

In its earliest years, the company began to assemble its own private military and police forces. After a particularly bloody massacre of company employees by the Dutch at Amboina, Indonesia, in 1623, the company realized it needed to hire some new and uniquely competent people to ply the trade routes. To stop smugglers from competing with their trade to North America, the company authorized its Governor of New York to hire Captain Kidd to clean up its trade routes by killing colonial smugglers and sinking their ships. When Kidd began secretly competing with the company on the side (an activity the company called smuggling and piracy) they had him captured and executed in 1701.

The company also approached the British Parliament, and asked for authority and protection by British military forces.

Thus, many of the seemingly "political" appointees of England to the early Americas were first and foremost employees of the East India Company.

One of many examples of how the company and the British military were connected is General Cornwallis. During the American Revolution, he lost the Battle of Yorktown in 1781, but later went on to "serve with great distinction in the company's service in India, and it was said of him that whilst he lost a colony in the West, he won one in the East."

FROM INDIA TO YALE, THE EAST INDIA COMPANY INFLUENCES

As its first century of existence was wrapping up, the company's reach had extended worldwide and proven enormously profitable for its stockholders. For example, during these years Thomas and Elihu Yale grew up in the American colonies and, like many American colonists, went to work for the East India Company. Elihu became the company's Governor of Madras, India, where he made a huge fortune for himself and the company, while his brother, Thomas, negotiated the company's first trade deals with China. Elihu returned home and made a large grant to the school he and his brother had attended, which, in grateful appreciation, renamed itself Yale College in 1718.

By the 1760s, the East India Company's power had grown massive and worldwide. It had taken control of much of the commerce of India, was aggressively importing opium into China to take control of that nation (which would lead to the Opium War of the late 1800s which China lost, ceding Hong Kong to Britain for 99 years), and had largely taken control of all international commerce to and from North America. However, this very rapid expansion, trying to keep ahead of the Dutch trading companies, was a mixed blessing, as the company went deep in debt to support its growth, and by 1770 found itself nearly bankrupt.

Among the company's biggest and most vexing problems were American colonial small businessmen and entrepreneurs, who ran their own small ships to bring tea and other goods directly into America without routing them through Britain or through the company. And there were many small-business tea retailers in North America who were buying their wholesale tea directly from Dutch trading companies instead of the East India Company. These two types of competition were very painful for the company.

THE FIRST PRO-CORPORATE TAX LAWS

The East India Company set a precedent that multinational corporations follow to this day: They lobbied for laws that would make it easy for them to put their small business competitors out of business. By 1681, most of the members of the British government and royalty were stockholders in the East India Company, so it was easy that year to pass "An Act For the Restraining and Punishing Privateers & Pirates." This law required a license to import anything into the Americas (among other British-controlled parts of the world) and the licenses were only rarely granted except to the East India Company and other large British corporations.

As trade to the American colonies grew, and under pressure from the East India Company, the British government passed a series of laws that increased the company's power and influence and reduced its competition and barriers to international trade, including the Townshend Acts of 1767 and the Tea Act of 1773.

The Tea Act was the most essential for the East India Company because the American colonies had become a huge market for tea—millions of pounds a month—which was largely being supplied at cheap prices by Dutch trading companies and American smugglers, also known as privateers because they operated privately instead of working for the company. (The company also often encouraged the British government to prosecute these entrepreneurial traders and smugglers as "pirates" under the 1681 law.)

Many people today think the Tea Act—which led to the Boston Tea Party—was simply an increase in the taxes on tea paid by American colonists. Instead, the purpose of the Tea Act was to give the East India Company full and unlimited access to the American tea trade, and *exempt* the company from having to pay taxes to Britain on tea exported to the American colonies. It even gave the company a *tax refund* on millions of pounds of tea they were unable to sell and holding in inventory.

One purpose of the Tea Act was to increase the profitability of the East India Company to its stockholders (which included the King), and to help the company drive its colonial small business competitors out of business. Because the company no longer had to pay high taxes to England and held a monopoly on the tea it sold in the American colonies, it was able to lower its tea prices to undercut the prices of the local importers and the mom-and-pop tea merchants and tea houses in every town in America.

This infuriated the independence-minded colonists, who were, by and large, unappreciative of their colonies being used as a profit center for the multinational East India Company corporation. They resented their small businesses still having to pay the higher, pre–Tea Act taxes without having any say or vote in the matter. (Thus, the cry of "no taxation without representation!") Even in the official British version of the history, the 1773 Tea Act was a "legislative maneuver by the British ministry of Lord North to make English tea marketable in America," with a goal of helping the East India Company quickly "sell 17 million pounds of tea stored in England . . ."

A clue to the anti-globalization agenda of the American revolutionaries is found right on the Web site of the modern East India Company, which states: ". . . the infamous Boston Tea Party in 1773 was a direct result of the drawback of the government in London of duties on tea which enabled the East India Company to dump excess stocks on the American colonies, and acted as a rallying point for the discontented."

The site also notes that American antipathy toward the corporation that had first founded, owned, ruled, and settled the original colonies continued even after the Revolution. After the Revolutionary War, the company tried to resume trading with America, offering clothing, silks, coffee, earthenware, cocoa, and spices, but, as their Web site observes, "Even after Independence the East India Company remained a highly competitive importer of goods into the United States, resulting in occasional flare-ups such as the trade war between 1812 and 1814."

AMERICA'S FIRST ENTREPRENEURS PROTEST

This economics-driven view of American history piqued my curiosity when I first discovered it. So when I came upon an original first edition of one of this nation's earliest history books, I made a sizable investment to buy it to read the thoughts of somebody who had actually been alive and participated in the Boston Tea Party and subsequent American Revolution. I purchased from an antiquarian book seller an original copy of *Retrospect of the Boston Tea-Party with a Memoir of George R. T. Hewes, a Survivor of the Little Band of Patriots Who Drowned the Tea in Boston Harbour in 1773*, published in New York by S. S. Bliss in 1834.

Because the identities of the Boston Tea Party participants were hidden (other than Samuel Adams) and all were sworn to secrecy for the next 50 years, this account (published 61 years later) is singularly rare and important, as it's the only actual first-person account of the event by a participant that exists, so far as I can find. And turning its brittle, age-colored pages and looking at printing on unevenly-sized sheets, typeset by hand and printed on a small hand press almost 200 years ago, was both fascinating and exciting. Even more interesting was the perspective of the anonymous ("by a citizen of New York") author and of Hewes, whom the author extensively interviewed for the book.

Although Hewes' name is today largely lost to history, he was apparently well-known in colonial times and during the 19th century. Esther Forbes' classic 1942 biography of Paul Revere, which depended heavily on Paul Revere's "many volumes of papers" and numerous late 18th- and early 19th-century sources, mentions Hewes repeatedly throughout her book. For example, when young Paul Revere went off to join the British army in the spring of 1756, he took along with him Hewes. "Paul Revere served in Richard Gridley's regiment," Forbes writes, noting Revere's recollection that the army had certain requirements for its recruits. "All must be able-bodied and between seventeen and forty-five, and must measure to a certain height. George Robert Twelvetrees Hewes could not go. He was too short, and in vain did he get a shoemaker to build up the inside of his shoes; but Paul Revere 'passed muster' and 'mounted the cockade.'"

Hewes wasn't of noble birth, according to Forbes. "George was of poor family. He had started out apprenticed to a shoemaker, ran away to sea and fished on the Grand Banks. At the time of the great inoculation, he was of age, back in Boston, and completing his apprenticeship to a shoemaker. In spite of his diminutive size and the dignity of his name, he was mixed up in every street fight, massacre, or tea party that occurred in the Boston of his day."

Even the wealthy John Hancock, who kept careful records of his philanthropy, knew Hewes. "He [Hancock] called that young scamp, George

Robert Twelvetrees Hewes, 'my lad' and 'put his hand into his breeches-pocket and pulled out a crown piece, which he placed softly in his hand,'" according to Forbes.

Hewes was present for the Boston Massacre, one of the early events that led to the Tea Party. "George Robert Twelvetrees Hewes, of course, was in the middle of it," writes Forbes. "He was a little fellow, but 'stood up straight . . . and spoke up sharp and quick on all occasions.' Recently he had married Sally Sumner, a young washerwoman. When Captain Preston and his men shoved their way across King Street, they had bumped smack into Hewes."

And when it came to the Boston Tea Party, Forbes notes, "No one invited George Robert Twelvetrees Hewes, but no one could have kept him home." She quotes him as to the size of the raiding party, noting, "Hewes says there were one hundred to a hundred and fifty 'indians'" that night.

Hewes apparently came to Boston through the good graces of America's first president. "George Robert Twelvetrees Hewes fished nine weeks for the British fleet until he saw his chance [to escape] and took it," writes Forbes. "Landing in Lynn, he was immediately taken to [George] Washington at Cambridge. The General enjoyed the story of his escape—'he didn't laugh to be sure but looked amazing good natured, you may depend.' He asked him to dine with him, and Hewes says that 'Madam Washington waited upon them at table at dinner-time and was remarkably social.' Hewes was one of the many Boston refugees who never went back there to live. Having served as a privateersman and soldier during the war, he settled outside of the state."

And there, outside the state, was where Hewes lived into his old age, finally telling his story to those who would listen, including one who published the little book I found. While Forbes doesn't list my book among her bibliography, she does note that "George Robert Twelvetrees Hewes was holding young listeners spellbound out in Oswego County, New York," in his old age, and references Peleg Chandler's *American Criminal Trials*, published in 1841 as a source that "gives what seems to me the most careful analysis of the [Boston] Massacre and I have used this book as my primary source, adding to it various contemporary accounts, especially George Robert Twelvetrees Hewes."

Reading Hewes' account, I learned that the Boston Tea Party resembled in many ways the growing modern-day protests against transnational corporations and small-town efforts to protect themselves from chain-store retailers or factory farms. With few exceptions, the Tea Party's participants thought of themselves as protesters against the actions of the multinational East India Company and the government that "unfairly" represented, supported, and served the company while not representing or serving the residents.

Hewes said that many American colonists either boycotted the purchase of tea or were smuggling or purchasing smuggled tea to avoid supporting the East India Company's profits and the British taxes on tea, which, according to Hewes' account of 1773, "rendered the smuggling of [tea] an object and was frequently practiced, and their resolutions against using it, although observed by many with little fidelity, had greatly diminished the importation into the colonies of this commodity. Meanwhile," Hewes noted, "an immense quantity of it was accumulated in the warehouses of the East India Company in England. This company petitioned the king to suppress the duty of three pence per pound upon its introduction into America . . ."

That petition was successful and produced the Tea Act of 1773: The result was a boom for the transnational East India Company corporation and a big problem for the entrepreneurial American "smugglers."

According to Hewes, "The [East India] Company, however, received permission to transport tea, free of all duty, from Great Britain to America . . ." allowing it to wipe out its small competitors and take over the tea business in all of America. "Hence," he told his biographer, "it was no longer the small vessels of private merchants, who went to vend tea for their own account in the ports of the colonies, but, on the contrary, ships of an enormous burthen, that transported immense quantities of this commodity, which by the aid of the public authority, might, as they supposed, easily be landed, and amassed in suitable magazines. Accordingly, the company sent its agents at Boston, New York, and Philadelphia, six hundred chests of tea, and a proportionate number to Charleston, and other maritime cities of the American continent. The colonies were now arrived at the decisive moment when they must cast the dye [sic], and determine their course . . ."

Interestingly, Hewes notes that it wasn't just American small businesses and citizens who objected to the new monopoly powers granted the East India Company by the English Parliament. The East India Company was also putting out of business many smaller tea exporters in England, who had been doing business with American family-owned retail stores for decades, and those companies began a protest in England that was simultaneous with the American protests against transnational corporate bullying and the East India Company's buying of influence with the British Parliament.

Hewes remarks that, "Even in England individuals were not wanting, who fanned this fire; some from a desire to baffle the government, others from motives of private interest, says the historian of the event, and jealousy at the opportunity offered the East India Company, to make immense profits to their prejudice.

"These opposers [sic] of the measure in England [the Tea Act of 1773] wrote therefore to America, encouraging a strenuous resistance. They represented to the colonists that this would prove their last trial, and that if they should triumph now, their liberty was secured forever; but if they should yield, they must bow their necks to the yoke of slavery. The materials were so prepared and disposed that they could easily kindle."

The battle between the small businessmen of America and the huge multinational East India Company actually began in Pennsylvania, according to Hewes. "At Philadelphia," he writes, "those to whom the teas of the [East India] Company were intended to be consigned, were induced by persuasion, or constrained by menaces, to promise, on no terms, to accept the proffered consignment.

"At New-York, Captain Sears and McDougal, daring and enterprising men, effected a concert of will [against the East India Company], between the smugglers, the merchants, and the sons of liberty [who had all joined forces and in most cases were the same people]. Pamphlets suited to the conjecture, were daily distributed, and nothing was left unattempted by popular leaders, to obtain their purpose."

Resistance was organizing and growing and the Tea Act was the final straw. The citizens of the colonies were preparing to throw off one of the corporations that for almost 200 years had determined nearly every aspect of their lives through its economic and political power. They were planning to destroy the goods of the world's largest multinational corporation, intimidate its employees, and face down the guns of the government that supported it.

A newsletter called *The Alarm* circulated through the colonies; one issue, signed by an enigmatic "Rusticus," made clear the feelings of colonial Americans about England's largest transnational corporation and its behavior around the world:

"Are we in like Manner to be given up to the Disposal of the East India Company, who have now the Assurance, to step forth in Aid of the Minister, to execute his Plan, of enslaving America? Their Conduct in Asia, for some Years past, has given simple Proof, how little they regard the Laws of Nations, the Rights, Liberties, or Lives of Men. They have levied War, excited

Rebellions, dethroned lawful Princes, and sacrificed Millions for the Sake of Gain. The Revenues of Mighty Kingdoms have centered in their Coffers. And these not being sufficient to glut their Avarice, they have, by the most unparalleled Barbarities, Extortions, and Monopolies, stripped the miserable Inhabitants of their Property, and reduced whole Provinces to Indigence and Ruin. Fifteen hundred Thousands, it is said, perished by Famine in one Year, not because the Earth denied its Fruits; but [because] this Company and their Servants engulfed all the Necessaries of Life, and set them at so high a Rate that the poor could not purchase them."

THE PAMPHLETEERING WORKED

After turning back the company's ships in Philadelphia and New York, Hewes writes, "In Boston the general voice declared the time was come to face the storm."

He writes about the sentiment among the colonists who opposed the naked power and wealth of the East India Company and the British government that supported them: "Why do we wait? they exclaimed; soon or late we must engage in conflict with England. Hundreds of years may roll away before the ministers can have perpetrated as many violations of our rights, as they have committed within a few years. The opposition is formed; it is general; it remains for us to seize the occasion. The more we delay the more strength is acquired by the ministers. Now is the time to prove our courage, or be disgraced with our brethren of the other colonies, who have their eyes fixed upon us, and will be prompt in their succor if we show ourselves faithful and firm.

"This was the voice of the Bostonians in 1773. The factors who were to be the consignees of the tea, were urged to renounce their agency, but they refused and took refuge in the fortress. A guard was placed on Griffin's wharf, near where the tea ships were moored. It was agreed that a strict watch should be kept; that if any insult should be offered, the bell should be immediately rung; and some persons always ready to bear intelligence of what might happen, to the neighbouring towns, and to call in the assistance of the country people."

Rusticus added his voice in a May 27, 1773 pamphlet saying, "Resolve therefore, nobly resolve, and publish to the World your Resolutions, that no Man will receive the Tea, no Man will let his Stores, or suffer the Vessel that brings it to moor at his Wharf, and that if any Person assists at unloading, landing, or storing it, he shall ever after be deemed an Enemy to his Country, and never be employed by his Fellow Citizens."

Colonial voices were getting louder and louder about their outrage at the giant corporation's behavior. Another issue of *The Alarm*, dated October 27, 1773 said, "It hath now been proved to you, That the East India Company, obtained the monopoly of that trade by bribery, and corruption. That the power thus obtained they have prostituted to extortion, and other the most cruel and horrible purposes, the Sun ever beheld."

THE PEOPLE CHALLENGE THE CORPORATION

And then, Hewes says, on a cold November evening, the first of the East India Company's ships of reduced-tax tea arrived. "On the 28th of November, 1773," Hewes writes, "the ship *Dartmouth* with 112 chests arrived; and the next morning after, the following notice was widely circulated.

"Friends, Brethren, Countrymen! That worst of plagues, the detested TEA, has arrived in this harbour. The hour of destruction, a manly opposition to the machinations of tyranny, stares you in the face. Every friend to his country, to himself, and to posterity, is now called upon to meet in Faneuil Hall, at nine o'clock, this day, at which time the bells will ring, to make a united and successful resistance to this last, worst, and most destructive measure of administration."

The reaction to the pamphlet—back then one part of what was truly a "free press" in America—was emphatic. Hewes' account was that, "Things thus appeared to be hastening to a disastrous issue. The people of the country arrived in great numbers, the inhabitants of the town assembled. This assembly which was on the 16th of December, 1773, was the most numerous ever known, there being more than 2,000 from the country present."

Hewes continued, "This notification brought together a vast concourse of the people of Boston and the neighbouring towns, at the time and place appointed. Then it was resolved that the tea should be returned to the place from whence it came in all events, and no duty paid thereon. The arrival of other cargoes of tea soon after, increased the agitation of the public mind, already wrought up to a degree of desperation, and ready to break out into acts of violence, on every trivial occasion of offence. . . .

"Finding no measures were likely to be taken, either by the governor, or the commanders, or owners of the ships, to return their cargoes or prevent the landing of them, at 5 o'clock a vote was called for the dissolution of the meeting and obtained. But some of the more moderate and judicious members, fearing what might be the consequences, asked for a reconsideration of the vote, offering no other reason, than that they ought to do every thing in their power to send the tea back, according to their previous resolves. This, says the historian of that event, touched the pride of the assembly, and they agreed to remain together one hour."

The people assembled in Boston at that moment faced the same issue that citizens who oppose combined corporate and co-opted government power all over the world confront today: Should they take on a well-financed and heavily armed opponent when such resistance could lead to their own imprisonment or death? Even worse, what if they should lose the struggle, leading to the imposition on them and their children an even more repressive regime to support the profits of the corporation?

THERE ARE CORPORATE SPIES AMONG US!

There was a debate late that afternoon in Boston, Hewes notes, but it was short because a man named Josiah Quiney pointed out that some of the people in the group worked directly or indirectly for the East India Company or held loyalty to Britain or both. Quiney suggested that if they took the first step of confronting the East India Company, it would inevitably mean they would have to take on the army of England. He pointed out they were really discussing the possibility of going to war against England to stop England from enforcing the East India Company's right to run its "ministerial enterprise," and that some who profited from that enterprise were right there in the room with them.

Hewes goes on to say, "In this conjuncture, Josiah Quiney, a man of great influence in the colony, of a vigorous and cultivated genius, and strenuously opposed to ministerial enterprises, wishing to apprise his fellow-citizens of the importance of the crisis, and direct their attention to probable results which might follow, after demanding silence said, 'This ardour and this impetuosity, which are manifested within these walls, are not those that are requisite to conduct us to the object we have in view; these may cool, may abate, may vanish like a flittering shade. Quite other spirits, quite other efforts are essential to our salvation. Greatly will he deceive himself, who shall think, that with cries, with exclamations, with popular resolutions, we can hope to triumph in the conflict, and vanquish our inveterate foes. Their malignity is implacable, their thirst for vengeance insatiable. They have their allies, their accomplices, even in the midst of us—even in the bosom of this innocent country; and who is ignorant of the power of those who have conspired our ruin? Who knows not their artifices? Imagine not therefore, that you can bring this controversy to a happy conclusion without the most strenuous, the most arduous, the most terrible conflict; consider attentively the difficulty of the enterprise, and the uncertainty of the issue. Reflict [sic] and ponder, even ponder well, before you embrace the measures, which are to involve this country in the most perilous enterprise the world has witnessed.'"

Most Americans today believe that the colonists were only upset that they didn't have a legislature they had elected that would pass the laws under which they were taxed: "Taxation without representation" was their rallying cry. And while that was true, Hewes points out, the thorn in their side, the pinprick that was really driving their rage, was that England was passing tax laws solely for the benefit of the transnational East India Company at the expense of the average American worker and America's small business owners.

Thus, "taxation without representation" also meant hitting the average person and small business with taxes while letting the richest and most powerful corporation in the world off the hook for its taxes. It was government sponsorship of one corporation over all competitors, plain and simple.

And the more the colonists resisted the predations of the East India Company and its British protectors, the more reactive and repressive the British government became, arresting American entrepreneurs as smugglers and defending the trade interests of the East India Company.

Among the reasons cited in the 1776 Declaration of Independence for separating America from Britain are, "For cutting off our Trade with all parts of the world: For imposing Taxes on us without our Consent." The British had used tax and anti-smuggling laws to make it nearly impossible for American small businesses to compete against the huge multinational East India Company, and the Tea Act of 1773 was the final straw.

Thus, the group assembled in Boston responded to Josiah Quiney's comment by calling for a vote. The next paragraph in Hewes' book says, "The question was then immediately put whether the landing of the tea should be opposed and carried in the affirmative unanimously. Rotch [a local tea seller], to whom the cargo of tea had been consigned, was then requested to demand of the governor to permit to pass the castle [return the ships to England]. The latter answered haughtily, that for the honor of the laws, and from duty towards the king, he could not grant the permit, until the vessel was regularly cleared. A violent commotion immediately ensued; and it is related by one historian of that scene, that a person disguised after the manner of the Indians, who was in the gallery, shouted at this juncture, the cry of war; and that the meeting dissolved in the twinkling of an eye, and the multitude rushed in a mass to Griffin's wharf."

A FIRST-PERSON ACCOUNT OF THE TEA PARTY

On what happened next, Hewes is quite specific in pointing out that not only were the protesters registering their anger and upset over domination by England and the company, but they were willing to commit a million-dollar act of vandalism to make their point. Hewes says, "It was now evening, and I immediately dressed myself in the costume of an Indian, equipped with a small hatchet, which I and my associates denominated the tomahawk, with which, and a club, after having painted my face and hands with coal dust in the shop of a blacksmith, I repaired to Griffin's wharf, where the ships lay that contained the tea. When I first appeared in the street after being thus disguised, I fell in with many who were dressed, equipped and painted as I was, and who fell in with me and marched in order to the place of our destination.

"When we arrived at the wharf, there were three of our number who assumed an authority to direct our operations, to which we readily submitted. They divided us into three parties, for the purpose of boarding the three ships which contained the tea at the same time. The name of him who commanded the division to which I was assigned was Leonard Pitt. The names of the other commanders I never knew.

"We were immediately ordered by the respective commanders to board all the ships at the same time, which we promptly obeyed. The commander of the division to which I belonged, as soon as we were on board the ship appointed me boatswain, and ordered me to go to the captain and demand of him the keys to the hatches and a dozen candles. I made the demand accordingly, and the captain promptly replied, and delivered the articles; but requested me at the same time to do no damage to the ship or rigging.

"We then were ordered by our commander to open the hatches and take out all the chests of tea and throw them overboard, and we immediately proceeded to execute his orders, first cutting and splitting the chests with our tomahawks, so as thoroughly to expose them to the effects of the water.

"In about three hours from the time we went on board, we had thus broken and thrown overboard every tea chest to be found in the ship, while those in the other ships were disposing of the tea in the same way, at the same time. We were surrounded by British armed ships, but no attempt was made to resist us.

"We then quietly retired to our several places of residence, without having any conversation with each other, or taking any measures to discover who were our associates; nor do I recollect of our having had the knowledge of the name of a single individual concerned in that affair, except that of Leonard Pitt, the commander of my division, whom I have mentioned. There appeared to be an understanding that each individual should volunteer his services, keep his own secret, and risk the consequence for himself. No disorder took place during that transaction, and it was observed at that time that the stillest night ensued that Boston had enjoyed for many months."

The participants were absolutely committed that none of the East India Company's tea would ever again be consumed on American shores. Hewes continues, "During the time we were throwing the tea overboard, there were several attempts made by some of the citizens of Boston and its vicinity to carry off small quantities of it for their family use. To effect that object, they would watch their opportunity to snatch up a handful from the deck, where it became plentifully scattered, and put it into their pockets.

"One Captain O'Connor, whom I well knew, came on board for that purpose, and when he supposed he was not noticed, filled his pockets, and also the lining of his coat. But I had detected him and gave information to the captain of what he was doing. We were ordered to take him into custody, and just as he was stepping from the vessel, I seized him by the skirt of his coat, and in attempting to pull him back, I tore it off; but, springing forward, by a rapid effort he made his escape. He had, however, to run a gauntlet through the crowd upon the wharf; each one, as he passed, giving him a kick or a stroke.

"Another attempt was made to save a little tea from the ruins of the cargo by a tall, aged man who wore a large cocked hat and white wig, which was fashionable at that time. He had slightly slipped a little into his pocket, but being detected, they seized him and, taking his hat and wig from his head, threw them, together with the tea, of which they had emptied his pockets, into the water. In consideration of his advanced age, he was permitted to escape, with now and then a slight kick.

"The next morning, after we had cleared the ships of the tea, it was discovered that very considerable quantities of it were floating upon the surface of the water; and to prevent the possibility of any of its being saved for use, a number of small boats were manned by sailors and citizens, who rowed them into those parts of the harbor wherever the tea was visible, and by beating it with oars and paddles so thoroughly drenched it as to render its entire destruction inevitable."

In all, the 342 chests of tea—over 90,000 pounds—thrown overboard that night were enough to make 24 million cups of tea and were valued by the East India Company at 9,659 pounds sterling or, in today's currency, just over a million U. S. dollars.

In response to the Boston Tea Party, the British Parliament immediately passed the Boston Port Act stating that the port of Boston would be closed until the citizens of Boston reimbursed the East India Company for the tea they had destroyed. The colonists refused. A year-and-a-half later, the colonists would again openly state their defiance of the East India Company and Great Britain by taking on British troops in an armed conflict at Lexington and Concord ("the shots heard 'round the world") on April 19, 1775.

That war—finally triggered by a transnational corporation and its government patrons trying to deny American colonists a fair and competitive local marketplace—would last until 1783.

4

JEFFERSON'S DREAM: THE BILL OF RIGHTS

Let monopolies and all kinds and degrees of oppression be carefully guarded against.

—SAMUEL WEBSTER, 1777

Although the first shots were fired in 1775 and the Declaration was signed in 1776, the war had just begun. These colonists, facing the biggest empire and military force in the world, fought for 5 more years—the war didn't end until General Cornwallis surrendered in October 1781. Even then, some resistance remained; the last loyalists and British left New York starting in April 1782, and the treaty that formally ended the war was signed in Paris in September 1783.

The first form of government, the Articles of Confederation, was written in 1777 and endorsed by the States in 1781. It was subsequently replaced by our current Constitution, as has been documented in many books. In this chapter, we want to take a look at the visions that motivated what Alexis de Tocqueville would later call America's experiment with democracy in a republic.

THE FIRST GLIMPSES OF A POWERFUL AMERICAN COMPANY

Very few people are aware that Thomas Jefferson considered freedom from monopolies to be one of the fundamental human rights. But it was very much a part of his thinking during the time when the Bill of Rights was born.

In fact, most of the founders of America never imagined a huge commercial empire sweeping over their land, reminiscent of Hewes' "ships of an enormous burthen" with "immense quantities" of goods. Rather, most of them saw an America made up of people like themselves: farmers.

In a speech before Congress on April 9, 1789, James Madison referred to agriculture as the great staple of America. He added, "I think [agriculture] may justly be styled the staple of the United States; from the spontaneous productions which nature furnishes, and the manifest preference it has over every other object of emolument in this country."

In a *National Gazette* article on March 3, 1792, Madison wrote, "The class of citizens who provide at once their own food and their own raiment, may be viewed as the most truly independent and happy. They are more: they are the best basis of public liberty, and the strongest bulwark of public safety. It follows, that the greater the proportion of this class to the whole society, the more free, the more independent, and the more happy must be the society itself."

The first large privately owned corporation to rise up in the new United States during the presidential terms of Jefferson (1801 to 1809) and Madison (1809 to 1817) was the Second Bank of the United States. By 1830, the bank was one of the largest and most powerful private corporations, and was even sponsoring its directors and agents as candidates for political office in order to extend its own power.

In President Andrew Jackson's annual message to Congress on December 3, 1833, he explicitly demanded that the bank cease its political activities or receive a corporate death sentence—revocation of its corporate charter. He said, "In this point of the case the question is distinctly presented whether the people of the United States are to govern through representatives chosen by their unbiased suffrages or whether the money and power of a great corporation are to be secretly exerted to influence their judgment and control their decisions."

Jackson succeeded in forcing a withdrawal of all federal funds from the bank that year, putting it out of business. Its federal charter expired in 1836, and was only revived as a state bank authorized by the state of Pennsylvania. It went bankrupt in 1841.

Although thousands of federal, state, county, city, and community laws restrained corporations vastly more than they are today, the presidents who followed Jackson continued to worry out loud about the implications if corporations expanded their power.

In the middle of the 30-year struggle, in May 1827, James Madison wrote a letter to his friend James K. Paulding about the issue. He said, "With regard to Banks, they have taken too deep and too wide a root in social transactions, to be got rid of altogether, if that were desirable. . . . they have a hold on public opinion, which alone would make it expedient to aim rather at the improvement, than the suppression of them. As now generally constituted, their advantages whatever they be, are outweighed by the excesses of their paper emissions, and the partialities and corruption with which they are administered."

Thus, while Madison saw the rise of corporate power and its dangers during and after his presidency, the issues weren't obvious to him when he was helping write the United States Constitution decades earlier. And that may have been significant when the Bill of Rights was being put together.

THE FEDERALISTS VERSUS THE DEMOCRATIC REPUBLICANS

Shortly after George Washington became the first President of the United States in 1789, his Secretary of the Treasury, Alexander Hamilton, proposed that the federal government incorporate a national bank and assume state debts left over from the Revolutionary War. Congressman James Madison and Secretary of State Thomas Jefferson saw this as an inappropriate role for the federal government, representing the potential concentration of too much money and power in the federal government. (The Bill of Rights, with its Tenth Amendment reserving powers to the states, wouldn't be ratified for 2 more years.)

The disagreement over the bank and assuming the states' debt nearly tore apart the new government, and led to the creation by Hamilton, Washington, and Vice President John Adams (among others, including Thomas and Charles Pinckney, Rufus King, DeWitt Clinton, and John Jay) of the Federalist Party.

Several factions arose in opposition to the Federalists, broadly referred to as the Anti-Federalists, including two groups who called themselves Democrats and Republicans. Jefferson pulled them together by 1794 into the Democratic Republican Party, united in their opposition to the Federalists' ideas of a strong central government that could grant the power to incorporate a national bank and bestow benefits to favored businesses through the use of tariffs and trade regulation.

During the Washington and Adams presidencies, however, the Federalists reigned, and Hamilton was successful in pushing through his programs for assuming state debts, creating a United States Bank, and a network of bounties and tariffs to benefit emerging industries and businesses.

In 1794, independent whiskey distillers in Pennsylvania revolted against Hamilton's federal taxes on their product, calling them "unjust, dangerous to liberty, oppressive to the poor, and particularly oppressive to the Western country, where grain could only be disposed of by distilling it."

The whiskey distillers tarred and feathered a tax collector and pulled together a local militia of 7,000 men. But President Washington issued two federal orders and sent in General Henry Lee commanding militias from Pennsylvania, Maryland, New Jersey, and Virginia. To demonstrate his authority as commander-in-chief, Washington rode at the head of the soldiers in their initial attack.

The Whiskey Rebellion was put down and the power of the Federalists wasn't questioned again until the election of 1800, which Jefferson's Democratic Republican party won in an election referred to as the Second American Revolution or the Revolution of 1800.

In the election of 1804, the Federalists carried only Delaware, Connecticut, and part of Maryland against Jefferson's Democratic Republicans (later to become the Democratic Party), and by 1832, as the Industrial Revolution was taking hold of America, the Federalists were so marginalized that they ceased to exist as an organized party.

JEFFERSON AND NATURAL RIGHTS

Back in the earliest days of the United States, Jefferson didn't anticipate the scope, meaning, and consequences of the Industrial Revolution that was just starting to gather steam in Europe about the time he was entering politics in the Virginia House of Burgesses. He distrusted letting companies have too much power, but he was focusing on the concept of "natural rights," an idea which was at the core of the writings and speeches of most of the Revolutionary-era generation, from Thomas Paine to Patrick Henry to Benjamin Franklin.

In Jefferson's mind, "the natural rights of man" were enjoyed by Jefferson's ancient tribal ancestors of Europe, were lived out during Jefferson's life by some of the tribal peoples of North America, and were written about most explicitly 60 years before Jefferson's birth by John Locke, whose writings were widely known and often referenced in pre-Revolutionary America.

Natural rights, Locke said, are things that people are born with simply by virtue of their being human and born into the world. In 1690, in his "Second Treatise on Government," Locke put forth one of the most well-known definitions of the natural rights that all people are heirs to by virtue of their common humanity. He wrote, "All men by nature are equal . . . in that equal right that every man hath to his natural freedom, without being subjected to the will or authority of any other man . . . being all equal and independent, no one ought to harm another in his life, health, liberty or possessions . . ."

As to the role of government, Locke wrote, "Men being . . . by nature all free, equal and independent, no one can be put out of his estate and subjected to the political power of another without his own consent which is done by agreeing with other men, to join and unite into a community for their comfortable, safe, and peaceable living . . . in a secure enjoyment of their properties . . ."

This natural right was asserted by Jefferson first in his "Summary View of the Rights of British America," published in 1774, in which he wrote, "The God who gave us life gave us liberty at the same time; the hand of force may destroy, but cannot disjoin them." His first draft of the Declaration of Independence similarly declared, "We hold these truths to be sacred and undeniable; that all men are created equal and independent, that from that equal creation they derive rights inherent and unalienable, among which are the preservation of life, and liberty, and the pursuit of happiness."

Individuals asserted those natural rights in the form of a representative government that *they controlled*, and that same government also protected their natural rights from all the forces that in previous lands had dominated, enslaved, and taken advantage of them.

THE DANGER OF PEOPLE HAVING FULL NATURAL RIGHTS

Hamilton and Adams' Federalists, as we can read in *The Federalist Papers*, strongly objected to Jefferson and Madison's notion that a government should be entirely elected and controlled by its people, with minimal taxation and military powers.

They were worried that if there wasn't a strong federal government, with a perpetual army, taxation powers, and at least half the legislature (the Senate) made up of an elite appointed by professional politicians from the states, the newly born United States might be too weak to fend off external foes like the French and Spanish—who both had stakes in North America at that time—or to put down possible future internal rebellions.

They suggested that Jefferson and Madison were idealists and dreamers, trying to recreate a utopian society in a dangerous world. Hamilton wrote about the risks of such idealism, responding to Madison, in *Federalist* No. 30, saying, "Reflections of this kind may have trifling weight with men [like you] who hope to see realized in America the halcyon scenes of the poetic or fabulous age; but to those [among us Federalists] who believe we are likely to experience a common portion of the vicissitudes and calamities which have fallen to the lot of other nations, they must appear entitled to serious attention. Such men [as those of us who would lead this nation] must behold the actual situation of their country with painful solicitude, and depreciate the evils which ambition or revenge might, with too much facility, inflict upon it."

Nonetheless, over the strong objections of the Federalists, James Madison pressed through Congress the Bill of Rights, which he had worked out in correspondence with Jefferson. Made up of the first 10 amendments to the Constitution, the Bill of Rights in its entirety was designed by Madison and Jefferson to prevent government from ever taking for itself the rights that they considered to be natural and God-given.

THE THREE THREATS

Thomas Jefferson's vision of America was quite straightforward. In its simplest form, he saw a society where people were first and institutions were second. In his day, Jefferson saw three agencies that were threats to humans' natural rights. They were:

- Governments (particularly in the form of kingdoms and elite groups like the Federalists)
- Organized religions (he rewrote the New Testament to take out all the "miracles" so that in *The Jefferson Bible* Jesus became a proponent of God-given natural rights)

- Commercial monopolies and the "pseudo aristoi," or pseudo aristocracy (in the form of extremely wealthy individuals and overly powerful corporations)

Instead, he believed it was possible for people to live by self-government in a nation in which nobody controlled the people except the people themselves. He found evidence for this belief both in the cultures of Native Americans such as the Cherokee and the Iroquois Confederation, which he studied extensively; in the political experiments of the Greeks; and in histories that documented the lives of his own tribal ancestors in England and Wales.

JEFFERSON CONSIDERS FREEDOM AGAINST MONOPOLIES A BASIC RIGHT

Once the Revolutionary War was over, and the Constitution had been worked out and presented to the states for ratification, Jefferson turned his attention to what he and Madison felt was a terrible inadequacy in the new Constitution: It didn't explicitly stipulate the natural rights of the new nation's citizens, and didn't protect against the rise of new commercial monopolies like the East India Company.

On December 20, 1787, Jefferson wrote to James Madison about his concerns regarding the Constitution. He said bluntly that it was deficient in several areas. "I will now tell you what I do not like," he wrote. "First, the omission of a bill of rights, providing clearly, and without the aid of sophism, for freedom of religion, freedom of the press, protection against standing armies, restriction of monopolies, the eternal and unremitting force of the habeas corpus laws, and trials by jury in all matters of fact triable by the laws of the land, and not by the laws of nations."

Such a bill protecting natural persons from out-of-control governments or commercial monopolies shouldn't just be limited to America, Jefferson believed. "Let me add," he summarized, "that a bill of rights is what the people are entitled to against every government on earth, general or particular; and what no just government should refuse, or rest on inference."

In 1788, Jefferson wrote about his concerns to several people. In a letter to Mr. A. Donald, on February 7, he defined the items that should be in a bill of rights. "By a declaration of rights, I mean one which shall stipulate freedom of religion, freedom of the press, freedom of commerce against monopolies, trial by juries in all cases, no suspensions of the habeas corpus, no standing armies. These are fetters against doing evil, which no honest government should decline."

Jefferson kept pushing for a law, written into the Constitution as an amendment, which would prevent companies from growing so large that they could dominate entire industries or have the power to influence the people's government.

On February 12, 1788, he wrote to Mr. Dumas about his pleasure that the U. S. Constitution was about to be ratified, but also expressed his concerns about what was missing from the Constitution. He was pushing hard for his own state to reject the Constitution if it didn't protect people from the dangers he foresaw. "With respect to the new Government," he wrote, "nine or ten States will probably have accepted by the end of this month. The others may oppose it. Virginia, I think, will be of this number. Besides other objections of less moment, she [Virginia] will insist on annexing a bill of rights to the new Constitution, i.e. a bill wherein the Government shall declare that, 1. Religion shall be free; 2. Printing presses free; 3. Trials by jury preserved in all cases; 4. No monopolies in commerce; 5. No standing army. Upon receiving this bill of rights, she will probably depart from her other objections; and this bill is so much to the interest of all the States, that I presume they will offer it, and thus our Constitution be amended, and our Union closed by the end of the present year."

By midsummer of 1788, things were moving along and Jefferson was helping his close friend James Madison write the Bill of Rights. On the last day of July, he wrote to Madison, "I sincerely rejoice at the acceptance of our new constitution by nine States. It is a good canvass, on which some strokes only want retouching. What these are, I think are sufficiently manifested by the general voice from north to south, which calls for a bill of rights. It seems pretty generally understood, that this should go to juries, habeas corpus, standing armies, printing, religion, and monopolies."

The following year, on March 13, he wrote to Francis Hopkinson about continuing objection to monopolies, "You say that I have been dished up to you as an anti-federalist, and ask me if it be just. My opinion was never worthy enough of notice to merit citing; but since you ask it, I will tell it to you. I am not a federalist. . . . What I disapproved from the first moment also, was the want of a bill of rights, to guard liberty against the legislative as well as the executive branches of the government; that is to say, to secure freedom in religion, freedom of the press, freedom from monopolies, freedom from unlawful imprisonment, freedom from a permanent military, and a trial by jury, in all cases determinable by the laws of the land."

All of Jefferson's wishes, except two, would soon come true. But not all of his views were shared universally.

THE RISE OF AN AMERICAN CORPORATE ARISTOCRACY

Years later, on October 28, 1813, Jefferson would write to John Adams about their earlier disagreements over whether a government should be run by the wealthy and powerful few (the pseudo-aristoi), or a group of the most wise and capable people (the "natural aristocracy"), elected from the larger class of all Americans, including working people.

"The artificial aristocracy is a mischievous ingredient in government," Jefferson wrote to Adams, "and provision should be made to prevent its ascendancy. On the question, what is the best provision, you and I differ; but we differ as rational friends, using the free exercise of our own reason, and mutually indulging its errors. You think it best to put the pseudo-aristoi into a separate chamber of legislation [the Senate], where they may be hindered from doing mischief by their coordinate branches, and where, also, they may be a protection to wealth against the agrarian and plundering enterprises of the majority of the people. I think that to give them power in order to prevent them from doing mischief, is arming them for it, and increasing instead of remedying the evil."

Adams and the Federalists were wary of the common person (who Adams referred to as "the rabble"), and many subscribed to the Calvinist notion that wealth was a sign of certification or blessing from above and a certain minimum level of morality. Since the Senate of the United States was elected by the state legislatures (not by the voters themselves, until 1913) and entirely made up of wealthy men, it was mostly on the Federalist side. Jefferson and the Democratic Republicans disagreed strongly with the notion of a Senate made up of the wealthy and powerful.

"Mischief may be done negatively as well as positively," Jefferson wrote to Adams in the next paragraph of that 1813 letter, still arguing for a directly elected Senate. "Of this, a cabal in the Senate of the United States has furnished many proofs. Nor do I believe them necessary to protect the wealthy;

because enough of these will find their way into every branch of the legislation, to protect themselves. . . . I think the best remedy is exactly that provided by all our constitutions, to leave to the citizens the free election and separation of the aristoi from the pseudo-aristoi, of the wheat from the chaff. In general they will elect the really good and wise. In some instances, wealth may corrupt, and birth blind them; but not in sufficient degree to endanger the society."

Jefferson's vision of a more egalitarian Senate—directly elected by the people instead of by state legislators—finally became law in 1913 with the passage of the Seventeenth Amendment, promoted by the Populist Movement and passed on a wave of public disgust with the corruption of the political process by giant corporations.

Almost all of his visions for a Bill of Rights—all except "freedom from monopolies in commerce" and his concern about a permanent army—were incorporated into the actual Bill of Rights, which James Madison shepherded through Congress and was ratified December 15, 1791.

But the Federalists fought hard to keep "freedom from monopolies" out of the Constitution. And they won. The result was a boom for very large businesses in America in the 19th and 20th centuries, which arguably brought our nation and much of the world many blessings.

But as we'll see in the way things have unfolded, some of those same principles have also given unexpected influence to the very monopolies Jefferson had argued must be constrained from the beginning. The result has sometimes been the same kind of problem the Tea Party rebels had risked their lives to fight: a situation in which the government protects one competitor against all others, and against the will of the people whose money is at stake—along with their freedom of choice.

As the country progressed through the early 1800s, corporations were generally constrained to act within reasonable civic boundaries. In the next chapter, we'll examine how Americans and their government viewed the role of corporations, up to the time of the Civil War and its subsequent amendments.

5

THE EARLY ROLE OF CORPORATIONS IN AMERICA

An effort is being made to build a railroad from Springfield to Alton. A [corporate] charter has been granted by the legislature, and books are now open for subscriptions to the stock. The chief reliance for taking the stock must be on the eastern capitalists; yet, as an inducement to them, we, here must do something. We must stake something of our own in the enterprise, to convince them that we believe it will succeed, and to place ourselves between them and subsequent unfavorable legislation, which, it is supposed, they very much dread.

—ILLINOIS CONGRESSMAN ABRAHAM LINCOLN, ADDRESSING THE LEADERS OF SANGAMON COUNTY, ILLINOIS, JUNE 30, 1847

Jane Anne Morris is a corporate anthropologist and writer in Madison, Wisconsin, and affiliated with POCLAD (the Program on Corporations, Law and Democracy), one of the leading organizations doing research and work in illuminating the story of corporate personhood.

She discovered that on the eve of his becoming Chief Justice of Wisconsin's Supreme Court, Edward G. Ryan said ominously in his 1873 address to the graduating class of the University of Wisconsin Law School, "[There] is looming up a new and dark power . . . the enterprises of the country are aggregating vast corporate combinations of unexampled capital, boldly marching, not for economical conquests only, but for political power. . . . The question will arise and arise in your day, though perhaps not fully in mine, which shall rule—wealth or man [sic]; which shall lead—money or intellect; who shall fill public stations—educated and patriotic freemen, or the feudal serfs of corporate capital. . . ."

In researching 19th-century laws regulating corporations, Morris found that in Wisconsin—as in most other states at that time:

- Corporations' licenses to do business were revocable by the state legislature if they exceeded or did not fulfill their chartered purpose(s).
- The state legislature could revoke a corporation's charter if it misbehaved.
- The act of incorporation did not relieve corporate management or stockholders/owners of responsibility or liability for corporate acts.
- As a matter of course, corporation officers, directors, or agents couldn't break the law and avoid punishment by claiming they were "just doing their job" when committing crimes, but instead could be held criminally liable for violating the law.
- State (not federal) courts heard cases where corporations or their agents were accused of breaking the law or harming the public.
- Directors of the corporation were required to come from among stockholders.
- Corporations had to have their headquarters and meetings in the state where their principal place of business was located.
- Corporation charters were granted for a specific period of time, like 20 or 30 years (instead of being granted "in perpetuity," as is now the practice).
- Corporations were prohibited from owning stock in other corporations in order to prevent them from extending their power inappropriately.
- Corporations' real estate holdings were limited to what was necessary to carry out their specific purpose(s).
- Corporations were prohibited from making any political contributions, direct or indirect.
- Corporations were prohibited from making charitable or civic donations outside of their specific purposes.

- State legislatures could set the rates that some monopoly corporations could charge for their products or services.
- All corporation records and documents were open to the legislature or the state attorney general.

Similar laws existed in most other states. It is important to understand that tens of thousands of entrepreneurs did business in the early Colonies and continue to do so today without being incorporated—the proverbial butcher, baker, and candlestick maker. To do business in America or most of the world does not require a corporate structure—people can run partnerships, individual proprietorships, or simply manufacture and sell products or offer services without any business structure whatsoever other than keeping track of the money for the IRS.

It's only when a group of people get together and put capital (cash) at risk and want to seek from the government legal limits on their liability and to legally limit their possible losses, that a corporate form becomes necessary. In exchange for these limitations on liability, governments demand certain responsibilities from corporations. The oldest historic one was that corporations "operate in the public interest" or "to the public benefit." After all, if the people, through their elected representatives, are going to authorize a legal limitation of liability for a group of people engaged in the game of business, it's quite reasonable to ask that the game be played in a way that throws off some benefit to the government's citizens, or at least doesn't operate counter to the public welfare.

But the bigger they got, the less America's corporations (or their investors) seemed to like regulation, and the more they started to seek more flexibility. Railroads, in particular, were finding themselves increasingly subject to local and state taxes, regulations, and tariff and passenger fare limits, which were specifically designed to keep prices affordable for the people and to limit the profits of the railroads to what the people's governments considered fair for state-authorized monopolies.

So, starting in the 1870s, the railroads and their owners began directing massive legal attacks against the power of governments to regulate them.

CORPORATIONS UNDER CONTROL

From the 1500s until 1886, corporations were considered the artificial creations of their owners and the state legislatures that authorized them. Because they were artificial legal entities, created only and exclusively by the states and sometimes referred to in the law as artificial persons, they were subject to control by the people of the state in which they were incorporated, who asserted their will through representative government. In American republican democracy, government's role is to serve the people and protect them from the predations of both foreign and domestic threats to their "life, liberty, and the pursuit of happiness." This has historically included control of corporate behavior.

Although until 1886 corporations operated in many of the same ways as today's corporations do, the local, state, and federal legislatures had what the owners of America's largest corporations considered a distressing tendency to limit their behaviors.

Pennsylvania corporate charters were required to carry revocation clauses starting in 1784, and in 1815, Massachusetts Justice Joseph Story said explicitly that corporations existed only because they were authorized by state legislatures. In his ruling in the *Terrett v. Taylor* case, he said, "A private corporation created by the legislature may lose its franchises by a misuser or nonuser of them. . . . This is the common law of the land, and is a tacit condition annexed to the creation of every such corporation."

THE SUPREME COURT TAKES OVER

But the states, as Charles and Mary Beard write in *The Rise of American Civilization*, "had to reckon with the Federalist interpretation of the Constitution by John Marshall, who, as Chief Justice of the Supreme Court of the United States from 1801 to 1835, never failed to exalt the [pro-business] doctrines of Hamilton above the claims of the states."

Marshall, appointed to the Court by Federalist John Adams (who had appointed—for life—only Federalists to all federal judgeships), was what would today be called a judicial activist. As the Beards wrote, "By historic irony, he [Marshall] administered the oath of office to his bitterest enemy, Thomas Jefferson; and for a quarter of a century after the author of the Declaration of Independence retired to private life, the stern Chief Justice continued to announce old Federalist rulings from the Supreme Bench."

In 1803, during the second year of Jefferson's presidency, Marshall took on a power for himself and future Supreme Courts, which made President Jefferson apoplectic. In the *Marbury v. Madison* case, as the Beards relate it,

"Marshall had been in his high post only two years when he laid down for the first time in the name of the entire Court the doctrine that the judges have the power to declare an act of Congress null and void when in their opinion it violates the Constitution. This power was not expressly conferred on the Court [by the Constitution]. Though many able men had held that the judicial branch of the government enjoyed it, the principle was not positively established until 1803 [by Marshall's ruling in this case] . . ."

Jefferson, shocked, bluntly expressed his concern to his old friend Judge Spencer Roane, the son-in-law of Patrick Henry and a Justice of the Virginia Supreme Court. "If this opinion be sound," Jefferson wrote, "then indeed is our Constitution a complete *felo de se* [legally, a suicide]. For intending to establish three departments, co-ordinate and independent, that they might check and balance one another, it has given, according to this opinion, to one of them alone, the right to prescribe rules for the government of the others, and to that one too, which is unelected by, and independent of the nation. . . .

"The Constitution," Jefferson continued in full fury, "on this hypothesis, is a mere thing of wax in the hands of the judiciary, which they may twist and shape into any form they please. It should be remembered, as an axiom of eternal truth in politics, that whatever power in any government is independent, is absolute also; in theory only, at first, while the spirit of the people is up, but in practice, as fast as that relaxes. Independence can be trusted nowhere but with the people in mass. They are inherently independent of all but moral law. My construction of the Constitution is very different from that you quote. It is that each department is truly independent of the others, and has an equal right to decide for itself what is the meaning of the Constitution in the cases submitted to its action; and especially, where it is to act ultimately and without appeal. . . .

"A judiciary independent of a king or executive alone is a good thing; but independent of the will of the nation is a solecism [an error or blunder], at least in a republican government."

In his decision putting the Supreme Court above the elected officials (the legislature and president), Marshall was echoing Hamilton's Federalist mistrust of any form of government constrained solely by those elected by the people. Kings had faced challenges, the Federalists argued, and fought back because as kings they could force decisions without having to wait for a consensus by the people. This powerful federal judiciary, only partially answerable to the people, the Federalists believed, was essential to the survival of the nation.

As Hamilton wrote in *The Federalist Papers* (No. 23), in a heated argument with James Madison about whether there should be constraints in the constitution that would prevent the U. S. government from operating outside the will of its people, "These [constitutional] powers ought to exist without limitation, BECAUSE IT IS IMPOSSIBLE TO FORSEE OR DEFINE THE EXTENT AND VARIETY OF NATIONAL EXIGENCIES, OR THE CORRESPONDENT EXTENT AND VARIETY OF THE MEANS WHICH MAY BE NECESSARY TO SATISFY THEM [capitals Hamilton's]. The circumstances that endanger the safety of nations are infinite, and for this reason no constitutional shackles can wisely be imposed on the power to which the care of it is committed."

Madison, an ally of Jefferson, replied with equal heat in numerous places, perhaps most eloquently in *Federalist* No. 39, when he wrote: "It is ESSENTIAL [capitals Madison's] to such a government that it be derived from the great body of the society, not from an inconsiderable proportion, or a favored class of it; otherwise a handful of tyrannical nobles, exercising their oppressions by a delegation of their powers, might aspire to the rank of republicans, and claim for their government the honorable title of republic."

Jefferson further elaborated his arguments for three *independent* and *equal-in-power* branches of government as well in numerous writings during the early years as the Constitution was being formed.

But that was then and this was 1803: The deed was done by Marshall, and the Federalists had won. That said, there is also no doubt that Marshall, like Hamilton, believed he was doing the best thing for the nation that he had served as a soldier during the Revolutionary War. In the 1819 *McCullough v. Maryland* decision, for example, he referenced government deriving all its power from and "by the people" no fewer than 11 times in his majority opinion. It was just that his notion of who "the people" were was more in line with Hamilton's and Adams' than with Jefferson's and Madison's.

RULINGS AND LAWS ON REVOKING CORPORATE CHARTERS

In a sense, a corporate charter is like a driver's license: It is permission to operate in a particular way, granted by the government. (The comparison is imperfect in technical details, but this point doesn't depend on those details.) Like a driver's license, a charter can be revoked if the privilege is abused.

In 1819, Marshall used the power he had given himself and the Supreme Court to alter the states' power to regulate or dissolve corporations.

King George III had chartered Dartmouth College in 1769 as a private college, but one part of Jefferson's agenda was to make a college education available to any citizen regardless of their ability to pay. In keeping with Jefferson's Democratic Republican philosophy of free public education, the state of New Hampshire dissolved Dartmouth's corporate charter and rechartered it as a public state school. Dartmouth sued to retain their private corporate charter status, claiming that their corporate charter granted by King George before the Revolution was still valid, and the case went to the Supreme Court.

Chief Justice Marshall, in an opinion clearly reflective of Federalist thought and opposed to Jefferson's plans, ruled that because the original corporate charter of Dartmouth College didn't contain a clause that would allow for its own revocation, and the charter "was a contract between the state and the College, which under the federal Constitution no legislature could impair," the State of New Hampshire had no authority to revoke the college's charter.

Even at this, Marshall was explicit about the need for restrictions on corporations, including that they are not citizens. As corporate historian and law professor James Willard Hurst notes, "The *Dartmouth College* case put states on warning that regulation of their corporate creatures must be compatible with the contract clause of the federal Constitution. Concerned to respect state control of corporate activity, the Court took pains to deny that a corporation was a 'citizen' of the chartering state so that it might claim in other states the benefits of the Constitution's privileges and immunities clause."

Even with this qualification, the response from the states—feeling that the Marshall Court had usurped their power to control or dissolve corporations—was furious. Newspapers wrote scathing editorials about the decision, citizens were outraged, and over the following years, numerous state legislators took action.

In response to the *Dartmouth* decision, Pennsylvania's legislature passed a law in 1825 that declared the legislature had the power to "revoke, alter or annul the charter" of corporations. New York state passed a similar law in 1828, including "Section 320" that said any acts by a corporation not specifically authorized in their charter were *ultra vires* (Latin for "beyond the power;" it basically means "you can't do that because you lack the legal authority") and grounds for revocation of the corporation's charter. Michigan,

Louisiana, and Delaware all passed laws in 1831 limiting the time of corporate charters.

In the following decade, Michigan, Delaware, Florida, and New York all passed laws that corporate charters could only be created or renewed by a two-thirds vote of the legislature. All together, during the 19th century 19 states passed laws in response to Marshall's ruling in the *Dartmouth* case, each specifying they had the authority to control corporations. Rhode Island's 1857 law is characteristic: "The charter or acts of association of every corporation hereafter created may be amendable or repealed at the will of the general assembly."

In 1855, the U. S. Supreme Court went along with the trend, ruling in the *Dodge v. Woolsey* case that the states have not "released their powers over the artificial bodies which originate under the legislation of their representatives." The Court added that, "combinations of classes in society . . . united by the bond of a corporate spirit . . . unquestionably desire limitations upon the sovereignty of the people. . . . But the framers of the Constitution were imbued with no desire to call into existence such combinations."

EARLY PRESIDENTS WARY OF CORPORATIONS

The Founders of America knew that without business there would be little progress in the new nation they had helped birth. Yet on commerce, Madison and many of the Founders were of mixed minds. They had seen firsthand the abuses of large monopolistic trusts and corporations like the East India Company, yet they also knew that the future of America was based in part on people pursuing entrepreneurial, mercantile dreams. In a letter to Edmond Randolph on September 30, 1783, Madison wrote, "Wherever Commerce prevails there will be an inequality of wealth, and wherever [an inequality of wealth prevails] a simplicity of manners must decline."

On the other hand, given the widespread nature of trade in his day, Madison knew it foolish to try to restrain it, at least unless it got as big as the ill-fated Bank of the United States. For example, in a speech to Congress on April 9, 1789, Madison said, "I own myself the friend to a very free system of commerce, and hold it as a truth, that commercial shackles are generally unjust, oppressive and impolitic—it is also a truth, that if industry and labour are left to take their own course, they will generally be directed to those objects which are the most productive, and this in a more certain and direct manner than the wisdom of the most enlightened legislature could point out."

When commerce was taken over by large corporate enterprises, however, Madison knew exactly where he stood. In 1817, he wrote, "There is an evil which ought to be guarded against in the indefinite accumulation of property from the capacity of holding it in perpetuity by . . . corporations. The power of all corporations ought to be limited in this respect. The growing wealth acquired by them never fails to be a source of abuses."

And in a letter to James K. Paulding on March 10, 1817, Madison made absolutely explicit a lifetime of thought on the matter. "Incorporated Companies," he wrote, "with proper limitations and guards, may in particular cases, be useful, but they are at best a necessary evil only. Monopolies and perpetuities are objects of just abhorrence. The former are unjust to the existing, the latter usurpations on the rights of future generations. Is it not strange that the Law which will not permit an individual to bequeath his property to the descendants of his own loins for more than a short and strictly defined term, should authorize an associated few, to entail perpetual and indefeasible appropriations . . ."

Because the Founders of America tended to agree with Thomas Hobbes that corporations had the potential to be "worms in the body politic," governments at all levels—municipal, county, state, and federal—had laws carefully circumscribing the behaviors of corporations.

After the American Revolution, it was a basic principle of democratic government to protect the people it represented from unrestrained corporate power. Thus, during the first few decades of the existence of the new United States of America, there were only a handful of corporations, most formed for international trade or banking.

Seeing in even these few corporations the possible reincarnation of an East India Company type of corporate plutocracy, in 1816 Thomas Jefferson wrote, "I hope we shall crush in its birth the aristocracy of our moneyed corporations which dare already to challenge our government in a trial of strength, and bid defiance to the laws of our country."

Those "moneyed corporations" grew in power and influence through Jefferson's lifetime and after his death in 1826. As mentioned in chapter 4, the rise of the Second Bank of the United States caused considerable consternation. Legislators railed against it for decades, particularly when the bank started involving itself in politics, and tried to terminate its corporate charter, an effort that finally succeeded when the bank went under in 1841.

President Martin Van Buren, in his first annual message to Congress in December 1837, said, "I am more than ever convinced of the dangers to which the free and unbiased exercise of political opinion—the only sure foundation and safeguard of republican government—would be exposed by any further increase of the already overgrown influence of corporate authorities."

EARLY GROWTH OF THE RAILROADS—AND THEIR LEGAL TACTICS

During the middle of the 19th century—roughly from the late 1820s to the early 1870s—the first incarnations of our modern economy evolved out of a previously agrarian and local small business economy. Other than the Second Bank of the United States, which was out of business by 1841, the dominant industries in America were the plantations, largely staffed by slaves, and the textile mills of the northeast, largely staffed by indentured immigrants from Europe.

Cheap coal, the cheap steel it made possible, and the telegraph brought dramatic changes to the landscape of America between 1820 and 1850. During this time, the railroads grew from obscurity to dominate the corporate and political landscape of the nation. Just 26 years after the steam locomotive was invented in England, the first public railway in the world opened in England in 1823. Four years later, with subsidies from the city of Baltimore, the first railroad in America—the Baltimore & Ohio, or B&O Railroad—was incorporated. In 1830, the first scheduled passenger train began operation, using the first U. S.-built steam locomotive, "The Best Friend of Charleston." In 1833, there were only 380 miles of track laid in the United States, and that year President Andrew Jackson became the first sitting president to ride a railroad, creating a new mass-transport sensation.

By 1840, though, more than 2,700 miles of track were in use in the United States, serving seven states, and by 1850, the total had exploded to over 9,000 miles of track. By 1860, largely through government subsidies to the new rail companies, over 30,000 miles of track were in regular use in the United States, and the railroads were the largest and most powerful corporations the nation had ever seen. By 1890, over 180 million acres of taxpayer-owned land had been deeded to the owners of the nation's largest railroads by various federal, state, and county governments.

ABE LINCOLN RELUCTANTLY JOINS THE RAILROADS

As the railroads grew in size, they also grew in political power. And they hired some of the nation's best lawyers. For example, in May 1853, the Illinois Central Railroad Company chose not to pay its property taxes to McLean County, Illinois, and sued the county in the Circuit Court to prevent collection. James F. Joy of Detroit, the head lawyer for the railroad, contacted a former Illinois state representative, now an attorney in private practice in the McLean County city of Bloomington, with an offer of employment.

But the young lawyer, who had already gained quite a reputation as an attorney and from his days in the legislature, felt that his personal loyalties in the case were with the county and not the railroad. So the attorney—young Abraham Lincoln—wrote a letter to T. R. Webber, the Champaign County Clerk of Court, asking for the job of defending the county against the railroad.

"An effort is about to be made to get the question of the right to so tax the [Railroad] Co. before the court and ultimately before the Supreme Court," Lincoln wrote, "and the [Railroad] Co. are offering to engage me for them. . . .

"I am . . . feeling that you have the first right to my services, if you choose to secure me a fee something near such as I can get from the other side."

Lincoln knew that the case would be big, the issues important, and the fee an attorney could earn from it would be a big help to his family. "The question in its magnitude to the [Railroad] Co. on the one hand and the counties in which the Co. has land on the other is the largest law question that can now be got up in the State," he wrote to the County's Clerk, "and therefore in justice to myself, I can not afford, if I can help it, to miss a fee altogether."

The county didn't answer his letter, and so Lincoln wrote to the railroad's attorney, Mason Brayman, saying, "Neither the County of McLean nor anyone on its behalf has yet made any engagement with me in relation to its suit with the Illinois Central Railroad on the subject of taxation, so I am now free to make an engagement for the [rail]road, and if you think of it you may 'count me in.'"

Brayman immediately sent Lincoln a check for $200 as a retainer, and Lincoln went to work for the railroad along with James Joy.

LINCOLN'S CASE FORESHADOWS A CORPORATE CLAIM OF PERSONHOOD

The case sailed through the Circuit Court and immediately went to the Illinois Supreme Court. In the May term of the court in 1854, Brayman and Lincoln represented the Illinois Central Railroad.

A brief written by Lincoln noted that Section Two, Article Nine of the Illinois State Constitution of 1847 required "uniform taxation" of all "persons using and exercising franchises and privileges." Arguing for the railroad, Lincoln claimed that they were a "person," and thus the nonuniform taxation of different railroad properties at different tax rates was unfair and unconstitutional under the Illinois State Constitution.

Lincoln both lost and won the case. The Illinois Supreme Court ruled unanimously that, on the one hand, the state legislature could "make exceptions from the rule of uniformity" with regard to corporations it had chartered, thus losing him the corporate personhood argument.

On the other hand, however, the Supreme Court ruled that the railroad's charter—which functioned also as a sort of contract between it and the state, since early railroad charters were more similar to modern-day state-subsidized public utilities than traditional private corporations—allowed for direct taxation of the railroad by the *state* based on its revenues, and therefore the *county* didn't have the authority to tax the railroad and the railroad didn't have to pay the tax bill.

LINCOLN SUES THE RAILROAD

Lincoln sent the Illinois Central Railroad—whose directors all lived in New York and thus had its headquarters there—a bill for his services in the case:

He asked for $5,000. James F. Joy refused to pay him that much, suggesting that Lincoln was asking for more than he was worth. (Joy's fee had been only $1200 for his work on the case.) "The simple truth is that the whole trouble was with Mr. James F. Joy . . . whom Mr. Lincoln afterward despised," a company memo later noted.

To resolve the issue, the railroad's president, William H. Osborne, suggested that Lincoln should simply sue the railroad and let a judge decide how much he should be paid. Lincoln preferred not to sue his client, and almost 3 years later, in March 1857, he traveled by railroad to New York, but was unsuccessful in prying his fee out of the railroad. With no other option, Lincoln filed a lawsuit against the railroad in McLean County Circuit Court, asking for his $5,000 legal fee.

The case opened on Thursday, June 18, 1857, then was postponed to the following Tuesday when it was well-attended, as Lincoln was a rising star and there was a huge curiosity factor. In the courtroom that day was a young law student, Adlai E. Stevenson, who, when he was later Vice President of the United States (1893 to 1897) would recall that, "It appeared to me in the nature of an amicable suit." In a process that took only a few minutes, the railroad agreed to pay Lincoln's $5,000 fee except that he had to reduce it by $200 as they had already advanced him that amount as a retainer. Lincoln admitted that he had forgotten about the $200 and agreed to the terms.

THE GREAT CORPORATE CRASH

Lincoln left the courtroom having won the judgment, but without any money. The railroad procrastinated in paying him, and on August 1, 1857 Lincoln had the sheriff issue a writ. On August 12, 1857, he was paid his $4,800 in a check, which he deposited and then converted to cash on August 31, 1857.

It was a fortunate date for Lincoln to get his cash, because just over a month later, in the Great Panic of October 1857, both the bank on which the check was drawn and the railroad itself were "forced to suspend payment."

Of the 66 banks in Illinois, the *Central Illinois Gazette* (Champaign) reported that by the following April, "27 have gone into liquidation" in a recession/depression that the *Chicago Democratic Press* declared on September 30, 1857, "The financial pressure now prevailing in the country has no parallel in our business history."

THE RAILROAD'S PRESIDENT AND HIS GENERALS

Attesting to the power of the railroads as an employer is that Lincoln, throughout the entire time he was negotiating with and suing the railroad, continued to work as their attorney. One of the railroad's attorneys noted, "We had a contract that Lincoln was to take no case against us and that I could call on him to help me when he was there; and when my clients [the railroads] wanted help I always got Lincoln."

Lincoln enjoyed, as did all of the railroad's lawyers, a free pass for unlimited travel, which no doubt helped when he was floating his candidacy for President—he served as a railroad lawyer up until the day of his nomination for President.

On March 19, 1860, just 2 weeks before the opening of the Republican Convention in Chicago where he was nominated as a candidate for President (on May 18), Lincoln defended the railroads in court in that same city and won the case, helping cement his credentials as a candidate for the Republicans.

Perhaps most interesting, and demonstrative of how tightly knit the railroads of the day were into the present and future leaders of the nation, is that while working for the railroad in Illinois, Lincoln met and befriended three men: George B. McClellan was, when Lincoln was first suing the railroad, the Vice President and Chief Engineer of the Illinois Central Railroad. Ambrose E. Burnside was Treasurer of the railroad. And a veteran of the Mexican war, Ulysses Grant, "was without success trying to win a livelihood at Galena, Illinois" and had apparently approached the railroad for employment.

Lincoln's biographer, Albert J. Beveridge, noted, "Within five years Lincoln was to make each of these [three] men a general in the Union army."

As the *History of the Illinois Central Railroad* notes, "Stephen A. Douglas, Abraham Lincoln, George B. McClellan, Ulysses S. Grant and Edward Harriman all played a major or minor role in the [railroad] line's development."

THE EMERGENCY OF THE CIVIL WAR

The Civil War was a huge boom for the largest corporations in America because government spending exploded for just about every conceivable commodity that was needed by the troops. By the time the war was over, several corporations that supplied war materials and transportation, particularly the railroads, were operating in multi-state and monopolistic ways that were raising alarm bells among citizens and in legislatures across the nation.

On July 1, 1862, President Lincoln signed into law under "military necessity" the Pacific Railway Bill, which granted to the Union Pacific and the Central Pacific Railroads ten sections of land along a right-of-way from Iowa to San Francisco. The bill also included government loans for building rail lines of $16,000 per mile for level ground, $32,000 per mile for railways crossing deserts, and $48,000 per mile for rails crossing mountains. The national railroad-building campaign became a frenzied activity, sloshing with money and manpower.

But the money was everywhere, and it spawned rampant corruption. As Attorney General Edward Bates wrote in his diary on March 9, 1863, "The demoralizing effect of this civil war is plainly visible in every department of life. The abuse of official powers and the thirst for dishonest gain are now so common that they cease to shock."

In his classic biography of Lincoln, Carl Sandburg wrote, "A procession of mouthpieces and fixers twined in and out of Lincoln's office from week to week . . ."

Sandburg notes that General James Grant Wilson wrote to Lincoln, "every contractor has to be watched" because "some of the most competent and most energetic contractors were the most dishonest, [and] could not be content with a fair profit." He quotes *Blackwood Magazine* of England as noting, "A great war always creates more scoundrels than it kills."

Between just June 1863 and June 1864, the War Department paid out more than $250,000,000. In the last year of the war, on November 21, 1864, Lincoln looked back on his actions and the growing power of the now-unleashed and enriched corporations, and wrote the following thoughtful letter to his friend Colonel William F. Elkins.

"We may congratulate ourselves that this cruel war is nearing its end. It has cost a vast amount of treasure and blood. The best blood of the flower of American youth has been freely offered upon our country's altar that the nation might live. It has indeed been a trying hour for the Republic; but I see in the near future a crisis approaching that unnerves me and causes me to tremble for the safety of my country.

"As a result of the war, corporations have been enthroned and an era of corruption in high places will follow, and the money power of the country will endeavor to prolong its reign by working upon the prejudices of the people until all wealth is aggregated in a few hands and the Republic is destroyed. I feel at this moment more anxiety than ever before, even in the midst of war. God grant that my suspicions may prove groundless."

THE RAILROADS RISE TO POWER

During the Civil War, the railroads rose to become the most powerful of the American corporations. Lincoln mentioned both their "great enterprise" and the conflicts that they were causing all over the nation by defying state and federal attempts to regulate them, and charging whatever prices they wanted for transportation of goods and people. Because most of the railroads were essentially monopolies (except where they met in large cities), as "the only game in town" they could charge whatever prices they wanted for transportation of goods and people.

The resulting expenses caused by this domination of the transportation industry by a few very large railroad corporations were increasingly passed along to consumers, government, and smaller companies who received their workmen or materials by rail. The unrestrained price increases that drove their profits were also driving a general inflation, even as they helped interconnect and build the nation.

"The great enterprise of connecting the Atlantic with the Pacific states by railways and telegraph lines has been entered upon with a vigor that gives assurance of success," Lincoln noted in his fourth annual message to the nation on December 6, 1864, "notwithstanding the embarrassments arising from the prevailing high prices of materials and labor."

At the same time, under the growing influence of railroad money and power, courts and legislatures were making business more risk-free for the railroad corporations. In 1864, Congress passed the Contract Labor Law, which allowed employers to exchange a year's low-cost or free labor for passage and immigration from a foreign nation to the United States. The main effect—and one of the main goals—of this legislation was to break up strikes and lower labor costs by increasing the labor pool and thus introducing greater competition among humans for jobs.

While the courts ruled that if a corporation broke a contract with another corporation, the aggrieved company would still have to pay for what it had already received, they also ruled that if a human broke a Contract Labor Law contract with a railroad corporation, that corporation wasn't obligated to pay the worker anything. As historian Howard Zinn points out, "The pretense of the law was that a worker and a railroad made a contract with equal bargaining power," the same as if two powerful corporations had entered into a contract with each other with equal legal resources. Thus, the railroads always won.

The first transcontinental railroad line, proposed by Lincoln during his campaign and started during his presidency, was completed on May 10, 1869. By 1871, over 45,000 miles of railroad track crisscrossed the nation. John D. Rockefeller was 11 years away from forming the Standard Oil Trust, and Andrew Carnegie's steel monopoly and J. P. Morgan's banking monopoly were rising in power and influence but not yet dominant forces in American business. At that time, railroads were king, the first truly huge American corporations, as the power to transport people and goods and crops from place to place and state to state energized the American economy and drove the westward expansion of the new nation.

The growth of the railroads, while supported in part by government grants of millions of acres of free land and millions of dollars of subsidies and tax abatements, also drew expressions of concern from the president and state legislatures. Transportation is a fundamental need, and people quickly became dependent on the railroads for fast long-distance transport, so the public became prey for predatory pricing practices.

On December 4, 1882, President Chester Arthur said in his annual address to Congress and the nation, "One of the incidents of the marvelous extension of the railway system of the country has been the adoption of such measures by the corporations which own or control the [rail]roads as have tended to impair the advantages of healthful competition and to make hurtful discriminations in the adjustment of freightage [prices]. These inequalities have been corrected in several of the States by appropriate legislation, the effect of which is necessarily restricted to the limits of their own territory."

As President Arthur noted, the states considered the railroad's ability to charge whatever they pleased as unfair, and by the mid-1880s, virtually all states had passed laws setting maximum fees and prices for fares (for people) and tariffs (for freight), or otherwise regulating the railroads. There was nationwide sentiment in favor of continuing to regulate the behavior of the country's largest and most aggressive corporations, particularly the railroads.

HOW FREEING THE SLAVES BECAME THE RAILROADS' SECRET WEAPON

On July 9, 1868, just after the Civil War, three-quarters of the states ratified the Fourteenth Amendment to the U. S. Constitution as part of a set of laws to end slavery. The intent of Congress and the states was clear: to provide full constitutional protections and due process of law to the now-emancipated former slaves of the United States. The Fourteenth Amendment's first article says, in its entirety, "All persons born or naturalized in the United States, and subject to the jurisdiction thereof, are citizens of the United States and of the state wherein they reside. No state shall make or enforce any law which shall abridge the privileges or immunities of citizens of the United States; nor shall any state deprive any person of life, liberty, or property, without due process of law; nor deny to any person within its jurisdiction the equal protection of the laws."

Along with the Thirteenth Amendment ("Neither slavery nor involuntary servitude . . . shall exist within the United States") and the Fifteenth Amendment ("The right of citizens of the United States to vote shall not be denied or abridged by the United States or by any State on account of race, color, or previous condition of servitude"), the Fourteenth Amendment guaranteed that freed slaves would have full access to legal due process within the United States.

Acting on behalf of the railroad barons, attorneys for the railroads repeatedly filed suits against local and state governments that had passed laws regulating railroad corporations. The main tool the railroad's lawyers tried to use was the fact that corporations had historically been referred to under law not as corporations but as artificial persons. Based on this, they argued, corporations should be considered persons under the free-the-slaves Fourteenth Amendment and enjoy the protections of the Constitution just like living, breathing, human persons.

Using this argument for their base, the railroads repeatedly sued various states, counties, and towns claiming that they shouldn't have to pay local taxes because different railroad properties were taxed in different ways in different places and this constituted the creation of different "classes of persons" and was thus illegal discrimination. For almost 20 years, these arguments did not succeed.

In 1873, one of the first Supreme Court rulings on the Fourteenth

Amendment, which had been passed only 5 years earlier, involved not slaves but the railroads. Writing in the lead opinion, Justice Samuel F. Miller minced no words in chastising corporations for trying to claim the rights of human beings.

The Fourteenth Amendment's "one pervading purpose," he wrote in the majority opinion, "was the freedom of the slave race, the security and firm establishment of that freedom, and the protection of the newly-made freeman and citizen from the oppression of those who had formerly exercised unlimited dominion over him."

The railroads, however, had a lot of money to pay for lawyers, and railroad lawyer S. W. Sanderson had the reputation of a pit bull. Undeterred, the railroads again and again argued their corporations-are-persons position all the way to the Supreme Court. The peak year for their legal assault was 1877, with four different cases reaching the Supreme Court in which the railroads argued that governments could not regulate their fees or activities or tax them in differing ways because governments can't interfere to such an extent in the lives of "persons" and because different laws and taxes in different states and counties represented illegal discrimination against the persons of the railroads under the Fourteenth Amendment.

By then, the Supreme Court was under the supervision of Chief Justice Morris Remick Waite, himself a former railroad attorney. Associate Justice Stephen Field, who was so openly on the side of the railroads in case after case that he annoyed his colleagues, also heavily influenced the Court. In each of the previous four cases, the Court ruled that the Fourteenth Amendment was not intended to regulate interstate commerce and therefore not applicable. But in none of those cases did Waite or any other justice muster a majority opinion on the issue of whether or not railroad corporations were persons under the Constitution, and so Miller's "one pervading purpose" of the Fourteenth Amendment as being to free slaves prevailed.

Having lost four cases in one year took a bit of the wind out of the sails of the railroads, and there followed a few years of relative calm. The railroads continued to assert that they were persons, but states and localities continued to call them artificial persons and pass laws regulating their activities.

Throughout the 1870s and 1880s, the issue of corporate personhood was frequently debated in newspapers and political speeches, with a handful of the nation's largest corporations arguing "for" and most of the voters, newspaper editorialists, and politicians arguing "against." Across America, politicians were elected repeatedly on platforms that included the regulation of corporations, particularly the railroads. And yet the legal fight continued.

THE RAILROADS CLAIM THERE WAS A "SECRET JOURNAL"

In 1882, the railroad's attorneys floated the claim in an 1882 Supreme Court pleading that when the Fourteenth Amendment was drafted, "a journal of the joint Congressional Committee which framed the amendment, secret and undisclosed up to that date, indicated the committee's desire to protect corporations by the use of the word 'person.'"

It was a complete fabrication and they lost the 1882 case: Nobody took the "secret journal theory" seriously except Justice Field, who had ruled in the railroad's favor in the Ninth Circuit Court, where he was a judge at the same time he was on the Supreme Court, and which brought the case before the Supreme Court.

In future cases, the railroad attorneys were unable to produce or even prove legislative reference to the secret journal of the congressional committee.

Years later, Supreme Court Justice Hugo Black wrote, in a dissenting opinion in the *Connecticut General Life Insurance Company v. Johnson* case, "Certainly, when the Fourteenth Amendment was submitted for approval, the people were not told that the states of the South were to be denied their normal relationship with the Federal Government unless they ratified an amendment granting new and revolutionary rights to corporations. This Court, when the Slaughter House Cases were decided in 1873, had apparently discovered no such purpose. The records of the time can be searched in vain for evidence that this amendment was adopted for the benefit of corporations.

"It is true [303 U.S. 77, 87] that in 1882, twelve years after its adoption, and ten years after the Slaughter House Cases, an argument was made in this Court that a journal of the joint Congressional Committee which framed the amendment, secret and undisclosed up to that date, indicated the committee's desire to protect corporations by the use of the word 'person.'

"A secret purpose on the part of the members of the committee, even if such be the fact, however, would not be sufficient to justify any such construction. The history of the amendment proves that the people were told that its purpose was to protect weak and helpless human beings and were not told that it was intended to remove corporations in any fashion from the control of state governments. The Fourteenth Amendment followed the freedom of a race from slavery.

"Justice Swayne said in the Slaughter Houses Cases, supra, [ruled] that: 'By "any person" was meant all persons within the jurisdiction of the State. No distinction is intimated on account of race or color.' Corporations have neither race nor color. He knew the amendment was intended to protect the life, liberty, and property of human beings. The language of the amendment itself does not support the theory that it was passed for the benefit of corporations."

The 1882 case, however, would not be the last time attorneys for the railroads would try to use this fabricated story in their attempts to change the meaning of the Constitution.

There's an important lesson here about the relative ability of different parties to use the legal system for their protection, or to gain advantage. A human individual might try to advance a ludicrous claim such as "There was a secret journal" without the slightest evidence. Indeed, from time to time we hear of defendants trying such things. But it's highly unlikely that an actual person would have the ability to carry claims to the Supreme Court year after year after year, even when they have so little to go on.

This is directly relevant to the issue of a level playing field: When one party has dramatically more power, property, and wealth than another, it makes no sense to assert that both require equal protection.

Indeed, one aspect of the concentration of wealth that worried Jefferson and most American legislatures in those decades was that with enough wealth, a corporation can keep trying in the courts for centuries (literally centuries, because they don't die), no matter how much it costs, until they get what they want.

And ultimately, that's what happened.

6

THE DECIDING MOMENT

The first thing to understand is the difference between the natural person and the fictitious person called a corporation. They differ in the purpose for which they are created, in the strength which they possess, and in the restraints under which they act.

Man is the handiwork of God and was placed upon earth to carry out a Divine purpose; the corporation is the handiwork of man and created to carry out a money-making policy.

There is comparatively little difference in the strength of men; a corporation may be one hundred, one thousand, or even one million times stronger than the average man. Man acts under the restraints of conscience, and is influenced also by a belief in a future life. A corporation has no soul and cares nothing about the hereafter. . . .

—WILLIAM JENNINGS BRYAN, IN HIS ADDRESS TO THE OHIO 1912 CONSTITUTIONAL CONVENTION

Part of the American Revolution was about to be lost a century after it had been fought. At the time, probably only a very few of the people involved realized that what they were about to witness could be a counterrevolution that would change life in the United States and ultimately, the world, over the course of the following century.

In 1886, the Supreme Court met in the U. S. Capitol building, in what is now called the Old Senate Chamber. It was May, and while the northeastern states were slowly recovering from the most devastating ice storm of the century just 3 months earlier, Washington, D. C., was warm and in bloom.

In the Supreme Court's chamber, a gilt eagle stretched its 6-foot wingspan over his head as United States Chief Justice Morrison Remick Waite glared down at the attorneys for the Southern Pacific Railroad and the county of Santa Clara, California. Waite was about to pronounce judgment in a case that had been argued over a year earlier, at the end of January 1885.

The Chief Justice had a square head with a wide slash of a mouth over a broomlike shock of bristly graying beard that shot out in every direction. A graduate of Yale University and formerly a lawyer out of Toledo, Ohio, Waite had specialized in defending railroads and large corporations. In 1846, Waite had run as a Whig for Congress from Ohio but lost before being elected as a Republican state representative in 1849. After serving a single term, he had gone back to litigation on behalf of the biggest and wealthiest clients he could find, this time joining the Geneva Arbitration case suing the British government for helping to outfit the Confederate Army with the warship *Alabama*. He and his delegation won an astounding $15.5 million for the United States in 1871, bringing him national attention in what was often referred to as the Alabama Claims case.

In 1874, when Supreme Court Chief Justice Salmon P. Chase died, President Ulysses S. Grant had real trouble selecting a replacement, in part because his administration was embroiled in a railroad bribery scandal. His first two choices withdrew; his third was so patently political it was certain to be rejected by the Senate; three others similarly failed to pass muster. On his seventh try, he nominated attorney Waite.

Waite had never before been a judge in *any* court, but he passed Senate confirmation, instantly becoming the most powerful judge in the most powerful court in the land. It was a position and power he relished and promoted, even turning down the 1876 Republican nomination for President to stay on the Court and to serve as a member of the Yale [University] Corporation.

Standing before Waite and the other justices of the Supreme Court that spring day were three attorneys each for the railroad and the county.

The Chief Legal Advisor for the Southern Pacific Railroad was again S. W. Sanderson, a former judge—a huge, aristocratic bear of a man, over 6 feet tall, with neatly combed gray hair and an elegantly trimmed white goatee. For more than 2 decades, Sanderson had made himself a rich man litigating for the nation's largest railroads—artist Thomas Hill included a portentous and dignified Sanderson in his famous painting *The Last Spike* about the 1869 meeting of the rail lines of the Union Pacific and Central Pacific Railroads at Promontory Summit, Utah.

The lead lawyer for Santa Clara County, California, was Delphin M. Delmas, a Democrat who later went into politics and by 1904 was known as the Silver-Tongued Orator of the West when he was elected a delegate to the Democratic National Convention from California. While Waite and Sanderson had spent their lives serving the richest men in America, Delmas had always worked on behalf of local California governments and, later, as a criminal defense attorney. For example, he passionately and single-handedly argued before the California legislature for a law to protect the remaining redwood forests. (See chapter 2.)

Fiercely defensive about the "rights of natural persons," Delmas was a fastidious, unimposing man, known to wear "a frock coat, gray-striped trousers, a wing collar and an Ascot tie," whose "voice thrummed with emotion" and was nationally known as the master dramatist of America's courtrooms. He had a substantial nose and a broad forehead only slightly covered in its center with a wispy bit of thinning hair. In the courtroom he was a brilliant dramatist, as the nation would learn in 1908 when he successfully defended Harry K. Thaw for murder in what was the most sensational case of the first half of the century, later made into the 1955 movie *The Girl in the Red Velvet Swing*, starring Ray Milland and Joan Collins. (Delmas was played by Luther Adler.)

The case about to be decided in the Old Senate Chamber before Justice Waite's Supreme Court was about the way Santa Clara County had been taxing land and rights-of-way of the Southern Pacific Railroad. Claiming the taxation was improper, the railroad had refused for 6 years to pay taxes levied by Santa Clara County, and the case had ended up before the Supreme Court, with Delmas and Sanderson making the main arguments before the Court.

Although the case on its face was a simple tax case, having nothing to do with due process or human rights or corporate personhood, the attorneys for the railroad nonetheless used much of their argument time to press the issue that the railroad was a person and should be entitled to human rights under the Fourteenth Amendment.

THE MYSTERY OF 1886 AND CHIEF JUSTICE WAITE

In the decade leading up to this May day in 1886, the railroads had lost every Supreme Court case that they had brought seeking Fourteenth Amendment rights. I've searched dozens of histories of the time, representing a wide variety of viewpoints and opinions, but only two have made a serious attempt to answer the question of what happened that fateful day—and their theories clash.

No laws were passed by Congress granting that corporations should be treated the same under the Constitution as living, breathing human beings, and none have been passed since then. It was not a concept drawn from older English law. No court decisions, state or federal, held that corporations were persons instead of artificial persons. The Supreme Court did not rule, in this case or any case, on the issue of corporate personhood.

In fact, to this day there has been *no* Supreme Court ruling that could explain why a corporation—with its ability to continue operating forever—a legal agreement that can't be put in jail and doesn't need fresh water to drink or clean air to breathe—should be granted the same constitutional rights our Founders explicitly fought for, died for, and granted to the very mortal human beings who are citizens of the United States to protect them against the perils of imprisonment and suppression they had experienced under a despot king.

But *something* happened in 1886, even though nobody to this day knows exactly what or why.

That year, Sanderson decided to again defy a government agency that was trying to regulate his railroad's activity. This time he went after Santa Clara County, California. His claim, in part, was that because a railroad was a person under the Constitution, local governments couldn't discriminate against it by having different laws and taxes in different places. In 1885, the case came before the Supreme Court.

In arguments before the court in January 1885, Sanderson asserted that corporate persons should be treated the same as natural (or human) persons. He said, "I believe that the clause [of the Fourteenth Amendment] in relation to equal protection means the same thing as the plain and simple yet sublime words found in our Declaration of Independence, 'all men are created equal.' Not equal in physical or mental power, not equal in fortune or social position, but equal before the law."

Sanderson's fellow lawyer for the railroads, George F. Edmunds, added his opinion that the Fourteenth Amendment leveled the field between artificial persons (corporations) and natural persons (humans) by a "broad and catholic provision for universal security, resting upon citizenship as it regarded political rights, and resting upon humanity as it regarded private rights."

But that wasn't actually what the case was about—that was just a minor point. The railroad was being sued by the county for back taxes. The railroad claimed six different defenses. The specifics are not important because the central concern is whether the Court ruled on the Fourteenth Amendment issue. As will be shown below, the Supreme Court's decision clearly says it did not. But to put the railroad's complaint in perspective, consider this:

- On property with a $30 million mortgage, the railroad was refusing to pay taxes of about $30,000. (That's like having a $10,000 car and refusing to pay a $10 tax on it . . . and taking the case to the Supreme Court.)
- One of the railroad's defenses was that when the state assessed the value of the railroad's property, it accidentally included the value of the fences along the right-of-way. The county, not the state, should have assessed the fences. So the railroad withheld *all* its taxes.

Yes, this is an exceedingly picayune distinction. All the tax was still due to Santa Clara County; the railroad didn't dispute that. But they said that the wrong assessor assessed the fences—a tiny fraction of the whole amount—so they refused to pay *any* of the tax, and they fought it all the way to the U. S. Supreme Court.

And as it happens, the Supreme Court of the United States agreed: " . . . the entire assessment is a nullity, upon the ground that the state board of equalization included . . . property [the fences] which it was without jurisdiction to assess for taxation . . ."

The Court rejected the county's appeal, and that was the end of it. Except for one thing. One of the railroad's six defenses involved the Fourteenth Amendment. As it happens, since the case was decided based on the fence issue, the railroad didn't need those extra defenses, and none of them were ever decided by the court. But one of them—related to the Fourteenth Amendment—still crept into the written record, *even though the Court specifically did not rule on it.*

Here's how the matter unfolded. First, the railroad's defense.

THE TREATMENT THAT THE RAILROAD CLAIMED WAS UNFAIR

In the Fourteenth Amendment part of their defense, the railroad said:

"That *the provisions of the constitution and laws of California . . . are in violation of the Fourteenth Amendment* of the Constitution, in so far as *they require the assessment of their property at its full money value, without making deduction*, as in the case of railroads [that are only] operated in one county, and of other corporations, and of natural persons, *for the value of the mortgages . . .*" (Italics added.)

The italic portions say, in essence, "The state is taxing us railroads on the whole value of our property, instead of deducting our mortgage the way people do. That's not fair. Nobody else gets taxed that way."

The implication, of course, is that the state has no right to decide that corporations get different tax rates than humans. And the railroad was using the former slaves' equal protection clause (the Fourteenth Amendment) as its shield.

THE LEGAL DIFFERENCE BETWEEN ARTIFICIAL AND NATURAL PERSONS

In the Supreme Court, cases are typically decided a year after arguments are presented, allowing the justices time to research and prepare their written decisions. So it happened that on January 26, 1885 (a year before the 1886 decision was handed down), Delphin M. Delmas, the attorney for Santa Clara County, made his case before the Supreme Court in exquisitely persuasive language:

"The defendant claims [that the state's taxation policy] . . . violates that portion of the Fourteenth Amendment which provides that no state shall deny to any person within its jurisdiction the equal protection of the laws. . . . In defending the provisions of our Constitution, permit me, in the first place, to reply to this attack made upon it, which, if tenable, would place the organic law of California in a position ridiculous to the extreme. . . . If this be so, it is safe to say that there is hardly a State in this Union whose revenue system is not in danger of overthrow. . . .

"The shield behind which [the Southern Pacific Railroad] attacks the Constitution and laws of California is the Fourteenth Amendment. It argues that the amendment guarantees to every person within the jurisdiction of the State the equal protection of the laws; that a corporation is a person; that, therefore, it must receive the same protection as that accorded to all other persons in like circumstances. . . .

"To my mind, the fallacy, if I may be permitted so to term it, of the argument lies in the assumption that corporations are entitled to be governed by the laws that are applicable to natural persons. That, it is said, results from the fact that corporations are [artificial] persons, and that the last clause of the Fourteenth Amendment refers to all persons without distinction.

"The defendant has been at pains to show that corporations are persons, and that being such they are entitled to the protection of the Fourteenth Amendment. . . . The question is, Does that amendment place corporations on a footing of equality with individuals?

"Blackstone says, 'Persons are divided by the law into either natural persons or artificial. Natural persons are such as the God of nature formed us; artificial are such as are created and devised by human laws for the purposes of society and government, which are called corporations or bodies politic.'

"This definition suggests at once that it would seem unnecessary to dwell upon, that though a corporation is a person, it is not the same kind of person as a human being, and need not of necessity—nay, in the very nature of things, cannot—enjoy all the rights of such or be governed by the same laws. When the law says, 'Any person being of sound mind and of the age of discretion may make a will,' or 'any person having arrived at the age of majority may marry,' I presume the most ardent advocate of equality of protection would hardly contend that corporations must enjoy the right of testamentary disposition or of contracting matrimony.

"The equality between persons spoken of in the Fourteenth Amendment obviously means equality between persons of the same nature or class, and not equality between persons whose very natures are absolutely dissimilar—equality between human beings, if the rights of natural persons are involved; equality between corporations of the same class, if the rights of artificial persons are involved. The whole history of the Fourteenth Amendment demonstrates beyond dispute that its whole scope and object was to establish equality between men—an attainable result—and not to establish equality between natural and artificial beings—an impossible result.

"The evolution of the Fourteenth Amendment began with the first Civil Rights Bill, which provided that—

"'*All persons born in the United States . . . are hereby declared to be citizens of the United States and such citizens of every race and color . . . shall have the same right in every state and territory in the United States to make and enforce contracts, to sue, be parties, and give evidence, to inherit, purchase, lease, sue, hold, and enjoy real and personal property, and to the full and equal benefit of all laws and proceedings for the security of person and property as is enjoyed by WHITE citizens.'* [capitals from Delmas' original text]

"That this law was intended to establish equality between men in their individual capacity, and had no reference to equality between men and corporations, is too plain for argument. The law took the rights of a white citizen as the standard of measurement, and simply commanded that the rights of all other citizens, whatever their race or color, should be equal to his. . . ."

At this point, Delmas cut right to the heart of the issue. Sanderson had before made his claim of the "secret committee" of Congress that helped write the Fourteenth Amendment and meant for it to equalize corporate persons and human persons. Delmas, if his performance before the Supreme Court was consistent with his later well-documented performances in criminal courtrooms, would have been trembling in righteous indignation as he said:

"Could Congress have by any possibility meant to confer upon artificial persons the same rights in the respects enumerated as were enjoyed by white citizens? Could it, for instance, have meant that a corporation should have the same right to 'give evidence' as a white citizen? And as to contracts, may not the state, which creates corporations, impose certain limitations upon their right or power to make contracts? . . . Under this leveling statute was it intended to abolish the right of a state to impose terms and limits upon its own creatures? . . .

"It is certain that this law has never been so understood or interpreted by any State. And if it is now so to be interpreted, what, I ask, is to become of the vast mass of legislation in all the States by which taxes, licenses, and exactions are demanded from corporations where none whatever is demanded from white citizens? . . .

"As of the broad meaning and generous scope of the Fourteenth Amendment, I yield my fullest assent. Standing in this presence, I would not attempt to dwarf the proportions of that historic provision by seeking to restrict its beneficent operation to a particular class or race. No. The law is as broad as humanity itself.

"Wherever man is found within the confines of this Union, whatever his race, religion, or color, be he Caucasian, African, or Mongolian, be he Christian, infidel, or idolater, be he white, black, or copper-colored, he may take shelter under this great law as under a shield against individual oppression in any form, individual injustice in any shape. It is a protection to all men because they are men, members of the same great family, children of the same omnipotent Creator.

"In its comprehensive words I find written by the hand of a nation of sixty millions in the firmament of imperishable law the sentiment uttered more than a hundred years ago by the philosopher of Geneva, and re-echoed in this country by the authors of the Declaration of the Thirteen Colonies: *Proclaim to the world the equality of man.*

"And realizing the dream of the poet, the philosopher, and the philanthropist, it may be that this great statute is destined to usher in the dawn of that era when national antipathies and animosities shall be appeased, national boundaries and barriers obliterated, and, under a system of universal justice, man shall be allowed to claim from man, in all climes and in all countries, equal protection, equal security, and equal rights.

"What, then, must a State of this Union do in order to bear its share in carrying out the behests of this great commandment, that all men shall be equal—shall receive the equal protection of the laws? The State must see to it that no man, no class, no order of men are granted privileges, immunities, distinctions that are denied upon the same terms to others; that no rank or superiority is accessible to one which is not upon equal conditions within the reach of all; that no badge of invidious discrimination or humiliating inferiority is affixed to any, the humblest member of the commonwealth.

"The State must see to it that the avenues leading to happiness are left equally open to all; that whatever pursuit is lawful for one is lawful equally for all; that whatever hopes aspirations, ambitions are licit for the most exalted shall be equally licit for the most humble; that into whatever paths leading to profit, place, or honor one man may venture to tread, all may upon an equal footing venture.

"To attain and accomplish all these ends in all the states is, I conceive, in some degree, the object of the Fourteenth Amendment. Its mission was to raise the humble, the down-trodden, and the oppressed to the level of the most exalted upon the broad plain of humanity—to make man the equal of man; but not to make the creature of the State—the bodiless, soulless, and mystic creature called a corporation—the equal of the creature of God. . . .

"Therefore, I venture to repeat that the Fourteenth Amendment does not command equality between human beings and corporations; that the state need not subject corporations to the same laws which govern natural persons; that it may, without infringing the rule of equality, confer upon corporations rights, privileges, and immunities which are not enjoyed by natural persons; that it may, for the same reasons, impose burdens upon a corporation, in the shape of taxation or otherwise, which are not imposed upon natural persons . . .

"I have now done. I am conscious of having occupied no inconsiderable portion of the time allotted by the court for the argument—not longer, I hope, however, than the importance of the questions at issue warrants. In saying this I am not unmindful of the propensity of counsel to magnify their causes. Self-complacency is ever ready to whisper exaggerated notions of the magnitude of our undertakings. Yet I cannot but think that the controversy now debated before your Honors is one of no ordinary importance. It is important to the people of California, not only on account of the very large amount [of tax money] at stake, but more, for that it involves the validity of their laws and Constitution. It is important to the many States . . . menaced by the same attack. It is important to every State of this Union whose sovereign attribute of taxation is here challenged."

A year and 5 months passed while the Supreme Court debated the issues in private. And then came the afternoon of May 10, 1886, the fateful moment for the fateful words of the Supreme Court, upon which hung much of the future of the United States and, later, much of the world.

CHIEF JUSTICE WAITE REWRITES THE CONSTITUTION (OR DOES HE?)

According to the record left to us, here's what *seems* to have happened. For reasons that were never recorded, moments before the Supreme Court was to render its decision in the now-infamous *Santa Clara County v. Southern Pacific Railroad Company* case, Chief Justice Waite turned his attention to Delmas and the other attorneys present.

As railroad attorney Sanderson and his two colleagues watched, Waite told Delmas and his two colleagues, "The court does not wish to hear argument on the question whether the provision in the Fourteenth Amendment to the Constitution, which forbids a state to deny to any person within its jurisdiction the equal protection of the laws, applies to these corporations. We are of the opinion that it does." He then turned to Justice Harlan, who delivered the Court's opinion in the case.

In the written record of the case, the court recorder noted, "The defendant corporations are persons within the intent of the clause in section 1 of the Fourteenth Amendment to the Constitution of the United States, which forbids a State to deny to any person within its jurisdiction the equal protection of the laws."

This written statement, that corporations were persons rather than artificial persons, with an equal footing under the Bill of Rights as humans, was not a formal ruling of the court, but was reportedly a simple statement by its Chief Justice, recorded by the court recorder.

- There was no Supreme Court decision to the effect that corporations are equal to natural persons and not artificial persons.
- There were no opinions issued to that effect, and therefore no dissenting opinions on this immensely important constitutional issue.

The written record, as excerpted above, simply *assumed* corporate personhood without any explanation why. The only explanation provided was the court recorder's reference to something he says Waite said, which essentially says, "that's just our opinion" without providing legal argument.

In these two sentences (according to the conventional wisdom), Waite weakened the kind of democratic republic the original authors of the Constitution had envisioned, and set the stage for the future worldwide damage of our environmental, governmental, and cultural commons. The plutocracy that had arisen with the East India Company in 1600 and been fought back by America's Founders, had gained a tool that was to allow them, in the coming decades, to once again gain control of most of North America and then the world.

Ironically, of the 307 Fourteenth Amendment cases brought before the Supreme Court in the years between Waite's proclamation and 1910, only 19 dealt with African Americans: 288 were suits brought by corporations seeking the rights of natural persons.

Supreme Court Justice Hugo Black pointed out 50 years later, "I do not believe the word 'person' in the Fourteenth Amendment includes corporations. . . . Neither the history nor the language of the Fourteenth Amendment justifies the belief that corporations are included within its protection."[82]

Sixty years later, Supreme Court Justice William O. Douglas made the same point, writing that, "There was no history, logic or reason given to support that view [that corporations are legally 'persons']."

There was no change in legislation, and President Grover Cleveland had not issued a proclamation that corporations should be considered the same as natural persons. The U. S. Constitution does not even contain the word "corporation," and has never been amended to contain it because the Founders wanted corporations to be regulated as close to home as possible, by the states, so they could be kept on a short leash—presumably so nothing like the East India Company would ever again arise to threaten the entrepreneurs of America.

But as a result of this case, for the past 100-plus years corporate lawyers and politicians have claimed that Chief Justice Waite turned the law on its side and reinvented America's social hierarchy.

"But wait a minute," many legal scholars have said over the years. Why would Waite say, *before* arguments about corporations being persons, that the court had already decided the issue—and then allow Delmas and Sanderson to argue the point anyway? Alternately, why would he say such a thing *after* arguments were already made? By all accounts, he was a rational and capable justice, so it wouldn't make sense that he would do either of those things.

Several theories have been advanced about what *really* happened. But first, let's look at what the Supreme Court decision actually said in the 1886 *Santa Clara* case.

WHAT THE COURT ACTUALLY SAID ABOUT PERSONHOOD

The Supreme Court generally tries to stay out of a fight. If a case can be thrown out or decided on simpler grounds, there's no need to complicate things by issuing a new decision. And in this case, the Court's decision specifically mentioned this. "These questions [regarding the Constitutional amendment] belong to a class which *this court should not decide* [emphasis added] unless their determination is essential to the disposal of the case . . ."

It continued, saying that the question of "unless it is essential to the case" depended on how strong the other defenses were. "Whether the present cases require a decision of them depends upon the soundness of another proposition, upon which the court . . . in view of its conclusions upon other issues, did not deem it necessary to pass." In other words, because of other issues (who should assess the fences), the Court wasn't even going to consider *whether* to rule on the Fourteenth Amendment corporate personhood issue.

The decision then identifies the fence issue, and concludes that there's nothing left to decide. "If these positions are tenable, there will be no occasion to consider the grave questions of constitutional law upon which the case was determined . . . as the judgment can be sustained upon this ground, it is not necessary to consider any other questions raised by the pleadings . . ."

So what actually happened? Why have people said, for all these years, that in 1886 the Waite Court in the *Santa Clara* case decided that corporations were persons under the Fourteenth Amendment? It turns out that the court said no such thing, and it can't be found in the ruling.

IT WAS IN THE HEADNOTES!

This apparent contradiction—lawyers and corporations and authors and courts saying for over 100 years that the Supreme Court had decided corporations are person, when the opinion itself does *not* say that and in fact explicitly says it didn't rule on constitutional issues—sent me to the law library in the Vermont Supreme Court building. Librarian Paul Donovan found for me Volume 118 of *United States Reports: Cases Adjudged in The Supreme Court at October Term 1885 and October Term 1886*, published in New York in 1886 by Banks & Brothers Publishers, and written by J. C. Bancroft Davis, the Supreme Court's reporter.

What I found in the book, however, were two pages of text that are missing from the online and official version. They were not part of the decision. They weren't even written by the Supreme Court justices, but were a quick summary-of-the-case commentary by Davis. He wrote commentaries like these for each case, "adding value" to the published book, from which he earned a royalty.

And there it was, in the notes. The very first sentence of Davis's note reads, "The defendant Corporations are persons within the intent of the clause in section 1 of the Fourteenth Amendment to the Constitution of the United States, which forbids a State to deny to any person within its jurisdiction the equal protection of the laws."

That sentence was followed by three paragraphs of small print that summarized the California tax issues of the case. In fact, the notes by Davis, further down, say, "The main—and almost only—questions discussed by counsel in the elaborate arguments related to the constitutionality of the taxes. This court, in its opinion *passed by these questions* [emphasis added], and decided the cases on the questions whether under the constitution and laws of California, the fences on the line of the railroads should have been valued and assessed, if at all, by the local officers, or by the State Board of Equalization . . ." In other words, the first sentence of "The defendant Corporations are persons . . ." has *nothing* to do with the case and wasn't the issue that the Supreme Court decided on.

Two paragraphs later, perhaps in an attempt to explain why he had started his notes with that emphatic statement, Davis remarks that, "One of the points made and discussed at length in the brief of counsel for defendants in error was that 'Corporations are persons within the meaning of the Fourteenth Amendment to the Constitution of the United States.' Before argument Mr. Chief Justice Waite said: 'The court does not wish to hear argument on the question whether the provision in the Fourteenth Amendment to the Constitution, which forbids a State to deny to any person within its jurisdiction the equal protection of the laws, applies to these corporations. We are all of the opinion that it does.'"

A half-page later, the notes ended and the actual decision, delivered by Justice Harlan, begins—which, as noted earlier, explicitly says that the Supreme Court is *not*, in this case, ruling on the constitutional question of corporate personhood under the Fourteenth Amendment or any other amendment.

I paid my 70 cents for copies of the pages from the fragile and cracking book and walked down the street to the office of attorney Jim Ritvo, a friend and wise counselor. I showed him what I had found and said, "What does this mean?"

He looked it over and said, "It's just headnotes."

"Headnotes? What are headnotes?"

He smiled and leaned back in his chair. "Lawyers are trained to beware of headnotes because they're not written by judges or justices, but are usually put in by a commentator or by the book's publisher."

"Are they legal? I mean, are they the law or anything like that?"

"Headnotes don't have the value of the formal decision," Jim said. "They're not law. They're just a comment, by somebody who doesn't have the power to make or determine or decide law."

"In other words, these headnotes by court reporter J. C. Bancroft Davis, which say that Waite said corporations are persons, are meaningless?"

Jim nodded his head. "Legally, yes. They're meaningless. They're not the decision or a part of the decision."

"But they contradict what the decision itself says," I said, probably sounding a bit hysterical.

"In that case," Jim said, "you've found one of those mistakes that so often creep into law books."

"But other cases have been based on the headnotes' commentary in this case."

"A mistake compounding a mistake," Jim said. "But ask a lawyer who knows this kind of law. It's not my area of specialty."

So I called Deborah L. Markowitz, Vermont's Secretary of State and one very bright attorney, and described what I had found. She pointed out that even if the decision had been wrongly cited down through the years, it's now "part of our law, even if there was a mistake."

I said that I understood that (it was dawning on me by then), and that I was hoping to have some remedies for that mistake in my book, but just out of curiosity, "What is the legal status of headnotes?"

She said, "Headnotes are not precedential," confirming what Jim Ritvo had told me. They are not the precedent. They are not the law. They're just a comment, with no legal status.

So how did it come that court reporter J. C. Bancroft Davis wrote that corporations are persons in his headnotes? And why have 100 years of American—and, now, worldwide—law been based on them? Here are the main theories that have been advanced regarding what happened.

THE REPUBLICAN CONSPIRACY THEORY THAT EMPOWERED FDR

In the early 1930s, the stock market had collapsed and the world was beginning a long and dark slide into the Great Depression and eventually to World War II. Millions were out of work in the United States, and the questions on many people's minds were, "Why did this happen? Who is responsible?"

The teetering towers of wealth created by American industrialists during the late 1800s and early 1900s were largely thought to have contributed to or caused the stock market crash and ensuing Depression. In less than 100 years, corporations had gone from being a legal fiction used to establish colleges and trading companies to standing as the single most powerful force in American politics.

Many working people felt that corporations had seized control of the country's political agenda, capturing senators, congressmen, the Supreme Court, and even recent presidents in the magnetic force of their great wealth. Proof of this takeover could be found in the Supreme Court decisions in the years between 1908 and 1914, when the Supreme Court, often citing corporate personhood, struck down minimum wage laws, workmen's compensation laws, utility regulation, and child labor laws—every kind of law that a people might institute to protect its citizenry from abuses.

Unions and union members were the victims of violence from private corporate armies and had been declared "criminal conspiracies" by both business leaders and politicians. It seemed that corporations had staged a coup, seizing the lives of American workers—the majority of voters—as well as the elected officials who were supposed to represent them. And this was in direct contradiction of the spirit expressed by the Founders of the country.

It was in this milieu that an American history book first published in 1927, but largely ignored, suddenly became a hot topic. In *The Rise of American Civilization*, Columbia University history professor Charles Beard and women's suffragist Mary Beard suggested that the rise of corporations on the American landscape was the result of a grand conspiracy that reached from the boardrooms of the nation's railroads all the way to the Supreme Court.

They fingered two Republicans: former senator (and railroad lawyer) Roscoe Conkling and former congressman (and railroad lawyer) John A. Bingham. The theory, in short form, was that Conkling, when he was part of the Senate committee that wrote the Fourteenth Amendment back in 1868, had intentionally inserted the word "person" instead of the correct legal phrase "natural person" to describe who would get the protections of the amendment. Bingham similarly worked in the House of Representatives to get the language passed.

Once that time bomb was put into place, Conkling and Bingham left elective office to join in litigating on behalf of the railroads, with the goal of exploding their carefully worded amendment in the face of the Supreme Court.

Thus "Republican lawmakers," the Beards said, conspired in advance to give full human constitutional rights to corporate legal fictions. "By a few words skillfully chosen," they wrote, "every act of every state and local government which touched adversely the rights of [corporate] persons and property was made subject to review and liable to annulment by the Supreme Court at Washington."

This conspiracy theory was widely accepted because the supposed conspirators themselves had said, very publicly, "We did it!" Earlier, in an 1882 case pitting the railroads against San Mateo County, California, Conkling testified (as a paid witness for the railroads) that he had slipped the "person" language into the amendment to ensure that corporations would one day receive the same civil rights Congress was giving to freed slaves. Bingham made similar assertions when appropriate during his turns as a paid witness for the railroads. As a result of these assertions, through the late years of the 1800s both were the well-off darlings of the railroads, basking in the light of their successful appropriation of human rights for corporations.

When the Beards' book was widely read in the early 1930s, it gave names and faces to the villains who had turned control of America over to what were then called the Robber Barons of industry. Conkling, Bingham, and Justice Waite were all dead by the time of the Great Depression, and all judged guilty by the American public of pulling off the biggest con in the history of the republic.

The firestorm of indignation that swept the country helped set the stage for Franklin D. Roosevelt's New Deal, using legislative means and packing the Supreme Court to turn back the corporate takeover—at least in part—and returning to average working citizens some of the rights and benefits they felt had been stolen from them in 1886.

It was widely accepted that Conkling and Bingham had pulled off this trick successfully, purposefully saying "person" instead of "natural person" or "citizen" when they helped write the Fourteenth Amendment, and corporate personhood was a fait accompli. It was done, and couldn't be undone. The Supreme Court, confronted with the reality of the language of the Fourteenth Amendment, had been forced to recognize that corporations were persons under the U. S. Constitution because of the precedent of the 1886 *Santa Clara* case.

Senator Henry Cabot Lodge apparently ratified the coup on January 8, 1915, when he unwittingly promulgated Conkling's myth in a speech to the Senate about the 1882 *San Mateo* case cited above.

"In the case of San Mateo County against Southern Pacific Railroad," Lodge said, "Mr. Conkling introduced in his arguments excerpts from the Journal [of the Senate committee writing the Fourteenth Amendment], then unprinted, to show that the Fourteenth Amendment did not apply solely to Negroes, but applied to persons, real and artificial of any kind. It was owing to this, undoubtedly, that the [Supreme] Court extended it to corporations."

The journal Lodge referenced is the secret journal that never existed. Nonetheless, it was a done deal, conventional wisdom suggested, and the

Supreme Court had been forced to acknowledge the reality of corporate personhood—or, some suggested, had gone along with it because Waite and the other justices were corrupt stooges of the railroads, but wielded the majority vote. In either case, it had been the intent of at least *some* of the legislators (Conkling and Bingham) who drafted the Fourteenth Amendment that corporations should have the constitutional rights of natural persons.

THE REPUBLICAN CONSPIRACY THEORY COLLAPSES

In the 1960s, author, attorney, and legal historian Howard Jay Graham came across a previously unexamined treasure in the personal papers of Chief Justice Waite, which had been gathering dust at the Library of Congress.

In Waite's private correspondences with Davis (his former Recorder of the Court's Decisions), Graham made a startling discovery: *The entire thing had been a mistake.*

What had vexed legal authorities for nearly 80 years was why Waite would say, "The Court does not wish to hear argument . . ." when the arguments were already finished. Further, why wasn't there any discussion of this explosive new doctrine of corporate personhood in the Court's ruling or in dissents? It was as if they said it, and then forgot they had said it. And complicating the situation further, if the Court had arrived at a huge constitutional decision with sweeping implications, why did the decision say it was based on a technicality about fences? It just didn't seem to add up.

Looking over Waite's personal papers, Graham found a note from Davis to Waite. At one point in the arguments, Waite had apparently told Sanderson to get beyond his arguments that corporations are persons and get to the point of the case. Court reporter Davis, apparently seeking to clarify that, wrote to Waite, "In opening, the Court stated that it did not wish to hear argument on the question whether the Fourteenth Amendment applies to such corporations as are parties in these suits. All the Judges were of opinion that it does.

"Please let me know whether I correctly caught your words and oblige."

Waite wrote back, "I think your mem. in the California Railroad Tax cases expresses with sufficient accuracy what was said before the argument began. I leave it with you to determine whether anything need be said about it in the report inasmuch as we avoided meeting the constitutional question in the decision."

Graham notes in an article first published in the *Vanderbilt Law Review* that Waite explicitly pointed out to court reporter Davis that the constitutional question of corporate personhood was *not* included in their decision. According to Graham, Waite was instead saying, "something to the effect of, 'The Court does not wish to hear further argument on whether the Fourteenth Amendment applies to these corporations. That point was elaborately covered in 1882 [in the *San Mateo* case], and has been re-covered in your briefs. We all presently are clear enough there. Our doubts run rather to the substance [of the case . . . the fence issue]. *Assume* accordingly, as we do, that your clients are persons under the Equal Protection Clause. Take the cases on from there, clarifying the California statutes, the application thereof, and the merits.'"

In my opinion, Waite was saying something to the effect of, "Every judge and lawyer knows that corporations are persons of the artificial sort—corporations have historically been referred to as 'artificial persons,' and so to the extent that the Fourteenth Amendment covers them, it does so on a corporation-to-corporation basis. But we didn't rule on the railroad's claim that corporations should have rights equal to human persons under the Fourteenth Amendment, so I leave it up to you if you're going to mention the debates or not."

Another legal scholar and author, C. Peter Magrath, was going through Waite's papers at the same time as Graham for the biography he published in 1963 titled *Morrison R. Waite: Triumph of Character*. In his book, he notes the above exchange and then says, "In other words, to the Reporter fell the decision which enshrined the declaration in the *United States Reports*. Had Davis left it out, *Santa Clara County v. Southern Pac. R. Co.* would have been lost to history among thousands of uninteresting tax cases."

It was all, at the very best, a mistake by a court reporter. There never was a decision on corporate personhood. "So here at last," writes Graham, "'now for then,' is that long-delayed birth certificate, the reason this seemingly momentous step never was justified by formal opinion." He adds, in a wry note for a legal scholar, "Think, in this instance too, what the United States might have been spared had events taken a slightly different turn."

GRAHAM'S CONSPIRACY THEORY

In *Everyman's Constitution*, Howard Jay Graham suggests that if there was an error made on the part of court reporter J. C. Bancroft Davis—as the record seems to show was clear—it was probably the result of efforts by Supreme Court Justice Stephen J. Field.

Field was very much an outsider on the Court, and despised by Waite. As Graham notes, "Field had repeatedly embarrassed Waite and the Court by close association with the Southern Pacific proprietors and by zeal and bias in their behalf. He had thought nothing of pressuring Waite for assignment of opinions in various railroad cases, of placing his friends as counsel for the railroad in upcoming cases, of hinting at times he and they should take, even of passing on to such counsel in the undecided *San Mateo* case 'certain memoranda which had been handed me by two of the Judges.'"

Field had presidential ambitions, and was relying on the railroads to back him. He had publicly announced on several occasions that if he were elected, he would enlarge the size of the Supreme Court to 22 so he could pack it with "able and conservative men."

Field also thought poorly of Waite, calling him upon his appointment "His Accidency" and "that experiment" of Ulysses Grant. Waite didn't have the social graces of Field, who was often described as a "popinjay," and even though he had been a lawyer for the railroads, the record appears to show that Waite did his best to be a truly impartial Chief Justice during his tenure, eventually literally working himself to death.

But Field was a grandstander who served on the Ninth Circuit Court of Appeals of California at the same time he was a Justice of the Supreme Court of the United States. It was often his "corporations are a person" decisions in California cases that led them to reappear before the U. S. Supreme Court—no accident on Field's part—including the *San Mateo* case in 1882 and the *Santa Clara* case in 1886.

And when the justices did *not* decide (contrary to what court reporter Davis published months after the decision) that constitutional issues were involved in the *Santa Clara County v. Southern Pacific Railroad* case, Justice Field was incensed. In his concurring opinion to the *Santa Clara* case, even though he agreed with the finding that fence posts should have a different tax rate than railroad land, he was clearly upset that the issue of corporate personhood was not addressed or answered in the case. He wrote, "[The court had failed in] its duty to decide the important constitution questions involved, and particularly the one which was so fully considered in the Circuit Court [where Field was also the judge], and elaborately argued here, that in the assessment, upon which the taxes claimed were levied, an unlawful and unjust discrimination was made . . . and to that extent depriving it [the railroad 'person'] of the equal protection of the laws. At the present day nearly all great enterprises are conducted by corporations . . . [a] vast portion of the wealth . . . is in their hands. It is, therefore, of the greatest interest to them whether their property is subject to the same rules of assessment and taxation as like property of natural persons . . . whether the State . . . may prescribe rules for the valuation of property for taxation which will vary according as it is held by individuals or by corporations. The question is of transcendent importance, and it will come here and continue to come until it is authoritatively decided in harmony with the great constitutional amendment (Fourteenth) which insures to every person, whatever his position or association, the equal protection of the laws; and that necessarily implies freedom from the imposition of unequal burdens under the same conditions."

In *Everyman's Constitution*, Graham documents scores of additional attempts by Supreme Court Justice Field to influence or even suborn the legal process to the benefit of his open patrons, the railroad corporations. Field's personal letters, revealed nearly a century after his death, show that his motivations, in addition to wealth and fame, were presidential aspirations—he wrote about his hopes that in 1880 and 1884 the railroads would finance his rise to the presidency, which may explain his zeal to please his potential financiers in 1882 in the *San Mateo* case and the 1886 *Santa Clara* case.

So, this conspiracy theory goes, after the case was decided—without reference to corporations being persons and without anybody on the court except Field agreeing with Sanderson's railroad arguments that they were persons under the Fourteenth Amendment—Justice Field took it upon himself to make sure the court's record was slightly revised: it wouldn't be published until J. C. Bancroft Davis submitted his manuscript of the Court's proceedings (titled *United States Reports*) to his publisher, Banks & Brothers in New York in 1887, and not released until Waite's death in 1888 or later.

After all, Waite's comments to reporter Davis were a bit ambiguous—although he *was* explicit that *no* constitutional issue had been decided. Nonetheless, recorder Davis, with his instruction from Waite that Davis himself should "determine whether anything need be said . . . in the report," may well have even welcomed the input of Field. And since Field, acting as the judge of the Ninth Circuit in California, had already and repeatedly ruled that corporations were persons under the Fourteenth Amendment, it doesn't take much imagination to guess what Field would have suggested court recorder Davis include in the transcript, perhaps even offering the language, curiously matching his own language in previous lower court cases.

Graham and Magrath, two of the preeminent scholars of the 20th century (Graham on this issue, and Magrath as Waite's biographer), both agree that this is the most likely scenario. At the suggestion of Justice Field, almost certainly unknown to Waite, "a few sentences" were inserted into Davis's final written record "to clarify" the decision. It wasn't until a year or more later, when Waite was fatally ill, that the lawyers for the railroads safely announced they had seized control of vital rights in the United States Constitution.

THE HARTMANN THEORY

Court recorders had a very different role in the 19th century than court reporters do today. It wasn't until 1913 that the Stenograph machine was invented to automate the work of court reporters. Prior to that time, notes were kept in a variety of shorthand forms, both institutionalized and informal. Thus, the memory of the reporter and his (in the 19th century, nearly all were men) understanding of the case before him, were essential to a clear and informed record being made for posterity.

Being a recorder for the Supreme Court was also not simply a stenographic or recording position. It was a job of high status and high pay. Although the Chief Justice in 1886 earned $10,500 a year, and the Associate Justices earned $10,000 per year, the Recorder of the Court could expect an income of more than $12,000 per year, between his salary and his royalties from publishing the *United States Reports*. And the status of the job was substantial, as Magrath notes in Waite's biography. "In those days the reportership was a coveted position, attracting men of public stature who associated as equals with the justices . . ."

Prior to his appointment to the Court, John Chandler Bancroft Davis was a politically active and ambitious man. A Harvard-educated attorney, Davis held a number of public service and political appointment jobs ranging from Assistant Secretary of State for two presidents to Minister to the German Empire to Court of Claims judge.

This was no ordinary court reporter, in the sense of today's professionals who do their jobs with clarity and precision but completely uninvolved in the cases or with the parties involved. He was a political animal, well-educated and traveled, and well-connected to the levers of power in his world, which in the 1880s, were principally the railroads.

In 1875, while Minister to Germany, Davis even took the time to visit Karl Marx, transcribing in their conversations one of what was considered one of the era's clearest commentaries about Marx. But Davis also left out part of what Marx said—Davis apparently viewed himself as both reporter and editor. In late 1878, a second reporter tracked down Marx and asked about Davis' omission. Here's an excerpt from that second article, as it appeared in the January 9, 1879 issue of the *Chicago Tribune*.

"During my visit to Dr. Marx, I alluded to the platform given by J. C. Bancroft Davis in his official report of 1877 as the clearest and most concise exposition of socialism that I had seen. He said it was taken from the report of the socialist reunion at Gotha, Germany, in May 1875. The translation was incorrect, he said, and he [Marx] volunteered correction, which I append as he dictated . . ."

Marx then proceeds to give this second reporter an entire Twelfth Clause about state aid and credit for industrial societies, and suggests that Davis had cooperated with Marx in producing a skewed record in recognition of the times and place where the discussion was held.

I own 12 books written by Davis, which give an insight into the status and role he held as recorder for the Supreme Court. My frayed, disintegrating copy of *Mr. Sumner, the Alabama Claims and Their Settlement*, published by Douglas Taylor in New York in 1878, is filled with Davis's personal thoughts and insights on a testimony before Congress. The book, first published as an article in the *New York Herald* by Davis, says such things as, "Like Mr. Sumner's speech in April 1869, this remarkable document would have shut the door to all settlement, had it been listened to. To a suggestion that we should negotiate for the settlement of our disputed boundary and of the fisheries, it proposed to answer that we would negotiate only on condition that Great Britain would first abandon the whole subject of the proposed negotiation. I well remember Mr. Fish's astonishment when he received this document."

He summarizes with extensive commentary such as, "I add to the foregoing narrative that Mr. Motley's friends were (perhaps not unnaturally) indignant at his removal, and joined him in attributing it to Mr. Sumner's course toward the St. Domingo Treaty . . ." He indirectly references his own time as Envoy to Germany when he writes, "They apparently forgot that the more brilliant, the more distinguished, and the more attractive in social life an envoy is, the more dangerous he may be to his country when he breaks loose from his instructions and communicates socially to the world and officially . . ." As you can see, Davis was fond of flowery writing, and thought well of himself.

And then I realized what I was reading. It related to the famous 1871 Geneva Arbitration Case, led by attorney Morrison Remick Waite, which won over $15 million for the U. S. government from England for their help of the Confederate army during the Civil War. Going to another book by Davis that I had purchased while researching this book, published in 1903 and titled *A Chapter in Diplomatic History*, I discovered that Davis had been quite active in the Geneva Arbitration Case.

During the negotiations with England, he writes, "I answered that I was very sorry at the position of things, but that the difficulty was not of our making; that I would carry his message to Lord Tenterden, but could hold out little hope that he would adopt the suggestion; and that, in my opinion, the Arbitrators should take up the indirect claims and pass upon them while this motion was pending.

"That evening I saw Lord Tenterden," Davis continues, "and told him what had taken place between me and Mr. Adams and the Brazilian arbitrator. . . . About midnight he came to me to say that he had told Sir Roundell Palmer what had passed between him and me, and that Sir Roundell had made a minute of some points which would have to be borne in mind, should the Arbitrators do as suggested. He was not at liberty to communicate these points to me officially; but, if I chose to write them down from his dictation, he would state them. I wrote them down from his dictation, and, early the next morning, convened a meeting of the counsel and laid the whole matter before them."

That Davis was playing more than just the role of a stenographer in this case was indisputable. And the case? It was, again, the Alabama Claims or Geneva Arbitration Case, which had made Morrison Remick Waite's career. Checking the University of Virginia's law school, I found the following notes on the Geneva Arbitration Case: "The United States' case was argued by former Assistant Secretary of State Bancroft Davis, along with lawyers Caleb Cushing, William M. Evarts, and Morrison R. Waite, under the direction of Secretary of State Hamilton Fish and Secretary of Treasury George Boutwell."

Waite and Davis had worked side-by-side on one of the most famous cases in American history (at the time), both in Geneva, Switzerland, and before the United States Congress. And all this a full 15 years before Davis was to put his pen to his understanding of the *Santa Clara County v. Southern Pacific Railroad* case when it came before the Supreme Court of which Waite was now Chief Justice and for which Davis was the head recorder.

Searching for traces of Davis on the Internet, I found an autograph for sale—it was a letter by President Ulysses Grant, signed by Grant, and also signed by Grant's Acting Secretary of State—J. C. Bancroft Davis.

And looking through the records of the City of Newburgh, New York, where Davis once lived, the Orange County New York Directory of 1878–1879 lists the following note about one of that city's distinguished citizens. "The Newburgh and New York Railroad Company was organized December 14th, 1864, the road was completed September 1st, 1869. J. C. Bancroft Davis was elected President of the Board of Directors . . . [on] August 1st, 1868."

Given his distinguished background, and his having worked with James Taylor and Jay Cooke of the railroads in late 1860s, it's hard to imagine that Davis would insert "corporations are persons" into the record of a Supreme Court proceeding without understanding full well its importance and consequences, even if he was encouraged to do so by Justice Field.

So here is the fourth and final possibility: John Chandler Bancroft Davis undertook to rewrite that part of the United States Constitution himself, for reasons that to this day are still unknown, but probably not inconsistent with his own personal political worldview and affiliation with the railroads, and that he did it with the encouragement of Fields.

Waite was so ill that he missed the entire session of the 1885 court, was very weak and sick in 1886 and 1887, and died in March of 1888: In all probability, he never knew what Davis had written in his name.

Whether it was a simple error by Davis, or Davis was bending to pressure from Fields, or if Davis simply took it upon himself to use the voice of the Supreme Court to modify the United States Constitution—the fact is that an amendment to the Constitution which had been written by and passed in Congress, voted on and ratified by the states, and signed into law by the president, was radically altered in 1886 from the intent of its post–Civil War authors.

And the hand on the pen that did it was that of J. C. Bancroft Davis.

7

THE CORPORATE CONQUEST OF AMERICA

The legal rights of the . . . defendant, Loan Company, although it be a corporation, soulless and speechless, rise as high in the scales of law and justice as those of the most obscure and poverty-stricken subject of the state.

—EXCERPT FROM JUDGE'S RULING IN
BRANNAN V. SCHARTZER, 25 OHIO DEC. 491 (1915)

While corporations can live forever, exist in several different places at the same time, change their identities at will, and even chop off parts of themselves or sprout new parts, the Chief Justice of the U. S. Supreme Court, according to its reporter, had said that they are "persons" under the Constitution, with constitutional rights and protections as accorded to humans. Once given this key, corporations began to assert the powers that came from their newfound rights.

- Claiming the First Amendment right of all "persons" to free speech, corporate lawsuits against the government successfully struck down laws that prevented them from lobbying or giving money to politicians and political candidates.
- Earlier laws (such as the Wisconsin laws noted in chapter 5) had said that a corporation had to open all its records and facilities to our governments as a condition of being chartered. But now, claiming the

Fourth Amendment right of privacy, corporate lawsuits successfully struck down such laws. In later years, they also sued to block OSHA laws allowing for surprise safety inspections of the workplace and stopped EPA inspections of chemical factories.

- Claiming the Fourteenth Amendment protection against discrimination (granting persons equal protection), the J. C. Penney chain store successfully sued the state of Florida, ending a law designed to help small, local business by charging chain stores a higher business license fee than locally owned stores.

On December 3, 1888, President Grover Cleveland delivered his annual address to Congress. Apparently, the President had taken notice of the *Santa Clara County* decision, its politics, and its consequences, for he said in his speech to the nation, delivered before a joint session of Congress, "As we view the achievements of aggregated capital, we discover the existence of trusts, combinations, and monopolies, while the citizen is struggling far in the rear or is trampled to death beneath an iron heel. Corporations, which should be the carefully restrained creatures of the law and the servants of the people, are fast becoming the people's masters."

WOMEN ASK, "CAN I BE A 'PERSON' TOO?"

Interestingly, during the era of the *Santa Clara County* decision granting the full protections of persons under the Constitution to corporations, two other groups also brought cases to the Supreme Court asking for similar protections. The first group was women. This was a movement with a fascinating history, its roots in the American Revolution itself.

In April of 1776, 32-year-old Abigail Adams sat at her writing table in her home in Braintree, Massachusetts, a small town a few hours' ride south of Boston. The war between the American colonists and their opponents, the governors and soldiers of the East India Company and its British protectors, had been going on for about a year. A small group of the colonists gathered in Philadelphia to edit Thomas Jefferson's Declaration of Independence for the new nation they were certain was about to be born, and Abigail's husband, John Adams, was among those men editing that document.

Abigail had a specific concern. With pen in hand, she carefully considered her words. Assuring her husband of her love and concern for his well-being, she then shifted to the topic of the documents being drafted, asking John to be sure to "remember the Ladies, and be more generous and favourable to them than [were their] ancestors."

Abigail knew that the men drafting the Declaration and other documents leading to a new republic would explicitly define and extol the rights of men, but not of women, and she and several other well-bred women were lobbying for the Constitution to refer instead to persons, people, humans, or "men and women." Her words are well-preserved and her husband later became President of the United States, so her story is better known than most of her peers.

By late April, Abigail had received a response from John, but it wasn't what she was hoping. "Depend on it," the future president wrote to his wife, "[that we] know better than to repeal our Masculine systems." Reflecting that attitude, Adams' friend and political ally Alexander Hamilton wrote in what became *The Federalist Papers* an explicit warning about the dangers to a new nation from the "intrigues of courtesans and mistresses."

Furious, Abigail wrote back to her husband, saying, "If perticular [sic] care and attention is not paid to the Ladies, we are determined to foment a Rebellion . . ."

All of Abigail's efforts were ultimately for nothing. Richard Henry Lee of Virginia introduced on June 7, 1776 a resolution that the colonies be free and independent states governed solely by free *men*, based on a document written by Thomas Jefferson and edited by John Adams and Ben Franklin. Adams played a strong role in the heated debate over the following month, which concluded with a vote to adopt the gender-specific language of Lee's resolution on July 2, 1776; Congress formalized it 2 days later as the Declaration of Independence.

Adams, Jefferson, Hamilton, and the other men of the assembly explicitly demanded rights for male citizens—and not for female citizens—when they crafted the Declaration. "Men" was not a generic reference to humans: The authors meant humans of the male gender. They wrote: "We hold these Truths to be self-evident, that all Men are created equal, that they are endowed by their Creator with certain unalienable Rights, that among these are Life, Liberty and the Pursuit of Happiness—That to secure these Rights, Governments are instituted among Men, deriving their just Powers from the Consent of the Governed . . ."

The men had won. Among the earliest laws of the Colonies were several legislating that men had power over women:

- A married woman was not allowed to make out a will because she was not allowed to own land or legally control anything else worthy of willing to another person.
- Any property she brought into the marriage became her husband's at the moment of marriage, and would revert to her only if he died and she did not remarry. But even then, she would get only one-third of her husband's property, and what third that was and how she could use it were determined by a male, court-appointed executor, who would supervise for the rest of her life (or until she remarried) how she used the third of her husband's estate she "inherited."
- When a widow died, the executor would either take the property for himself or decide to whom it would pass; the woman had no say in the matter because she had no right to sign a will. Women could not sue in a court of law except under the same weak procedures allowed for the mentally ill and children, supervised by men.
- If the man of a family household died, the executor would decide who would raise the wife's children, and in what religion: She had no right to make those decisions and no say in such matters. If the woman was poor, it was a virtual certainty that her children would be taken from her.
- It was impossible in the new United States of America for a married woman to have legal responsibility for her children, control of her own property, own slaves, buy or sell land, or even obtain an ordinary license.

WOMEN WORK FOR, THEN AGAINST, THE FOURTEENTH AMENDMENT

After the American Revolution, educated women picked up Abigail Adams' chant and began to quietly foment her "rebellion." They wrote poems and seemingly innocuous letters to the editors of newspapers, speaking indirectly about their demands for equal rights. Word spread. By the early 1800s, women's voices were getting louder, and many were demanding an amendment to the Constitution to give equal rights to women or prohibiting discrimination against women.

But women didn't gain any legislative successes until 1868, and that turned out to be a nonvictory. It was the Fourteenth Amendment, passed after the Civil War, which guaranteed due process of law to all "persons." Oddly, when it was being drafted in 1866, suffragettes Susan B. Anthony and Elizabeth Cady Stanton had argued strongly against it because it was the first time the word "male" was used in the Constitution or any constitutional amendments. The Fourteenth Amendment has two provisions, one guaranteeing due process of law to all persons and the other defining how lines would be drawn to decide how representation was to be apportioned in the House of Representatives. Section 2 includes the phrase "the proportion which the number of such male citizens shall bear to the whole number of male citizens."

Stanton wrote in 1866 that, "if the word 'male' be inserted [in this Amendment] it will take a century to get it out again." Despite her objections to its sexually discriminatory language, the Fourteenth Amendment was passed and ratified by enough states to become law. And Stanton was off in her prediction by only 2 years: The Equal Pay Act of 1963 and the Civil Rights Act of 1964 required equal pay for women and men and prohibited discrimination against women by any company with more than 24 employees.

WOMEN TEST THE FOURTEENTH AMENDMENT

In an attempt to test the Fourteenth Amendment, Susan B. Anthony went to her local polling station and cast a vote on November 1, 1872. Justifying her vote on the grounds of the Fourteenth Amendment, on November 12, Anthony wrote, "All persons are citizens—and no state shall deny or abridge the citizen rights . . ."

Six days later, however, she was arrested for illegally voting. The judge, noting that she was female, refused to allow her to testify, dismissed the jury, and found her guilty. Lacking the resources available to huge corporations, she was unable to repeatedly carry her cause to the Supreme Court as the railroads customarily did, and that judge's decision stood.

One year later, in the 1873 *Bradwell v. Illinois* decision, the Supreme Court ruled that women were *not* entitled to the full protection of persons under the Fourteenth Amendment. Justice Bradley wrote the Court's concurring opinion, which minced no words: ". . . the family institution is repugnant to the idea of a woman adopting a distinct and independent career from that of her husband. So firmly fixed was this sentiment in the founders of the common law that it became a maxim of that system of jurisprudence that a woman had no legal existence separate from her husband, who was regarded as her head and representative in the social state . . ."

Corporations had full legal existence and the constitutional rights of persons, but women could derive these rights only through their husbands. They didn't even *exist* separate from their husbands. And the Supreme Court said that the Fourteenth Amendment didn't apply to them, even though the Amendment explicitly said "persons."

Women didn't get the vote until 1920, and the Equal Rights Amendment that says, "Equality of rights under the law shall not be denied or abridged by the United States or by any state on account of sex," still hasn't been ratified by enough states to amend the Constitution and was most recently reintroduced to the Senate by Ted Kennedy in 2000.

FREED SLAVES ASK, "CAN I BE A 'PERSON,' TOO?"

The second group to petition the Supreme Court to be recognized as persons under the Fourteenth Amendment were the people for whom it was passed: freed slaves and their descendants. But 10 years after giving corporations full rights of personhood, the Supreme Court ruled in *Plessy v. Ferguson* that any person more than "⅛th Negro" was not legally entitled to full interactions with white "persons."

Justice Brown delivered the near-unanimous (one dissenter) opinion of the court, which established nearly a century of Jim Crow laws, saying, "Gauged by this standard we cannot say that a law which authorizes or even requires the separation of the two races in public conveyances is unreasonable, or more obnoxious to the Fourteenth Amendment than the acts of Congress requiring separate schools for colored children in the District of Columbia, the constitutionality of which does not seem to have been questioned, or the corresponding acts of state legislatures."

Court reporter J. C. Bancroft Davis, in the headnotes he wrote as commentary to the *Plessy v. Ferguson* case, said that the case had come about when

Plessy, "being a passenger between two stations within the State of Louisiana, was assigned by the officers of the [railroad] company to the coach used for the race to which he belonged, but he insisted upon going into a coach used by the race to which he did not belong."

Davis then quotes the Fourteenth Amendment, and says afterward, "The object of the amendment was undoubtedly to enforce the absolute equality of the two races before the law, but in the nature of things it could not have been intended to abolish distinctions based upon color, or to enforce social, as distinguished from political equality, or a commingling of the two races upon terms unsatisfactory to either."

This institutionalization of segregation by the 1896 *Plessy* case prompted U. S. Supreme Court Justice Hugo Black to note in 1938 that, "Of the cases in this court in which the Fourteenth Amendment was applied during its first fifty years after its adoption, less than one half of one percent invoked it in protection of the Negro race, and more than fifty percent asked that its benefits be extended to corporations."

FROM WOMEN'S RIGHTS LOST TO WORKER'S RIGHTS LOST

Fast on the heels of the passage and then Supreme Court interpretations of the Fourteenth Amendment, a new type of feudalism emerged in America with the Industrial Revolution, and included women, people of color, and first-generation immigrants. The explosion of factories in the East and Midwest was so great and so rapid that millions of workers emigrated from Europe to the United States, many of them arriving deeply in debt and indentured to their new employers.

My wife and I once bought a truckload of slate from a local quarry to pave an area in front of our home in Vermont. The quarry owner who delivered the stone told us, "This is from a huge pile of seconds that were mined over 150 years ago by indentured Welshmen." Looking into the history of the quarry industry in New England, I discovered that the incredibly difficult and often deadly job of quarryman was filled for more than 100 years in New England almost exclusively by indentured men freshly arrived from Wales, Scotland, and Ireland.

It turns out, according to author Peter Kellman, "Roughly half the immigrants to the English colonies were indentured servants. At the time of the

War of Independence, three out of four persons in Pennsylvania, Maryland, and Virginia were or had been indentured servants, people who had exchanged a certain number of years of bonded work (usually 4 to 25) for passage to America and/or to reduce family debts or avoid prison back in Europe." Increasing the labor pool with immigrants so that more people were forced to compete for the same jobs reduced the problem of strikes or workers demanding a living wage.

ELIMINATING COMPETITION

Over 2,000 corporations had been chartered between 1790 and 1860. They helped protect themselves from economic disasters by keeping a tight control of the economy and markets within which they operated. In this, they echoed the Federalist ideas of Hamilton and Adams.

Many companies deal with competition by working hard to earn our business, just as Adam Smith envisioned. But others don't—they feel that the best way to deal with competition is to eliminate it. And, as the East India Company had shown, two ways to do so were by getting the government to grant a monopoly or special tax favors, or by crushing or buying out one's competition.

Railroads were the leaders in the movement of monopoly grants, convincing lawmakers to use the government's power of eminent domain to seize land from farmers and settlers and grant it, free, to the railroads, to provide convenient and financially low-risk rights-of-way. In just 7 years after 1850, over 25 million acres of land were given to railroads, and often it was alleged to be the consequence of bribes. For example, the LaCrosse and Milwaukee Railroad in Wisconsin passed out $900,000 worth of stocks and bonds to the governor, 13 senators, and 59 assemblymen . . . and soon after received a million acres in free land and freedom from competition.

Another way of limiting the risk of competition was for large corporations to become larger. Some did this by buying their competitors, although many states had outlawed such practices in the 19th century. An easier method was to form consortiums, trade associations, and what were later called trusts, to muscle upstart entrepreneurs out of the marketplace.

By the time of *Santa Clara*, the generation that knew the East India Company was dead, and the corporate excesses that would eventually bring about the Great Depression hadn't yet happened. So most of these associations were quite open and free in declaring their intent to control prices, markets, and competition.

The American Brass Association, for example, came right out and said that their purpose in organizing was "to meet ruinous competition." Similar language was found in the charters, articles, or publications of trade groups that organized to protect large companies, in business categories as diverse as selling cotton, manufacturing matches, and distributing steel.

THE EARLIEST MERGERS AND ACQUISITIONS

The railroads made possible the rapid growth of other industries that previously had been hampered by an inability to quickly and easily transport their raw materials or finished goods. After the Civil War, this growth took on explosive proportions. Entrepreneurs of every stripe were starting and building companies, and the competition was cutthroat.

To deal with this excessive competition, companies joined together within industries to fix prices and control markets. By 1889, there were at least 50 of these consortiums operating in the United States; most were called trusts. They were essentially the same as what are today called corporate mergers, with each participating company selling their company to the trust in exchange for stock in the larger entity. This method would allow 8, 10, or 20 companies to become a single company, with the attendant benefits of larger economies of scale, joint purchasing, and the ability to control a large market while crushing smaller competitors.

A committee of the New York State Senate noted on March 6, 1888, "That combination [anticompetitive collusion] is the natural result of excessive competition there can be no doubt. The history of the Copper Trust, the Sugar Trust, the Standard Oil Trust, the American Cotton Oil Trust, the combination of railroads to fix the rates of freight and passenger transportation, all prove beyond question or dispute that combination grows out of and is a natural development of competition . . ."

When that New York Senate committee pursued their investigation in 1888, they called witnesses from trusts representing meat, milk, oil, sugar, cottonseed oil, oilcloth, and glass, among others. They learned that in just the 6 years since its creation in 1882, John D. Rockefeller's Standard Oil Trust increased the value of its holdings to the point where dividends paid out to trustees in 1888 were over $50 million. Simultaneously, the trust drove thousands of small oil and kerosene dealers out of business. The Sugar Trust had caused the price of sugar to soar nationally, and the Bagging Trust had doubled the price of bags in the previous decade. The Copper Trust had succeeded in raising the cost of copper from 12 to 17 cents a pound, making all of the copper companies profitable but hitting small businesses and consumers hard.

The revelations of the trusts' wild profits hit the newspapers as a big story, and the U. S. House of Representatives began their own investigation of trusts in April 1888, under the leadership of Representative Henry Bacon of New York.

Testimony before Congress showed that the trusts played hardball with entrepreneurs and small businesses who tried to compete with them. Unrelated trusts even cooperated with each other to wipe out small businesses in each other's markets.

A small businessman named Harlan Dow testified before Congress that when he tried to market kerosene in West Virginia in competition with Rockefeller's Standard Oil Trust, the railroads raised their prices to him for transporting his product. He tried to survive by shipping his kerosene in his own horse-drawn wagon, but in response to this, the Standard Oil Trust cut their price to consumers for kerosene in the areas where Dow was trying to sell it. "I stopped the wagon and it has been idle in the stable ever since," Dow told the investigating committee.

One of Standard's distributors, a man named F. D. Carley, even corroborated Dow's testimony, bragging about how he had been able to destroy every small competitor who tried to enter the marketplace or stay in business. "For instance," Carley said, "a man named Pettit got on some [oil] tanks at New Orleans . . . I dropped the price on him pretty lively." In the absence of competition and free choice, giant corporations have the power to do this, and consumers have nowhere else to go.

As newspapers nationwide screamed headlines about how the fat cats of industry were raking in millions while wiping out small businesses and fixing prices, the states got into the act. While most states already had laws or constitutional prohibitions against restraint of trade, the years from 1887 to 1896 saw dozens of new laws enacted. The first were in 1887 in Texas, then 1889 in Idaho, Kansas, Tennessee, and Michigan; by 1892 virtually every state had passed some sort of legislation, with one of the most powerful being passed in New York that year. The corporate charters of the Standard Oil Trust in

California and the Sugar Trust in New York were both revoked in this early wave of reaction.

SENATOR SHERMAN TRIES TO PROTECT SMALL BUSINESSES AND ENTREPRENEURS

Both of the major political parties denounced trusts in the 1888 Cleveland-Harrison presidential campaigns, and on December 4, 1889, Senator John Sherman of Ohio submitted Senate Bill No. 1, “A bill to declare unlawful, trusts and combinations in restraint of trade and production.” In promoting his bill, Sherman said that the people “are feeling the power and grasp of these combinations, and are demanding from every legislature and of Congress a remedy for this evil. . . . Society is now disturbed by forces never felt before.”

The bill was championed by Senators George of Mississippi, Edmunds of Vermont, and Hoar of Massachusetts, passed by an almost unanimous vote, and then signed into law by President Harrison in 1890. The Sherman Anti-Trust Act of 1890, in its entirety, says:

“Section 1: Every contract, combination in the form of trust or otherwise, or conspiracy, in restraint of trade or commerce among the several States, or with foreign nations, is declared to be illegal. Every person who shall make any contract or engage in any combination or conspiracy hereby declared to be illegal shall be deemed guilty of a felony, and, on conviction thereof, shall be punished by fine not exceeding ten million dollars if a corporation, or, if any other person, three hundred and fifty thousand dollars, or by imprisonment not exceeding three years, or by both said punishments, in the discretion of the court.

“Section 2: Every person who shall monopolize, or attempt to monopolize, or combine or conspire with any other person or persons, to monopolize any part of the trade or commerce among the several States, or with foreign nations, shall be deemed guilty of a felony, and, on conviction thereof, shall be punished by fine not exceeding ten million dollars if a corporation, or, if any other person, three hundred and fifty thousand dollars or by imprisonment not exceeding three years, or by both said punishments, in the discretion of the court.”

The Standard Oil Trust was clearly in violation of the new law, and of state laws that mirrored it. Six days after the state of Ohio ruled his trust an anticompetitive monopoly that violated the law, John D. Rockefeller announced on March 10, 1892 that his Standard Oil Trust would be dissolved into separate companies. By then, federal and state prosecutions of trusts were underway nationwide.

BUT THEY'RE STILL PERSONS

In 1906, President Theodore Roosevelt proposed campaign finance reform legislation in his annual address to Congress on December 3, saying, "I again recommend a law prohibiting all corporations from contributing to the campaign expenses of any party. . . . Let individuals contribute as they desire; but let us prohibit in effective fashion all corporations from making contributions for any political purpose, directly or indirectly."

Teddy Roosevelt made another run at trying to rein in the new corporate "persons" a year later, when in December 1907 he addressed Congress and said, "The fortunes amassed through corporate organization are now so large, and vest such power in those that wield them, as to make it a matter of necessity to give to the sovereign—that is, to the Government, which represents the people as a whole—some effective power of supervision over their corporate use. In order to ensure a healthy social and industrial life, every big corporation should be held responsible by, and be accountable to, some sovereign strong enough to control its conduct."

The result was the Tillman Act of 1907, the first law to bar (in a very limited fashion) corporate money from political campaigns. The Republican Roosevelt followed this by building a popular reputation as "the trustbuster" through his aggressive enforcement of the Sherman Anti-Trust act, using it to break up more than 40 large corporations during his presidency.

From 1909 to 1913, President Taft continued Teddy Roosevelt's tradition by further breaking up John D. Rockefeller's Standard Oil Trust into 33 separate companies, and breaking up American Tobacco. Working people loved him for it, as did entrepreneurs who again had opportunities in the newly freed marketplace.

But in the first year of the Wilson administration, the corporations reacted by trying to use the same law—the Sherman Anti-Trust Act—to get unions outlawed. They essentially argued that if it was illegal for corporate persons to conspire or form monopolies for their own benefit, then it should be equally illegal for human persons to do the same in the form of unions.

When corporations started using the Sherman Act against unions, going against the spirit of an act that was passed to protect the average person from excessive corporate power, the U. S. Congress passed the Clayton Anti-Trust Act of 1914 at the urging of President Woodrow Wilson. It specifically outlawed tying together multiple products, price discrimination, corporate mergers, and interlocking boards of directors. The Clayton Act also mandated the creation of the Federal Trade Commission (FTC). The FTC's original job was to control corporate wrongdoing, and it still carries that mission.

Through the Roaring Twenties, little was done to enforce these various acts by the corporate-friendly administrations of Calvin Coolidge ("the business of America is business") and Herbert Hoover. Seven years after the onset of the Great Depression, however, Franklin D. Roosevelt again began to enforce the Sherman Act, and it was pretty much the law of the land from that time until Ronald Reagan was elected President.

OTHER ATTEMPTS TO PUT HUMANS FIRST FAIL

On the one hand, legislation was being pushed through state legislatures right and left granting corporations human and superhuman powers. In the state of Ohio, for example, Senate Bill No. 8 "became effective on March 8, 1927, amending over 70 statutes and enacting more than 50 others." It repealed the "single purpose" requirement of incorporation, streamlined the processes, insulated corporate owners and managers from personal liability for corporate wrongdoing, and, in an sweepingly phrased provision, enabled Ohio corporations to "perform all acts," both within and outside the state, that could be performed by a natural person.

In 1936, the Robinson-Patman Act was passed, which made price discrimination illegal in an attempt to revive the Sherman Anti-Trust Act: It is still law, yet it is largely ignored today. And in 1950, the Celler-Kefauver Antimerger Act (another attempt to update and re-empower the Sherman Anti-Trust Act) was passed: It, too, is still law, yet it is now largely ignored.

Since 1950, no legislation of any consequence has passed that would put corporate power or personhood under the control of the people and their democratically elected governments, and most of the earlier laws have been watered down substantially.

For example, the Hart-Scott-Rodino Anti-Trust Improvements Act of 1976, itself a watering down of the Sherman Anti-Trust Act, was amended during the 2000 term of Congress, through passage of the Commerce-State-Justice appropriations bill, to reduce by about half the number of corporate mergers that would come under Federal Trade Commission review. Other mergers could proceed without such regulation.

THE WORKING CLASS TESTS THE FOURTEENTH AMENDMENT

Between the Civil War and the Great Depression, workers tried many times to gain equal rights with corporations and thus bargain on a level playing field for fair wages and decent working conditions. Carl Sandburg, in his biography of Lincoln, points out that the word "strike" was so new during the Civil War era that newspapers put it in quotes in their headlines. And, Sandburg notes, Lincoln was the first U. S. president to explicitly defend the rights of strikers, intervening in several situations where local governments were planning to use police or militia to break strikes and preventing the local governments from cooperating with the local corporate powers.

Nonetheless, from the time of Lincoln's death to the era of the Great Depression and Franklin D. Roosevelt, strikes were most often brutally put down, and corporations sometimes used intimidation, violence, and even murder to keep their workers in line. Probably the biggest turning point in the union movement, however, happened on February 11, 1937, when striking workers at General Motors won recognition for their union in the Great Sit-Down Strike in Flint, Michigan.

After the Great Depression, in the 3 years between 1937 and 1940, union membership more than tripled in the United States and the American working class became, for the first time since the Jefferson-Madison-Monroe era, a class with some powers of self-determination. Along with it, however, came the exploitation of workers by their own union bosses. All forms of organized business activity where there is money or power at stake, it seems, are equally susceptible to these corrupting forces, although unions never achieved as much power as corporations because more laws were passed to limit union behaviors . . . and they never achieved personhood status under the Fourteenth Amendment.

CHARTERMONGERING AND THE RACE TO THE BOTTOM, CIRCA 1900

As we've seen, throughout most of the 18th and 19th centuries, states were moving to restrict corporate activities by placing limits on the term, activities, and powers a corporation could take in their charter of incorporation. When Ohio broke up the Standard Oil Trust in 1892, Rockefeller and other corporate giants with similar problems began looking for states where they could recharter their corporations without all of the restrictions that Ohio and most other states had placed on them.

New Jersey was the first state to engage in what was then called chartermongering—changing its corporate charter rules to satisfy the desires of the nation's largest businesses. In 1875, its legislature abolished maximum capitalization limits, and in 1888, the New Jersey legislature took a huge and dramatic step by authorizing—for the first time in the history of the United States—companies to hold stock in other companies.

In 1912, New Jersey Governor Woodrow Wilson was alarmed by the behavior of corporations in his state, and "pressed through changes [that took effect in 1913] intended to make New Jersey's corporations less favorable to concentrated financial power."

As New Jersey began to pull back from chartermongering, Delaware stepped into the fray, by passing in 1915 laws similar to but even more liberal for corporations than New Jersey's. Delaware continued that liberal stance to corporations, and thus, as the state of Delaware says today, "More than 308,000 companies are incorporated in Delaware including 60 percent of the Fortune 500 and 50 percent of the companies listed on the New York Stock Exchange. The Delaware Corporation Law, the Court of Chancery, and the customer service–oriented staff at the Division of Corporations are all sound reasons why Delaware leads the nation as a major corporate domicile."

As New Jersey and then Delaware threw out old restrictions on corporate behavior, allowing corporations to have interlocking boards, to live forever, to define themselves for "any legal purpose," to own stock in other corporations, and so on, corporations began to move both their corporate charters and, in some cases, their headquarters to the chartermongering states. By 1900, trusts for everything from ribbons to bread to cement to alcohol had moved to Delaware or New Jersey, leaving 26 corporate trusts controlling, from those states, more than 80 percent of production in their markets.

CHARTERMONGERING GOES NATIONAL, THEN INTERNATIONAL

Between 1900 and 1970, in order to remain competitive, nearly all U. S. states rolled back their state constitutions or laws to make it easier for large corporations to do business in their states without having to answer to the citizens of the state for what they do or how they do it. At the same time, America's largest corporations—including the burgeoning defense industry—began to look overseas and see a whole new frontier of minerals and wood and raw materials owned by poor or powerless people, and great new places to build factories because the people would work for extremely low wages compared to workers in the United States who were trying to maintain a middle-class lifestyle. Not to mention all those potential customers for their products.

The race to the bottom of costs, regulation, taxes, and prices was underway, and would bring with it a race to the top in wealth for a few hundred multinational corporations and the politicians and media commentators they supported.

And soon that race would turn worldwide.

8

TRANSNATIONAL CORPORATIONS: THE GHOST OF THE EAST INDIA COMPANY RISES AGAIN

Curtin, what do you think of those fellows in Wall Street who are gambling in gold at such a time as this? . . . For my part, I wish every one of them had his devilish head shot off.

—PRESIDENT ABRAHAM LINCOLN, PERSONAL LETTER TO PENNSYLVANIA GOVERNOR ANDREW CURTIN, APRIL 25, 1864

It was the last week of June 1944, and the war wasn't going well for Adolf Hitler. The killing machines of his death camps were running full out, straining his resources and creating consternation as word leaked out across Europe. His forces were falling back before the Soviets and his generals openly worried about an Allied invasion on the French coast. On Thursday, June 29, almost all of the 1,800 Jews of Corfu were murdered upon their arrival at Auschwitz, while 20,000 Jewish women were relocated to the concentration camp at Stutthof. On Friday, June 30, more than 1,000 Parisian Jews arrived at Auschwitz.

This same weekend that opened July 1944, a 3-week meeting was convened in an isolated hotel in New Hampshire's White Mountains near the town of Bretton Woods. Bankers, economists, and representatives of the governments of 44 nations arrived for the meeting, which was convened as the International Monetary and Financial Conference of the United and Associated Nations.

The official history of the meeting suggests it was a group of nations getting together to work out a new international economic world order that would prevent a repeat of the Great Depressions and European inflations that had occurred in the 1930s and driven Hitler to prominence and power with his promises to "restore Germany to greatness."

Four years earlier, in November 1940, the German minister of finance, Walther Funk, had suggested a "New Order" for the world's finances and banking that would be dominated by Germany. Partly in response to this, John Maynard Keynes had begun, in 1942, to create a plan for an International Clearing Union (ICU), which formed part of the eventual basis of the Bretton Woods discussions.

According to Raymond F. Mikesell, who was present at the meetings, the legend of the time was that on the night of December 13, 1941, the U. S. Secretary of the Treasury, Henry Morganthau, "dreamed about an international currency," and the next morning called his Undersecretary, Harry Dexter White, to ask him to write up a paper on how it could be brought to pass.

"Two weeks later," Mikesell wrote, "White responded with a general outline of an International Stabilization Fund (ISF) and a (World) Bank."

During these 3 weeks and in subsequent meetings, the attendees hammered out the Bretton Woods Agreement, which created the International Monetary Fund (IMF), the World Bank, and laid early foundations for the General Agreement on Tariffs and Trade (GATT), which gave birth to the World Trade Organization (WTO). The group selected as the first U. S. Executive Director of the IMF the lead U. S. representative to the meeting and then–U. S. Undersecretary of the Treasury, Harry Dexter White.

The Bretton Woods Agreement wasn't ratified in whole by the United States until Bill Clinton's administration roughly 50 years later.

THE FEAR OF THE WORLDWIDE COMMUNIST CONSPIRACY

The main obstacle to ratification was that conservative conspiracy theorists—both in and outside the U. S. government but particularly in the U. S. Congress—suspected that the Bretton Woods meeting was an early attempt to use the United Nations to impose a "one-world government" on the United States, perhaps even in collaboration with what they saw as an international Communist conspiracy. That the meetings to work out the agreement began more than a year before the war ended was evidence, in the minds of some of those suspicious of the agreement, that there was something up the sleeves of those who met to hammer out the agreements.

Although GATT's predecessors were worked out before the end of World War II as part of Bretton Woods, the Eisenhower, Kennedy, Johnson, Nixon, Ford, Carter, and Reagan administrations couldn't or didn't work to get anything like it ratified by the U. S. Congress. As far as I could find, the first President to overtly push for full ratification of GATT was George Herbert Walker Bush, as part of his "New World Order" agenda.

In the early years after World War II, members of both parties in the U. S. Congress were wary of one-world government and an internationalist agenda. They not only refused to ratify all parts of the Bretton Woods Agreement but also went after Harry Dexter White, the IMF's first U. S. Executive Director.

In 1948, conservatives dragged White and Alger Hiss before a federal grand jury in New York City and accused them of "advocating the overthrow of the U. S. government by force" as agents of the Soviet Union, which in the 3 years since the end of WWII had gone from anti-Nazi ally to Communist enemy.

While White himself ultimately wasn't charged, his name was dragged through the newspapers along with Alger Hiss, who was indicted along with 12 others under the Smith Act. White, looking back on that time and the anti-Soviet hysteria in Congress, later noted that none of the organizers of Bretton Woods thought there would one day be such enmity on the part of the United States toward the Soviet Union, or that fear of the Soviets would sabotage their attempts to create a single worldwide banking and trading network.

He wrote, "It was expected that the early post-war world would witness a degree of unity and good-will in international political relationships among the victorious allies [including Russia] never before reached in peace-time. It was expected that the world would move rapidly . . . toward 'One World.' . . . No influential person, as far as I can remember, expressed the expectation or the fear that international relations would worsen during those years."

Mikesell, in his memoir of the Bretton Woods meetings, mentioned a private meeting he had with White the evening of April 19, 1947, just a few weeks before White was scheduled to testify before Joseph McCarthy's House Committee on Un-American Activities. "Some say he committed suicide to avoid testifying before the House Committee," wrote Mikesell about White's self-inflicted death shortly after their meeting. "I do not believe it," he added, although he offered no other explanation for White's death.

Joe McCarthy's concern about any sort of "one-world agenda" persisted: GATT wasn't ratified until roughly half a century later.

THE WORRISOME POWER OF TREATIES

Congress was reluctant to accept all the provisions of the Bretton Woods Agreement for an important reason: International treaties almost always supersede national laws. If the United States signed a treaty with, for example, Saudi Arabia that said, "In exchange for a cheap oil deal, all American gas stations must display a picture of the King of Saudi Arabia out front," then that would become the binding law of the United States from coast to coast, even though neither Congress nor the American citizens had ever voted on it. If you didn't put a picture of the king on your gas station, you could be subject to fines or imprisonment.

As former Secretary of State John Foster Dulles said on April 11, 1952, before a Louisville, Kentucky, American Bar Association meeting, "Treaties make international law and also they make domestic law. Under our Constitution, treaties become the supreme law of the land. . . ."

The language that provides for this is in the Constitution. Clause 2 of Article VI of the U. S. Constitution says, "This Constitution and the laws of the United States which shall be made in pursuance thereof, and all treaties made, or which shall be made, under the authority of the United States, shall be the supreme law of the land; and the judges in every state shall be bound thereby, anything in the constitution or laws of any state to the contrary notwithstanding." In other words, treaties and some agreements can supersede federal, state, or local law, or court decisions, with the single possible exception of constitutionally defined rights.

That's why the Founders were so wary of treaties. Knowing how draconian this treaty power was, the framers of the Constitution made it difficult for treaties to be ratified, by requiring a full two-thirds vote of the Senate instead of just a simple majority as with normal legislation. Such concerns kept the GATT from being ratified for years.

REAGAN, BUSH, AND CLINTON MAKE A FAST TRACK AROUND THE CONSTITUTION

The Reagan administration ushered in an era of mergers and acquisitions that in many ways resembled the trusts of the late 1800s and the 1920s. Corporations were well-represented in the corridors of power, and their power to combine into market behemoths was again blessed by an American president.

Time magazine reported in their August 3, 1981 issue, "President [Reagan] appointed William Baxter, a Stanford law professor who firmly believes in the virtues of large-scale enterprises unfettered by excessive Government regulation, to be his antitrust chief in the Justice Department. Baxter's boss, Attorney General William French Smith, succinctly stated the new Administration's philosophy in an oft-quoted speech before the District of Columbia Bar. Said Smith: 'Bigness in business is not necessarily badness. Efficient firms should not be hobbled under the guise of antitrust enforcement.'"

According to supply-side booster George Gilder, during the Reagan era there were ". . . 42,621 merger and acquisition deals worth $3.1 trillion, $89.9 billion in shareholder gains, [and] the doubling of stock market value in real terms . . ."

In addition to merging into giants that could keep out small competitors and largely control entire marketplaces, multinational corporations wanted the government to ease up on restrictions on their activities overseas. The U. S. Constitution specifically states that the president "shall have Power, by and with the Advice and Consent of the Senate, to make Treaties, provided two thirds of the Senators present concur."

That two-thirds-of-the-Senators requirement, however, made for a slow and contentious process, particularly when it came to issues that could affect American jobs. During the Ford era, the administration proposed that the Senate go around the Constitution and turn their power to negotiate and define the details of treaties over to the sole person of the president. They did this by using an obscure provision of the 1974 Trade Act that gave the president the right to negotiate trade treaties and then let him submit them to Congress for a straight up-or-down vote with no amendments allowed. Under these rules, debate is limited to 45 days in committee and 15 days on the floor of the House or Senate.

Called fast-track authority, each president from Richard Nixon to the first George Bush pushed to get this authority for himself. Bush pushed for ratification of the GATT agreement, but was unsuccessful.

But Bill Clinton, in the final days of his first 4-year term, joined with Senate leader Bob Dole to use political pressure, fast-track procedures, and careful timing (just before the Christmas recess) to bring the GATT agreement to pass.

Thus, after much lobbying and giving out of substantial campaign contributions by multinational business interests and a Senate vote to invoke cloture—a procedure that allowed only 30 hours of Congressional debate and forbade amendments—the final parts of the Bretton Woods Agreement and its offspring were ratified in November 1994, just as Congress was in a hurry to head home for the holidays. Most of the members of Congress didn't read the document they voted on, but it became the law of the land in any case. One month later, GATT gave birth to the U. N. World Trade Organization.

SOMEBODY READ THE AGREEMENT

Of course, the legislation had been around for a long time, but the record at the time, based on statements by at least one member of Congress, is that only one senator, Hank Brown of Colorado, actually read the agreement. He was a supporter of the trade agreements when he first decided to read their nearly 30,000 pages. By the time Brown finished reading it, however, he had changed his mind. On December 9, 1994, he wrote, "The GATT, which cleared Congress December 1, creates a form of world government limited to trade matters without fair representation for the U. S., and an international court system without due process. The details of this new government called the World Trade Organization (WTO) are buried in the thousands of pages of the Agreement.

"Fifty new committees, boards, panels and organizations will be created by the WTO making it an international bureaucracy of unprecedented size. The United States could be responsible for up to 23 percent of the cost of running the WTO, yet will have less than 1 percent of the control of how the money is spent. The WTO courts' (Dispute Settlement Body Panels) proceedings will be secret and decisions will be rendered anonymously by unaccountable bureaucrats. No conflict of interest rules exist to ensure impartial panelists. . . . Unfortunately, efforts which I supported to block the passage of the GATT implementing legislation (H. R. 5110/S. 2467) failed. The final measure, which I voted against, passed the Senate by a margin vote of 76-24." Senator Brown resigned after his one term and became a director of a multibillion-dollar corporation. Both the World Bank and the WTO were now reality.

Bretton Woods biographer Mikesell, looking back on the Bretton Woods Agreement, wrote in 1994 that, "There is little resemblance between the present functions and operations of the Fund and Bank and the way they were conceived at Bretton Woods." He noted that over a period as long as 50 years, most organizations either change or disappear. The IMF and World Bank changed, but didn't die. "They had too much money to fail," Mikesell remarked, "and they have increased their assets, and their staff, at a rate that rivals the postwar growth of the largest international behemoths."

GATT/WTO/NAFTA BECOME THE LAW OF THE LAND

The result of the fast-track implementation of these trade agreements was both swift and dramatic. For example, back in 1972, in response to consumer outcries and 25 years of lobbying by the Humane Society of the United States, Congress passed the Marine Mammal Protection Act, which barred U. S. tuna fishermen from using purse seine nets that killed hundreds of thousands of dolphins each year. (Dolphins often swim above schools of tuna.) In 1988, after extensive lobbying by American voters concerned about imported tuna, the law was strengthened with a provision banning the importation of tuna caught in purse seine nets anywhere in the world, and allowing for a "dolphin safe" label on tuna.

In 1995, the first year after ratification of GATT/WTO, Mexico challenged the United States under the rules of the WTO, claiming that the Marine Mammal Protection Act and subsequent laws that strengthened it were illegal violations of free trade. The Clinton administration took Mexico's side in the arguments, and the WTO prevailed: It is now legal to catch and import into the United States purse seine–netted tuna from anywhere in the world.

The WTO ruling was a problem for American packagers of imported and domestic tuna, because consumers loved the dolphin-safe labeling. So they lobbied Congress and U. S. regulatory agencies to get rules passed that as long as the fishing corporation certified that "no dolphins were *observed* being killed or seriously injured during a particular net set [catch]," tuna could still be labeled "dolphin safe."

Although the evidence is clear that dolphin populations have again begun to crash worldwide, oddly no fisherman has yet stepped up to notify his company that their catch should be thrown back into the ocean because he saw a dolphin die in the same nets that everybody admits killed millions of dolphins between 1959 and 1972.

According to Dr. Noreena Hertz of Cambridge University, as of 2001 in every environmental or species dispute that had come before the WTO, "the WTO has ruled in favor of corporate interests against the wishes of democratically elected governments."

THE ROLE OF NAFTA AND GATT/WTO

The biggest hit on the average family in the developed world has been the result of changes in how international trade is regulated. While Ross Perot stepped up to the podium during the presidential campaign and warned about "giant sucking sounds" from the south, both Bill Clinton and the elder George Bush supported the U. S. ratification of the North American Free Trade Agreement (NAFTA), saying that it would produce 170,000 new jobs.

NAFTA did, in fact, create that many new jobs and more—in Mexico. But in the United States, more than 420,000 jobs vanished by 1996 as a result of NAFTA, and over $28,000,000,000 in business was lost to U. S.-based workers. When job losses because of other international trade deals and the resultant U. S. trade deficit are factored in, more than 2.6 million U. S. jobs have vanished since the 1970s, most of them year-round and full-time, although many have been replaced by part-time or low-pay service sector jobs, thus the "net loss" of "only" 420,000 jobs.

Speaking in opposition to giving George W. Bush new fast-track authority, Congressman Bernie Sanders of Vermont wrote in the December 14,

2001 *Burlington Free Press*, ". . . our current trade policy has resulted in a record-breaking trade deficit in goods of more than $400 billion in 2000, including a trade deficit with China of more than $80 billion. Anyone with even a modest understanding of economics has to realize that a net [out]flow of $400 billion a year is a disaster. And it is.

"The result has been the loss of millions of decent-paying jobs as companies go abroad in search of cheap labor, or are forced to shut down because they can't compete against companies who set up shop in developing countries so they can pay starvation wages. . . .

"Today, the average American worker is working longer hours for lower wages than was the case 28 years ago—before the explosion of 'free trade.' This wage crisis is especially acute for entry-level workers without a college education. For men with less than six years in the work force and no college education, average real wages fell about 28 percent between 1979 and 1997."

Congressman Sanders noted and then refuted the argument that the WTO free trade agreements "would benefit the poorest people in the developing world. Really? Since the passage of NAFTA, more than 1 million more Mexicans work for less than the minimum wage of $3.40 per day, and 8 million Mexicans have fallen from the middle class into poverty."

An earlier editorial in the Gannett-owned *Burlington Free Press* in favor of fast track and free trade had noted how many people in Pakistan are now employed making clothing for Americans.

Congressman Sanders replied, "The *Free Press* mentions that fabric and apparel factories employ 60 percent of the industrial work force in Pakistan. True. But the *Free Press* forgets to mention that while the apparel industry in America has been decimated, and tens of thousands of jobs have been lost here, the average Pakistani worker is paid 25 cents an hour. The *Free Press* may think that the Tommy Hilfiger company is producing shirts in Pakistan because they want to help the poor people there. I think they're there because they can pay slave wages and increase their profit margin."

The bottom line is that neither the average working people of rich nations nor those of poor nations have benefited from free trade or its corollaries: The gains have gone to a few hundred corporations that are each larger, economically, than most nations. These treaties and agreements, Sanders concluded, "simply encourage a 'race to the bottom,' pushing wages down here and exploiting poor people abroad so that multinational corporations can expand their profits."

And now Americans are discovering that WTO can bite back when it comes to internal domestic tax policy. On January 15, 2002, the Associated Press reported that the WTO had concluded that American tax laws that let American-based transnational corporations exempt themselves from paying American taxes on income they earned abroad was illegal.

"The WTO appeals panel in Geneva ruled against a U. S. law granting multibillion-dollar tax breaks to Microsoft, Boeing, and thousands of other American companies operating overseas," the article said, indicating "the EU [European Union] could ask the WTO for permission to start imposing up to $4 billion in sanctions almost immediately." The Trade Representative for the United States, Robert Zoellick, said, "We are disappointed with the outcome."

THE NEW "HARMONIZATION": LEVELING TO THE LOWEST COMMON DENOMINATOR

Since 1995, virtually every area of consumer and industrial product has been affected by the new WTO or NAFTA regulations, which have the force of law in those countries where they're ratified. Thousands of U. S., Canadian, European, and other safety and consumer protection laws and regulations have been overturned or, through a process called harmonization, weakened to the point of irrelevance.

Harmonizing is a term that refers to bringing the laws of different nations into alignment. The effect is usually to force all nations to accept the most corporate-friendly and least restrictive laws of any of the member nations. Anti-globalization folks have referred to the process as leveling all nations to the standards of the lowest common denominator. Supporters point out that harmonization increases profits for corporations who participate, and assert that has a positive social benefit.

These trade agreements use tribunals and Dispute Resolution Panels (DRPs) to review complaints. Their largest effect has been to put corporations on a level ground with national governments. Corporations can sue countries under NAFTA, and many have successfully won tens of millions of dollars for "unfair restraint of trade" because of laws designed to protect the environments or workers. So far, no countries have sued a corporation.

If a DRP decides a law is obstructing corporations from their right to engage in free trade across national borders, then fines are assessed unless *all* of the WTO members vote within 60 days to dispute the DRP's decision. As of this writing, this has rarely happened. If a nation continues to try to enforce laws ruled antitrade by a DRP, it suffers huge ongoing fines, must pay reparations, and can be branded a renegade nation and suffer massive trade penalties.

Thus, the DRPs are among the most powerful groups in the world—they can pressure governments to repeal or change laws that were legally passed by the people of those nations, and enforce their judgments with penalties, sanctions, and fines. Even with all this worldwide power, the DRPs are not democratic, not elected by the people, not controllable by the voters of *any* nation, and they don't meet in public.

The Dispute Resolution Panels meet in private in Geneva, Switzerland. Their panels constitute three to five members in total. The public is forbidden from watching, listening, or participating in the meetings, the experts on whom the panels rely for testimony are never publicly named or identified, and the documents resulting from the meetings are forever sealed from the public.

NAFTA (North American Free Trade Agreement) actually allows corporations to sue companies, although its scope is limited to the United States, Canada, and Mexico. It may soon extend to 30 more South and Central American nations. It operates similar programs and offices out of its headquarters in Dallas, Texas, and its decisions are equally binding on the nations they affect. (NAFTA's Chapter 11 processes are even more draconian than are similar rules of the WTO.)

Here are a few examples of laws in the United States or Europe that were passed by elected legislatures and supported by citizens, but were overturned because of the unelected, secret Dispute Resolution Panels of NAFTA or WTO:

- The state of Massachusetts and 30 other local governments in the United States had passed laws that banned imports of products that were manufactured with slave or child labor from the repressive dictatorship of Myanmar, formerly known as Burma. Facing a WTO challenge from Japan and the European Union, the Supreme Court struck down these laws, making now illegal the kind of boycott that led to the freedom of Nelson Mandela and the end of apartheid in South Africa.

- Laws in England and France restricting the use of asbestos in construction were challenged by Canada, which exports asbestos.
- Asian laws that barred the marketing of tobacco products were overturned.
- The Venezuelan government successfully challenged the U. S. Clean Air Act's provisions banning the import of "dirty gasoline" reformulated in refineries of Venezuela.
- Laws in several European countries restricting the import of lumber cut from old-growth forests or by environmentally destructive clear-cutting were successfully challenged by Canada's Department of Foreign Affairs and International Trade.
- Japanese laws proposed to reduce automobile emissions by cars sold in that country were successfully challenged by the United States.
- U. S. laws banning the import of shrimp taken from regions where the shrimp industry is destroying habitats of endangered sea turtles were successfully challenged by several nations and corporations.
- European laws banning the importation of genetically modified organisms, or GMOs, were successfully challenged by the United States.
- A Canadian ban on the gasoline additive MMT (methylcyclopentodieny manganese tricarbonyl), which can cause disabling neurological impairments in movement and speech, was struck down and the Canadian government paid millions to MMT's American manufacturer for the economic harm to that corporation caused by Canada's law to protect its citizens.
- A California ban on the gasoline additive MTBE (methyl tertiary butyl ether) that the EPA had found to be a "known animal carcinogen and probable human carcinogen" was challenged. MTBE is manufactured by a Canadian corporation, which sued the United States for three-quarters of a billion dollars to make up for their loss of profits in California because they cannot now sell their product in that state.
- European laws, passed by elected legislatures, that banned beef laced with hormones, regulated cosmetic testing on animals, and banned the import of furs caught with steel-jaw leg holds were all thrown out.

Under NAFTA, a corporation can sue a foreign government and can also force the taxpayers of the defendant nation to pay the corporation for any profits it might have earned if the nation had not passed laws that restricted free trade. The effect of the treaties has been to not only validate the *Santa Clara* contention that corporations have human rights but also expand those rights and powers to the point where multinational corporations have greater powers even than governments.

For example, a Canadian multinational corporation lost a court case in Mississippi when a jury ruled that they had engaged in fraudulent and predatory trade practices; the corporation paid $175 million to settle the case after losing in the jury trial. Rather than appealing the jury's ruling to a higher court and eventually to the U. S. Supreme Court, however, the Canadian corporation went over the Supreme Court by appealing directly to a NAFTA-authorized tribunal, demanding $725 million in damages. The NAFTA tribunal, like the WTO's DRPs, meets in secret, does not allow in the public or report their discussions to the public, and is accountable to no democratically elected government. The government being sued by the corporation, in fact, does not even have the right to be present at the deliberations, and there is no possibility of an appeal to any nation's Supreme Court.

Reactions to these and other changes in the international trade landscape brought about by the International Monetary Fund and the World Bank have been mixed. The news media owned by multinational corporations have tended to either ignore such events or report them as victories for free trade.

At the citizen level across the world the response has also been mixed. When the World Bank demanded that Argentina cut social programs and services to its citizens so that it could speed up payments of its debt to the Bank, the resulting loss of much of that nation's social safety net led to riots, martial law, and the resignation of that nation's president the week before Christmas 2001. Similar scenes have been repeated in nations across the world, as over 100 nations are now required by the World Bank to adopt "budgetary austerity, trade liberalization and privatization." Local liberation movements are demanding that their governments stop privatizing their commons by selling natural resources to transnational corporations.

Jock Gill was Director of White House Special Projects in the Clinton administration, and as such, had occasion to work with many people in governments around the world both during and after his time in the White House. He reports a chilling effect of WTO regulations on the rights of government to oversee the commons of its people.

Recalling the benefits Roosevelt's Rural Electrification Administration (REA) and Truman's telephony program had on rural America, he related a conversation he had after leaving the White House. "When I asked some representatives of the Mexican Telephone Company if they could institute a program in Mexico modeled after the REA and Truman's solution to rural telephony and electrification," Gill said, "they said, 'Absolutely not.' Why? Because the WTO treated such plans as outlaw solutions requiring drastic penalties."

Imagine if the WTO had been in power in the time of Teddy Roosevelt, who said, "This country, as Lincoln said, belongs to the people. So do the natural resources which make it rich. They supply the basis of our prosperity now and hereafter. In preserving them, which is a national duty, we must not forget that monopoly is based on the control of natural resources and natural advantages, and that it will help the people little to conserve our natural wealth unless the benefits which it can yield are secured to the people."

THE PROBLEM OF INTERNATIONAL POVERTY

The United Nations Millennium (2000) Report submitted to member nations and the world by Secretary-General Kofi Annan pointed out that:

- More than 2.8 billion people, close to half the world's population, live on less than the equivalent of $2 per day. More than 1.2 billion people, or about 20 percent of the world population, live on less than the equivalent of $1 per day.
- More than 1 billion people do not have access to safe water; some 840 million people go hungry or face food insecurity.
- About one-third of all children under the age of 5 suffer from malnutrition.
- The top fifth (20 percent) of the world's people who live in the highest income countries have access to 86 percent of world gross domestic product (GDP). The bottom fifth, in the poorest countries, has about one percent.
- The assets of the world's three richest men exceed the combined gross domestic products of the world's 48 poorest countries.
- In 1998, for every $1 that the developing world received in grants, it spent $13 on debt repayment.

The need (and the moral imperative) for developed-world citizens to help bring people up out of poverty in most of the world is very real. The advocates of corporatism suggest that the way to bring this about is to unleash corporations and let them roam freely from nation to nation to "create jobs" and "recover resources" (to use phrases common in modern corporate PR). And it's important to acknowledge that when corporations do this—moving manufacturing from high-labor-cost nations to low-labor-cost nations, or mining/drilling/cutting in nations with lax environmental regulations, they are doing so not for humanly immoral reasons, but for reasons that are at the very core of corporate morality—profits.

Yet this profit-driven behavior that does, over the short term, create jobs in and extract resources from the developing world, is placing the very nations who are trying to emerge from poverty at high risk of social upheaval because of the natural tension between democratic social stability and corporatism.

Many of those same corporations who are now providing jobs for wage earners in low-wage nations also explicitly warn those countries that if their workers begin to demand higher standards of living and their wages go too high, the corporations will simply move elsewhere—as has already happened to the United States, Japan, the developed European nations, Korea, Taiwan, and Thailand. Each struggles with the social crises brought about by this form of unconstrained global free trade that allows the unrestricted movement of corporations in constant search of cheaper resources such as human labor.

The result is that most of the workers of the developed world experience a continuous decline in their standard of living, while developing nations find themselves in a competitive battle against each other for corporate largesse, which is also socially destabilizing and antidemocratic. In this competition, these nations essentially have only two things they can use to raise their standard of living in the direction demanded by their citizens who watch American-produced TV and movies: sell off their natural resources to the highest bidders, and do whatever they can to suppress labor movements and other efforts within their nations to raise living standards to the point where they'll no longer be "competitive" with poorer nations.

The end result is that the nations are strip-mined of their natural resources, corporations "play the spread" between labor costs among nations to skim off the cream, and the developed-world countries (where the corporations are based) play the role England once did for the East India Company—building a huge military with worldwide reach so that it can act as the suppressor of local independence movements all around the world where "our" corporations are mining local resources or labor. And often those suppressed movements for local culture bite back: When the United States did it in 1776, we called our citizen-soldiers patriots. Today, however, when other nations' peoples do it against us we most often call them terrorists.

HOW TO RESPOND TO POVERTY?

So what can we do about this? On the one hand, there is the very real problem of poverty around the world, and the reality that in many ways industrialization helps that problem over the short-term. On the other hand, there is the very real problem of how such development becomes antidemocratic (both in the developing and developed worlds) and eventually leads to political crises in emerging nations.

The corporate position is clear: Let the "invisible hand" of the marketplace work things out, while they pry as many of the natural resources of the commons as possible out of the hands of democratically elected governments and put them into the invisible hands of corporations.

But both Adam Smith and history tell us that such privatization schemes and the invisible hand only works to place more and more wealth into the pockets of the corporations and their stockholders. Citizens and their elected officials must intelligently constrain that invisible hand, or it will end up holding those officials and the resources of the citizens by the throat, as we can so clearly see in the entanglement of Enron and governments all over the world.

The response the Founders of America came up with when they faced this same sort of problem was to encourage business, but at the same time to place controls and limits on what corporations could do both domestically and internationally. Developed and developing nations both need essential economic stability, but when corporations operate in what they call a free environment (creaming off labor and natural resources then moving on to greener pastures when it's profitable to do so), stability is threatened worldwide as indigenous peoples' cultures are destroyed and the natural world is spoiled.

The suggestion I'm putting forth in this book is to try democracy—government of, by, and for "we, the people"—and to encourage it in nations all around the world once it is reinstated in the United States and other developed nations.

Because raw or free trade corporatism is essentially undemocratic—it answers to stockholders instead of citizens, and drives to the moral imperative of profit, thus ignoring future generations and long-term consequences to environments, cultures, and governments—there is a natural and dynamic antagonism between corporatism and democracy. The Founders of the United States faced this in the Boston Tea Party and the Revolutionary War, and solved the problem in early America with the passage of thousands of laws—all put into place by citizens or officials elected by citizens—to control and constrain corporate behavior. Since the *Santa Clara* mistake, however, corporatism has steadily been overwhelming democracy, both in the developed and developing worlds.

GLOBALISM DRIVES A PERMANENT DEFENSE INDUSTRY

In the novel *1984* by George Orwell, the way a seemingly democratic president kept his nation in a continual state of repression was by having a continuous war. The lesson wasn't lost on Richard Nixon, who, some suggest, extended the Vietnam war specifically so it would run over an election cycle, knowing that a wartime president's party is more likely to be reelected and has more power than a president in peacetime.

As he was leaving office, the old warrior president Dwight D. Eisenhower had looked back over his years as President and as a General and Supreme Commander of the Allied Forces in France during World War II, and noted that the Cold War had brought a new, Orwellian type of war to the American landscape—a perpetual war supported by a perpetual war industry.

"Our military organization today bears little relation to that known by any of my predecessors in peacetime, or indeed by the fighting men of World War II or Korea," Eisenhower said. "Until the latest of our world conflicts, the United States had no armaments industry. American makers of plowshares could, with time and as required, make swords as well. But now we can no longer risk emergency improvisation of national defense; we have been compelled to create a permanent armaments industry of vast proportions. Added to this, three and a half million men and women are directly engaged in the defense establishment. We annually spend on military security more than the net income of all United States corporations."

Nonetheless, Eisenhower added, "This conjunction of an immense military establishment and a large arms industry is new in the American experience. The total influence—economic, political, even spiritual—is felt in every city, every State house, every office of the Federal government. We recognize the imperative need for this development. Yet we must not fail to comprehend its grave implications. Our toil, resources, and livelihood are all involved; so is the very structure of our society.

"In the councils of government, we must guard against the acquisition of unwarranted influence, whether sought or unsought, by the military-industrial complex. The potential for the disastrous rise of misplaced power exists and will persist.

"We must never let the weight of this combination endanger our liberties or democratic processes. We should take nothing for granted. Only an alert and knowledgeable citizenry can compel the proper meshing of the huge industrial and military machinery of defense with our peaceful methods and goals, so that security and liberty may prosper together."

WAR PROFITS FOR THE LARGEST TRANSNATIONAL CORPORATIONS

War has become big business in America, and we're now not only a big user of military equipment, we sell it to the world: We're the world's largest exporter of weapons of virtually all sizes and types. While some consider the U. S. defense budget excessive, others argue that we live in a dangerous world and a strong military is necessary. After all, there are sociopaths and psychopaths out there, and sometimes they rise to the highest levels of power with nations and threaten life and liberty around the world.

But in a nation where the political process is more strongly influenced by the profit value than by human and life-based values—where corporations have human rights but not human vulnerabilities—Eisenhower's warning becomes more of a concern.

Military spending is the least effective way to help, stimulate, or sustain an economy for a very simple reason: Military products are used once and destroyed.

When a government uses taxpayer money to build a bridge or highway or hospital, that investment will be used for decades, perhaps centuries, and will continue to fuel economic activity throughout its lifetime. But when taxpayer dollars are used to build a bomb or a bullet, that military hardware will be used once and then vanish. As it vanishes, so does the wealth it represented, never to be recovered.

As Eisenhower said in an April 1953 speech, "Every gun that is made, every warship launched, every rocket fired, signifies, in the final sense, a theft from those who hunger and are not fed, those who are cold and are not clothed. The world in arms is not spending money alone. It is spending the sweat of its laborers, the genius of its scientists, the hopes of its children."

It was a brilliant articulation of human needs in a world increasingly dominated by nonbreathing entities whose values were not human values. But it was a call unheeded and today, it is nearly totally forgotten.

Meanwhile, the ruling elites of the Third World, aligned with transnational corporations, generally become richer and more well-armed as their people become poorer. The world, in part as a result of the notion contained in the *Santa Clara* ruling—that corporations have the rights of persons—is becoming more unequal day by day.

PART 3
UNEQUAL CONSEQUENCES

In our every deliberation, we must consider the impact of our decisions on the next seven generations.

–FROM THE GREAT LAW (OR CONSTITUTION) OF THE IROQUOIS CONFEDERACY

9

UNEQUAL USES FOR THE BILL OF RIGHTS

Of the cases in this court in which the Fourteenth Amendment was applied during its first fifty years after its adoption, less than one half of one percent invoked it in protection of the Negro race, and more than fifty percent asked that its benefits be extended to corporations.

–JUSTICE HUGO BLACK, 1938

The statistic in this chapter's epigraph is sobering indeed. It says corporations sought protection under the Fourteenth Amendment 100 times more often than did the people it was intended to protect. And this is not a victimless shift—there have been real and substantial consequences. In the years following the *Santa Clara* decision and the cases that referred to it, companies have used their personhood rights in an amazing variety of ways. What follows in this chapter is a small selection.

FIRST AMENDMENT

Supreme Court Justice Oliver Wendell Holmes noted in the landmark 1919 *Shenck v. United States* case that shouting "Fire!" in a crowded theater does not constitute free speech; the Bill of Rights guarantees that a person's opinion can be expressed, not that there are no limits on what one can do. But consider how this fundamental freedom has been bent by corporations since *Santa Clara*.

- By claiming the same right as humans to express themselves, companies won approval to spend whatever they want on lobbyists in Washington. At one point, there was a full-time tobacco lobbyist for every two legislators on Capitol Hill. As of this writing, there are roughly 38 registered lobbyists for every member of Congress—over 20,000 in total—and 138 of them are former members of Congress.
- The American Academy of Pediatrics has proposed that the federal government initiate controls on advertising directed at children, and has recommended that parents educate their children about how advertising can manipulate them. Corporations, using their First Amendment rights to freedom of expression, have instead *increased* their spending on ads to children.
- The California Public Utility Commission ordered a public utility to include a statement-stuffer in their bills informing consumers of a key point. In a move that was startlingly reminiscent of the *Santa Clara* case, the utility (a government-authorized monopoly) sued the state that gave it the monopoly and took the case all the way to the U. S. Supreme Court and won. They asserted that they didn't have to comply because they had a First Amendment right "not to speak" and so could avoid informing their customers about issues as they chose. The Supreme Court, extending the logic of the *Santa Clara* case, agreed.
- Lawyers at a 1988 judicial conference recommended that corporations "use the First Amendment to invalidate a range of Federal regulations, including Securities and Exchange Commission disclosure requirements that govern corporate takeovers, and rules affecting stock offerings."

FOURTH AMENDMENT

The Fourth Amendment, instituted to prevent soldiers from bursting into homes and unreasonably searching and seizing property, has been used by corporations to avoid government regulators as if they were British dragoons.

Supreme Court cases in 1967 and 1978 affirmed that corporations do not have to submit to random inspections because as persons, they are entitled to privacy and freedom from unreasonable searches. Corporations have pursued this logic for many years:

- Referencing the 1886 *Santa Clara* decision, the Supreme Court granted Fourth Amendment privacy rights to a corporation in 1906, just 16 years after the Sherman Act had been passed. As William Meyers notes in *The Santa Clara Blues: Corporate Personhood versus Democracy*, "This ruling made it difficult to enforce the Sherman anti-monopoly act, which naturally required the papers of corporations in order to determine if there existed grounds for an indictment."
- An electrical and plumbing corporation in Idaho cited the Fourth Amendment and deterred a health and safety investigation.
- In a 1986 Supreme Court case, a corporation sued the Environmental Protection Agency because the EPA hired a professional photographer to fly over the plant with a camera after the corporation had turned down a request by the EPA for an on-site inspection of the plant. The Court acknowledged the corporation's right to privacy from inspections by the EPA within its buildings. Meyers says that, "Without random inspections it is virtually impossible to enforce meaningful anti-pollution, health, and safety laws."

FIFTH AMENDMENT

Like the Fourth Amendment, the Fifth Amendment was written to prevent a recurrence of government abuses from colonial days. Among other things, it says that a person cannot be compelled to testify against himself (as often happened under English royal rule) or be tried twice for the same crime. This was in a time when the balance of power was definitely in favor of the government, which could and routinely did execute people.

Today the shoe is on the other foot: Business, the more powerful party, is claiming protection, again to avoid government investigation of its alleged misdoings. Convicted once of *criminal* misdoing in an anti-trust case, a textile supply company used Fifth Amendment protections and barred retrial.

IN A DEMOCRACY . . .

The constitutional protections of free speech, privacy, and protection from overzealous prosecution were all the results of the Founders of the United States having lost these rights to a multinational corporation and the government that supported its right to so-called free trade. They and the Fourteenth Amendment that was part of the post–Civil War legislation necessary to free slaves in the United States were all put in place specifically to benefit and protect humans.

The core concept of American democracy, as established in the writings of the Founders, is that *all* institutions, from churches that claim to be created by gods to businesses created by the wealthy or ambitious to the very government itself—*all institutions*—are authorized by the people to exist and are answerable to the people for their existence. And when their behavior "becomes destructive of these ends, it is the Right of the People to alter or to abolish it . . . as to them shall seem most likely to effect their Safety and Happiness."

10

UNEQUAL REGULATION

There can be no effective control of corporations while their political activity remains.

—THEODORE ROOSEVELT, SPEECH, AUGUST 31, 1910

There's a side to regulation that most people don't think about, and it has far-reaching effects if representatives of corporations are writing the rules. Once a regulation is passed saying "you can emit no more than 10 ppm of mercury," then *you can legally emit up to 10 ppm*. Before that rule was passed, any amount you emitted might subject you to potential lawsuits from nearby humans made ill by your emissions, by other states, or even the federal government. The regulatory rule essentially legalizes what a corporation is doing. In the best of worlds, this wouldn't be a problem. But in practice, it means business interests are often directly involved in writing the regulations that they themselves will have to obey.

REGULATIONS CAN LEGALIZE ACTIVITY THAT CAUSES PUBLIC HARM

During the Reagan administration, Robert Monks and Nell Minow worked with the Presidential Task Force on Regulatory Relief. Monks says, "We found that business representatives continually sought more rather than less regulation, particularly when [the new regulations] would limit their liability or protect them from competition."

Monks and Minow became disenchanted with the process. In their 1991 book *Power and Accountability*, they say, "The ultimate commercial accomplishment is to achieve regulation under law that is purported to be comprehensive and preempting and is administered by an agency that is in fact captive to the industry." In this way, corporations find an actual government shield for their actions. For example:

- Tobacco companies point to the government-mandated warnings on their labels, saying that the labels relieve them of responsibility for tobacco-related deaths because they're obeying government rules.
- Producers of toxic wastes can't be sued or attacked if they are releasing their toxins within guidelines defined by a government agency.
- Telemarketing companies push for laws and regulations that define their practice, thus legalizing it.
- Manufacturers of genetically modified products can bring them to market without labeling, as long as their products are made within the guidelines of the regulations.

THE FOX GUARDING THE CHICKEN COOP

Before there was a single genetically modified food product on the market, Monsanto, a leading provider of agricultural products to farmers, including Roundup, the world's best-selling herbicide, and a pioneer in genetically altered crops, sent lobbyists to the White House in late 1986 to meet with Vice President George Bush. "There were no products at the time," Leonard Guarraia, one of the Monsanto executives at the meeting, told the *New York Times* in 2001. "But we bugged him for regulation. We told him that we have to be regulated."

And so, the *Times* reports, "the White House complied" and Monsanto got the regulations they wanted from the EPA, USDA, and FDA.

Those regulations evolved throughout the Reagan and Bush administrations into a regulatory policy, announced by Vice President Dan Quayle on May 26, 1992, when he said, "We will ensure that biotech products will receive the same oversight as other products, instead of being hampered by unnecessary regulation." Certainly there would be no unnecessary regulation, but the regulations that were now in place were necessary for the industry. Said the *New York Times*, "the new policy strictly limited the regulatory reach of the FDA."

Under the regulations shepherded through government agencies by the

White House, the dangers of genetically modified foods would be determined by the manufacturers, not the government, and testing would occur only when the companies wanted it to. And consumers were not to be notified if their food contained genetically modified organisms (as does now a substantial percentage of the American food supply). "Labeling was ruled out as potentially misleading to the consumer, since it might suggest that there was reason for concern," notes *Times* reporter Kurt Eichenwald. In the meantime, gene-altered corn accounted for about 32 percent of the 1998 U. S. crop, 38 percent for soybeans, and 58 percent for Canadian canola oil.

In the summer of 2000, the Clinton administration had to select an American representative to the WTO talks on genetically modified foods. Ignoring the nomination of a scientist from the Consumers Union, they instead chose a former lobbyist for one of the largest companies in the business of genetically modified foods.

And in one of the most notorious cases, a multinational chemical and agricultural-products company's attorney quit his job with the company's law firm, went to work for the FDA where he wrote a regulation that allowed that company's product into the food supply, then quit the FDA and went to work for the USDA where he participated in writing regulations eliminating labeling of the product for consumers, and then quit his job at USDA and went back to work for the law firm representing the multinational. Unfortunately, because of "Veggie Libel Laws" passed in numerous states after much lobbying by pesticide manufacturers and others in the agricultural products industry (under which Oprah Winfrey was sued for her hamburger remarks), it would be a crime in at least 14 states (where, hopefully, this book will be for sale) for me (or any reporter) to give you the details of this episode.

The GMO regulations followed a pattern set out years before by the chemical industry. As Paul Hawken pointed out in 1994 in *The Ecology of Commerce*, the industry launched such a huge lobbying effort to fight regulations on toxic chemicals after the passage of the 1970 Clean Air Act that by 1990, "the agency has been able to muster regulations for exactly 7 of the 191 toxins that fell under the original legislation."

A decade later, things are still problematic, with profit driving the equation at every turn. 1999 is the last year for which EPA statistics are available on the release of toxic chemicals into the environment by industry, and in that year, 7.7 billion pounds of toxins were released directly into our air and water, most with unknown short- or long-term effects. And as huge as that statistic may sound, it's actually only the tip of the iceberg:

- Lobbyists defined EPA regulations so that now only 650 of the more than 80,000 chemicals being used in industry have to be reported—which means that the 7.7 billion pound total represents only 1 percent of the possible chemicals in use.
- Only America's largest chemical manufacturers are required to report their figures.
- Those figures include only accidents and spills. As the Worldwatch Institute's Anne Platt McGinn noted in a commentary titled "Detoxifying Terrorism" on November 16, 2001, "releases during routine use are not included" in that 7.7 billion pound figure. Platt added that we don't yet even know how dangerous or carcinogenic are "over 71 percent of the most widely used chemicals in the United States today" because the data simply doesn't exist or hasn't been released by the industry.

THE IMPACT ON SMALL BUSINESS

Small businesses rarely lobby Congress, the White House, or regulatory agencies for more regulations. But because large businesses have an infrastructure to deal with regulations, the burden of regulations on small businesses sometimes wipes them out. Many regulations come along with benefits. Farm subsidies represent a huge transfer of tax money to corporations, but only a very small portion goes to family farmers.

In the agriculture industry, four multinational corporations control 82 percent of the beef cattle market; five companies control 55 percent of the hog-packing marketplace. Although large agricultural corporations numerically own only 6 percent of U. S. farms, that 6 percent accounts for almost two-thirds of all farm income.

In a growing trend known as contract farming, farmers are forced (because they can't compete against large-scale multinational purchasing) to sell their farms to agribiz companies and then work on the land they once owned. The United States lost 300,000 family-owned farms between 1979 and 1998. As agriculture writer Julie Brussell notes, "This agrarian 'genocide' mirrors the descent of much of America's rural country into economic serfdom." The result, as documented by the Community Environmental Legal Defense Fund's (CELDF) Thomas Linzey, is that, "Suicides have replaced equipment-related deaths as the number one cause of farmer deaths."

11

UNEQUAL PROTECTION FROM RISK

Corporations are neither physical nor metaphysical phenomena. They are socioeconomic ploys—legally enacted game-playing—agreed upon only between overwhelmingly powerful socioeconomic individuals and by them imposed upon human society and its all unwitting members.

—BUCKMINSTER FULLER

When corporations gained the protections that had been written for persons in the United States, a substantial shift began in who bears what risk, resulting in an imbalance that now affects virtually all parts of the world. Most companies handle risk responsibly, but many corporations are legally allowed to avoid responsibility in ways that would never be permitted for an individual.

Risk is a matter of who suffers when something goes wrong. Corporations and their shareholders may risk loss of income or even loss of their investment, but that pales in comparison to the risks humans share as a result of a corporate activity—such as degradation of the environment, higher rates of cancer and other diseases, job-related disfigurement or death, or community and family breakdown after a factory is closed and jobs shipped overseas, and even a life with no income or health insurance if we choose not to affiliate with a corporation.

Large companies rarely risk anything nearly that serious. They rarely undergo corporate death (charter revocation) or disfigurement. The burden of risk is unqual and one source of this inequality is the changes in laws and regulations that happened after companies gained access to the law-making process when they were declared to share the same rights as persons.

THE NATURE OF RISK

Risk means different things to different people, and it has meaning only in context. Sometimes creating a risk to humans—manufacturing cancer-causing chemicals or designing risky gas tanks—is a source of profit to a company. If regulations are imposed or scandals erupt from human deaths, our current system of accounting and measuring risk does not allow us to factor in the value of human life or the loss of quality of life from pollution or other consequences of corporate activity.

We have strayed far indeed from America's founding laws in the 1700s under which corporate behavior was suspect and tightly controlled and the 1800s when states exercised control of corporate behavior and could revoke a corporation's "driver's license" if it harmed people.

In a classic Darwinian sense, corporations have learned how to manage risks by anticipating them and doing what they can to eliminate them. There's nothing inherently wrong with that, per se, but as William Jennings Bryan said at the 1912 Ohio Constitutional Convention, when one group is vastly larger than another so it has far more ability to bend events in its favor, the result is unfair and unequal.

UNEQUAL ACCOUNTABILITY

Humans are responsible for the effects of their actions. If they violate laws, they can be fined or imprisoned; if they violate the rights of another person, they can be sued. They can even be sued or prosecuted for failing to anticipate the effects of their actions. Companies, too, can be sued (though big corporations are rarely if ever driven out of business that way). But one group bears no responsibility whatsoever for the effects of its actions: Investors have no liability for the actions they enable through their investments.

Of course, few investors, if any, mean any harm when they invest. When the United States was founded, the concept of limiting the financial liability of corporate stockholders was defined by the states in which the corporations were chartered. So, too, was liability for the *behavior* of the corporation, or of the people making decisions for the corporation. As the Supreme Court said, "The individual liability of stockholders in a corporation is always a creature of statute. It does not exist at common law."

It wasn't until 1811 that New York was the first state to pass a law that put a barrier (sometimes called the corporate veil) between the behavior of corporations and the responsibilities for that behavior that may otherwise have fallen to the corporation's stockholders. During the chartermongering period of the late 1800s, this became more common, although many states still reserved the right to hold stockholders, officers, directors, and/or managers responsible for the behaviors and impacts of the corporations that they owned and/or controlled.

Different states have different laws about what corporations must and must not do to continue to exist in their states. To remedy this situation, the American Bar Association, Section of Business Law, Committee on Corporate Laws, has proposed a new set of state laws regulating corporations, called the Model Business Corporation Act (MBCA). Today, 7 states have laws based on the 1969 version of this, and variations on the updated version had been adopted by an additional 24 states as of 1999.

This proposal gives corporate shareholders no responsibility whatsoever for the acts or debts of the corporation that they own. They can invest without legal risk, only financial risk. They might lose the money itself, but if their money is used to commit crimes or to support business decisions that knowingly lead to deaths, the shareholders are considered to have nothing to do with it legally. Some question the logic of a doctrine that somebody who funds an operation should be allowed to share in its profits if it succeeds, but have no responsibility for what it does or whether it harms others while getting those profits.

Under this setup, it's little wonder that shareholders rarely tell executives to behave themselves. In contrast, if shareholders carried even a small liability for the consequences of what they sponsor, it stands to reason that in their hiring and firing decisions, the shareholders and board members might take into account the ethics and legal tendencies of the executives. But Section 6.22 of the MBCA concerns shareholder liability and explicitly says, " . . . (b) Unless otherwise provided in the articles of incorporation, a shareholder of a corporation is not personally liable for the acts or debts of the corporation except that he may become personally liable by reason of his own acts or conduct."

This particular language is now law in Arkansas, Colorado, Connecticut, Georgia, Idaho, Indiana, Kentucky, Mississippi, Montana, Nebraska, New

Hampshire, North Carolina, Tennessee, South Carolina, Utah, Vermont, and Wyoming. According to the ABA's *Model Business Corporation Act Annotated, Third Edition*, Arizona and Iowa have similar laws, and New York and Wisconsin do also. (In New York and Wisconsin, stockholders are at least liable for wage claims, but in the other states, they are not.)

WHERE DOES THIS IMMUNITY COME FROM?

Interestingly, not all states have adopted these laws. And the Constitution does not limit shareholder liability for debt, crimes, or other acts of corporations. Nor is there such a provision in English common law. So what happens in those other states?

In the 1965 case *Fields v. Synthetic Ropes, Inc.* the Delaware Supreme Court said, "A stockholder of a corporation is not personally liable for the corporate debts." When attorney Dan Brannen Jr. researched this, however, he noted that, "The court, however, cited no statute for this proposition, and I find none in Delaware's current corporate code."

Apparently the Delaware Supreme Court isn't the only one to have such notions. In a CERCLA (The Comprehensive Environmental Response, Compensation, and Liability Act, usually referred to as the EPA's Superfund) case before the U. S. Supreme Court in 1998, Justice David Souter said on behalf of the unanimous Court, "It is a general principle of corporate law deeply ingrained in our economic and legal systems that a parent corporation . . . is not liable for the acts of its subsidiaries. . . . Thus it is hornbook law that the exercise of the control which stock ownership gives to the stockholders . . . will not create liability beyond the assets of the subsidiary. . . . Although this respect for corporate distinctions when the subsidiary is a polluter has been severely criticized in the literature . . . nothing in CERCLA purports to reject this bedrock principle, and against this venerable common law backdrop, the congressional silence is audible."

In other words, the U. S. Supreme Court unanimously said in this decision:

- In practice, parent companies have not been held responsible for the illegal polluting acts of their subsidiaries.
- Many people have said it's wrong (Souter said, "severely criticized in the literature") to pretend that the subsidiary is not part of the parent company ("this respect for corporate distinctions").

- But Congress has conspicuously done nothing about it.
- So the Court says it's not illegal. A company can form a subsidiary that it knows is a notorious polluter, and not only are the executives legally blameless, even the parent *company* is completely blameless.

Reading this, I wondered what would happen if Congress were to break its silence. Certainly, the congresses of virtually every state in the union have done so at various and numerous times before 1886. Attorney Brannen's thoughts were more blunt. He wrote to me, citing the above, "This is scary. At our country's birth, corporations were state creations, with stockholder liability subject to state control. Today, American jurisprudence has given corporations life under the Fourteenth Amendment and [then, since that time,] declared their distinctiveness to be a matter of American corporate law too basic and obvious to challenge."

That's especially ironic, considering that the Supreme Court did *not* actually give corporations such rights to life. It was an 1886 court reporter's mistake that's been institutionalized into law to the point where we have become accustomed to it.

Let's look at a practical, real-world effect of this principle in today's world, using as an example who is accountable for the risks of newly developed chemicals, in the United States and elsewhere, and what it means to our children.

THE BENEFITS OF MARKETING UNTESTED CHEMICALS OUTWEIGH THE RISK?

In America, newly developed chemicals are usually put into the environment before there has been time to do studies on their long-term low-dose human toxicity. But what are we doing to our children and our grandchildren? Where did we get the idea that anyone (corporate or real person) has every right to market what they developed, whether or not we know what effect it has? And where did we get the idea that we can't change that rule?

In effect, we and our children are the lab animals for modern new chemicals, as were our parents with DDT, PCBs, and lead in gasoline. The product is put on the market, and if it turns out to be carcinogenic, everyone finds out the hard way. And the developer isn't responsible because it was a company "regulated" by a government agency.

It wasn't that way in the past. Whole books have been written on this subject. Here is one current example, and some statistics to indicate how big the issue is:

- PCE (perchloroethylene) is an industrial solvent used for a variety of purposes ranging from dry cleaning to plastics and electronics fabrication. In 1968, it was used in pipes and glues for 650 miles of plastic-lined concrete water main on Cape Cod, Massachusetts. Decades later, clusters of cancer were discovered where the chemical had leached into the water supply. By the time the possible link was discovered, "people had been drinking contaminated water, some for as long as 10 years," Boston University's lead researcher Ann Aschengrau said in an interview with the *Cape Cod Times.*
- The EPA classifies 3,800 chemicals as "high production volume chemicals." A study by the Environmental Defense Fund in the late 1990s found that fewer than half of them had *ever* been tested for the possibility of toxic effects on humans.
- It's even more rare (fewer than 10 percent of those 3,800 chemicals) that we test chemicals for their impact on developing children.

THERE'S ANOTHER WAY: THE PRECAUTIONARY PRINCIPLE

The alternative system—used widely in Europe—is known as the precautionary principle. It was written into the 1992 Treaty of the European Union. It moves risks from human persons to the manufacturer: A substance is considered potentially dangerous until proven beyond any reasonable doubt that it is safe, and the burden of proving its safety is with the corporation that would profit from its release, whether it's a new chemical or a genetically modified organism. In other words, just as was the intention of our country's Founders, a company is welcome to do business as long as the welfare of the community is respected.

Interestingly, although American business often portrays this as a fanatical idea, it's the principle we already use in America to approve new drugs and medical devices. It was even invoked by former New Jersey governor Christine Todd Whitman, who is usually reviled by environmentalists, when in October 2000 she told the National Academy of Sciences in Washington, D. C., that "policymakers need to take a precautionary approach to environmental protection. . . . We must acknowledge that uncertainty is inherent in managing natural resources, recognize it is usually easier to prevent environmental damage than to repair it later, and shift the burden of proof away from those advocating protection toward those proposing an action that may be harmful."

But the precautionary principle is not law in the United States. In the United States, a company is entitled to calculate risks, assess the *economic risk* of potential casualties without considering any impact on humans, and decide solely on that basis.

UNEQUAL RISK OF LAWSUIT

The Fourteenth Amendment was written to ensure equal protection under the law for people, including the ability to sue for these protections. In practice, however, it has turned out to give humans very little protection against wealthy corporations that wish to shut them up.

SLAPP suits are defined in *Black's Law Dictionary* as: "*abbr*. A strategic lawsuit against public participation—that is, a suit brought by a developer, corporate executive, or elected official to stifle those who protest against some type of high-dollar initiative or who take an adverse position on a public-interest issue (often involving the environment)."

SLAPP suits started out as suits by polluters, toxic waste sites, nuclear facilities, and the like, against people who get up in public venues like town meetings or public hearings and offer anti-pollution or anti-nuclear opinions. The next thing they know, they're SLAPPed—having to spend thousands of dollars in legal fees to defend themselves for having exercised what they thought was their First Amendment right of free speech—and it often shuts people up in a hurry. This variety of lawsuit has expanded over the years beyond just public hearings, and the suing corporations usually charge slander, libel, harassment, or interference with contract.

The bottom line is that the corporation initiating the lawsuit is often not intending to win in court; they're just working to shut people up or wipe them out by forcing them to pay huge legal bills to defend themselves. In the eyes of the law, since 1886, a corporate person with billions of dollars and a human person who works for a living are entitled to equal protection under the law. But the people across America who have been SLAPPed certainly could not intimidate a corporation by threatening to drive it bankrupt with legal bills.

Further irony is that under the most recent tax laws, the corporation could deduct from its income taxes the cost of its lawyer to SLAPP sue an individual, counting it as an ordinary cost of doing business. A working person, however, though legally equal, cannot deduct the costs of defending himself. As Delphin M. Delmas so eloquently pointed out in his pleadings before the Supreme Court in the 1886 *Santa Clara* case, the law has come to "a position ridiculous to the extreme."

IN A DEMOCRACY . . .

So we see that there are some very unequal risks here. Corporations risk profits but rarely anything else, while humans risk much more.

At the moment, the world's largest corporations are able to influence—and, in most cases today, even write—legislation that benefits them because their personhood gives them the constitutionally protected right of free speech, assembly, and to meet with "their" elected representatives.

If we were to return to the idea that only humans are persons, then perhaps our human legislators would drift back to supporting the communities they represent. It would be a first step toward equaling the now very unequal risks between corporations and humans.

12

UNEQUAL TAXES

You must pay the price if you wish to secure the blessings.

—U. S. PRESIDENT ANDREW JACKSON

It costs money to run a government, and the more you want the government to do, the more it usually costs. One point to consider is *how much do we want our government to do*? Another is, *who should pay for it*? Tax policy is how government funds its services and also one way it fulfills the will of the people who elect it by providing tax incentives or disincentives for particular types of behaviors. Consider how home mortgage interest deductibility has fueled home-buying, for example.

As we have seen, starting well before *Santa Clara*, some companies have worked hard to get out of paying for anything, including taxes. Some even spent years resisting paying taxes on land the government had given them for free, and then worked the issue to a ludicrous extent. The *Santa Clara* case involved going to the Supreme Court to fight a tax of 1⁄10 of a percent.

You and I could never afford to do such a thing, but economies of scale mean that for huge property owners, such efforts can have very big paybacks. Motivated to pursue the subject, with the means to do so, and in the absence of regulations preventing it, they do the obvious thing, as Adam Smith predicted anyone would: They act in their own self-interest.

The result has been an additional inequity that could not possibly have been intended by the framers of the Fourteenth Amendment. After Santa Clara (and subsequent cases continuing well into the 20th century), increased corporate access to lawmakers has resulted in a shift in the tax burden that rivals the shift in risk from corporate to individual shoulders. In this chapter, we will cover four aspects of this issue:

- A shift in income tax burden from corporations to workers
- A shift in property tax burden from corporations to residents
- The use of federal tax breaks and subsidies to help large corporations
- The use of tax breaks at state and regional levels to lure businesses

There is an appropriate concern about not overtaxing corporations; to do so could endanger the survival of business. But as you will see, this particular pendulum has swung very far away from that risk. To the contrary, the additional shift in tax burden being proposed today is financially crushing individuals who can least afford it.

THE START OF INCOME TAXES

The main purpose of a business corporation is as an instrument for the accumulation of wealth, and it has worked well in that respect. In the Robber Baron era of the late 1800s and early 1900s, wealth was being concentrated at an amazing rate among the owners of the trusts. If you've ever had a chance to visit Newport, Rhode Island, to see the mansions of the rich from those days, you know how much wealth there was. For example, The Breakers is the 70-room Italian Renaissance–style villa of Cornelius Vanderbilt II, President and Chairman of the New York Central Railroad. The Elms is the French-style chateau of Edward Berwind, who made his millions providing coal to the railroads.

And these were their summer homes—cottages, as they called them. In New York City, Vanderbilt's "real" home filled the length of a city block along Fifth Avenue from 57th to 58th Street. Illustrating that the Newport house was truly just a cottage, the Victorian mansion in New York City had 137 rooms. "I have been insane on the subject of moneymaking all my life," he told the New York *Daily Tribune*.

The poor, however, who at that time constituted the vast majority of people in America and Europe, were truly poor: A middle class was largely unknown, outside of self-sufficient farming communities. At the turn of the century, more than half a worker's wage went to cover rent—often in slum tenements—and the remainder barely covered food and clothing. Children worked to supplement the family income because, as Annie S. Daniel documented in 1905, 4-year-old boys "can sew on buttons and pull basting threads" and a girl "from 8 to 12 can finish trousers as well as her mother." The Supreme Court declared a minimum wage unconstitutional and illegal, and it wasn't unusual for people to work 14-hour days, with two half-hour meal breaks, 6 days a week for $1.00 a day. As is always the case in situations of poverty, infant mortality in these communities was high.

Nobody filed income tax returns because nobody paid income taxes. Both the wealthy and the poor, however, *were* paying taxes—essentially a form of sales tax—but it affected the poor far more than the rich. Here's how it worked.

To support itself, the government first taxed the things that people wanted but didn't need, and also taxed things that people were willing to pay to import from abroad. In 1912, for example, 42 percent of the money that ran the federal government came from taxes on alcohol and tobacco, which were heavily marketed to and used by the working poor. Another 45 percent of revenues came from taxes or duties on imported goods, which ran from necessities to luxuries. These taxes were paid to the government by the importers, wholesalers, or retailers, and were passed on to the consumers.

The net effect was that the working poor were paying large percentages of their incomes in taxes on the products they bought. The wealthy, who saved or invested much of the money they brought in so it could earn more money, paid only the pass-through duties when they purchased things. It was a dramatically smaller portion of their income, particularly if they chose to live frugally.

In 1913, during the Progressive movement, a constitutional amendment initiated the federal income tax, which allowed spreading the cost of government over a much wider base—not just what was spent but what was earned. Thus, the wealthy could no longer pocket almost all of their income. They shared the burden, which laid the foundation for the middle class.

By 1922, tariffs on tobacco and alcohol represented only 8 and 9 percent of federal government tax revenue respectively, whereas income taxes on wealthy individuals produced 13 percent of government revenue and taxes on corporations paid 19 percent of the cost of running the governments that authorized their existence. This sharing has been increasingly reversed in recent years, however.

- Corporate taxes as a share of the nation's tax revenues plunged from 28 percent in 1956 to only 11.8 percent in 1996.

- Family income taxes rose from 17.3 percent of median income in 1955 to 37.6 percent in 1998.
- In the past 2 decades, after-tax income of the middle class, which had been rising, has collapsed to inflation-adjusted 1969 levels, and, according to statistics compiled by the AFL-CIO, "average hourly wage of production and nonsupervisory workers in the U. S. economy was $12.77 last year [2001]—down 9 percent compared with 1973."
- The share of all property taxes paid by corporations has dropped from 45 percent in 1957 to 16 percent in 1995.
- During the first year of the Reagan administration's "tax reforms," General Electric actually received a tax refund—an omen of things to come.
- *Austin Chronicle* columnist Jim Hightower pointed out, "Forty-one of America's largest corporations earned $25.8 billion in profits between 1996 and 1999, yet not only did they avoid paying their fair share of taxes—they got $3.2 billion in rebate checks from taxpayers. Among these tax dodgers are such brand-names as Chevron, PepsiCo, Pfizer, J. P. Morgan, Saks, Goodyear, Ryder, Enron, Colgate-Palmolive, MCI, Weyerhaeuser, GM, and Northrop Grumman."
- By setting up almost 900 subsidiaries in tax havens such as the Cayman Islands and through exploiting the tax-deductibility of stock options given to senior executives, Enron Corporation was able to pay *no* federal taxes in 4 of the 5 years prior to its implosion in 2002. As the *Washington Post* pointed out, in 2000 the corporation was successful in converting a $112 million potential tax bill into a $278 million tax refund.
- According to the U. S. General Accounting Office, almost a third of all "large" corporations (assets of at least a quarter-billion dollars) in the United States paid no income tax whatsoever between 1989 and 1995 (the last year such a study was done), and more than 60 percent of such companies paid less than $1 million in taxes.
- Looking at *all* U. S. corporations, the GAO concluded, "in each year between 1989 and 1995, a majority of corporations, both foreign- and U. S.-controlled, paid no U. S. income tax."

A similar shift has occurred within the human domain, with the wealthy carrying less of the burden than the middle class. The decline in corporate income taxes has been paralleled by a decline in the income taxes paid by the CEOs and senior executives of those corporations.

- The wealthiest 1 percent of Americans paid $46,726 less in taxes in 1996 than they would have paid if there had been no changes in the tax laws since 1977. But among those earning less than $80,000, those "tax reductions" were worth an average of only $115.
- In 1981, the Reagan administration pushed through the Economic Recovery Tax Act, which, added to a Kennedy-era tax cut, slashed the income tax for America's top 1 percent of families by over 50 percent.
- The George W. Bush administration has recently driven the top income bracket's taxes even lower—from a high averaging around 80 percent between 1935 and 1963, to a 2002 low of 33 percent.

This may not be financially healthy, even for the wealthy. The figures for the period leading up to the crash of 1929 are startlingly similar to those above:

- The 1926 tax cut reduced income taxes for millionaires from 60 percent to 20 percent just 3 years after the minimum wage was repealed in 1923.
- America's top 1 percent of families reaped a 75 percent increase in after-tax income during the 1920s.
- From 1920 to 1929, corporate profits rose 62 percent and dividends rose 65 percent.

WHAT HAPPENS WHEN CORPORATE INSIDERS RUN THE GOVERNMENT

In May of 2001, the idea of taxation without representation came full circle when a government leader proposed that we shift *all* tax burden back onto the people, lowering corporate income tax to zero. Paul O'Neill is a multimillionaire who has been a top executive at Alcoa and International Paper, two of the world's largest multinational corporations. At the time of this writing, O'Neill is Secretary of the United States Treasury, appointed by the Bush administration and approved by the Senate.

In May 2001, O'Neill suggested that corporations should be totally exempt from all income tax. He said that the roughly 10 percent of federal funds they currently pay in corporate income taxes to provide for and administer our commons is too much; corporations should be just as tax-exempt as churches and synagogues.

O'Neill also called for the abolition of Social Security, Medicaid, and Medicare for working people because, he told a reporter for London's *Financial Times*, "able-bodied adults should save enough on a regular basis so that they can provide for their own retirement, and, for that matter, health and medical needs." In O'Neill's opinion, corporations should pay *no* taxes and individuals should pay *all* costs of the federal government while also saving to pay for their retirement *and* all of their own medical costs.

Social Security is half-paid by the employer. If companies don't have to pay for it, the difference does not pass through to the employee—the worker's total tax burden goes up by another 7¾ percent of her income, and the employer's labor cost goes down correspondingly.

YES, HE REALLY SAID IT

While O'Neill's proposal was widely reported in England's business press, the media of the United States chose to ignore it, with the single exception of the suburban New York tabloid *Newsday*. When *Newsday* columnist Paul Vitello called the Treasury Department, he reported the following conversation:

VITELLO: "The secretary didn't really mean to say that no matter how old, no person who has paid into the Social Security system all his or her life would be entitled to benefits until he or she is physically no longer able to work? He didn't really mean to say that ExxonMobil and Time Warner should be treated as we treat the church—as tax exempt?"

TREASURY DEPARTMENT SPOKESMAN: "Yes, that is our position. The quotes were all accurate."

Checking Vitello's work (and somewhat incredulous myself), I called O'Neill's Washington, D. C., office on June 20, 2001. I was eventually connected to a friendly and helpful woman at the Public Liaison Office. She confirmed that yes, that's what the secretary said. She added, "We were surprised we didn't hear anything back about this [from the American media]. We were waiting for it, but nothing came."

UNEQUAL TAX BREAKS

In the early 1990s, Paul Hawken, author of *Ecology of Commerce*, found data indicating that the nation's corporations were net consumers, rather than producers, of tax monies. Several recent books on corporate welfare point to similar trends and conclusions, although hard data are difficult to come by because the statistics necessary to compile are spread across literally thousands of separate local, state, and federal government agencies and their reports. "It was almost certainly the case, when I did my initial research in 1992," Hawken told me, "that the nation's corporations took more out of the economy in tax dollars than they pay in."

Around the same time as Secretary O'Neill's modest proposal, a major aerospace corporation illustrated how much power it has in the economy. It announced that it would relocate its corporate headquarters and then played the offers of three cities against each other. By the time the decision was announced on May 10, 2001, the *New York Times* announced that the winning destination had "promised tax breaks and incentives that could total $60 million over 20 years . . ." to seal the deal.

This is far from rare. According to a 1996 report from the Cato Institute, businesses in America receive direct tax subsidies of over $75 billion annually. That equates to every household in America paying a $750 annual subsidy to corporations, according to author and former faculty member of the Harvard Graduate School of Business Dr. David C. Korten.

The way that this happens clearly illustrates the consequences of unrestrained "freedom of expression" in the halls of a government that was designed to serve the public good. In a situation that is reminiscent of the chartermongering era, companies can once again be aggressive in getting local governments to offer tax breaks that are never offered for humans. All of the following have the effect of cash taken out of human pockets and put into company pockets:

- In Louisiana, a multinational chemical company was given a $15 million tax break.
- In Ohio, $2.1 billion worth of business property was taken off the tax rolls, leaving public schools struggling to find resources since they depend most on the now-eviscerated property tax revenues.
- New York State companies had, from just 1991 to 1992, "earned" $242 million in tax credits and held $938 million in "unused" tax credits they could "use" in future years.
- Arkansas helped a snack-food processor with $10 million.
- Alabama offered $153 million to a German automobile company to

build a factory there, an amount equal to about $200,000 per job created.

- Illinois gave a national retail chain $240 million in land and tax breaks to keep them from moving out of state.
- New York City gave tax breaks of $235 million, $98 million, and $97 million to three corporations to keep them from moving to New Jersey, and $25 million to a media corporation to keep it in town. (Few of these breaks created any new jobs anywhere.) Says the *New York Times*, "Since Mr. Giuliani took office in 1994, he has provided 34 companies with tax breaks and other incentives totaling $666.7 million."
- The state of Indiana borrowed millions from its citizens by a bond issue and gave that money as an "upfront cash subsidy," along with other grants and tax breaks that totaled $451 million, to an airline to build a maintenance facility.
- Pennsylvania gave a Norwegian transnational corporation $235 million in economic incentives to build a shipyard, an amount that cost the state, according to *Time* magazine, $323,000 per job.
- Kentucky gave nearly $140 million to two steel manufacturers—more than $350,000 per job created.
- In Louisiana over a 10-year period, just the top 10 corporations getting breaks (there were others) received $836 million to "create jobs." *Time* magazine did the math and found that the cost to the state's taxpayers per job created among those 10 ranged from $900,000 to $29 million.
- The State of Michigan created the Michigan Economic Growth Authority (MEGA), which as of 1999 had awarded over $900 million in tax breaks and grants to corporations, costing Michigan taxpayers, according to the Mackinac Center for Public Policy, $40,000 per job created or moved from other states into Michigan.

In almost every case, benefits to one community were subtracted from another. "No new jobs are created in the process," of most of these sorts of tax breaks, according to former United States Secretary of Labor Robert B. Reich, quoted in the *New York Times*. "They're merely moved around. Meanwhile, the public spends a fortune subsidizing these companies. But there's no way that mayors or governors can withstand the heat once a major company announces it is thinking about leaving."

The list could easily go on for pages, and extends from the local to the national. Indeed, entire books and Web sites are devoted to "corporate welfare." On November 6, 2001, the *Barre-Montpelier Times Argus* ran a syndicated article from the Knight Ridder News Service by Micah L. Sifry about proposals put before Congress within days and weeks of the September 11 terrorist attacks. The title speaks for itself: "At a Time of Sacrifice, Corporations Are Picking Our Pockets." After the attacks, corporations began lobbying hard for a Bush administration proposal to repeal retroactively the Alternative Minimum Tax passed in 1986. The result, if passed:

- $250 million for Enron
- $572 million for Chevron Texaco Inc.
- $671 million for General Electric
- $184 million for American Airlines
- $833 million for General Motors
- $608 million for TXU Corporation
- $241 million for Phillips Petroleum Company
- $600 million for DaimlerChrysler Corporation
- $1.424 billion for IBM

The consumer advocacy group Common Cause estimated that there may be a relationship between the $4.6 million given by 10 of America's largest corporations to the Democrats, the $10-plus million they gave the Republicans, and the $6.305 *billion* dollars in tax rebates just those 10 corporations would receive as result of the "economic stimulus package" lobbyists were promoting after the September 11 tragedy.

With or without that legislation, 7 of America's 82 largest corporations paid "less than zero" in federal income taxes in 1998 (they got rebates instead), and 44 of the 82 didn't pay the standard federal corporate income tax rate of 35 percent.

THE TREND GOES INTERNATIONAL

Trends of business influencing government are becoming more uniform worldwide. In a famous recent case, a coalition of Deutsche Bank, Dresdner Bank, Allianz, Daimler-Benz, BMW, and the Germany energy group RWE all threatened to leave Germany if they didn't get tax breaks and subsidies from the government. (In the past 20 years, corporate profits in Germany had gone up over 90 percent and corporate tax revenues had actually fallen by half, but this wasn't enough.) Finance Minister Oskar Lafontaine tried to fight them, but in the end he himself was crushed. When he quit his job over the issue in 1999, Lafontaine said, "The heart isn't traded on the stock market yet."

As the *Washington Post* pointed out on March 15, 1999, Lafontaine's experience "shows the limits of any single politician, or any single country, to stem the tide of global capitalism."

The next voice from the German government, Chancellor Gerhard Schröder's top aide, Bobo Hombach, apparently got the message, and said, "Things will be different now. We have to move in a different direction." The companies got their money and stayed in Germany: Human taxpayers and family-owned businesses will make up the difference.

Often, however, corporations don't have to make threats to get their cash from the government: They make "investments."

- In the late 1980s and early 1990s, the tobacco companies donated over $30 million to various Republican and Democratic politicians and their parties. In 1997, Trent Lott and Newt Gingrich inserted a single and mostly unnoticed 46-word sentence into that year's massive tax law. The sentence granted the tobacco industry a $50 billion tax break.
- As Charles Lewis documented in his book *The Buying of the President*, a large national bank gave the Democratic National Committee a $3.5 million line of credit at an attractive interest rate 2 weeks after Democrats helped push through the 1994 Fair Trade in Financial Services Act, which netted that same bank $50 million a year in savings.

The final irony is that while all of this fiscal benefit has accrued to companies through their personhood privileges and they shift the tax burden to humans, they continue to claim exemptions from liability. Additionally, because the structure and culture of corporations is driven to maximize quarterly profits, otherwise well-intentioned people working in company boardrooms find themselves pushed to make decisions that may not be in the best interest of the long-term, of the commons, or even of the company's employees.

In a democracy, the citizens—the voters—would decide these issues without pressure or influence from corporate or other special interests groups.

13

UNEQUAL RESPONSIBILITY FOR CRIME

A wicked big interest is necessarily more dangerous to the community than a wicked little interest.

—TEDDY ROOSEVELT, OHIO CONSTITUTIONAL CONVENTION, 1912

Consider this August 3, 2001 White House press briefing, in which the editor of *Corporate Crime Reporter*, Russell Mokhiber, asked a question of White House Press Secretary Ari Fleischer.

MOKHIBER: Ari, the Federal Communication Commission requires that if you're going to have a broadcast license you have to be of sound moral character. So when you make the application, you have to answer whether you've ever been convicted of a felony. They are now going after a gentleman in Missouri who's been convicted of a felony—

FLEISCHER: Be careful, there are many broadcasters in this room.

MOKHIBER: I understand, that's why I'm raising the question. This gentleman was convicted of a felony, child molestation, and they're trying to strip him of five radio licenses. On the other hand, General Electric, which owns NBC, has been convicted of felonies, and they're not being stripped of their license. Why the double standard?

FLEISCHER: I think you need to talk to the FCC about their standards. That's their jurisdiction to deal with licensing. [Looks around the room at another reporter] Ron?

MOKHIBER: I understand, but generally, does the President have a position on—?

At that point, Fleischer cut off Mokhiber and moved on.

The case Mokhiber cited is not unique. In 1982, a study of America's 500 largest corporations reported that "23 percent of them had been convicted of a major crime or had paid more than $50,000 in penalties for serious misbehavior during the previous decade."

IF CORPORATIONS ARE PERSONS, WHY AREN'T THEIR CRIMES IN THE STATISTICS?

In December 2001, the FBI issued a press release on their Uniform Crime Reporting Program, which determines the "Nation's Crime Index." It reports crimes by persons—but it excludes corporate persons, even when the corporations have been convicted of felonies. In its entire history, the FBI has never issued an annual report on crimes by corporate persons, although its reports on crimes by human persons are well-researched and well-publicized. The upshot of this is that when you ask people how most money and property are stolen, or how most people are killed, they think of burglars and muggers and bank robbers and crimes of passion. They think of human persons.

The reality, though, is that more money and property are stolen by or lost to corporate criminals than human criminals. Mokhiber's *Corporate Crime Reporter* notes that in 1998, when the FBI estimated robberies and burglaries at almost $4 billion, the cost of corporate crimes was in the hundreds of billions . . . as it is every year. These include:

- Securities scams that ran around $15 billion that year
- Car-repair fraud that hit around $40 billion
- Insurance swindles and corporate fraud found on your health insurance/HMO/hospital billings that runs between $100 billion and $400 billion a year . . . a hundred times greater than all the burglaries in the country combined.

Then there are the occasional "really big crimes" like the savings and loan scandal that then–Attorney General Dick Thornburgh called the biggest white-collar swindle in history.

DEATHS FROM CORPORATE ACTIONS ARE NOT INCLUDED

More people die as a result of corporate activity than because of the actions of deranged killers or overwrought spouses. According to *Corporate Crime Reporter*, the FBI reported that 1998 saw about 19,000 Americans murdered at the hands of other people. But that same year 56,000 people died from work-related diseases like black lung and asbestosis—that were unreported by the FBI—and many times that number died from "the silent violence of pollution, contaminated food, hazardous consumer products, and hospital malpractice."

Much of the human death caused by corporate activity has arguable benefits—for example, the many cancers caused by compounds associated with plastics or pesticides. But the cost of these deaths isn't factored into the unit cost of the products, so there's no financial incentive for industry to develop toxin-free or toxin-reduced alternatives, or to use the more expensive but less toxic alternatives that already exist.

And then there are the Big Mistakes.

In 1998, one of America's largest meatpacking companies replaced a refrigeration unit on one of their processing lines. Shortly thereafter, the detectors they have in place on the line to look for deadly cold-loving bacteria like *Listeria monocytogenes* started to react, indicating high levels of bacterial contamination.

The company's response was immediate. Caroline Smith DeWaal of the Center for Science in the Public Interest told reporters Russell Mokhiber and Robert Weissman, "Then their tests started coming up positive, so they stopped testing." This company's Fourth Amendment right to privacy blocked surprise inspections by the government.

The detectors were apparently turned off for a full month before the Centers for Disease Control used DNA fingerprinting to track the bacteria that was causing a national outbreak of *Listeria* back to the plant, provoking a nationwide recall of a million pounds of product.

But during that month, hundreds of people consuming this company's products were sickened by *Listeria*, and 21 humans died from it.

The U. S. Attorney's office, according to Mokhiber and Weissman, "said there was insufficient evidence to bring a felony charge" against the company. Instead, the company paid a $200,000 fine and issued an unprecedented joint press release with the Bush administration's USDA . . . that managed to say that the company had paid the fine without ever mentioning the brand name of the product that had been contaminated and caused the deaths.

Mokhiber and Weissman raised the case at the White House with Press Secretary Ari Fleischer. Here's the transcript of the interaction.

QUESTION: Ari, has the President expressed a view on the death penalty for corporate criminals—that is, revoking the charter of a corporation that has been convicted of a crime that resulted in death?

FLEISCHER: The President does not weigh in on those matters of justice. They should not be dictated by decisions made at the White House.

QUESTION: No, Ari, wait a second. Ari, Ari, wait a second. He's in favor of the death penalty for individuals generally. Is he in favor of the death penalty for corporations convicted of crimes that result in death?

FLEISCHER: These are questions that are handled by officials of the Justice Department—not by people at the White House.

The White House hasn't commented further. And because the FBI doesn't report on such deaths, or on workplace deaths, it's hard to know how many deaths every year could have been prevented.

IN A DEMOCRACY . . .

The risk to a person who kills another is high: prison, and, in some states, execution. But the risk of killing people is relatively low to a corporation, and industry lobbies to keep it that way. For instance, when Congress considered putting criminal penalties into the National Traffic and Motor Vehicle Safety Act, the auto industry lobbied hard against it and won.

As a result, today if you or I were to knowingly and willfully repair or build a car for somebody that killed them, we could go to prison for manslaughter or even murder. But if a corporation knowing and willfully were to repair or build a car that killed a human, they now have a legal exemption. They would face only civil penalties and fines under the act.

Many human deaths are a result of corporate activities that are permitted by the government—but even deaths that result from corporate felony convictions are not included in FBI crime statistics. In a democracy, we can do better.

14

UNEQUAL PRIVACY

The right of the people to be secure in their persons, houses, papers, and effects, against unreasonable searches and seizures, shall not be violated . . .

—FOURTH AMENDMENT TO THE CONSTITUTION OF THE UNITED STATES, GUARANTEEING PRIVACY FROM GOVERNMENT SNOOPING

Who reads your mail? Nobody? It depends what system you use for communication.

Paper mail that is delivered by the government-run Post Office carries legal protections for the privacy of our communications. Nobody, at least without a court order, can read our letters or track what we send and receive.

But if you send an e-mail, the corporation that provides your Internet access can read everything you write and keep track of who you correspond with, what Web sites you visit, and everything you write, read, and view. Even after the terrorist attacks on the World Trade Center and Pentagon in September 2001, the FBI needed an act of Congress to get that kind of power, even in limited form. But the corporations who transmit our e-mail have had it from day one.

And not only *can* multinational media corporations track our individual Internet activity, they do. If I walk around in my local bookstore, Bear Pond Books, nobody is following me and noting every book I pick up and look over. But when I browse the Web, both my Internet provider and the owners of the Web sites I visit may know who I am and what I've looked at. In fact, unless we intentionally install or activate security software, it's highly likely that they do know where we've been. That's because when I click a mouse on a Web site, it sends a coded signal through my Internet company and to the Web site host. Both of them can easily record my clicks—at practically no cost to themselves.

In our increasingly electronic age, there's more: The corporation that sells me telephone service keeps complete records of whom I call, where, and when. If I had digital interactive cable television, the cable corporation could keep a list of every program I watch and when.

Microsoft got a lot of publicity because, according to the online journal PCWorld.com, "it was unaware that a feature in its Windows 98 operating system was transmitting a hardware serial number to a Microsoft server, even if the user had requested that the number not be sent." Microsoft said it would take 2 months to make it stop sending the information. In a similar glitch, Microsoft said its Office software was accidentally inserting a unique ID code into documents that could be used to track where a document originated.

Many corporations today are responding to consumer pressure and heeding privacy initiatives, which is good. One thing Americans value very highly is their Fourth Amendment right to privacy, and polls have shown that it's one of the few issues that will get Americans out of their seats on election day. That fact could be even more persuasive to legislators than campaign contributions.

But that only works if the consumer realizes their information is being collected—and they are rarely notified as companies scrutinize all of this information to determine their habits, desires, and ability to pay for new products.

While the names of only a few of the participants in the Boston Tea Party are known today, more than 220 years later, such anonymity is impossible. And without anonymity, the skeptics argue, anybody who would try to shift power away from corporations back to the people will be neutralized before they have a chance to be effective. Access to the media would be denied, they would find themselves unemployable and without resources, and, in a worst-case scenario, they may suffer the fate of Karen Silkwood, who died on her way to share corporate inside information with a reporter.

CORPORATIONS WANT PRIVACY—FOR THEM, BUT NOT FOR HUMANS

Although corporations keep all their constitutional rights as a person intact throughout the business day and night, 7 days a week, 365 days a year, the

Supreme Court has ruled that when a human steps onto the corporate-owned property of his or her employer, that human is voluntarily giving up their constitutional rights to privacy, freedom from search, and free speech.

Your employer can read your e-mails, monitor your computer use, secretly photograph you, listen in on your telephone calls, fire you if you say things they don't like (even unrelated to work), and even demand that you provide them with samples of your bodily fluids or subject you to external and internal physical examinations.

At the same time, however, the corporation you work for continues to assert their full constitutional rights against these same types of "interference" by the representative of humans, the government. The EPA can't inspect a chemical factory without the permission of the corporation that owns it, but that same corporation can inspect its employees in the minutest detail without asking their permission.

Additionally, information about U. S.-based multinational corporations are *not* available in the following areas because those corporations are entitled, as persons with privacy rights, to keep secret:

- How much they pay overseas workers
- How many overseas employees they have, or where
- Levels of toxic emissions from their plants overseas, or of those of their contractors
- Where they have overseas plants or contractors

IN A DEMOCRACY . . .

Not only was it *not* always this way in America, but it's probably the opposite of what the Founders of this nation intended. In a democracy, this can change.

15

UNEQUAL CITIZENSHIP AND ACCESS TO THE COMMONS

fas-cism (fâsh'iz'em) n. *A system of government that exercises a dictatorship of the extreme right, typically through the merging of state and business leadership, together with belligerent nationalism. [Ital.* fascio, *group.] -fas'cist* n. *-fas-cis'tic (fa-shis'tik)* adj.

–THE AMERICAN HERITAGE DICTIONARY
HOUGHTON MIFFLIN COMPANY, 1983

There are resources and there are resources. For corporations, resources include raw materials, labor, the property and equipment they use, the talents of the people they employ, and cash. For humans, resources include air, water, food, shelter, clothing, health care, and the means of exchange to ensure these.

I remember growing up 50-plus years ago in an America where an employer's responsibilities to their community were so well understood that bosses who laid off people were considered either evil or failures. There was a dramatic recalibration of this during the 1980s, as the word "layoff" was replaced with the more politically tolerable euphemism "downsizing"... and then further euphemized to "rightsizing." In Europe, the same event is described much more directly: "I was made redundant."

This chapter is about what has happened to humans as their protections have been given to entities (corporations) that have entirely different values.

Ironically, the bigger companies get, the more ability they have to influence people's lives for better or worse—but the bigger they get, the fewer choices are available to workers and customers. And in recent years, health researchers have identified that the inability to do anything about one's problems is a key contributing factor to stress.

STRESS KILLS

For many Americans, a lengthening workweek, increasing debt, and dwindling job security are now part of life. Not surprisingly, this triad produces stress. Debt carries risk. A longer workweek reduces options for enjoying life and for escaping from debt. The decline of job security increases the risk of complete economic disaster—a scenario that corporations rarely have to confront.

The ratification of NAFTA and GATT/WTO made it possible to shift manufacturing and production jobs from the United States to the Third World. The American situation is mirrored throughout the world, as industrialized nations lose manufacturing jobs and Third World countries become spotted with sweatshops like a child with measles. Humans require passports and visas to travel from nation to nation, but corporations can now move anywhere with virtually no restrictions.

- The U. S. Centers for Disease Control notes that, "From 1952 to 1995, the incidence of suicide among adolescents and young adults nearly tripled. From 1980 to 1997, the rate of suicide among persons aged 15 to 19 years increased by 11 percent and among persons aged 10 to 14 years by 109 percent."
- Between 1972 and 1994, the number of Americans living below the poverty line almost doubled from roughly 23 million to about 40 million.
- Across Latin America, Africa, and Asia, the United Nation's International Labor Organization catalogues over 250 million children between the ages of 5 and 14 working in hazardous industries and slave labor.
- The World Health Organization lists unemployment as one of its risk factors for child abuse.
- When the Asian financial crisis hit Japan, for the first time in 50 years corporations could no longer afford the *keiretsu* system, which dictated

> that corporations provide workers with health care, local schools, and housing. Citizens of company towns found themselves scrambling for employment, housing, education, and health care. As a result, noted the *New York Times* in 2001, "The suicide rate in Japan among males rose during the 1990s to a higher point than it was in the post–World War II era."

While this has been tragic for the people who are affected, a cynical view is that an increase in the number of desperate people can be beneficial to business: Wages drop when more people are out of work and competing for available jobs. In fact, wages are lowest when the worker literally has *no* choice.

THE PRISONER AS EMPLOYEE

Under the new WTO and NAFTA rules, an importing country cannot consider the conditions under which a product was produced. So, some corporations have discovered that they can profit by using prison labor to manufacture export products or perform services for offshore clients.

Although corporations can't be put in prison, they find it very profitable to put humans there: Corporations in nations like Burma, China, and the United States have opened manufacturing or service facilities in prisons, paying their laborers anywhere from a few cents an hour down to nothing at all. It's an enormously profitable enterprise, and some nations have moved to capitalize on it by passing laws that are easy to violate (so people end up in prison who would not otherwise have been there), increasing the severity of penalties for existing crimes, more heavily criminalizing health problems (drug use), or criminalizing "anti-state" behaviors (such as practicing religion in China). While China and Burma don't publish their figures, in the United States (the nation with the world's highest incarceration rate), we find:

- The "correctional population" of the United States was 5.9 million adults in 1998, resulting in 1 in every 34 Americans (2.9 percent of the U. S. adult population) in jail, on parole, or on probation. The consequence was a substantial pool of potential prison labor: According to the U. S. Department of Justice, "At year end 2000, 1 in every 143 U. S. residents were incarcerated in State or Federal prison or a local jail."

- Since the 1985 passage of new laws increasing criminal penalties for drug use and sale, drug convictions accounted for over 80 percent of the increase in the federal prison population between then and 1996, driving up the budget of the Federal Bureau of Prisons by 1,954 percent.
- From its birth in the 1980s, the American private prison industry has grown to be worth more than a billion dollars today, and is now moving international with the two largest players having moved into direct construction or alliance partnerships in over 60 nations.
- The percentage of American prisoners in private prisons who are now working for multinational corporations more than doubled between 1993 and 1998, according to www.prisonactivist.org. (Detailed statistics are hard to come by since the industry is not required to release such information and therefore chooses not to.) At the same time, American prisons carry the highest rates of tuberculosis and HIV infection (and new infections) in the nation, and have a suicide rate 20 times higher than the country as a whole.
- But they can be *very* profitable: On February 8, 2002, America's largest private prison corporation "reported record high annual revenues for fiscal year 2001 of $2.8 billion, a 12.1 percent increase over its 2000 revenues of $2.5 billion," and that the security part of their business was doing well. The company's president said, "The North American security operations had a very strong quarter and year with a margin increase of 20 basis points for the fourth quarter, and a margin increase of 80 basis points for the year."

PRIVATIZING THE COMMONS

Privatization is the idea of taking commons functions or resources out of the hands of elected governments responsible to their voters and handing the management or ownership of them over to private enterprise answerable to shareholders. Many arguments have been advanced about privatization; those in favor arguing that corporations run for a profit can be more efficient than government, and those opposed usually arguing that the resources of the commons should always be held in the hands of institutions that are only answerable to the people who use them—the citizens—and thus must be managed by elected and responsive governments.

Opponents of privatization of the commons also usually point out that whatever increases in efficiency a corporation may bring to a utility, the savings produced by those increases in efficiency rarely make their way to the consumer, but instead are raked off the top by the corporation and distributed to shareholders as profits. One of the more high-profile examples is that of Enron and their role in the privatization of electricity worldwide, with particular focus on how Enron's privatization of electricity in California worked to the detriment of California's citizens but produced millions in profits for a small group of Texas stockholders, or an Enron subsidiary's meetings in 1999 with Governor Jeb Bush of Florida in which they proposed to privatize and take over much of the state's water supply.

Supporters of privatization point to the creative ways corporations can figure out how to extract profits from things governments previously just supervised in a boring and methodical fashion. For example, an article in the *Houston Chronicle* in January 2001 titled "Enron Is Blazing New Business Trail" noted the "extraordinary year" the Houston-based company was having, with most of the company's revenues coming "from buying and selling contracts in natural gas and electricity."

The article quoted Kenneth Lay who, the newspaper said, "has a doctorate in economics," as extolling the virtues of profiting from trading in previously regulated or government-run commodities. "The company's emphasis on trading to hedge against risk has been emulated by other firms in energy," the article said, including "Duke Energy, Dynegy, Williams Energy—and increasingly in other industries."

WHO OWNS THE WORLD'S WATER?

While Enron had started the discussion going in Florida in 1999 about privatizing that state's water supplies and the Everglades, the process was already a done deal in Bolivia. In 1998, the Bolivian government requested a $25 million loan guarantee to refinance their water services in the community of Cochabamba. The World Bank told the Bolivian government that they would guarantee the loan only if Bolivia privatized the water supply, so it was handed over to Aguas del Tunari, a subsidiary of several large transnationals, including an American corporation that is one of the world's largest private construction companies.

The next year, Aguas del Tunari, in an effort to squeeze profits out of

Bolivia's water, announced that water prices were doubling. For minimum wage or unemployed Bolivians, this meant water would now take half their monthly income, costing more than food. The Bolivian government, acting on suggestions from the World Bank and Aguas del Tunari, declared all water corporate property, so that even to draw water from community wells or to gather rainwater on their own properties, peasants and small farmers had to first pay for and obtain permits from the corporation.

The price of water was pegged to the U. S. dollar to protect the corporation, and the Bolivian government announced that none of the World Bank loan could go to poor people to help with their water bills.

With over 90 percent of the Bolivian people opposing this move, a people's rebellion rose up to de-privatize the water system. A former machinist and union activist, Oscar Olivera, built a broad-based coalition of peasants, workers, and farmers to create La Coordinadora de Defensa del Agua y de la Vida, or La Coordinadora. Hundreds of thousands of Bolivians went on a general strike, brought transportation in Cochabamba to a standstill, and evoked violent police response in defense of the Aguas del Tunari corporation's right to continue to control the local water supply and sell it for a profit. Victor Hugo Danza, one of the marchers, was shot through the face and killed: He was 17.

The government declared martial law, and members of La Coordinadora were arrested and beaten in the middle of an early April night. The government seized control of the radio and television stations to prevent anticorporate messages from being broadcast. But the uprising continued and grew.

The situation became so tense that the directors of the American corporation and Aguas del Tunari abandoned Bolivia on April 10, 2000. They took with them key files, documents, computers, and the assets of the company—leaving a legal shell with tremendous debt.

The Bolivian government handed the debts and the water company, SEMAPA, to La Coordinadora. The new company is now run by the activist group—essentially a local government itself, now—and its first action was to restore water to the poorest southern neighborhoods, over 400 communities, which had been cut off by the for-profit company because the residents didn't have the money to pay profitable rates for water. Throughout the summer of 2000, La Coordinadora held hearings through the hundreds of neighborhoods they now served.

In the meantime, the American corporation moved its holding company for Aguas del Tunari from the Cayman Islands to Holland so that they could legally sue the government of Bolivia (South America's poorest country) under WTO and Bilateral Investment Treaty (BIT) rules that Bolivia had signed with Holland.

As of this writing, the lawsuit for $40 million is proceeding, while at the same time a disconcerting pattern of harassment, surveillance, infiltration, and physical violence has stepped up against members of La Coordinadora.

Why such extraordinary steps against such a poor country? There's more at stake than the immediate situation. If this citizen's group is successful in turning a water supply back from private to government hands, and thus improving water service and making it more egalitarian and less expensive in this poverty-stricken country, it could threaten water-privatizing plans of huge corporations all around the world.

The stakes are high, even as cities across India, Africa, and other South American countries hand their local water systems to for-profit corporations. Nonetheless, politicians around the world are stepping up the rate at which they're pushing for a transfer of the commons to the hands of for-profit corporations. Checking voting records and lists of corporate contributors, it's hard not to conclude that there is a relationship between this political activity and the generous contributions these corporations give to pro-privatization politicians.

HOSTILE TAKEOVERS CAN ERASE A FIRM'S VALUES

In today's business environment, when corporations are run in ways that benefit the environment or their workers as much as their stockholders, they're at risk. When good salaries and pension plans are cut, it's referred to as unnecessary fat that can be trimmed. (Note that such cuts are made much more feasible when wages are forced down by exporting jobs from the local economy.) Similarly, behaving in a more expensive but environmentally friendly way is not "efficient."

In an article in *Yes!* magazine, economist and author David C. Korten pointed out that for many years the Pacific Lumber Company was, in many regards, a model corporate citizen. They paid good salaries, fully funded their pension fund, offered an excellent benefit package to employees, and even had an explicit no-layoffs policy during soft times in the lumber economy. Perhaps most important to local residents who weren't employed by the company, Pacific Lumber "for years pioneered the development of sustainable logging practices on its substantial holdings of ancient redwood timber stands in California."

In a nation where such employee- and nature-friendly values were both valued and defended, Pacific Lumber Company would have a bright future. But in a world where profit is the prime value, and humans and ancient trees are merely excess fat, Pacific Lumber was a sitting duck.

As Korten documents in his article, a corporate raider "gained control in a hostile takeover. He immediately doubled the cutting rate of the company's holding of thousand-year-old trees, reaming a mile-and-a-half corridor into the middle of the forest that he jeeringly named 'Our wildlife-biologist study trail.' He then drained $55 million from the company's $93 million pension fund and invested the remaining $38 million in annuities of the life insurance company which had financed the junk bonds used to make the purchase and subsequently failed. The remaining redwoods were the subject of a last-ditch effort by environmentalists to save from clearcutting." In the end, the government stepped in to save some of the old-growth forests.

Once upon a time, America had laws that corporations couldn't own other corporations. If that were still true, then situations like that chronicled by Korten would become illegal rather than the norm. The reason Madison and Jefferson—and even Hamilton and Adams—worried so loudly about "associations and monopolies" growing too large and powerful is that they would begin to usurp the very lives and liberties of the humans who created them. It becomes particularly problematic when companies are bought and stripped of their assets by other companies who aren't even in their industry, but simply asset hunting.

In the realm of government, the Founders kept power close to the people with the Tenth Amendment and other constitutional references to the powers of states over the federal government. A similar principle could apply to corporations.

The breakup of AT&T between 1974 and 1984 led to a vigorous growth in the telecommunications industry, although that industry is once again reconsolidating in the absence of government pressure or incentives to stay small and local.

SEIZING OTHER NATIONS' COMMONS VIA PATENT

Because the only inventions recognized by most countries' patent laws are those patented in those countries, and international courts have recently held that life forms and their by-products are patentable, multinational corporations in wealthy nations have been busily patenting the living products of poorer nations.

For example, people in India have been using the oil of the neem tree as a medicine for millennia: Over 70 patents have now been granted on the tree and its by-products in various nations. One European patent on its use as a fungicide was recently thrown out, but others stand.

In similar fashion, Maggie McDonald notes in the British magazine *New Scientist* that, "a botanical cure for hepatitis traditionally used in India can be patented in the U. S." She notes that Vandana Shiva documents how this is not a process that is driving innovation or competition, as multinationals often claim, but instead, "a survey in the U. S. showed that 80 percent of patents are taken out to block competitors."

Ironically, that same issue of *New Scientist* has a feature on recruitment news that extols the wonders of becoming a patent agent. In the new world of international biotechnology, the article says, "Wealth is measured not in gold mines, but in the new currency of 'intellectual property.'" Eerily echoing Shiva's claim, the article on getting a job in the patent business says, "The aim is to lock away these prize assets so they can't be plundered by commercial rivals."

And the business of locking up these assets pays very well. Ted Blake of Britain's Chartered Institute of Patent Agents is quoted as saying, "You're looking at six-figure salaries for those who make it as partners in an agents' firm." But not only is the pay good, the work is also very chic. Reiner Osterwalder of the European Patent Office told the magazine, "Patents are no longer stuck in a dusty corner. They're sexy, and touch questions of world order."

The BBC notes that not only can plants and their uses be patented, but the very genetics of the plants can be nailed down. In an article about the patenting of the neem tree published in 2000 on the BBC Web site, they say, "Genes from nutmeg and camphor have also been patented with the aim of producing their oils artificially—a move which would hit producers in developing countries."

And it's in developing countries where the race to patent indigenous life forms is most rapid, particularly by American-based companies, because U. S. patent law doesn't recognize indigenous use of a product as "prior art," meaning once a use for a plant is "discovered" by an American company—even if that plant has been used that way for 10,000 years by local tribes, it's considered new and thus patentable. The Web site www.globalissues.org notes that, "In Brazil, which probably has the richest biodiversity in the world, large multinational corporations have already patented more than half the known plant species."

The consequences of this behavior are profitable for corporations, but can be devastating to the humans who find that their food or medicinal plants are now the property of a multinational corporation. Corporations say that this is necessary in order to ensure profits, but the thriving herbal products industry—made up mostly of domestic plants that cannot be patented—testifies to the untruthfulness of this assertion. Selling plants may not be as profitable as selling tightly controlled and patented plants, but it can be profitable nonetheless.

This is not to say plants should or should not be patentable. In a democracy, the benefits or liabilities of corporations patenting life forms would be discussed and decided by popular vote. Because of the *Santa Clara* decision and its consequences, however, corporations have exercised their "right" to get patent laws changed and exemptions established that would be difficult to impossible for an ordinary human to accomplish.

CHANGING YOUR CITIZENSHIP IN A DAY

For a human to change their citizenship from one country to another is a process that can take years, sometimes even decades, and, for most of the world's humans, is practically impossible. Corporations, however, can change their citizenship in a day. And many do.

The New Hampshire firm Tyco International moved their legal citizenship from the United States to Bermuda and, according to a 2002 report in the *New York Times*, saved "more than $40 million last year alone" because Bermuda does not charge income tax to corporations, while the United States does. Stanley Works, which manufactures in Connecticut, will save $30 million. Ingersoll-Rand saves $40 million a year.

Offshore tax havens figured big in the Enron debacle, as that corporation spun off more almost 900 separate companies based in tax-free countries to shelter income and hide transactions. Through this device, the company paid no income taxes whatever in 4 of the past 5 years, and received $382 million in tax rebates from Uncle Sam.

Generally when a human person changes citizenship, they are also required to change their residence—they have to move to and participate in the country where they are a citizen. But Bermuda and most other tax havens have no such requirement. All you need do is be a corporate person instead of a human person, pay some fees (it cost Ingersoll-Rand $27,653), and, as Ingersoll-Rand's Chief Financial Officer told the *New York Times*, "We just pay a service organization" to be a mail drop for the company.

Ironically, the Bush administration justified rounding up human people and holding them incommunicado in jails without normal due process after September 11 because as noncitizens, they lacked the full protections of citizens under the U. S. Constitution. Similarly, if you or I were to open a post office box in Bermuda and then claim that we no longer had to pay U. S. income taxes, we could go to jail.

Corporate persons, however, keep their rights intact when they decide to change citizenship, and save a pile in taxes. And, notes the *New York Times*, "There is no official estimate of how much the Bermuda moves are costing the government in tax revenues, and the Bush administration is not trying to come up with one."

IN A DEMOCRACY . . .

One of the foundational principles of democracy is that all people are treated equally in regard to issues of the law, citizenship, and their access to the commons. As Lawrence Mitchell, John Theodore Fey Research Professor of Law at the George Washington Law School and author of *Corporate Irresponsibility* said, "The function of corporations in light of their constitutional personhood is effectively to foreclose access to the commons for most citizens. The entire proposition that a corporation is a person is ridiculous."

16

UNEQUAL WEALTH

I care not how affluent some may be, provided that none be miserable in consequence of it.

—THOMAS PAINE, 1796

In the absence of the controls recommended by the Founders and early state regulation, corporations have continued to grow in size and power without limit. But they haven't done it just by creating new wealth in the economy. Much of it, instead, has been accomplished by increasingly consolidating existing wealth. Of course, some new wealth has been generated, but nowhere near enough to explain the observable facts.

CONSOLIDATION: MERGERS, ACQUISITIONS, INTERLOCKING BOARDS

I noted in chapter 2 that if you were to define and rank nations according to their gross domestic product (GDP), 52 of the world's 100 largest "nations" are actually corporations. Tracking the growth of the largest companies can be problematic because they're constantly merging with or buying other companies. This trend has accelerated in the decreased regulatory environment of the 1980s and 1990s—just a few generations after Americans busted the trusts during the Populist movement of Teddy Roosevelt and William Jennings Bryan.

One-third of 1980's Fortune 500 companies no longer existed in 1990—not because they failed, but because they had been merged or acquired. This accelerated in the 1990s: Two-fifths of the Fortune 500 vanished in the 5 years from 1900 to 1995. They're still there and still powerful; it's just that now they're even more powerful and wealthy, and they have less competition.

The combined GDP of the world's 200 largest corporations is greater than all but nine nations, and just as the European royal families are interrelated, so too are the boards of directors of most of the world's largest corporations.

Corporate observer Robert A. G. Monks reports that today 86 percent of billion-dollar company boards contain at least one CEO of another company, while 65 percent of outside directors serve on two or more boards. He documents how 89 percent of inside directors are outside directors on other companies' boards, and 20 percent of all directors serve on four or more company boards. Ralph Nader has testified about this extensively before Congress, suggesting these interlocking boards violate antitrust statutes, and there are entire Web sites devoted to it, such as www.theyrule.net.

For example, the following companies are interconnected in that each has at least one board member who's also a board member on another, creating a continuous daisy-chain (all information was current as of early 2002; stats cited from www.theyrule.net):

- IBM shares a board member with Coca Cola
- Which shares a board member with AT&T
- Which shares a board member with Citigroup
- Which shares a board member with Lucent Technologies
- Which shares a board member with Chevron
- Which shares a board member with Hewlett Packard
- Which shares a board member with Boeing
- Which shares a board member with Sara Lee
- Which shares a board member with Bank One Corporation
- Which shares a board member with Cardinal Health
- Which shares a board member with Freddie Mac
- Which shares a board member with Lehman Brother Holdings
- Which shares a board member with PepsiCo

- Which shares a board member with Bank of America
- Which shares a board member with Motorola
- Which shares a board member with J. P. Morgan Chase
- Which shares a board member with ExxonMobil
- Which shares a board member with SBC Communications (owns Ameritech, PacBell, Southwestern Bell, among others)
- Which shares a board member with PG&E Corporation
- Which shares a board member with Home Depot
- Which shares a board member with General Electric
- Which shares a board member with Delphi Automotive Systems
- Which shares a board member with Goldman Sachs Group
- Which shares a board member with Ford Motor Company
- Which shares a board member with Sprint
- Which shares a board member with Allstate
- Which shares a board member with AMR (owns American Airlines)
- Which shares a board member with Aetna
- Which shares a board member with Dell Computer
- Which shares a board member with Prudential Insurance
- Which shares a board member with Dow Chemical
- Which shares a board member with Met Life
- Which shares a board member with Verizon
- Which shares a board member with USX (formerly U. S. Steel)
- Which shares a board member with Lockheed Martin
- Which shares a board member with Enron
- Which at this writing shares board member Ken Lay with Compaq
- Which shares a board member with Dynergy
- Which shares a board member with CVS/Pharmacy
- Which shares a board member with Fannie Mae
- Which shares a board member with Conoco
- Which shares a board member with E. I. du Pont de Nemours
- Which shares a board member with IBM

- Which shares a board member with Coca Cola (which is where we started)

There is strong evidence that this much concentration of wealth and power is not healthy, and prior to the last century it was considered criminal behavior in many states, as interlocking boards were often banned and most states had specific caps on the size a corporation could not exceed.

But that was then and this is now. Today, the world's largest 200 corporations, which employ fewer than 0.8 percent of the world's workforce, account for over 27 percent of the world's total economic activity, more than all nations in the world *combined* except the top 10.

The corporations of Samuel Adams' day, like the East India Company, were the bald economic instruments of monarchy and imperial power, but during and after the American Revolution they were put firmly under the control of state legislatures and local municipalities. Today, empowered with human rights, they roam free, with few checks on their power or growth.

- The United Nations reports that "about two-thirds of all world trade" is in the hands of transnational corporations, who "increasingly shape trade patterns" of the planet.
- Corporations reaching out from their home countries and into other countries have become "the main force in international economic integration," according to the U. N.'s Trade and Development Conference.
- Sales of the 200 largest corporations in the world equal 27.5 percent of world's GDP.
- If you added together the sales of every nation in the world except the top 10, the total would be less than the combined sales of the world's 200 largest corporations.
- The 1999 sales of General Motors were greater than the GDP of 182 nations. The same is true of Wal-Mart, Exxon-Mobil, Ford Motor, and DaimlerChrysler.
- The 82 largest American corporations contributed $33,045,832 to political action committees in the year-2000 election cycle (and that doesn't include "soft money," for which statistics are unavailable), outspending labor unions by 15 to 1. This was apparently useful to candidates: In 94 percent of U. S. House of Representatives races, the candidate who spent the most money won.

As this shift in income has happened, along with it came a shift in who owns pretty much everything.

- In 1976, the richest 10 percent of America's population owned 50 percent of American wealth. By 1997, they owned 73 percent. (In other words, 23 percent of America's total wealth shifted from the poor and middle-class to the very wealthy in 21 years.)
- This was not just because the economic pie got bigger—44 percent more people work multiple jobs than did in 1970, and American workers are putting in, on average, a full month more at work than they did 20 years ago. And hourly earnings of America's nonsupervisory workers, in 1998 dollars, have fallen by 9 percent since 1973, from $14.09 to $12.77.
- Looking at the same numbers from "the other end of the telescope," in 1976 the lower 90 percent of the population owned half the wealth. By 1997, their share was down to 27 percent.
- In 2000, the top 1 percent of American households have financial wealth greater than that of the bottom 95 percent combined.
- In 1998, the net worth of just one American, Bill Gates, at $46 billion, was greater than the bottom 45 percent of all American households *combined.*
- It's not just an American phenomenon any more. Worldwide, according to the United Nations Development Program, the difference between the richest and poorest nations in the world was 1 to 3 in 1820, 1 to 35 in 1950, and 1 to 72 in 1992. The gap has continued to grow since then.

How can this be? What's happening?

SPENGLER'S *THE DECLINE OF THE WEST*

In his book *The Decline of the West*, first published in German in 1918 and then in English in 1926, Oswald Spengler suggested that what we call Western Civilization was then beginning to enter a "hardening" or "classical" phase, in which all the nurturing and supportive structures of culture would become, instead, instruments of the exploitation of a growing peasant class to feed the wealth of a new and growing aristocracy.

Culture would become a parody of itself, peoples' expectations would decline while their wants would grow, and a new peasantry would emerge which would cause the culture to stabilize in a "classic form" that, while Spengler doesn't use the term, seems very much like feudalism—the medieval system in which the lord owned the land and everyone else was a vassal (a tenant who owed loyalty to the landlord).

Spengler, considering himself an aristocrat, didn't see this as a bad thing. In 1926, he prophesied that once the boom of the Roaring Twenties was over, a great bust would wash over the Western world. While this bust had the potential to create chaos, its most likely outcome would be a return to the classic, stable form of social organization, what Spengler calls High Culture and I call neofeudalism.

He wrote, "In all high Cultures, therefore, there is a *peasantry*, which is breed stock, in the broad sense (and thus to a certain extent nature herself), and a *society* which is assertively and emphatically 'in form.' It is a set of classes or Estates, and no doubt artificial and transitory. But the history of these classes and estates is *world history at highest potential.* It is only in relation to it that the peasant is seen as historyless." (All italics are Spengler's from the original text.)

More recent cultural observers, ranging from billionaire George Soros in his book *The Crisis of Global Capitalism*, to professor Noreena Hertz in *The Silent Takeover: Global Capitalism and the Death of Democracy* have pointed to deep cracks in the foundational structure of Western Civilization, traceable to the current legal status of corporations versus humans. The extent of the problems within our structures is laid bare with startling and sometimes frightening clarity by a wide variety of books.

The origin of many of modern global society's problems are clearly laid out in *The Trap* by now-deceased billionaire speculator Sir James Goldsmith, and it appears that perhaps that "crazy old coot" (as the media would have us believe) Ross Perot, with his charts and graphs and warnings about corporate money in the political process, GATT, and NAFTA was right in many regards, at least from a nationalistic American point of view.

The summary version of these and dozens of other books documenting Spengler's decline of the West is this: We're entering a new and unknown but hauntingly familiar era. It's new because it represents a virtual abandonment of the egalitarian archetypes the Founders of the United States put into place in our Constitution and Bill of Rights. And it's hauntingly familiar because it resembles in many ways one of the most stable and long-term of all social structures to have ever established itself in the modern history of Europe—feudalism.

Boston Tea Party participant George R. T. Hewes mentioned the idea that the situation then was beginning to resemble feudalism, and there are those today who have made the same comparison.

THE NEW FEUDALISM

Feudalism doesn't refer to a point in time or history when streets were filled with mud and people lived as peasants (although that was sometimes the case). Instead, it refers to an economic and political system, just like democracy or communism or socialism or theocracy. The biggest difference is that instead of power being held by the people, the government, or the church, power is held by those who own property and the other necessities of life. At its essential core, feudalism could be defined as "government of, by, and for the rich."

Marc Bloch is one of the great 20th-century scholars of the feudal history of Europe. In his book *Feudal Society*, he points out that feudalism is a fracturing of one authoritarian hierarchical structure into another: The state disintegrates as local power brokers take over.

In almost every case, both with European feudalism and feudalism in China, South America, and Japan, "feudalism coincided with a profound weakening of the State, particularly in its protective capacity." Given most accepted definitions of feudalism, feudal societies don't emerge in civilizations with a strong social safety net and a proactive government.

There is a slight debate, in that some scholars like Benjamin Guérard say feudalism must be land-based, whereas Jacques Flach and others suggest that the structure of power and obligation is the key. But the consensus is that when the wealthiest in a society take over government and then weaken it so that it no longer can represent the interests of the people, the transition has begun into a new era of feudalism. "European feudalism should therefore be seen as the outcome of the violent dissolution of older societies," Bloch says.

Whether the power and wealth agent that takes the place of government is a local baron, lord, king, or corporation, if it has greater power in the lives of individuals than does a representative government, the culture has dissolved into feudalism. Bluntly, Bloch states, "The feudal system meant the rigorous economic subjection of a host of humble folk to a few powerful men."

This doesn't mean the end of government, but instead, the subordination of government to the interests of the feudal lords. Interestingly, even in feudal Europe, Bloch points out, "The concept of the State never absolutely disappeared, and where it retained the most vitality men continued to call themselves 'free' . . ."

The transition from a governmental society to a feudal one is marked by the rapid accumulation of power and wealth in a few hands, with a corresponding reduction in the power and responsibilities of government. Once the rich and powerful gain control of the government, they turn it upon itself, usually first eliminating its taxation process as it applies to themselves. Says Bloch, "Nobles need not pay *taille* [taxes]."

Bringing this to today, consider that in 1982, just before the Reagan-Bush "supply side" tax cut, the average wealth of the Forbes 400 was $200 million. Just 4 years later, their average wealth was $500 million each, aided by massive tax cuts. Today, those 400 people own wealth equivalent to one-eighth of the entire GDP of the United States.

EXTREME CONCENTRATIONS ARE DESTABILIZING

Too much concentration of anything makes it vulnerable to toppling. Most historians and economists recognize that a root cause of the Great Depression was a severe economic imbalance. The sharp increase in concentration of wealth described in this chapter also has much in common with the statistics of the 1920s.

This is also the history of civilizations. As wealth and power accumulate into fewer and fewer hands, the rest of the populace loses its sense that there's any point in trying to keep up. Whether on a national or a worldwide stage, revolutions and terrorism result when enough people perceive too great a gap between the most rich and the average poor.

In the 1980s, the Reagan and Bush administrations effectively ceased enforcement of the Sherman Anti-Trust Act, just as the Coolidge administration had done in the 1920s. This led to a mania for mergers, acquisitions, and neo-trusts, just as happened in the Roaring Twenties, and with a similar reconsolidation of power and wealth and rise in the stock market. Hopefully, the same cycle will not play itself out: If we act promptly, we can set in motion forces that will change the direction of the current trend.

THE END OF THE AMERICAN DREAM?

Martin Luther King, Jr., in his "I have a dream" speech, referred to how the people who wrote the Declaration of Independence and the U. S. Constitution "were signing a promissory note to which every American was to fall heir." The contents of that note King referred to were identified by Jefferson when he wrote, "We hold these truths to be self-evident, that all men are created equal, that they are endowed by their Creator with certain unalienable Rights, that among these are Life, Liberty and the pursuit of Happiness."

The American dream is something every schoolchild understands. It's the heart and soul of democracy. It means opportunity and freedom, the ability to raise a family or pursue one's own dreams. It means the strong participate in the protection of the weak, lest they lose their own rights if they become oppressors.

In *The Federalist Papers* No. 51, Alexander Hamilton wrote, "In a society under the forms of which the stronger faction can readily unite and oppress the weaker, anarchy may as truly be said to reign . . ." and under such circumstances, eventually, even "the more powerful factions or parties will be gradually induced, by a like motive, to wish for a government which will protect all parties, the weaker as well as the more powerful."

Are we approaching that time Hamilton mentioned?

- At the same time that the concentration of wealth has taken place over the past 3 decades, the entry-level wage of an American male high school graduate has declined 28 percent (in real dollars).
- Twenty percent of American workers now earn income below the official poverty rate defined by the U. S. government—and that doesn't include the unemployed.
- The top 1 percent of Americans in 1998 in terms of income equaled the lowest wage earning 100 million Americans. (And there are only a total of about 140 million working Americans, according to the Bureau of Labor Statistics.)
- The top 20 percent of American families have seen their income go up by 97 percent in the past 2 decades. Meanwhile, the bottom 20 percent fell 44 percent in their real income, although most were working harder, working longer hours, and many carried multiple jobs.

Oswald Spengler noted that cycles of growth and collapse are built into the culture, and at a certain point it "hardens" and then becomes feudal or "classical." The warning signs, he says, are easily seen: replacement of human and spiritual values with slogans and self-indulgence, concentration of wealth into the hands of a few as poverty increases exponentially, citizens who are politically disengaged and ignorant, and a culture that becomes a parody of itself as it obsesses on its slogans and symbols but ceases to live out its ideals.

The fall of the Roman Empire is a classic example, and we may be another.

- In a 1998 survey of American teens, 2.2 percent could name the Chief Justice of the Supreme Court (William Rehnquist), but 59.2 percent could name Curly, Larry, and Moe as the fictional Three Stooges.
- An impressive 74.3 percent of teens knew that Bart Simpson lives in Springfield, Massachusetts, but only 12.2 percent recognized that Abraham Lincoln lived most of his life in Springfield, Illinois.
- 21.1 percent knew there are 100 U. S. Senators, 1.8 percent could identify James Madison as a father of the Constitution, and a thin 25 percent knew what human right the Fifth Amendment protects. But 98.7 percent knew that Leonardo DiCaprio starred in the hit movie *Titanic*, and 75.2 percent knew the zip code associated with the popular television show *Beverly Hills 90210.*

Ironically, and probably unknown to the National Constitution Center at the time they designed their poll, the Three Stooges, Bart Simpson, the movie *Titanic*, and the television show *Beverly Hills 90210* are all owned by the same multinational corporation. Such single-corporation influence over popular culture would not have been the case 200 years ago, or even 50 years ago.

To blame all or even most of this on the *Santa Clara* decision would be overreaching: Wealth was concentrating and moving around the world well before the modern corporation came along. Rome had concentrations of wealth, as did Sumeria and Greece. Medieval Europe and Japan were cultures of extreme wealth and poverty, as was India with its multi-millenia caste system. Even Victorian England, not so very long ago, was a hellhole for all but the well-born and the industrialists, as Charles Dickens reminds us in graphic, tragic prose. "This is nothing new," some would say.

But it is. The difference between then and now is twofold:

1. The wealth in those days had a face and a name. Without corporations to blur who does what, the warlords and nobles and the high-caste

were identifiable. We know who the kings and queens of old were, from Gilgamesh 6,000 years ago in Sumeria to the King of France before the revolutionaries executed him and his family. Because that wealth had a face, saying things like "Let them eat cake" could be dangerous for one's survival.

2. More important, those governments never claimed to be democratic. In the past 6,000 years of modern worldwide agriculture-driven civilization, there were only two governments—Athens for about 2 centuries, and the United States for a century or so—which rose out of a dominator culture and claimed that they were truly democratic, truly government by the people, even the poorest of the people. Since the American experiment, dozens of countries have joined the club in various forms, but it's still very much a new experiment worldwide, one that was only once tried before in all these millennia—Athens, 300 BCE—and they were conquered and thrown back into oppression by the concentrated wealth and power of Alexander the Great.

IN A DEMOCRACY . . .

The "great experiment" of a democratic republic is at a critical crossroads. Can it recover the "government of, by, and for the people" ideal that it held so recently, and implement it again in the halls of governments in America and across the world?

Or has de Tocqueville's worried vision come to pass? Have we become anesthetized and helpless as humans in the face of a mighty machine that puts on a good face but, when push comes to shove, takes no prisoners and destroys its competitors without a second's thought?

The answer will depend, in some part, on whether the fateful *Santa Clara* decision is allowed to stand. Will the people take back their government and assert democratic controls over the misdeeds of the fabulously powerful corporations among them?

To some extent, that will depend on whether We The People demand that our elected officials return to the time-tested principles of national trade policy and fair trade, instead of the "free for multinationals trade" that has been so aggressively peddled to the world in the past 2 decades.

17

UNEQUAL TRADE

In the great days of the USA, Henry Ford stated that he wanted to pay high wages to his employees so that they could become his customers and buy his cars. Today we are proud of the fact that we pay low wages. We have forgotten that the economy is a tool to serve the needs of society, and not the reverse. The ultimate purpose of the economy is to create prosperity with stability.

—BILLIONAIRE SPECULATOR SIR JAMES GOLDSMITH, 1993

Equal trade, fair trade, honest, decent trade requires reasonable balance between trading partners and strong domestic economies. When that happens, Adam Smith's model works pretty well: Prices for labor, materials, and finished goods all settle near the area where they "naturally" should be.

But as we've seen from the immensely imbalanced statistics on distribution of wealth in chapter 16, something is not working the way Smith envisioned. Wages appear to be dwindling and the number of strong, healthy competitors appears to be shrinking.

TEDDY ROOSEVELT WEIGHS IN

President Theodore Roosevelt brilliantly defined the American dream in the context of the dynamic difference between a business that is a builder of community and one that hollows out community. "We are a business people,"

Roosevelt said at the Ohio Constitutional Convention in Columbus, Ohio, in 1912. "The tillers of the soil, the wage workers, the business men—these are the three big and vitally important divisions of our population. The welfare of each division is vitally necessary to the welfare of the people as a whole.

"The great mass of business is of course done by men whose business is either small or of moderate size. The middle-sized business men form an element of strength which is of literally incalculable value to the nation. Taken as a class, they are among our best citizens. They have not been seekers after enormous fortunes; they have been moderately and justly prosperous, by reason of dealing fairly with their customers, competitors, and employees. They are satisfied with a legitimate profit that will pay their expenses of living and lay by something for those who come after, and the additional amount necessary for the betterment and improvement of their plant. The average business man of this type is, as a rule, a leading citizen of his community, foremost in everything that tells for its betterment, a man whom his neighbors look up to and respect; he is in no sense dangerous to his community, just because he is an integral part of his community, bone of its bone and flesh of its flesh. His life fibers are intertwined with the life fibers of his fellow citizens . . .

"So much for the small business man and the middle-sized business man. Now for big business. . . .

"It is imperative to exercise over big business a control and supervision which is unnecessary as regards small business. All business must be conducted under the law, and all business men, big or little, must act justly. . . . 'Big business' in the past has been responsible for much of the special privilege which must be unsparingly cut out of our national life.

"I do not believe in making mere size of and by itself criminal. The mere fact of size, however, does unquestionably carry the potentiality of such grave wrongdoing that there should be by law provision made for the strict supervision and regulation of these great industrial concerns doing an interstate business, much as we now regulate the transportation agencies which are engaged in interstate business. The antitrust law does good in so far as it can be invoked against combinations which really are monopolies or which restrict production or which artificially raise prices. . . .

"The important thing is this: that, under such government recognition as we may give to that which is beneficent and wholesome in large business organizations, we shall be most vigilant never to allow them to crystallize into a condition which shall make private initiative difficult. It is of the utmost importance that in the future we shall keep the broad path of opportunity just as open and easy for our children as it was for our fathers during the period which has been the glory of America's industrial history—that it shall be not only possible but easy for an ambitious man, whose character has so impressed itself upon his neighbors that they are willing to give him capital and credit, to start in business for himself, and, if his superior efficiency deserves it, to triumph over the biggest organization that may happen to exist in his particular field. Whatever practices upon the part of large combinations may threaten to discourage such a man, or deny to him that which in the judgment of the community is a square deal, should be specifically defined by the statutes as crimes. And in every case the individual corporation officer responsible for such unfair dealing should be punished. . . .

"We grudge no man a fortune which represents his own power and sagacity exercised with entire regard to the welfare of his fellows. We have only praise for the business man whose business success comes as an incident to doing good work for his fellows. But we should so shape conditions that a fortune shall be obtained only in honorable fashion, in such fashion that its gaining represents benefit to the community. . . .

"We stand for the rights of property, but we stand even more for the rights of man. . . . We will protect the rights of the wealthy man, but we maintain that he holds his wealth subject to the general right of the community to regulate its business use as the public welfare requires."

In this speech, Roosevelt identified the key distinction and pointed directly to the situation the world finds itself in now. Corporations have become so large and powerful that "we, the people"—citizens and their governments around the world—no longer have the ability to control or restrain corporate misbehavior when it endangers the common good. And so we have epidemics of cancer, acid rain, ozone holes, and massive species die-offs as multinational corporations roam the world, strip-mining it for human labor, minerals, fossil fuels, and the fragile remaining bounty of its forests and oceans.

The ultimate in unequal trade has ensued from increasing corporate influence. Very large corporations—Roosevelt's "big businesses"—have now become able to sue an entire nation, in a court that they, the companies, lobbied to create, and can overturn the laws of independent nations with virtually no appeal. And unlike any court in the civilized world, this court is as secret, private, and difficult to appeal as any military tribunal.

FREE TRADE RAVAGES NATIONAL ECONOMIES

"Free trade" is a phrase behind which multinational corporations have essentially strip-mined both the developed and the developing world. That's strong language, but the metaphor holds up under examination. In strip-mining, a company comes in, strips off anything necessary to get at what it wants, and leaves. Similarly, the developing world is being mined for its resources, including human labor. At the same time, the already-developed world is being mined for its wealth, as its middle class and working poor sink further into debt while multinational corporations become richer than any historic kingdom the planet has ever seen.

To understand what we can do about this, we first need to understand the mechanism. And there most definitely is a mechanism. When properly executed, it works quite reliably.

Every product from shoes to nails to computers requires some human labor to manufacture. For the cost of one American or European or Australian laborer, a company can hire between 15 and 50 laborers in a developing country. As transnational corporate lobbying succeeded in bringing about a world opened for free trade, about 4 billion people suddenly came into the same labor market that was once a protected space occupied by about a half-billion.

The first result of this was that companies that moved manufacturing from the developed world to the developing world were able to decrease labor costs and increase earnings (profits). As companies used this principle to their advantage and built empires in industries from shoes to retailing by selling products made in low-labor-cost nations into the retail channels of the high-labor-cost nations, it seemed like it was a good thing. Cheaper products were available in the wealthy nations, jobs were created in the poorer nations, and the people who made it all happen got rich. But there were complications.

- If a company wanted to compete with the one that had gone offshore for labor, it faced only two choices: 1) shut their domestic factories and move manufacturing offshore, or 2) go out of business. The result—on a vast scale—has been that the larger companies have moved offshore and the smaller companies who lacked the resources to do that have gone out of business. The number of competitors has dwindled and markets have become concentrated in fewer hands.

- As a consequence, well-paying manufacturing jobs in the developed world have evaporated at a startling pace. This echoes all the way up from the local level, through state and national economies, finally showing up as a general lowering of the standard of living in the developed world. Wages drop, benefits vanish, jobs become scarce, and people become insecure.
- Along with the economic changes come social changes. The worst of it shows up at the bottom first—the number of people in prison explodes, as do other negative social indicators. Antidepressant drug use goes up, suicide goes up (particularly among teenagers, who are developmentally most fragile and are watching their future earnings prospects evaporate), and spouses and even children go to work to help support the household. Debt goes up as the society becomes progressively poorer.
- Wealthy nations respond to the offshore challenge by trying to be competitive, which means lowering wages and benefits further. Companies may even cut promised benefits to their longtime employees who have already retired. But even if the local company cuts wages in half (doing enormous damage to the local economy), a transnational corporation is still able to hire a dozen or more workers for the same job in a poor nation. Consequently, the race to the bottom gathers momentum—the bottom is where more than 6 billion people compete for the same work that was, until recently, performed in a tariff-protected economy of 1 billion people (the developed world). Resources won't stretch that far. The bottom is worldwide poverty supervised by a wealthy few, also known as feudalism.
- In the developing nations where these "new jobs are created," people who have been doing traditional farming leave the land for the sweatshops, and the land is turned over to intensive corporate agriculture. People who in previous generations were independent, self-sufficient farmers become urban slum-dwellers, the working poor, dependent on corporate farmers and supermarkets for their food.
- When the new sweatshop nation's urban working poor begin demanding higher wages and benefits, the corporations move to another country where labor is cheaper. It happened in the 1990s when a mass exodus of multinational corporations left Korea, Taiwan, and Thailand for the ultracheap labor of Vietnam, Burma, and China, leaving

the economies of those former "Asian tigers" shattered and desperate. Poverty explodes as slums overflow with crime, drugs, and prostitution: the symptoms of people seeking some sort of income when the real jobs are gone. It is just like strip-mining, and it's a sign of the worst sort of corporate citizen—one without the slightest concern for the impact it has.

- In the process, the multinational corporations become richer, moving their "mining" activities from one nation to another as profits dictate. As multinational corporate wealth increases, stock prices go up and the top few percent of the socioeconomic pyramid become wealthier. Nations learn to watch the stock market, thinking—in complete error—that it is an accurate indicator of the nation's wealth and economic health. In fact, from the Dutch Tulip Market collapse in 1637 to the U. S. stock market rise and crash of 1929, rapidly increasing markets have historically been indicators of an economy on the edge of implosion or undergoing radical social transformation.

As Sir James Goldsmith suggested in the epigraph of this chapter, we have forgotten that the purpose of economies—the whole reason why humans began trading with each other from the earliest days—was to provide for social stability. Your country makes good cheese, we make good clothing, another country makes good wine: Let's all trade these products with each other so all three of us can enjoy good cheese, clothing, and wine.

But in a free trade world dominated by corporate values instead of human values, social stability is not a consideration unless or until it affects profits. This is the lesson of unequal values. And when a country becomes socially unstable, rather than working to restore the stability of the nation, multinationals simply leave town and go somewhere else, as Asian nations learned in the 1990s and Argentina learned in 2002.

This is not a new model, by the way. It's how the East India Company treated India, the early American colonies, and numerous smaller countries that it considered its property. It reflects the mentality not of communities but of pirates, a mentality that gives birth to phrases like "corporate raider."

Herman Daly and Robert Goodland used to work at the World Bank. They didn't like what they saw. Consider this prophetic 1992 comment, 2 years before GATT was approved. They foresaw that with the entire world open and companies able to come and go as they please, the entire world economy would be dragged down to the price of the lowest bidder, doing immense economic damage to any country that was improving in the ways the World Bank was asking them to do. "If by wise policy or blind luck, a country has managed to control its population growth, provide social insurance, high wages, reasonable working hours and other benefits to its working class (i.e., most of its citizens), should it allow these benefits to be competed down to the world average by unregulated trade?

" . . . This leveling of wages will be overwhelmingly downward due to the vast number and rapid growth rate of under-employed populations in the third world. Northern laborers will get poorer, while Southern laborers will stay much the same."

And this is exactly what we have seen happening.

THE CORRECTIVE, BALANCING POWER OF TARIFFS

Historically, nations used tariffs or taxes on imported goods to equalize differences between nations. Expensive-labor nations would charge tariffs on imported goods that were labor-intensive in their manufacture, to protect their domestic industries. Nations that wanted to protect unique natural resources or products would use import/export policy to ensure their long-term survival and wise use. Trade was possible—it's always happened among nations—but it was *fair trade*, fair to the *humans* in the trading nations.

Now, multinational corporations have lobbied nations to dump their import/export policies and drop their tariffs, a process called free trade. In so doing, they have finally succeeded in freeing themselves from the constraints of social commitment to any nation whatsoever. In the absence of tariffs, they are free to roam anywhere on a moment's notice, looking for labor, minerals, cheap rainforests. And since increasingly all money flows through them, they have essentially infinite power in all negotiations.

Finally, in a replay of events on American shores, they have in some cases taken roles in governments around the world. Over 100 corporations have joined the WTO and are now dangling the carrot of cash to the leaders of the poorer nations. We've seen this movie before; it's easy to tell what happens next. These governments readily comply, join the WTO, and subscribe to free trade. But what they get may not be quite what they bargained for. That's what happened to no less a power than America.

HOW U. S. LEGISLATORS REACT

The world's largest transnational corporations are among the biggest contributors to politicians in America, and most members of Congress have supported the WTO even if they get a bit testy when the Dispute Resolution Panels rule against their favorite legislation. One good example comes from a speech to Congress by Representative John Dingell of Michigan on June 21, 2000.

He said, "Our major trading partners, including Japan, Korea, and the EU (European Union nations), have turned the WTO dispute settlement process into a *de facto* appeals court that reviews U. S. trade agency determinations and strikes down our trade laws. Japan and Korea have gone so far as to say they will launch WTO appeals of every U. S. trade determination that is adverse to their interests. Already, WTO decisions are gutting the effectiveness of U. S. trade remedies in ways that the Administration and Congress expressly rejected during the negotiations on the agreement establishing the WTO."

Increasingly, both governments and citizens of nations all over the world are expressing concern about the WTO's process of leveling the corporate playing field across 134 member nations. Corporations manufacturing and exporting from countries that have lax or minimal environmental and labor laws are aggressively challenging and striking down the stronger laws passed in more developed nations.

Countries with laws that banned the import or marketing of products they consider dangerous to their citizens are finding those laws struck down because other countries with weaker laws can now, to some extent, define the standard to which every WTO-member nation must be held accountable. They do this through WTO's primary trade-law model, which says that a country cannot ban the import of a product because of how or with what type of labor it was produced.

OVERTURNING OUR LAWS

Thus, it's now largely illegal to ban the import of products made by slaves or under inhumane conditions, or using chemicals that poison the local environment. This has sparked an explosion of industrial activity in labor-cheap and environmentally lax nations. At the same time, the industrial core of more developed nations has been hollowed out in just the past few decades, leaving vast landscapes of abandoned factories and a populace increasingly on edge about employment security.

In a developing nation where there is little or no cost or penalty to dumping toxins into the air or water, manufacturing is vastly more profitable than in a developed nation where toxins must be captured, stored, tracked, and cleanly disposed of in environmentally friendly ways. In the developed world, we have minimum wage laws, maximum hours that may be worked per week laws, and safety and environmental laws. In the past, if an offshore product wasn't made in ways we approved, we either banned its import or added taxes or tariffs to give our cleaner domestic companies a competitively level playing field.

For example, say there's an hour's work in the manufacture of a pair of American-made shoes. In the United States that hour costs $12.77 including benefits and overhead. That same labor may be 10 cents an hour in Malaysia. So for the past century or so, the United States would have added a tariff, or tax, of $12.67 on any shoe imported from Malaysia that had an hour's labor in it. That way, U. S. shoe manufacturers could stay in business. It would level the playing field between the two cultures and nations, thus providing for fair trade.

Nations have often used tariffs to discourage manufacturing operations from moving their factories and jobs to less regulated nations.

But according to WTO, those tariffs are considered "restraint of free trade." It's illegal under WTO rules to consider how or who makes a product or at what level of pay it is manufactured. The loss of jobs to offshore began decades ago, but the elimination of tariffs accelerated it markedly. In the past few decades, millions of Americans in labor-intensive industries have lost their jobs.

The other upshot of this is a dramatic increase in people around the world who are working either as overt slaves or at a wage rate that makes them virtual slaves in an environment of company stores and company housing. The First World, and particularly the United States, at first appeared to have benefited tremendously from this. It allows our consumer-based economy to continue to hum, with low inflation and rising profits, just as the American South benefited so much from cheap slave labor before the Civil War. But at best this is a short-term benefit.

THE "NEW WORLD ORDER"

In most nations of the world today, there are basically two types of political parties. Those two parties stand on either side of a nearly invisible line—one party huge and imposing and the other thin and sickly, a political sumo wrestler pitted against an aging and infirm Woody Allen. The parties, regardless of local labels, are "We Who Represent The Interests Of Multinational Corporations" and "We Who Represent The Interests Of Human Beings." The first group have gotten laws passed that allow the easy movement of capital from nation to nation under rules far different and more relaxed than those for humans.

In the United States and most other developed nations, most of the distinctions between politicians are becoming increasingly blurred, and in many nations *all* the local politicians have joined the parties of the corporations. Those parties and politicians that exist to represent the interests of human beings have been marginalized or overwhelmed by the parties and politicians that exist to represent the interests of the corporations. The reason for this is simple—most of the world has followed our lead regarding "free speech" campaign contributions.

After the end of apartheid in South Africa, American corporations donated the services of corporate lawyers to help draft the new South African constitution. Pointing to the 1886 *Santa Clara* case, they essentially said that in America, corporations have the same constitutional status as humans, so you should write this into your constitution, too.

South Africa did that, as have many other countries that have emerged or developed or separated from the former Soviet Union. It's a challenge to find the details and statistics, and I'm hopeful that this book may spur somebody to do that hard, nation-by-nation research, but it appears that many of the countries of the world have written corporations-as-persons into their constitutions or laws, thinking that they were following the original intent of framers of the United States Constitution, which, of course, is not the case.

The result is that corporations have functionally taken control of governments the world over, particularly through their participation in the funding of the electoral process. Thus, corporations have become the honey pot from which many politicians and political parties draw their nourishment.

IN A DEMOCRACY . . .

In the 1996 election cycle in the United States, 96 percent of Americans didn't make any direct contribution whatsoever to a politician or political party, and fewer than one-quarter of 1 percent of Americans gave more than $200. By contrast, each of America's top 500 corporations gave over a half-million dollars to the Democrats and Republicans during the decade preceding the 1996 elections.

In the 1998 election cycle, which was not even a presidential election year, those corporations contributed $660 million to candidates, while the last remaining organized groups that represent workers—unions, which are *not* considered persons in the United States and most other countries, but are instead regulated as artificial persons—were able to pony up only $60 million in campaign contributions raised from their members.

Unions have to operate under the same types of rules and laws that corporations did before 1886, and, in fact, additional restrictions have been placed on them since then. So-called "paycheck protection" legislation is being promoted by corporate lobbyists that would essentially criminalize union contributions to candidates. Unions can't claim free speech the way corporations can because they're not persons like corporations are. And, increasingly, in corporate-controlled nations around the world, unions are being deemed illegal, political, or even labeled as terrorist organizations and ferociously stamped out.

Can it change? I believe so. But only if the word gets out . . .

18

UNEQUAL MEDIA

Our liberty depends on the freedom of the press, and that cannot be limited without being lost.

—THOMAS JEFFERSON, LETTER TO JAMES CURRIE, JANUARY 28, 1786

In researching this book I ran across an astonishing piece of writing from our nation's early years. It's a fitting prologue for this chapter. In May 1831, a young Frenchman named Alexis de Tocqueville arrived in the young nation of the United States of America. He was here at a pivotal time in American history. In the "Revolution of 1800," Thomas Jefferson had ousted John Adams' minority Federalist Party (largely made up of what Jefferson called "the rich and the well born") and shifted control of the government to the Jeffersonian Democrats. To de Tocqueville (and most Europeans), American democracy was still very much an unproven experiment.

In 1835, just 52 years after the end of the American Revolution and 42 years after the French Revolution, he closed his book *Democracy in America* with a chapter titled "What Sort Of Despotism Democratic Nations Have To Fear." Fascinated by that chapter title, which I had first seen on the Internet, I bought an 1869 edition. One of the best-selling books of that century, it was probably read 20 years earlier by Abraham Lincoln, as it was by almost all American politicians and most citizens. Turning the timeworn pages and reading the young de Tocqueville's thoughts, I was astounded. It was as if he had seen America in the late 20th and early 21st centuries.

De Tocqueville had a clear and prescient inkling of danger. He saw a nation where people had become isolated in their own homes, uninformed about the rest of humanity, addicted to some entertainment that was so powerful it separated them from their fellow humans. He imagined that despotism, in the remnants of a democracy, would take a different form than despotism under authoritarian rule; it would take the form of creating an *illusion* of choice, and he struggled to find words to express what it would be. "It would seem that, if despotism were to be established amongst the democratic nations of our days, it might assume a different character; it would be more extensive and more mild; it would degrade men without tormenting them. . . .

"I am trying myself to choose an expression which will accurately convey the whole of the idea I have formed of it, but in vain; the old words despotism and tyranny are inappropriate: the thing itself is new; and since I cannot name it, I must attempt to define it.

"The first thing that strikes the observation is an innumerable multitude of men, all equal and alike, incessantly endeavoring to procure the petty and paltry pleasures with which they glut their lives. Each of them, living apart, is as a stranger to the fate of all the rest—his children and his private friends constitute to him the whole of mankind; as for the rest of his fellow-citizens, he is close to them, but he sees them not;—he touches them, but he feels them not; he exists, but in himself and for himself alone; and if his kindred still remain to him, he may be said at any rate to have lost his country."

His description, written in 1831, sounds astonishingly like our world today, which is so often observed as being centered around gratification—and isolation. And the mechanism for this despotism, he said, is the sort of perpetual gratification that keeps people happy.

He continued, "Above this race of men stands an immense and tutelary [care-taking] power, which takes upon itself alone to secure their gratifications, and to watch over their fate. That power is absolute, minute, regular, provident, and mild. It would be like the authority of a parent, if, like that authority, its object was to prepare men for manhood; but it seeks, on the contrary, to keep them in perpetual childhood: it is well content that the people should rejoice, provided they think of nothing but rejoicing. . . .

"Thus, it every day renders the exercise of the free agency of man less useful and less frequent; it circumscribes them well within a narrower range, and gradually robs a man of all the uses of himself. The principle of equality has prepared men for these things: it has predisposed men to endure them, and oftentimes to look on them as benefits.

"After having thus successively taken each member of the community in its powerful grasp, and fashioned him at will, the supreme power then extends its arm over the whole community. . . . The will of man is not shattered, but softened, bent, and guided: men are seldom forced by it to act, but they are constantly restrained from acting: such a power does not destroy, but it prevents existence; it does not tyrannize, but it compresses, enervates, extinguishes, and stupefies a people, till each nation is reduced to be nothing better than a flock of timid and industrious animals . . ."

De Tocqueville also said that the press is the *most important* of all our democratic institutions; only a free press could preserve American democracy, and the loss of it to government or corporate powers would be the end of the democratic experiment. "I think that men living in aristocracies may, strictly speaking, do without the liberty of the press: but such is not the case with those who live in democratic countries. . . . servitude cannot be complete if the press is free: the press is the chief democratic instrument of freedom."

THE PURPOSE OF A FREE PRESS IS FREE EXPRESSION

The gadfly of American journalism in the first half of the 20th century, Joe (A. J.) Liebling, commented, "Freedom of the press belongs to the man who owns one." It's become even more true today, although you can replace the word "man" with the word "corporation." And today, there are fewer of those truly free resources than ever before. This is materially limiting the amount of information available to the public, creating the sort of environment de Tocqueville warned about in the quote above. We'll cover the following issues:

- The effects of consolidation of who owns the presses since fewer presses means fewer different voices reporting the news, and fewer owners means less diversity and dissent
- The effect of heavily financed lawsuits that squelch expression in the media, such as the well-known suit against Oprah Winfrey for her comments about hamburger
- The effects of the press being owned by a business that has pressure to deliver profits

Each of those issues is, in a different way, a consequence of the changes in America that have flowed from the *Santa Clara* decision.

Is this subject really important to our democracy? Aside from the advice of the far-sighted de Tocqueville, consider these diverse opinions:

- John Adams, Jefferson's eternal *opponent*, said, "The liberty of the press is essential to the security of the state."
- Napoleon Bonaparte made a serious attempt at conquering his part of the civilized world. His opinion was that, "Three hostile newspapers are more to be feared than a thousand bayonets."
- George Orwell, author of *Animal Farm* and *1984*, said, "Freedom of the Press, if it means anything at all, means the freedom to criticize and oppose."
- Richard Nixon said, "The media are far more powerful than the President in creating public awareness and shaping public opinion, for the simple reason that the media always have the last word."
- In a move to block media access, George W. Bush moved his records and papers as governor of Texas into his father's presidential library, while on February 11, 2002, the elder Bush said in a paid speech to roofing contractors that the press was a group "which I now confess I hate."

When people from Adams to Bush, Napoleon to Orwell all have such *different* ways of saying that the press is immensely powerful, it's a sign that we ought to pay attention to what happens to it. Let's look first at the shrinking diversity of outlets for news and information.

CAN I GET A WIDE RANGE OF VIEWS IN THE MEDIA?

Less so than you might think, and far less so than when you were growing up. In 1984, according to media observer Ben Bagdikian, 50 corporations dominated the nation's "daily newspapers, magazines, radio, television, books, and movies." Following the deregulation and merger craze in the 1980s, that number dropped to 20 by 1993. Today, it's just 10.

On a longer time scale, the shift is even more startling. Bagdikian observes that in 1946, 80 percent of all American newspapers were owned by individuals and independent local companies. Today, it's the opposite. "80 percent [are] owned by corporate chains," and only three corporations control "most of the business of the country's 11,000 magazines."

In 1993, when NAFTA was before Congress for a vote, Vermont congressman Bernie Sanders points out that about half of all Americans opposed ratification of the treaty. Of the hundreds of corporate chain–owned city newspapers across the country, only *two* ran editorials questioning NAFTA, while all the rest, echoing the position of America's largest corporations, came out in support of it.

Looking at *all* media in the United States, Bagdikian notes, "Today, despite more than 25,000 outlets in the United States, twenty-three corporations control most of the business in daily newspapers, magazines, television, books, and motion pictures."

If you've noticed that no matter where you are in the United States you can hear the same radio shows, there's a reason: the FCC has recently allowed four giant media corporations to buy up radio stations nationwide to the point where those four companies now control 90 percent of total advertising revenues.

Only 10 percent of Americans even have a meaningful choice as to their local telephone company. In Vermont, a small local company named Sovernet has begun offering high-quality local phone service along with DSL Internet access. So, in 2002, lobbyists for the big telecommunications companies got introduced into the Vermont legislature a "freedom in telecommunications" bill that would block Sovernet's access to Verizon's lines, effectively putting Sovernet out of the phone business. The bill has not been debated as of this writing.

Many of us are accustomed to viewing the Web as a wellspring of a vast number of sources of information, free of restraining influence. Indeed, if properly used by knowledgeable people, it can be. But in practice, perhaps not as much as we would think. In August 2001, the authoritative Jupiter Media Metrix research company reported that just four corporations own the Web sites that more than 50 percent of Americans spend their time viewing.

Additionally, with intelligent and programmable switching and routing systems, Internet service providers now have the ability to favor certain Web sites over others: Your ISP can program their systems to give you quick access to Web sites of corporations who pay a fee to them, and subtly (or not so subtly) slow your access to the rest of the Internet. Although many Internet users think of the World Wide Web as a commons of ideas, it's a commons whose access is now almost entirely controlled by a small number of very large corporations.

EVEN INTERNET SEARCH ENGINES

And the once-independent search engines are now selling the right to be displayed at the top of the list to the highest bidder. As a recent ad for search engine placement noted, "Eighty-five percent of all traffic is generated via search queries and over 90 percent of that traffic is driven to the top 30 results. If you're not in the top 30, you're not in a position to compete!" At virtually all the current search engines, top placement, sponsor placement, or top-of-fold ad placement are for sale on keyword searches.

Similarly, much has been written about the homogenizing effects of media mergers, further reducing diversity and trying to find the lowest common denominator to produce the best earnings, at the cost of sacrificing the good reporting that Americans used to take for granted.

The pressure to homogenize is economic, driven by the business incentive to generate economies of scale by being big and by being able to offer advertisers the largest audience size or attractive demographics at a low rate. Another major factor is the increasing amount of capital that's required today to be a broadcaster because of an important change that happened in the 1980s—a change implemented by the government at the request of corporations. At that time, a major piece of the commons was auctioned off to the highest bidder. Not surprisingly, the winners were big corporations.

WHO OWNS THE AIRWAVES?

The theory used to be that the airwaves over which television and radio signals pass were part of the national infrastructure, just like the national highway system or the air traffic control system. Nobody could own them since they are the ether that floats above the nation, the property of the people, yet some regulation of them was necessary to prevent chaos. Cable systems run under or over public streets, just like the public utilities and airwaves, and so similarly are part of the public's infrastructure, the commons.

It was also felt that the airwaves were part of the free press that the Founders and the Constitution asserted was so essential and crucial to a vibrant and living democracy and informed citizenry. Therefore, the Federal Communications Commission was formed to regulate the usage and content of what freely passes over the airwaves of America to Americans.

During the 1980s, however, the media corporations successfully lobbied that the national airwaves should no longer be the shared property of the citizens. Instead, they said, the airwaves and channels should be carved up by region and frequency, and sold off to the highest bidders at frequency auctions. When we auctioned off this part of the commons, it went into the hands of parties that already enjoy many unequal advantages over humans.

This was followed in 1996 by the Telecommunications Act, the product of prodigious lobbying on Capitol Hill and which, according to media watchdog Ben Bagdikian, "swept away even the minimal consumer and diversity protections of the 1934 act that preceded it."

Auctioning off the airwaves had a secondary effect that was perhaps more important than who owned them. When we auctioned off the airwaves, the corporations who bought them claim that we gave up the right to have a say in their use. The free press became corporate-owned, and today groups like Fairness and Accuracy In Reporting (FAIR) regularly chronicle examples of news programs and journalists concealing corporate misdeeds and crimes, or offering up publicity stories about the products of network owners or major advertisers. It's not just a matter of running flattering stories; it affects the process of filtering which investigative stories get on the air. And this is not just the opinion of a watchdog group; it's reported by those on the inside.

A Pew Center for the People and the Press poll in 2000 found that 61 percent of investigative reporters thought corporate owners influenced news decisions, and 41 percent of reporters could list specific examples of recent times they themselves had chosen or been forced to change or avoid news stories to further or benefit the interests of their media corporation.

COST OF ACCESS IS UNDEMOCRATIZING ELECTIONS

Along with the airwaves at the auctions went the notion of public service announcements. During the same administration, the FCC requirement that television and radio stations give free time for political debates was repealed. This gave corporations who owned radio and television stations a double windfall—they get to own what they had rented and now politicians have to pay for advertising if they want to get their message to the public. Again, the effect is that ordinary humans find it harder than ever to get heard because the previous equal-time provision no longer applies: You have to pay.

And campaign airtime doesn't come cheap. The average U. S. Senate campaign now costs over $6 million, whether the candidate wins or loses. That's $6 million to raise in 6 years: a million dollars a year, $20,000 dollars a week. Can you imagine starting every day in your office knowing, as corporate lobbyists begin to file in to visit you and promote their causes, that by the end of the day you have to raise another $4,000 or you won't have your job after the next election?

And the price is rising. During the 1998 House and Senate elections, over $1 billion was paid to media corporations for ads by parties, politicians, and interest groups seeking to get their word out to the public. That's double what was spent in 1992, and *seven times* the amount paid to media corporations by candidates and political parties in the 1978 elections—before the frequency auction and the end of the equal-time rule. In just the first 4 months of his 2000 campaign, George W. Bush raised and spent more money than Bill Clinton and Bob Dole *combined* had raised and spent in the entire election cycle 4 years earlier.

There are serious questions about whether the way our government works today is giving everyone in this democracy a fair chance of having their voice heard. Increasingly, the only voices we can hear are those backed by corporations with plenty of money.

THE IMPACT ON LOCAL AND NATIONAL POLITICS

For the most part, average Americans have stopped voting. During the 2000 election, about 55 percent of eligible American voters—over 100 million people—didn't bother to vote. Ask them why, and you'll most often hear, "What difference does it make?"

According to the Federal Election Commission, in that election about 50 million who were registered didn't show up to vote. In a "To Whom It May Concern" Web letter during the 2000 election, author and political filmmaker Michael Moore wrote about the impact of corporate ownership of the media and corporate influence of the electoral process—and how working Americans are reacting. He addressed his letter to the new American majority—those who have given up on voting.

"The reason you, the majority, no longer vote in America," he wrote, "is because you, the majority, realize there is no real choice on the ballot." He pointed out that over 80 percent of American voters didn't bother to show up for the primaries—that's more than 160 million nonvoters. He suggests that in a world where "six multinational corporations" deliver the majority of all information Americans get from radio, television, newspapers, and the Internet, American voters apparently feel their political process no longer offers them any choices worth voting for.

We're not as bad as the Soviet Union, of course, but Moore continues, echoing the widespread American concern that, "A handful of companies now call all the shots. They own Congress. They own us. . . . To keep our jobs we have had to give up decent health care, the 8-hour day and time with our kids, the security that we'll even have a job next year, and any unwillingness we may have to compete with a 14-year-old Indonesian girl who gets a dollar a day."

THE EFFECT OF THE NEWSROOM BEING A PROFIT ENTERPRISE

Earlier, we noted that smaller businesses tend, in general, to be focused on the nature of their trade. When they're absorbed into bigger businesses, especially the biggest ones, pressure tends to increase to deliver value for the shareholders—that is, to make money. In news operations, almost all the money comes from advertising—and ad prices depend on how many people are watching. So business managers are necessarily required to do what they can to improve income.

Once again, our point in pursuing this issue is not to decry profit. The point is that when corporations are allowed to operate with that goal *to the detriment of other values*, it can harm how well the system performs the functions we depend on, particularly those necessary to a vital democracy.

A month after the September 11 attacks on America, in a C-SPAN interview with Marvin Kalb on October 13, CBS News anchor and managing editor Dan Rather made a sobering admission. "We were asleep," he said, speaking of a time that he identified as starting in the 1980s and picking up steam throughout the 1990s and into mid-2001. "We went for titillation," he said, in apparent reference to the Monica Lewinsky and Gary Condit stories the press relentlessly pursued. They had ignored the "clear warnings" of earlier attacks such as the 1993 truck bombing of the World Trade Center, which should have told both America's news and intelligence agencies that there were people intent on harming us.

Rather pointed out that international news bureaus were being closed during the 1990s, and the press had failed to focus on news, going instead for what he called "the sensational" and "the personal."

Legendary newsman Walter Cronkite, who in his time was rated "the most credible man in America," recently told www.mediachannel.org, "Like you, I'm deeply concerned about the merger mania that has swept our industry, diluting standards, dumbing down the news, and making the bottom line sometimes seem like the only line. It isn't, and it shouldn't be."

USING LAWSUITS TO SUPPRESS INFORMATION

There's a completely different way in which some companies influence what shows up in the media: Some will sue to keep people from saying anything bad about them or their products, even if there's plenty of evidence. Because of their unequal resources, they can threaten (and follow through on) lawsuits, which can be effective at squelching criticism. People who fight back may be financially ruined, and many people simply quit before things reach that point.

The same concern applies to news outlets that might be sued. After all, if a company will weigh the dollar value of a safer gas tank versus the cost of victims' lawsuits, aren't they likely to perform a similar risk assessment here? And if the only parameter that's measured is cash, then cash will become the basis of the decision. An engineering decision, or a journalist's editorial decision, becomes a profit decision.

A key turning point on this issue may have been 1989. When CBS's *60 Minutes* reported that a pesticide used on apples may pose health risks to humans, the apple growing industry lost millions of dollars in sales. In response, 13 states passed "veggie libel laws" making it a crime to disparage the food supply. The most famous case of laws being used this way was the suit filed by Texas beef producers against Oprah Winfrey for casually remarking (some would say joking) on her show that she was personally going to stop eating hamburgers after interviewing a guest about Mad Cow Disease.

Seattle attorney Bruce Johnson, who defended CBS in the initial suit by the apple industry, said these laws "are designed specifically to stop the Rachel Carsons of the world from alerting the public to food-safety risks. If these were in effect in 1962 [when Carson published *Silent Spring*, her groundbreaking book about the dangers of DDT], they would have sued her and forced her into bankruptcy."

Similarly, in early 1998 when investigative reporters Jane Akre and Steve Wilson produced a 3-part series on how a synthetic product routinely given to American cattle could be causing cancer in America (and not in Europe, where it's banned), their television station fired them after they refused to "tone down" the story. Why? The station is owned by a well-known media conglomerate, and the manufacturer of the chemical—a massive and powerful multinational corporation—apparently threatened to sue them if the story ran, which would have decreased the media chain's profits from their news operations.

Our representatives have passed whistle-blower laws to protect people who make such discoveries. But if you're in court and you simply don't have the resources to stick with it—the playing field is simply not level with that of a billion-dollar corporation—the law can be defeated by the wealthier party's lawsuits. As it happened, the fired reporters sued under Florida's whistle-blower law and a jury ruled in their favor. But the suits and appeals and countersuits have exhausted these two reporters' funds . . . and the trials are still continuing as of this writing.

This is a perfect, living example of how the playing field is anything but level when an immortal, nonbreathing corporation is given the same protections as humans.

SUPPRESSION OF "ADVOCACY" ADS

When www.adbusters.org tried to purchase airtime on ABC, CBS, and NBC television networks for their "Buy Nothing Day" commercials, the networks refused them, year after year. The ads have an "in your face" edge to them, but they aren't at all violent or pornographic: They encourage people to "give it a rest"—take a single-day break from consumerism.

When asked why the networks wouldn't allow the American people to see the ads—for any price—a spokesman at one of the networks said it quite directly: "We don't want to accept any advertising that's inimical to our legitimate business interests." So much for their stewardship of the commons in the public interest.

The Vice President of Program Practices at another of the Big Three networks brought up a more commonly used dodge. "We can't run your ad," he told Adbusters. "It's an advocacy ad."

"I came from Estonia where you were not allowed to speak up against the government," says former advertising executive Kalle Lasn, head of Adbusters. "Here I was in North America, and suddenly I realized you can't speak up against the sponsor. There's something fundamentally undemocratic about our public airways."

Corporate influence of broadcast content happens in radio, too. Folksy "man of the people" Jim Hightower's radio show was syndicated by one of the Big Three American networks in 150 markets with over 2 million listeners until that network was bought out by an even larger entertainment conglomerate. Hightower mentioned on the air that his new parent corporation had replaced some of their full-time workers with contract laborers recruited from a local homeless shelter. On another show, he accused his network of "bending down and kissing the toes" of a tobacco company advertiser. Soon, his show was cancelled.

The reason given to the press was that his show wasn't making enough money from advertising, but Hightower pointed out that he would have been very profitable if the network had allowed him to run $250,000 worth of ads that the unions had tried to buy. Those ads, however, were "advocacy advertising," the network said, and so they never made it to the air. Remember, unions are *not* persons under the Fourteenth Amendment.

THE EFFECT ON CRIME REPORTING

Corporate influence on news content continues to have serious ramifications on what we know, and thus how well-prepared we are to make fundamental decisions for our communities and ourselves.

Consider crime reporting. Everybody who watches American television knows about the repeated troubles of Rodney King since his famous (and much-televised) beating by the Los Angeles police or Mike Tyson's difficulties with rage. But how many Americans know that in a 1982 study of America's largest 500 corporations, it was found that in the past 10 years, 23 percent of them had been convicted of a major crime or had paid more than $50,000 in penalties for serious misbehavior or both?

Stories about welfare moms make the news with no problem, but stories of the billions in taxpayer money given to oil companies appear mainly in the business press—where they're recognized as triumphs for the companies involved, events that will favorably raise their stock value.

As I watched Kalb's interview of Dan Rather, it seemed that Rather often came close to raising these topics. But it seemed neither wanted to step into the role of the fictional Howard Beal in the startlingly predictive movie *Network*, when he yelled about corporate/political influence on news, "I'm mad as hell and not going to take it anymore!"

DOESN'T THE FCC PROTECT THE FIRST AMENDMENT?

As of this writing and since his appointment by George W. Bush in early 2001, the Chairman of the Federal Communications Commission is Michael Powell, the son of Secretary of State Colin Powell, a former director of media giant AOL. Michael Powell was apparently rather new to the ideas of de Tocqueville and Jefferson when he took his job. As the *Columbia Journalism Review* reported in their May/June 2001 issue, "Asked at his maiden news conference for his definition of 'the public interest,' Powell joked, 'I have no idea.' The term can mean whatever people want it to mean, he said. 'It's an empty vessel in which people pour in whatever their preconceived views or biases are.'"

Those biases at the FCC have since become clear, as Powell's team shows. Other FCC commissioners included two former industry lobbyists. Powell's chief of staff is a former Disney lobbyist, and his legal advisor is a former lobbyist for another media giant.

The week of his appointment, media analyst Tom Wolzien said, "I think you'll see a little bit more of a free-market approach, perhaps less attention to consumer groups and more of letting companies do more of what they want."

According to Fairness and Accuracy In Media (FAIR), "One of Powell's first acts as chairman was to approve 62 pending radio station acquisitions, handing still more outlets to two of the country's largest and grabbiest conglomerates . . ." On April 24, 2001, Powell told the Associated Press that "there is something offensive to First Amendment values about that limitation [on concentration of television station ownership]" because, FAIR notes, "it restricts the number of people one company can talk to." In a December 2000 speech before a corporate-sponsored group in Washington, the *Chicago Tribune* quotes Powell as having said, "Our bureaucratic process is too slow to respond to the challenges of Internet time. One way to do so is to clear away the regulatory underbrush to bring greater certainty and regulatory simplicity to the market."

When the proponents of corporations having personhood suggest that corporations should have the ability to aggregate media so the largest multinational corporations among us will have free speech, they often trot out the argument that deregulating the media (or any other industry) encourages competition. The actual effect, as Bagdikian so eloquently documents, is the reverse: There are fewer and fewer competitors, less variety and fewer viewpoints for consumers to choose among, and a massive grab of media by a small number of huge multinational corporations.

One of the most visible results of this is that business coverage has become an important part of every corporate-owned newspaper and radio and TV programming (even though 42 percent of stock market gains between 1989 and 1997 went to America's top 1 percent of individuals, and 86 percent of stock market gains went to the top 10 percent), reflecting the prime moral value of corporate culture: profit. At the same time, the 100 percent of American citizens who are consumers and who confront a 1 in 3 chance of contracting cancer in their lifetimes find virtually no mention of issues relating to shoddy products, criminal business practices, or environmental toxins in the mainstream corporate-owned media.

Indeed, as Bagdikian notes, "From 1987 to 1994, the purchasing power of the minimum wage dropped 35 percent," an issue that hits 12 million more Americans in a powerfully real way than the Dow Jones Average (even considering stocks in pension plans held by the middle class). "If the Dow Jones Industrial Average had dropped 35 percent in seven years it would have been an ongoing and urgent issue in newscasts and on page one in newspapers, with insistence that official action be taken," Bagdikian says. But these are not issues that hurt profits—they *enhance* profits. So instead, we hear that when more people become unemployed, the Dow goes up because it means corporations can then negotiate lower labor costs. The human toll is apparently not an issue.

And that media competition extolled by FCC Chairman Powell? FAIR remarks, "Powell opposed the opening of the bandwidth to new microradio [small, local community stations with limited transmission range] voices on grounds that it might dilute audience share (and ad revenue) for commercial stations."

IN A DEMOCRACY . . .

As the last century closed, corporate-controlled media was reaching the most distant corners of the world and its effects were seen in strange ways. In 1995, parts of the island of Fiji, which had never before seen television, got the tube. Three years later, researchers talked with several groups of Fijian girls whose average age was 17. They found that before television, only 3 percent had ever thrown up to try to control their weight. After 3 years of television, however, 15 percent of those teenage girls were clinically bulimic.

The first step in a values-driven advertising campaign is to disempower humans—convince people that there's something wrong or deficient about them. The teenage girls of Fiji sure got the message and got it quick. While in the United States, with its own startlingly high prevalence rate of bulimia among young girls, we say, "It's a serotonin deficiency" that can be cured with antidepressant drugs, but the Fiji example tells us it may be easier to cure it by removing the television set.

After you read this page, set down this book and walk around for the next 5 minutes—indoors or out—and notice how many advertising messages and logos you see or hear. Have any of them suggested you should slow down your life, spend more time with your family, or seek deeper meaning and richer states of consciousness? Or are they all "Buy from us, we'll make you happy" messages?

Daily exposure to these messages has produced—no doubt as an unintended consequence, but real nonetheless—a deep angst and existential emotional and spiritual crisis across the world. We will successfully confront this existential angst when corporations no longer have the same rights as humans.

Then, our politicians can go back to being statesmen and stateswomen, and our doctors won't have to deal with an insurance industry that controls life-and-death decisions based solely on cost. Then, our commons can be clean because we—the people—decided that's how it should be.

Then, making money will be back in perspective: a fine thing to do, but please don't overwhelm our media, wreck our world, and harm our children's future in the process.

19

UNEQUAL INFLUENCE

The resources in the treasury of a business corporation . . . are not an indication of popular support for the corporation's political ideas. They reflect instead the economically motivated decisions of investors and customers. The availability of these resources may make a corporation a formidable political presence, even though the power of the corporation may be no reflection of the power of its ideas.

–U. S. SUPREME COURT JUSTICE WILLIAM J. BRENNAN, JR.

"The people have got to know if their President is a crook," U. S. President Richard Nixon told a national television audience on November 11, 1973, when asked at a press conference if donations from the dairy industry had caused him to reverse his position on dairy price supports. He added, "Well, I am not a crook."

A bit over 2 years earlier, however, Nixon had a meeting at the White House with representatives of the dairy industry, who had apparently just given him a $2 million campaign pledge. With the tape running on March 23, 1971, Nixon said, "Uh, I know . . . that, uh, you are a group that are politically very conscious . . . And you're willing to do something about it. And, I must say a lot of businessmen and others . . . don't do anything about it. And you do, and I appreciate that. And I don't have to spell it out."

When the men from the trade association left, John Connally, one of Nixon's advisors who didn't realize that Nixon had bugged his own office, said to Nixon, "They are tough political operatives. This is a cold political deal."

Two days later, as Dairy Education Board executive director Robert Cohen documents, Nixon announced to his Cabinet a stunning change in administration position that would bring the dairy industry over $300 million in additional revenue for the following year.

Similarly, as somebody involved in education issues (I'm on the board of directors of a private school in New Hampshire, and have written six education-related books) I had wondered why the Bush administration would propose doubling the testing burden on public schoolchildren when both good science and common sense say that decreasing classroom size, increasing teacher training and resources, and other less expensive and more local methods are far more effective at helping children learn.

Then the office of Senator Jim Jeffords gave me a study from the Congressional Research Service from July 9, 2001, titled "Educational Testing: Bush Administration Proposals and Congressional Response." The report, produced for members of Congress and not generally available to the public, noted, "Estimated aggregate state-level expenditures for assessment programs in FY2001 are $422.8 million."

Suddenly, it all made sense: Most standardized tests are sold to schools by a small number of very large corporations, and those corporations are now scheduled to make hundreds of millions more dollars under the Bush proposals.

In fact, the report notes that the Senate version of the Bush plan would "authorize a total of $400 million for state assessment development grants for FY2002;" "authorize $110 million for expansion of NAEP state assessments;" and "authorize $50 million for state performance awards"—all in addition to the current $422 million that the states were already spending on testing. The testing industry would more than double in size in a single year, helping a handful of large corporations get very much richer from this redistribution of tax dollars, whether it helps kids learn or not.

The daily payoffs in Washington, the hundreds of millions that are funneled from corporate bank accounts to politicians' campaigns, often producing results that are of questionable benefit to anybody but the donor corporations, evoke a response of cynicism among most Americans.

A POLITICAL BACKLASH

Political optimists see a different possibility than today's rampant cynicism. And although most registered voters no longer bother to vote, some do believe that politicians who are truly dedicated to the public good can return power to the people. Those who believe that it is the role of government and not corporations to ensure our rights to "Life, Liberty, and the Pursuit of Happiness" view the increasingly populist talk of some national politicians as good news.

For example, Vermont Congressman Bernie Sanders published an article on his Web site on August 17, 2001, titled "The U. S. Needs a Political Revolution." He wrote, "At a time when more and more Americans are giving up on the political process, and when the wealthy and multi-national corporations have unprecedented wealth and power, it is imperative that we launch a grass-roots revolution to enable ordinary Americans to regain control of their country. . . .

"It is no accident," Sanders continued, "that while pharmaceutical and insurance companies donate huge sums of money into the political process, American citizens must pay, by far, the highest prices in the world for prescription drugs. Those same companies and their political donations ensure that the United Stares remains the only industrialized nation that does not have a national health care program providing health care to all.

"The rich hold $25,000-a-plate fundraisers for their candidates. Why would they pay so much for a chicken dinner? The answer is, they want access and special favors. It is no accident that after raising more money from the wealthy for his campaign than any candidate in history, President Bush and the Republican leadership passed a $1.3 trillion dollar tax bill which provides $500 billion in tax breaks for the wealthiest 1 percent of Americans. It is no accident that, rather than raising the minimum wage, the President and congressional leadership are providing billions in tax breaks and subsidies to the major oil, gas, and coal companies. It is also, sadly, no accident that almost 20 percent of our children live in poverty, schools throughout the country are physically deteriorating, college graduates begin their careers deeply in debt, and millions of working class people are unable to find affordable housing."

My read of it is that Sanders is suggesting that we again try real "republican democracy": a government truly of, by, and for humans. That we begin to put people first and the rights and powers of corporations (and governments, churches, and any other human-made institutions) second.

This brings us back to those two meta-political parties: the politicians who work on behalf of corporations, and the politicians who work on behalf of humans. Increasingly, citizens of democratic nations are setting aside labels like Republican, Democrat, Tory, or Labor when considering their politicians. Instead, the labels in people's minds are: "working in the interests of corporations" and "working in the interests of individual citizens."

HOW PUBLIC OPINION IS INFLUENCED BY CONCENTRATED MONEY

Poll after poll has shown that Americans overwhelmingly support reform of our health-care system. People are concerned about costs and quality of care. Yet in 1993, when President Bill Clinton proposed that the government should offer some form of health-care protection to the nation's 40-plus million uninsured, the insurance industry spent an estimated $100 million on lobbying, $60 million on advertising, and provided members of Congress with around 350 free trips.

What actually happened as a result of all this spending is extraordinarily ironic. Industry polls showed that people cared more about being able to choose their own doctor than most other medical issues. Taking advantage of this, an infamous series of ads featuring "Harry and Louise" warned Americans that under a government-run health insurance program, they would lose their ability to select the doctor of their choice.

The advertising worked. Panicked, American public opinion swung from strong support for Clinton's proposals to overwhelming fear of them. The Internet became flooded with insulting e-mails about the evils of "Hillary's" insurance proposal.

Even more ironically, those fears have been realized today—*without* the Clinton proposal. Back in 1993, you could pretty much go to any doctor you wanted (assuming you were insured), and your insurance would almost always pay for it. Overtly restricting that ability was never part of the Clinton proposal, but because of the power of the Harry and Louise ads, people came to *believe* it was.

And within a few years, insurance companies and HMOs began to crack down on consumers who wanted to select their own doctors. Today, fewer Americans have that privilege than in 1993, even though it's fully available to citizens of virtually every country that has a national health-care program . . . which is every developed country in the world except the United States.

It turns out there is a strong reason why the insurance industry was eager to invest so much cash in advertising and lobbying to keep the government from competing with them in the realm of health care: *profits*. For every $100 that passes through the hands of the government-administered Medicare programs, between $2 and $3 is spent by Medicare on administration, leaving $97 to $98 to pay for medical services and drugs. But of every $100 that flows through corporate insurance programs and HMOs, $10 to $24 sticks to corporate fingers along the way. As Yale University Professor of Public Policy Theodore Marmor, author of *The Politics of Medicare*, said, "The costs of administering private insurance are somewhere between 5 and 10 times the costs of administering Medicare."

After all, Medicare doesn't have lavish corporate headquarters, corporate jets, or pay expensive lobbying firms in Washington to work on its behalf. It doesn't pay out profits in the form of dividends to its shareholders. And it doesn't compensate its top executive with over a million dollars a year, as do each of the largest of the American insurance companies. The result, as Professor Marmor points out, is that Canadians—who receive health care at one-sixth the cost of the United States because no insurance companies are in the middle—"are somewhat healthier than citizens of the United States, use more hospital days per thousand, and visit their physicians more often," because services are freely available.

Yet most citizens of the United States have no idea what it's like to live in a country with national health care. When our family lived in Germany for a year a bit over a decade ago, we were amazed at how smoothly their health-care system works: We could make any appointment with any physician, and they were excellent at what they did. But even describing the reality of that experience draws uncomprehending stares from Americans, who have been fed a steady corporate diet of very one-sided information.

POLLUTERS PASS "GO"

In 1995, the new governor of Texas responded to the needs of the "polluting industries" who had contributed more than $4 million (about 20 percent of the total) to his election campaign the year before. George W. Bush signed into law the Texas Environmental Health and Safety Audit Privilege Act, also known as the polluter immunity law. This new law, which has since been emulated in 25 other states and is now being considered at a federal level, allows polluting industries to avoid prosecution for pollution violations if they themselves report their own crimes to themselves in an internal audit. It also gives them the ability to prevent the public from knowing about their violations.

As Arizona's Assistant Attorney General David Ronald said, "Only the business with something to hide would benefit from a law that turns data gathered from environmental audits into secret information." Some of these laws even provide for a year in jail and a $10,000 fine for any human who reveals to the public or government agencies any corporate pollution discovered in an audit, thus discouraging investigative reporting or whistle-blowing employees.

Like with health-care policy, these laws that increase the power and profitability of the nation's largest corporations at the expense of smaller companies who play by the rules from the beginning are influenced by enormous amounts of "corporate free speech" in the form of cash for politicians and political parties.

IN A DEMOCRACY . . .

There are those who argue that health care should be included in understanding the meaning of the phrase "Life, Liberty, and the Pursuit of Happiness." Others point out that the Founders wrote the Constitution and didn't put into place a national health-care system then, so clearly they didn't mean for there to be one. Both arguments have their backers and make good points.

My goal here in this chapter was not to argue for national health care, but rather to point out how one of the more important of our national dialogues is skewed by the presence of corporate money, both in lobbying and advertising. And that money is spent under the "right of free speech" that corporations claim, hearkening back to the *Santa Clara* decision. Corporate personhood and its claim to First Amendment rights is one of the most powerful weapons wielded by insurance and HMO corporations to access politicians and use the airwaves to mold public opinion.

The point for a democracy, though, is *what is the will of the people?* That will may change over time, but it is undemocratic when it is shaped by the single voice that shouts the loudest because there are profits to be made. Democracy is more important than any single debate, and this is a classic example of how democratic republican processes have been twisted because of the concept of corporate personhood.

20

CAPITALISTS AND AMERICANS SPEAK OUT FOR COMMUNITY

"In America, no other distinction between man and man had ever been known but that of persons in office exercising powers by authority of the laws, and private individuals. Among these last, the poorest laborer stood on equal ground with the wealthiest millionaire, and generally on a more favored one whenever their rights seem to jar."

—THOMAS JEFFERSON: ANSWERS TO DE MEUSNIER QUESTIONS, 1786

Although we have much that we might change about our government and business, it's clear that we also have a great and noble heritage on which to build and many great leaders in whose footsteps we can follow. Unlike America's Founders, however, we don't have to start from a blank piece of paper.

The Founders set the principles for us and they inspired the formation of governments the world over—from the French Revolution to Tiananmen Square. Our job is to pick up the torch of liberty.

As this part of the book draws to a close, let's take one last look around and ask, "Is this a biased view, or do others see a problem, too?" This time, we'll look to three powerful proponents of capitalism and free enterprise: a billionaire, a Nobel laureate who was Chief Economist of the World Bank, and *Business Week* magazine.

THE CHARITABLE BILLIONAIRE

George Soros is one of the most successful capitalists in history. He has made billions and has given away enormous amounts to charity. He clearly understands how the system works—his financial success is proof of that—and he is worried about it, on a global scale.

Soros wrote the cover story for the February 1997 issue of *Atlantic Monthly*. The subtitle asked, "What kind of society do we want? 'Let the free market decide!' is the often-heard response. That response, a prominent capitalist argues, undermines the very values on which open and democratic societies depend."

Soros' article, titled "The Capitalist Threat," directly addressed the issue of whether government should intervene in economic affairs, or if corporations should be unconstrained by elected officials (often referred to as *laissez-faire* capitalism). He wrote, "Although I have made a fortune in the financial markets, I now fear that the untrammeled intensification of *laissez-faire* capitalism and the spread of market values into all areas of life is endangering our open and democratic society. The main enemy of the open society, I believe, is no longer the communist but the capitalist threat."

Four years later, he wrote in *Newsweek* magazine, "We need new ideas for fighting global poverty, ideas as sweeping as those that set the stage for global recovery after World War II. . . . The globalization of financial markets makes it more difficult for individual states to provide public goods. National governments find it harder to impose taxes and regulations because capital can go elsewhere."

He went on to propose the creation of a fund managed by the International Monetary Fund, which would serve three types of programs: "Global campaigns to provide such public benefits as eliminating HIV/AIDS," "Government-sponsored programs to alleviate poverty," and "Nongovernmental development programs [which] would be particularly valuable in countries with repressive or corrupt regimes."

Clearly, the principles of the common good proposed by Jefferson and other Founders, and espoused by so many of our presidents, are not at all incompatible with modern capitalist thinking. The problem, according to this billionaire, is in restriction of choices and excessive concentration of corporate power.

THE NOBEL LAUREATE FROM THE WORLD BANK

Stanford University Professor Emeritus Joseph E. Stiglitz won the Nobel Prize for Economics in 2001 just after quitting his job at the World Bank. His remarks are timely.

"As the chief economist at the World Bank from 1997 to 2000, I have seen firsthand the dark side of globalization—how the liberalization of capital markets, by allowing speculative money to pour in and out of a country at a moment's whim, devastated East Asia; how so-called structural-adjustment loans to some of the poorest countries in the world 'restructured' those countries' economies so as to eliminate jobs, but did not provide the means of creating new ones, leading to widespread unemployment and cuts in basic services. . . . The voices of those most affected by globalization are barely audible in discussions about how the table should be reshaped and who should have a seat at it."

Once again, Jefferson's dream is being thwarted by the influence of decisions being made on the basis of income regardless of human cost. Those are exactly the sort of decisions the Founders fought *against* at great peril to themselves. They literally put their personal fortunes and lives on the line, risked everything, to fight the corporate and political tyranny of the day and gain democracy. Stiglitz gave up his position as chief economist of the World Bank. Clearly, compassion and concern for one's community are not incompatible with capitalist thinking—even for a world-leading economist.

BUSINESS WEEK POLL OF THE AMERICAN PUBLIC

Finally, we turn to the American public, to gauge its mood. Has big business overstepped its bounds? Should it behave responsibly toward its community? What do Americans think?

In September 2000, a *Business Week*/Harris poll asked whether "business has gained too much power over too many aspects of American life." Between 72 and 82 percent of Americans said "yes." And 95 percent of Americans agreed that American corporations "owe something to their workers and the communities in which they operate, and should sometimes sacrifice profit for the sake of making things better."

By any measure, 72 to 82 percent of public opinion is an overwhelming majority, and the remarks of Soros and Stiglitz show that reasonable restrictions on businesses are not at all incompatible with *success* in business. Yet we see around us the sort of imbalance and injustice that our early presidents warned us about, in which so many large corporations misuse the protections that were created to protect humans *from* the biggest and most powerful. As Justice Black said, it was never meant to be this way.

IN A DEMOCRACY . . .

We need to level the playing field and return to the balance envisioned by our Founders, in which the highest priority actually accrues to humans and their communities—not to any massive authority, be it government or business. The first step in getting back to those values will be to end corporate personhood.

PART 4
RESTORING DEMOCRACY AS THE FOUNDERS IMAGINED IT

The Fourteenth Amendment followed the freedom of a race from slavery. . . . The amendment was intended to protect the life, liberty, and property of human beings. The language of the amendment itself does not support the theory that it was passed for the benefit of corporations.

—U. S. SUPREME COURT JUSTICE HUGO BLACK

21

END CORPORATE PERSONHOOD

We are made wise not by the recollection of our past, but by the responsibility for our future.

—GEORGE BERNARD SHAW

Arizona changed their law after 1886 so that the word "person" would include nonliving as well as living legal entities: "'Person' includes a corporation, company, partnership, firm, association or society, as well as a natural person."

Many states have varying definitions of "person" depending on the part of law at issue. For example, there was a 1998 U. S. Supreme Court case in which a large part of the argument had to do with whether or not the Federal Trade Commission had the authority, under California law, to act as a person in enforcing a judgment against a telemarketer.

LIMIT-SETTING LEGISLATION ISN'T ENOUGH

As we've seen through the history of the Sherman Anti-Trust Act and other legislative attempts to control corporate behavior, the problem faced by citizens as well as directors and stockholders of corporations is systemic and rooted in how corporations are defined under law.

Virtually every legislative session since the 1800s has seen new attempts to regulate or control corporate behavior, starting with Thomas Jefferson's unsuccessful insistence that the Bill of Rights protect humans from "commercial monopolies." Ultimately, most have either failed or been co-opted because they didn't address the underlying structural problem of corporate personhood.

To solve this problem, then, new laws controlling corporations aren't the ultimate answer. Instead, what is needed is a foundational change in the definition of the relationship between living human beings and the nonliving legal fictions we call corporations. Only when corporations are again *legally* subordinate to those who authorized them—humans, and the governments representing them—will true change be possible.

To bring this about will require a grassroots movement in communities all across America and the world to undo corporate personhood, leading to changes in the definitions of the word "person."

PERSISTENCE

I'm not so naive as to think this is something that will happen quickly, easily, or start at a national level. It will begin with you and me, at a local level, and percolate up from there, just as every substantial reformation movement has, from the American Revolution to the populist trust-busting movement of Teddy Roosevelt's era to the civil rights movement. Change happens when citizens stand up and say "I won't have it anymore."

If history is any indicator, it won't be a short or direct path. It may be in my children's or their children's lifetime that humans finally take back their governments and their planet from corporations, and it may even be generations beyond that. On the other hand, sometimes the Constitution is amended quickly in response to an overall public uprising, as happened with the amendment to end Prohibition and the amendment to lower the voting age to 18 that was passed in response to the rage of teenagers being forced to serve in the Vietnam War over which they had no voting power.

TOWNSHIPS FIGHT BACK

In 2001, several townships in Pennsylvania passed ordinances forbidding corporations from owning or controlling farms in their communities. "They chose to go that route instead of the regulatory route," said attorney Thomas Linzey of the Community Environmental Legal Defense Fund (CELDF). "If we just got a regulation passed about, for example, odor from factory farms, then the entire debate from then on would be about odor. But what we want to challenge is the right for these huge corporate farming operations to exist in our communities in the first place."

In December 2001, Gene Mellott, the Secretary for Thompson Township, Pennsylvania, said his township had adopted several such ordinances, including, "An ordinance forbidding confined animal feeding operations from being owned and operated by a corporation," and "one that deals with corporations who have a previous history of violations, denying them access to starting up an animal feeding operation."

Mellott noted that at the time of our interview, one farmer was actually going through the processes specified by the ordinance, cooperating with the township, prior to opening a new animal feeding operation.

Other townships weren't so lucky, though, Mellott said. "In one township, the agribiz corporations threatened to sue the directors of the Township, both as directors and personally. They didn't have the personal funds to fight that, so they decided not to pass the ordinance."

I asked Linzey how a corporation could sue a township official for proposing legislation, and he said, "They allege that the township officials are planning to infringe on their civil rights."

"Civil rights?" I said.

"Yes, civil rights. Because they claim they're persons, just like the township officials, so they can sue them, person to person, so to speak. That also immediately throws it into federal court, where the local officials will have to pay more for defense and won't have the easy support of their local community."

If corporations weren't persons, they couldn't use such forms of harassment to prevent local officials from trying to protect their citizens from what may be unpleasant corporate neighbors. And that's really the bottom line for township officials like Mellott, who said, "These ordinances were passed *to protect our citizens* [emphasis added] from pollution or side-effects of factory farms, water usage problems where they may draw down our reserves and making wells go dry, that sort of thing. We felt that a business that large should be regulated. I've heard the farm bureau is opposed to this, but the majority of the citizens of the township are in favor of them if they're passed, and they're the ones who elected us to represent their interests."

CHANGING LOCAL LAWS FIRST

So how to make these changes? As with the family farmers in Pennsylvania with their and CELDF's battle against corporate factory-farming operations that risk fouling their air, polluting their wells and river waters, and degrading their land, it will start at the local level.

I've helped fund an effort by attorneys Daniel Brannen and Thomas Linzey to check the laws of every single state in the Union and Washington, D. C., to figure out how to best phrase local ordinances denying corporate personhood. You'll find the proposed Model Ordinances to Rescind Corporate Personhood on page 294.

In many communities, you'll have to get a city councilperson or other elected official to propose the law; in others, individuals can place initiatives on ballots or before town meetings themselves. Call your town hall to find out; ask, "How do I go about submitting a new law? What's the process?" In so doing, you will be joining all those down through the centuries who have initiated change in democracies across the world.

And, just as those who worked for civil rights for specific groups of humans came up against resistance, there may be opposition to your proposal.

When Linzey helped local farmers and elected officials pass ordinances keeping corporate factory farms out of their communities, he said, "A ranking Republican state senator demanded that CELDF be banned from [speaking out in public] panels. The Farm Bureau actively interfered in one local government's effort to pass the ordinance. And factory farm operatives began attending local government meetings."

But that was just the beginning, Linzey notes. Next, "The Pennsylvania Chamber of Commerce became more active, doing what the Chamber is designed to do—painting people like me and public officials who believe in democracy as rabble-driven advocates of no growth and no jobs. The Chamber also labeled as 'anti-agriculture' residents who supported our ordinance."

And then the corporate P. R. machine turned itself on. Linzey says, "Our work made the cover of the Chamber's monthly *Advocate for Pennsylvania Business*, with an article titled 'There's No Business Like No-Bizness in Wayne Township' and a graphic of the township surrounded by barbed wire."

Nonetheless, remembering former Speaker of the House of Representatives Tip O'Neill's comment that, "All politics is local," there's little doubt that the best strategy is to start where we humans live, town by town, city by city, county by county. Corporations may have corrupted many of our political processes, but you and I still retain the right to vote. The ballot box has the potential to be the great leveler, the remedy of past errors and current inequalities.

CHANGING STATE LAWS

When enough local communities have passed laws denying corporate personhood, eventually a corporation will challenge one of these laws and it'll end up before the Supreme Court. This could be a golden opportunity for the court to rectify the error made by reporter J. C. Bancroft Davis in his headnotes for the 1886 *Santa Clara* case. If the Court were to rule that the Founders didn't intend to give corporations human protections under the Bill of Rights and the Fourteenth Amendment, step one would be finished.

But if the Court rules that the new anti–corporate personhood laws are unconstitutional, then it will be necessary to move up the ladder and amend the state and federal constitutions. To support that effort, you'll also find ready-to-use draft amendments on page 315.

I've spoken with a number of attorneys, constitutional scholars, and a few politicians about all of this, and most agree that starting on a local level is probably best. But most also suggest that people should concurrently begin the process of amending state constitutions since corporate charters are issued and controlled by—in virtually all cases—the states themselves.

MAKING CHANGE HAPPEN

Taking on the conventional wisdom and a hierarchical power structure is no small or easy task. The civil rights and Native American rights movements tell us how true social change happens: from the bottom up. The Supreme Court, for example, doesn't just go out and right social or legal wrongs. Instead, legislatures pass laws, and people challenge those laws. When the challenges have worked their way up through the courts, they end up before the Supreme Court, which then has an opportunity to rule on the laws in the context of their relationship to the Constitution.

For humans to take back control of our governments by undoing corporate personhood, we'll have to begin with the governments that are the closest and most accessible to us. It's almost impossible for you or me to go to Washington, D. C., and have a meeting with our Senator or Representative—most of us usually can't even get them on the phone unless we're a big contributor. But most of us can meet with our city council members or show up at their meetings. Lobbying within the local community is both easy and effective. Local politicians are the closest to the people they represent, and generally the most responsive to the people they represent.

When enough local communities have passed ordinances that directly challenge corporate personhood, state legislatures will begin to notice. As with the issues of slavery, women's suffrage, and Prohibition (among others), when local communities take actions that are followed by states, eventually the federal government will get on board.

AN OPPORTUNITY FOR THE SUPREME COURT TO NOW RIGHT A WRONG

These new laws will surely meet with lawsuits, which will bring the question back to the courts. Just as the railroads themselves sought change in the courts, ordinary citizens across the land are standing up and saying, "This is not what we want." It may take decades, as it did to create the wrong in the first place, but eventually, the movement will lead to explicit legislation, or an amendment to the United States Constitution, or to the Supreme Court reversing the *Santa Clara* precedent as it has reversed so many other error-filled cases over the years.

The ultimate change would be to clarify that the Fourteenth Amendment's reference to "persons" meant "natural persons." But whatever change you might choose to seek, at the end of this book you'll find a start: proposed ordinances, state constitutional amendments, and a federal constitutional amendment, all returning to "natural persons" what Locke and Jefferson called our natural rights as *human* persons.

The result could be a new flowering of freedom, democracy, *and* economic opportunity in America and around the world.

22

A NEW ENTREPRENEURIAL BOOM

To widen the market and to narrow the competition is always the interest of the dealers. . . . The proposal of any new law or regulation of commerce which comes from this order, ought always to be listened to with great precaution, and ought never to be adopted, till after having been long and carefully examined, not only with the most scrupulous, but with the most suspicious attention. It comes from an order of men, whose interest is never exactly the same with that of the public, who have generally an interest to deceive and even to oppress the public, and who accordingly have, upon many occasions, both deceived and oppressed it.

–ADAM SMITH, *THE WEALTH OF NATIONS*, BOOK I, CHAPTER XI

For some people, particularly the young and the old, the local mall or big-box retailer or superstore is an important part of their social lives. They get exercise by walking up and down the aisles, greet friends they see only there, and have a special and often inexpensive meal. They notice what's on sale and what's new in stock, making both intentional purchases and the occasional impulse buy.

ARE SUPERSTORES AND MALLS "THE NEW DOWNTOWN"?

In a way, a mall or superstore is like a small town's downtown. Instead of a library, there's the bookstore where you can browse books, thumb through magazines, and read today's newspapers. Instead of the old corner coffee shop, there's the food court. Most of the retail categories in a traditional downtown area are represented, from the clothing stores to the drug store to the optometrist. The mall has its own police force and its own street-sweepers and maintenance crew. There are even sitting areas—the equivalent of the old parks, although they're usually lacking in squirrels and pigeons.

Shopping malls and big-box retailers are so much like downtowns that in most of the world's suburban communities where they exist, they've replaced the downtown areas of previous centuries. From the outside, it looks like a change of location and style, but not one of great significance. So people now shop at the mall instead of downtown. So what? Isn't it just one business replacing another? Isn't that the way of commerce? Well . . . no. It's not the same thing.

THE LOCAL MONEY RECYCLING SYSTEM WE LOST

There is one huge difference between a mall full of chain stores or a big-box retailer and a downtown area full of small businesses, and it's a difference that is destroying local communities on the one hand and creating mind-boggling wealth for a very few very large corporations on the other. Here's how it works.

When I shop in downtown Montpelier, Vermont, and buy a pair of pants, for example, at the Stevens Clothing Store on Main Street, at the end of the day the store's owner, Jack Callahan, takes his proceeds down to the Northfield Savings Bank and deposits them. From Stevens, I walk next door to Bear Pond Books and buy today's newspaper, a magazine, and a copy of Thomas Paine's *Rights of Man*, a book that is as fascinating today as when it was first written in 1791. At the end of the day, Bear Pond's manager, Linda Leehman, will take my money down to the Chittenden Bank and deposit it. From Bear Pond I go to one of the dozen or so local restaurants, and exchange some of my cash for a good meal. At day's end, that cash, too, will end up in one of Montpelier's local banks.

The next day, Montpelier's banks are richer by my purchases, as are Stevens, Bear Pond, and the restaurant. If my daughter the Web designer wanted to start her own design firm in an office on Main Street (or from her home), she could visit one of those banks, and if her credit was good, they could loan her some of the money that was deposited with them the night before from the townspeople's purchases.

If her work is good, Stevens or Bear Pond or the restaurant may decide they want to hire her to design their Web site, using the profits they made from my and others' purchases to pay for her work. She'll put her money into the local bank, increasing its deposits available for local lending. Thus, by keeping money within the community, the community grows. This is how communities in America and most of the rest of the world have historically grown.

In the process of patronizing local businesses, people get their social and exercise needs met by walking into and around in downtown areas, *and* they contribute wealth to the local community, which eventually recycles back to them in the form of an improved quality of life, local taxes for local services like schools and police and parks, and a thriving entrepreneurial environment. That's a healthy local economy.

THE OUT-OF-TOWN MONEY VACUUM

Consider, though, if my shopping trip had been to a mall full of chain stores or to a national superstore. Strict management of cash flow is the name of the game for such businesses, and some of them make deposits several times a day. But the money stays in town for only a day, at best.

At the end of every day, somebody somewhere pushes a button and all the money from each of the national or international chain's outlets all over the world goes "whoosh" to a distant location (usually near the headquarters of the chain). Of course, some of the money comes back into the local community in the form of wages, rent, taxes, and purchased services. But it's a fraction of what it would be if it had all stayed in the community from beginning to end. And none of the profit ever finds its way back into the local community unless, coincidentally, there are local stockholders.

At the moment, one of the main things that prevent local communities from defining and protecting their own local economies from these cash vacuums is based on the *Santa Clara* ruling.

HOW *SANTA CLARA* SET THE STAGE

When Thomas Jefferson pushed so hard for 2 years for the Bill of Rights to include "freedom from monopolies," he may well have anticipated the very problem I just identified: the dominance of distant mega-merchants such (as the East India Company) over local merchants. On the other hand, his Federalist opponents thought a strong central government could prevent the rise of monopolies while controlling the entrepreneurial engine that could drive great prosperity for a new nation in a vast, relatively untouched commons.

As America industrialized through the 1800s, it went from a minor agricultural nation to an industrial powerhouse central to the world's economy. This brought vast and rapid leaps in what we would call progress, but also left huge areas soiled by industrial waste and strip-mining, and resulted in one of the most rapid and dramatic losses of topsoil in the history of the world. Overall, though, most Americans today would consider it a good foundation laid for contemporary comforts.

While our history books tend to focus on the rich and powerful of the past—the John Rockefellers, Andrew Carnegies, and Prescott Bushes—the reality is that hundreds of thousands of small businesspeople built much of America and the rest of the modern industrial world.

These small businessmen and women didn't just create personal wealth for their families; they also kept wealth circulating in the communities where they lived. They provided employment, improvements, and economic vigor to their towns or neighborhoods, and responded to the needs of those communities—because they lived in them.

State and local governments recognized the value and importance of having local entrepreneurs responsible for the local business, rather than out-of-state monopolies, chains, or multinational corporations. Most states, for example, taxed out-of-state or multinational businesses at a higher rate than local entrepreneurs, to discourage the distant and encourage the local.

But this was overthrown in 1933 when the J. C. Penney chain sued the state of Florida, claiming that since their corporation was actually a person under the Constitution (citing *Santa Clara*), it was illegal discrimination under the Fourteenth Amendment for a state to give preferential treatment to a person in their own state while not offering that same treatment to a person from out of state. The Supreme Court, looking back to 1886, sided with the Penney corporation, and now states and local communities all over the nation find themselves without the legal tools to encourage and nurture local businesses.

Like the *Santa Clara* case, this one too went all the way to the Supreme Court because a very large corporation could litigate over an astonishingly small amount of money: $25. At that time, local businesses were assessed a $5 annual fee, and out-of-state businesses were charged $30 in Florida.

CHAINS AND CATEGORY-KILLERS: NO MORE BUILDING FOR POSTERITY

The fallout from that 1933 decision has been far-reaching. Just as individual humans are woefully outmatched by a corporation that wants to fight them, so are local communities outmatched.

A related effect is that individuals today are far less able to build an enterprise that will last in their community. And due to the attraction of enormous amounts of money from distant areas, they're often not even interested in doing so.

I first noticed the change in the mid-1980s, although it was probably underway for a decade or more. A young friend was pursuing the American dream—starting his own business—and as a fellow entrepreneur, he had adopted me as a mentor.

"People who start businesses aren't always the best to run them as they get larger," I advised him. "Leadership and management are two different skill sets, and only in very rare individuals do you find both together. When your company gets large enough that it needs real, day-to-day management of the details, I recommend you plan in advance now to hire somebody to replace yourself, so you can move into either sales, idea-hatching, or some other function that you still find fun but doesn't get in the way of the bean counters you'll need to bring in."

"Not gonna be a problem for me," he said. "I have no intention of keeping this business beyond its initial growth phase."

"Why not?" I said, reflecting that small businesses were what had built and sustained virtually every American community over the past 300 years.

Why go to the trouble of starting one if you weren't going to let it sustain you for your lifetime?

"Because that's not how things work anymore," he said, reversing our advice-giving roles. "People don't start businesses anymore thinking they'll have security for their old age or something to pass along to their children. Whether it's a restaurant or a retail store or a software company, the plan now is to grow big enough and fast enough to be noticed by one of the big guys, and then cash out before they squash you like a bug. Make it easier and cheaper for them to buy you out than for them to spend the time and effort running you out of business or simply stealing your idea. And to succeed, you've gotta do it quickly."

After that meeting while driving home in suburban Atlanta, I noticed with new eyes the stores that lined the main roads. Nearly all were large corporate chains, from the video stores to the bookstores to the fast-food outlets. The crafts store was a chain, as was the bicycle store. Nearly all the entrepreneurial ventures that had populated the area up until the late 1970s and mid-1980s had died, replaced by such a numbing sameness of product and presentation that I could just as easily have been driving down a suburban street in Dallas, San Diego, Seattle, Memphis, Detroit, or Boston. Or, increasingly, Paris, London, Frankfurt, Rio, or Taipei.

Retail has been taken over. There's a good reason that national superstore chains are known in the business press as category killers. When such a chain enters an industry, whether it's hardware or stationery or anything else, it typically puts dozens to hundreds of local, family-owned businesses into bankruptcy. Other local merchants, having seen the fate that awaits them, "get while the getting's good," closing down before they lose everything they've earned in decades of business. In either case, the category killer relocates locally generated profits to its distant corporate headquarters. And the local, community-oriented, full-service merchants are gone.

Manufacturing, too, has been moved far away from the local economy, to labor-cheap countries. Taking Amtrak from Boston to New York, you see miles of empty, decaying, vandalized factory buildings once serviced by the railroads, their products now manufactured in China or Indonesia, their former workers now flipping burgers.

Big, nonlocal corporations have largely inhaled even service industries, traditionally the last bastion of lower-paying local labor: fast-food chains, day care and learning center chains, home-service franchises, and hospital and medical chains.

RELOCALIZING OUR ECONOMIES

In summary, consider these benefits of local communities being allowed to give special breaks to local companies, or regulate out-of-town companies, to support their local economy:

- They keep cash local.
- Local companies are more sensitive and responsive to regional issues—they are far less likely to be "bad citizens" because their families have to live with the consequences.
- They are more heterogeneous and responsive in the services and products supplied.
- They preserve regional culture, personality, and perspective.
- They provide greater stability, given that the economies become more self-contained. The demise of a business or two won't prove nearly as devastating as when a large employer decides to shut down a plant and move production to Mexico.

This is not to say we shouldn't have large businesses. Instead, they must be kept in an appropriate context, and submit to regulation by the *local* communities in which they operate.

RECOVERING AN ENTREPRENEURIAL BOOM

According to the U. S. Small Business Administration (SBA), "Industries dominated by small firms created jobs at a rate almost 60 percent faster than those dominated by large businesses." Their report adds, "Approximately 86 percent of small businesses are legally organized as proprietorships or partnerships."

The same trends are found worldwide, and attested to by the enormous success of microlending projects such as run by the Grameen Bank in Bangaladesh, which was started in 1976 when Bangladeshi economics professor Muhammad Yunus loaned $26 to 42 Bangladeshi villagers, thus starting the Grameen Bank. Yunus's bank has since loaned $2 billion to more than 2.2 million people, mostly poor women, with an average loan size of $160 and a repayment rate (including interest) of 98 percent. Through the small businesses that have been started with these microloans, over a third of

Grameen's clients have now been raised out of poverty, and microlending is a growing tool of nonprofits and charities around the world.

The challenge to a new entrepreneurial boom is found in the type of neoliberal corporate person–based economics practiced by the World Bank, WTO, and big-business advocates of what is called free trade. It's a system that does exactly what corporations are chartered to do: move and aggregate wealth into the corporation. But with corporate personhood openly allowing corporations to corrupt political processes and roam the world unrestrained, the consequences have been unhealthy for humans. The result of today's situation is well summarized by Jeff Gates, author of *Democracy at Risk*, in an article published in the Summer 2002 issue of *Reflections*, MIT's Journal of the Society for Organizational Learning. Gates notes the following nine clear and troubling trends, which all track back to the current corporate laws and structures for the very largest of the corporations we allow to do business here (quoted verbatim from Jeff's article with permission):

1. **From the bottom to the top.** The wealth of the Forbes 400 richest Americans grew an average $1.44 billion each from 1997 to 2000, for a daily increase in wealth of $1,920,000 per person. The financial wealth of the top 1 percent now exceeds the combined household financial wealth of the bottom 95 percent. The share of the nation's after-tax income received by the top 1 percent nearly doubled from 1979 to 1997. By 1998, the top-earning 1 percent had as much combined income as the 100 million Americans with the lowest earnings. The top fifth of U. S. households now claim 49.2 percent of the national income while the bottom fifth gets by on 3.6 percent. Between 1979 and 1997, the average income of the richest fifth jumped from 9 times the income of the poorest fifth to 15 times. The pay gap between top executives and their average employees in the 365 largest U. S. companies widened from 42 to 1 in 1980 to 531 to 1 in 2000.
2. **From democracies to plutocracies.** Today's capital markets–led "emerging markets" development model is poised to replicate U. S. wealth patterns worldwide. For instance, World Bank research found that 61.7 percent of Indonesia's stock market value is held by that nation's 15 richest families. The comparable figures are 55.1 percent for the Philippines and 53.3 percent for Thailand. Worldwide, there is now roughly $60 trillion in securitized assets (stocks, bonds, and so

on), with an estimated $90 trillion in additional assets that will become securitizable as this model spreads.

3. **From the future to the present.** Unsustainable production methods are now standard practice worldwide, owing largely to globalization's embrace of a financial model that insists on maximizing net present value (chiefly, what stock values represent). That stance routinely and richly rewards those who internalize gains and externalize costs such as paying a living wage or cleaning up environmental toxins.
4. **From poor nations to rich.** The neoliberal version of globalization assumes that unrestricted economic flows will benefit the 80 percent of humanity living in developing countries as well as those 20 percent living in developed countries. Yet the U. N. Development Program (UNDP) reports that the richest fifth of the global population now accounts for 86 percent of all goods and services consumed, while the poorest fifth consumes just over 1 percent.
5. **From developing nations to developed nations.** In all three ecosystems suffering the worst declines (forests, freshwater, and marine), the most severe damage has occurred in the southern temperate or tropical regions. Industrial nations (located mainly in northern temperate zones) are primarily responsible for the ongoing loss of natural capital elsewhere in the world. In its July 2001 report, the International Panel on Climate Change confirms that relentlessly rising global temperatures—due primarily to hydrocarbon use in the 30 most developed economies—are poised to create catastrophic conditions worldwide. Agriculture, health, human settlements, water, animals—all will feel the impact on a planet that is warming faster than at any time in the past millennium. Throughout the panel's 2,600 pages of analysis, one theme remains constant: The poor of the world will be hardest hit. According to GEO 2000, a U. N. environmental report, "The continued poverty of the majority of the planet's inhabitants and excessive consumption by the minority are the two major causes of environmental degradation."
6. **From families to financial markets.** The work year for the typical American has lengthened by 184 hours since 1970. That's an additional 4½ weeks on the job for about the same pay. Parents in the United States also spend 40 percent less time with their children than in 1970.

7. **From free-traders to protectionists.** OECD nations channel $362 billion a year in subsidies to their own farmers while restricting agricultural imports from developing countries and insisting that debtor nations repay their foreign loans in foreign currency, which they can earn only by exporting.
8. **From debtors to creditors.** In 1999, leaders of the G7 nations agreed to a debt initiative for Heavily Indebted Poor Countries, aiming to cap debt service for the world's 41 poorest countries at [a steep] 15 to 20 percent of [their] export earnings. By comparison, after World War I, the victors set German reparations at 13 to 15 percent of exports.
9. **From law abiders to law evaders.** Roughly $8 trillion is held in tax havens worldwide, ensuring that globalization's most well-to-do can harvest the benefits of globalization without incurring any of the costs.

Denying corporate personhood isn't a panacea, but it's a huge first step. Corporations will still have extraordinary constitutional protections (the contracts clause and the commerce clause, for example), as they have had from the founding of the United States. Personhood status won't by any means leave them unprotected in court, any more than they were before 1886.

But when states, counties, townships, and communities can once again define corporate behavior, they can again encourage entrepreneurial activity. Then people can start and run small businesses without worrying that a giant corporation will come along and crush them without the slightest thought.

Communities would see the money spent in their neighborhoods circulate and be reinvested in their own area, building strong and vital towns, counties, and states. And corporations won't be able to intimidate local politicians by suing them personally for violations of the very civil rights laws that were first enacted to protect human beings.

An entrepreneurial boom awaits America and the rest of the world.

- The U. S. State Department notes that only 1 percent of the corporations in America (and most other developed nations) are "large" (more than 500 employees); 99 percent of all American companies are small businesses.
- That 99 percent accounts for 52 percent of all nonfarm jobs (keep in mind that about a third of all other workers are employed by governments and nonprofits) and 47 percent of all sales.

- America's 500 largest manufacturing firms cut almost 2 million workers from their payrolls in the United States between 1986 and 1994 (after that, the statistic gathering system changed and it's not broken out any more) as the focus of large companies moved from making things in America to selling them in America.
- But during the years 1990 to 1995 (the last years for which there are current statistics broken out in this fashion), more than three-quarters of *all* new jobs were created by small businesses.
- The U. S. Small Business Administration (SBA) says, "Overall, employment in establishments owned by small firms grew 10.5 percent over the period (noted above), compared with 3.7 percent employment growth in establishments owned by firms with more than 500 employees."
- Small businesses obtain more patents per sales dollars than large firms, and produce 55 percent of all significant innovations.
- The Bureau of Labor Statistics projects that 88 percent of all new job creation in the years up to 2005 will come from small businesses.

As the SBA notes in their "Annual Report on Small Business and Competition," "Small firms make two indispensable contributions to the American economy:

- "First, they are an integral part of the renewal process that pervades and defines market economies. New and small firms play a crucial role in experimentation and innovation that leads to technological change and productivity growth. . . .
- "Second, small firms are the essential mechanism by which millions enter the economic and social mainstream of American society. Small businesses enable millions, including women, minorities, and immigrants, to access the American Dream. . . . In this evolutionary process, community plays the crucial and indispensable role of providing the 'social glue' and networking opportunities that bind small firms together in both high tech and 'Main Street' activities."

And few to none of these small businesses would be affected in an adverse way by the elimination of corporate personhood.

- Small businesses don't have the time or money to field full-time lobbyists in Washington or to funnel millions of dollars to presidential or congressional campaigns, and thus don't assert First Amendment personhood rights. (Or, if they do, it's usually the business owner who contacts an elected official as a private citizen with a concern.)

- They don't claim the First Amendment right to free speech in spending hundreds of millions on national advertising designed to affect the political processes.
- They don't sue the government, declaring a person's Fourth Amendment right to privacy as a means to prevent OSHA or EPA inspectors from looking into toxic wastes or labor practices in chemical factories or steel mills.
- They don't demand Fourteenth Amendment rights of equal protection to knock down local community laws designed to keep out large corporations that have been convicted of corporate crimes or have the ability to unfairly compete.
- They don't sit on the councils of NAFTA and the WTO and make decisions that wipe out domestic high-paying jobs and create offshore kingdoms in tax havens or low-wage nations.
- Most small businesses don't even make use of the limited liability provisions of corporate law: Banks and venture capitalists almost always demand that a small business *owner*—an individual—personally sign for and secure loans and other transactions.

In fact, small and medium-size businesses make little to no use whatsoever of corporate personhood. Eliminating corporate personhood would help them, inasmuch as it could help restore democratic processes, empower local communities in which small businesses are rooted, and give politicians the ability to begin anew to enforce anti-monopoly legislation.

Denying the personhood of the handful of very large corporations who exploit it will allow the passage of laws getting them out of undue influence in politics, which in turn will hinder efforts to influence government to maintain trust and monopoly status. Federal, state, and local governments will be able to enforce laws, if the citizens want, that require corporations to operate to the benefit of the states and communities in which they are incorporated and do business.

This will open millions of doors of opportunity for the entrepreneurial energies and imagination of people all over the world, and could easily create a boom every bit as dramatic as the agricultural revolution, the industrial revolution, or the technological revolution.

23

A DEMOCRATIC MARKETPLACE

The prevalence of the corporation in America has led men of this generation to act, at times, as if the privilege of doing business in corporate form were inherent in the citizen; and has led them to accept the evils attendant upon the free and unrestricted use of the corporate mechanism as if these evils were the inescapable price of civilized life, and, hence, to be borne with resignation.

Throughout the greater part of our history a different view prevailed.

Although the value of this instrumentality in commerce and industry was fully recognized, incorporation for business was commonly denied long after it had been freely granted for religious, educational, and charitable purposes.

It was denied because of fear. Fear of encroachment upon the liberties and opportunities of the individual. Fear of the subjection of labor to capital. Fear of monopoly. Fear that the absorption of capital by corporations, and their perpetual life, might bring evils similar to those which attended mortmain. There was a sense of some insidious menace inherent in large aggregations of capital, particularly when held by corporations.

So at first the corporate privilege was granted sparingly; and only when the grant seemed necessary in order to procure for the community some specific benefit otherwise unattainable.

—U. S. SUPREME COURT JUSTICE LOUIS BRANDEIS, 1933

Although the increasingly unrestrained marketplace that George Soros and Louis Brandeis warn of makes it hard for many companies to emphasize community values, some still do. Others are recognizing the need to respond to human demands for a cleaner, safer, less toxic world.

Additionally, many people are fortunate enough to work in an industry they love, and the love of railroads or automobiles or flying or medicine has motivated the startup and ongoing operation of many of what are now the world's best companies.

In my experience in business, it's the people who care about their industry or area of expertise who are the most likely to be successful. And companies with mission statements and standards of behavior that let people ethically live out their passions can be wonderful places to work.

As people take back control of their governments and begin to again regulate how far businesses can go, the vast majority of ethical and appropriately run corporations can begin to operate in ways that are more long-term and more community oriented.

REVOKING CORPORATE CHARTERS IS NOT AT ALL NEW

The process of revoking corporate charters goes back to the very first years of the United States. Beginning in 1784 (4 years before the U. S. Constitution was ratified), Pennsylvania demanded that corporations include a revocation clause in corporate charters.

As the United States grew, laws were passed requiring revocation clauses in the corporate charters (permissions) of insurance companies in 1809 and banks in 1814. From the founding of America to the late 1800s, governments routinely revoked corporate charters, forcing liquidation and sale of assets. Banks were shut down for behaving in a "financially unsound" way in Ohio, Mississippi, and Pennsylvania. And when corporations that ran the turnpikes in New York and Massachusetts didn't keep their roads in repair, those states gave the corporations the death sentence.

In 1825, Pennsylvania passed laws making it even easier for that state to "revoke, alter, or annul" corporate charters "whenever in their opinion [the operation of the corporation] may be injurious to citizens of the community," and by the 1870s, 19 states had gone through the long and tedious process of amending their state constitutions expressly to give legislators the power to terminate the existence of corporations that originated in those states.

Presidents have even run for public office and won on platforms including the revocation of corporate charters. One of the largest issues of the election of 1832 was Andrew Jackson's demand that the corporate charter of the Second Bank of the United States not be renewed.

Following his lead, states all over the nation began examining their banks and other corporations, and in just the year 1832, the state of Pennsylvania pulled the corporate charters of 10 corporations, sentencing them to corporate death "for operating contrary to the public interest."

Oil corporations, match manufacturers, whiskey trusts, and sugar corporations all received the corporate death penalty in the late 1800s in Michigan, Ohio, Nebraska, and New York. And when, in 1894, the Central Labor Union of New York City campaigned for the New York state supreme court to revoke the charter of Standard Oil Trust of New York for "a pattern of abuses," the court agreed and dissolved the company.

It was the beginning of a bandwagon that only ended, for all practical purposes, with the election of President Warren G. Harding in 1921 with his promise to have "less government in business and more business in government."

LEGISLATIVE REMEDIES

Whether the threat is one of economic penalty, regulation, or even dissolution, the fact is that laws do change corporate behavior. For example, literally millions of corporate decisions are made daily around the world in response to tax laws. In Germany, where a government-imposed energy tax causes oil and gasoline to cost more than twice what it does in the United States, industry is roughly twice as energy-efficient as American companies and with significantly lower toxic and atmosphere-destabilizing discharges as a result. When the three-martini lunch became no longer deductible under U. S. tax law, most American companies changed their guidelines for employee behaviors and reimbursements.

Thus, if humans were to again decide that they wanted corporations to behave in a way that protected the living environment that sustains all life forms (including humans), we could indeed pass laws making it unprofitable or dangerous for corporations to do otherwise. Taking it a step further, we could even pass laws that give corporations incentives to actively help the environment.

With the end of corporate personhood, it will be possible for the humans of the United States and every nation in the world to define the terms of a new economy. With natural persons once again in charge of government, we can redefine the rules of business so that corporations are profitable when their actions lead to sustainability and a clean environment, respond to values defined by local communities, and promote and develop renewable forms of energy. We can strip out the strings and harnesses put into regulatory law by corporate lobbyists so that the government agencies charged with protecting us from malefactors and criminals can once again work.

ELIMINATING THE CORPORATE PERSONHOOD BARRIER

Once corporate personhood is eliminated and corporations are again seen as they really are—the fictitious legal creatures of the states that authorized and created them—all this can change. The rightful representatives of humans—our governments—can then pass laws like the ones that were once part of this nation and its states, forbidding corporations from attempting to influence the laws and regulatory agencies that oversee their activities.

As stated in the Wisconsin law that stood until it was finally noticed and struck down in 1953, "No corporation doing business in this state, shall pay or contribute, or offer, consent or agree to pay or contribute, directly or indirectly, any money, property, free service of its officers or employees or thing of value to any political party, organization, committee or individual for any political purpose whatsoever, or for the purpose of influencing legislation of any kind, or to promote or defeat the candidacy of any person for nomination, appointment or election to any political office."

RETURNING POLITICAL POWER TO THE PEOPLE

When decisions are made locally, their full range of impacts, including all present and future costs, are more likely to be considered. If a community knows that extracting a mineral from its soil will produce environmental damage, it can require the mining corporation to pay for that damage in advance or as product is extracted, without worrying that because some other community has chosen not to so tax the corporation, they're trampling the "rights" of the corporation under the Fourteenth Amendment's equal protection clause.

Wolfgang Sachs, the German historian and author, noted in an interview with former California governor Jerry Brown that, "Nature has only been minimally present in the market. The market thrives on the fact that nature doesn't cost anything." Except to the local communities who must suffer with the effects of strip-mining, toxic waste, loss of topsoil, and the destruction of local ecosystems.

When corporations are changed from natural person to artificial person status, then the natural persons who live in these regions can begin to legislatively regulate the actions of any corporation that seeks to exploit their local part of nature.

Once again in America, as Thomas Jefferson hoped would always be the case, "the people, being the only safe depository of power, should exercise in person every function which their qualifications enable them to exercise, consistently with the order and security of society."

DEMOCRACY IN THE GLOBAL MARKETPLACE

On January 20, 1949, President Harry Truman in his inaugural address committed the United States to helping lift much of the world out of poverty. It was the first time a national leader had used the word "development" to describe a national goal outside the United States, or "undeveloped" to describe what we now call the Third World. Truman was quite clear and specific about his vision.

"We must embark on a bold new program for making the benefits of our scientific advances and industrial progress available for the improvement and growth of underdeveloped areas," he said. "More than half the people of the world are living in conditions approaching misery. Their food is inadequate. They are victims of disease. Their economic life is primitive and stagnant. Their poverty is a handicap and a threat both to them and to more prosperous areas."

Pointing out that the United States had the resources and knowledge to help lift people around the world out of poverty and misery, Truman demanded that corporations who had an eye to exploiting the Third World be restrained. He said, "The old imperialism—exploitation for foreign profit—has no place in our plans."

Instead, he added, the poorer people of the world must have the ability to determine their own fates and control for themselves the extent of our companies' participation in their nations as well as the extent of their own development. "Democracy alone can supply the vitalizing force to stir the peoples of the world into triumphant action," Truman said, "not only against their human oppressors, but also against their ancient enemies—hunger, misery, and despair."

The role of government is to protect, defend, and represent the interests of its own people, he said. "Democracy maintains that government is established for the benefit of the individual, and is charged with the responsibility of protecting the rights of the individual and his freedom in the exercise of his abilities." Citing Locke's concept of Natural Rights, he added, "Democracy is based on the conviction that man has the moral and intellectual capacity, as well as the inalienable right, to govern himself with reason and justice."

Truman's vision was a challenge to the *Santa Clara* decision, but NAFTA, GATT, WTO and fast-track authority have sidetracked it. Ending corporate personhood would allow communities to correct this situation and empower them to enforce clean and ethical corporate behavior.

24

RESTORING THE GLOBAL DREAM OF GOVERNMENT OF, BY, AND FOR THE PEOPLE

All constitutions, those of the States no less than that of the nation, are designed, and must be interpreted and administered so as to fit human rights.

—THEODORE ROOSEVELT, IN A SPEECH GIVEN ON FEBRUARY 12, 1912

Thomas Paine said it best. "It has been thought," he wrote in *The Rights of Man* in 1791, ". . . that government is a compact between those who govern and those who are governed; but this cannot be true, because it is putting the effect before the cause; for as man must have existed before governments existed, there necessarily was a time when governments did not exist, and consequently there could originally exist no governors to form such a compact with. The fact therefore must be, that the *individuals themselves*, each in his own personal and sovereign right, *entered into a compact with each other* to produce a government: and this is the only mode in which governments have a right to arise, and the only principle on which they have a right to exist."

Every culture and every religion of what we call the civilized world carries, in one form or another, a mythos or story about a time in the past or future when humans lived or will live in peace and harmony. Whether it's referred to as Valhalla or Eden, Shambhala or A Thousand Years of Peace, the *Satya Yuga* or *Jannat*, stories of past or coming times of paradise go hand-in-hand with hierarchical cultures.

Such prophecies were clearly in the minds of America's Founders when they first discussed integrating Greek ideas of democracy, Roman notions of a republic, Masonic utopian ideals, and the Iroquois Federation's constitutionally organized egalitarian society, which was known to Jefferson, Washington, Adams, and Franklin. The creation of the United States of America brought into the world a dramatic new experiment in how people could live together in a modern state.

While most of the rest of the world watched this new experimental democracy with skepticism, the citizens of France took our revolution to heart and initiated the French Revolution just 6 years after ours ended.

America grew swiftly and steadily for nearly a century, and many other countries of the world began to experiment with their own versions of democracy. As America was convulsed by the Civil War, the world held its breath, but America remained intact and the period of industrialization following the war led to one of the most rapid periods of worldwide growth in history. This growth cemented for the world the concept of the American ideal, as millions escaped their homelands to settle in the new "land of opportunity and freedom."

AMERICAN DEMOCRACY IS THE MODEL FOR THE GLOBAL DREAM

Thus, America has come to represent the world's archetypal concept of freedom and egalitarianism. On May 29th, 1989, 20,000 people gathered around a 37-foot-tall statue in Beijing's Tiananmen Square. They placed their lives in danger, but that statue was such a powerful representation that many were willing to die for it . . . and some did. They called their statue the Goddess of Democracy: It was a scale replica of the Statue of Liberty that stands in New York harbor on Liberty Island.

From the French Revolution in 1789 to the people's uprising in Beijing in 1989, people around the world have used language and icons borrowed from the pen of Thomas Jefferson and his peers. Even if we didn't implement it fully in our early efforts, and even if it's been strained since its inception, the Greek-Roman-Masonic-Iroquois-American idea of a government "deriving its just Powers from the Consent of the Governed" is probably one of the most powerful and timeless ideas in the world today. It is the Global Dream.

While there are pockets of those in the world who hate us and even foist terrorist acts upon us, there are billions more who desperately wish to embrace the principles upon which our nation was founded. We in the United States of America hold a sacred archetype for the world: the Dream of freedom and individual liberty. Can we reclaim the Global Dream in the land of its birth? I believe we still can:

- In the last century, a citizen-led effort resulted in passage and ratification of the Nineteenth Amendment, guaranteeing women the right to vote—despite long tradition and past court decisions.
- Similar efforts led to constitutional amendments banning, and then rescinding the ban on, alcohol.
- Most recently, the Twenty-Sixth Amendment lowering the voting age from 21 to 18 was ratified, in part in response to demands from servicemen and women in Vietnam and veterans of that war. And a popular protest song, "The Eve of Destruction," was a prominent voice for this popular sentiment, saying, "You're old enough to kill, but not for votin'."

In each of these cases, citizens spoke out and the Constitution was changed. Today, a growing movement has begun in the United States to bring back the Global Dream, restoring *human* personhood to its rightful place at the top of the priority sheet. For example, on April 25, 2000, the city of Point Arena, California, passed a City Council Resolution On Corporate Personhood, "rejecting the notion of corporate personhood," in which they "urge other cities to foster similar public discussion" on the issue.

RESTORING JEFFERSON'S DREAM

The Dream of egalitarian democracy in America was taken captive, but it lives on. Today, the captivity is so obvious that as the 21st century began, people protested in Seattle and Genoa, facing police beatings to register their hope that the Dream be reawakened. They faced risks similar to those faced by the Americans who stood up against tyranny at the Boston Tea Party.

Presidents warned us, and the railroads fought their restrictions for decades. The Dream was finally, formally stolen in 1886 when U. S. Supreme Court reporter J. C. Bancroft Davis wrote that Chief Justice Waite had said, "Corporations are persons," and courts read his headnotes as if they were a Supreme Court ruling, changing the course of world history.

It seems especially ironic that the whole premise of the founding of this country was that "all Men are created equal," and companies have sought protection on that premise; yet in reality, the words of William Jennings Bryan are far more accurate: Men are indeed fairly equivalent, but a company can be a million times more powerful.

Equal protection was designed to protect the disenfranchised, not to further empower the mighty. We can right the wrong; we can balance the scales; we can write new laws. We can restore the intent of the Constitution's authors by declaring that these protections apply to *natural persons*, and in so doing, begin the process of restoring and reinvigorating the world's democracies.

25

OUR FIRST STEPS FORWARD

It is rather for us to be here dedicated to the great task remaining before us . . . that we here highly resolve that these dead shall not have died in vain—that this nation, under God, shall have a new birth of freedom—and that government of the people, by the people, for the people, shall not perish from the earth.

—ABRAHAM LINCOLN, FROM THE GETTYSBURG ADDRESS, NOVEMBER 19, 1863

When I first shared my concept for this book with a noted—and friendly—constitutional scholar, he replied in an e-mail that he'd had to pick himself up from the floor over the shock that anybody would seriously propose laws and constitutional amendments to correct the current situation. I hope that he has come around to seeing the possibilities, as he and many others—across the political spectrum—now agree that there is a very real crisis in the political, financial, and business structure of the developed world, and that it is rapidly spreading across the world.

As in the story of the Emperor's New Clothes, we've recently discovered we have a problem. The belief in so-called "free markets" has reached a near-religious frenzy, particularly in the press, while corporations greenwash and bluewash themselves with advertisements extolling their commitment to nature and community. But corporations were not created as institutions of environmental preservation or social justice, nor are they true agents of either free markets or democracy: They are legal devices to accumulate wealth, pure and simple.

As law professor Lawrence Mitchell noted earlier, "The entire proposition that a corporation is a person is ridiculous." And if they are not people? He says, "If they are not people, then we should take them out of the political process."

As Richard Cohen noted in a January 21, 2002 article in the *Washington Post* about the Enron debacle, "What we have here is a an updated form of feudalism."

And like the feudal systems that held Europe, Asia, South America, and Japan in their grip for centuries, this new feudalism isn't going to easily submit to transformation or simply morph back into the representative republican democracy from which it emerged and has now largely taken over.

Instead, it will fight back, and if Alexis de Tocqueville was right, the main tool it will use will be the media it owns or has easy access to with its advertising and P. R. dollars, keeping people passively lulled into the twin beliefs that they are powerless, and that the world's largest corporations do know, after all, how to run the planet and therefore everything is just fine and there's no need to worry about or do anything.

But no matter how much they try to convince us that "global warming is a good thing" or "toxic sludge is good for you," humans *know*. We've figured out that the ideals and dreams of Jefferson and Madison, Washington and Adams—even allowing for their differences—have been stolen.

Abraham Lincoln well understood the stakes. Standing in the same room where Jefferson's Declaration of Independence was read and signed, he said that the American Revolution "was not the mere matter of separation of the colonies from the motherland, but of that sentiment in the Declaration of Independence, which gave liberty not alone to the people of this country, but hope to all the world, for all future time. It was that which gave promise that in due time the weights would be lifted from the shoulders of all men, and that all should have an equal chance. This is the sentiment embodied in the Declaration of Independence. . . . I would rather be assassinated on this spot than surrender it."

SUCCESSFUL GRASSROOTS MOVEMENTS

Article V of the United States Constitution says that a constitutional amendment may be offered to the states for approval when it's been approved by two-thirds of both the House and the Senate, or submitted to the Congress by two-thirds of the states. In order to become law and actually amend the Constitution, three-quarters of the states must then approve, or ratify, the amendment. Those two-thirds and three-quarters thresholds have proven a substantial (and intentional) obstacle to changing the Constitution of the United States.

As of this writing, the most recent successful amendment to the Constitution became law in 1992, an amendment to ensure that when legislators vote themselves a pay raise, the benefits of it aren't enjoyed until after the next election cycle. Over 18,000 amendments have been proposed in Congress, but since 1789, only 33 have emerged with the required two-thirds majority of both the House of Representatives and the Senate (or submitted by the states) to be passed along to the states for ratification. Of those 33, only 27 have been ratified into law by three-quarters of the states.

As with nearly all social movements, most of these started at a grassroots level and grew from there. People passed or defied laws on a local level that produced echoes all the way up to the federal legislature or Supreme Court. The effort to again put people first in America and the rest of the free world will, no doubt, work the same way. As anthropologist Margaret Mead said, "Never doubt that a small group of thoughtful, committed citizens can change the world. Indeed, it is the only thing that ever has."

Nonetheless, it won't be rapid or easy. Consider the history of another group who set out to establish equality in America: women of the Revolutionary era, and their successors.

WOMEN AMEND THE CONSTITUTION

The history of the women's rights movement, like that of the civil rights movement, is complex and well beyond the scope of this book, but it claimed its first major victory in 1920 with the passage of the Nineteenth Amendment, which gave women the right to vote.

But that was just the beginning. A hundred and one years after Susan B. Anthony was arrested for casting a vote, the U. S. Supreme Court referenced the Fourteenth Amendment a total of 17 times regarding people in the 1973 *Roe v. Wade* case, as they finally decided that men don't have the power to control the behaviors of women. That decision, combined with broad changes in public sentiment and corporate behavior, effectively overturned the 1873 *Bradwell v. State* Supreme Court decision which had said that "the Law of the Creator" defined the "paramount destiny and mission" of women as limited to "the noble and benign offices of wife and mother."

The process began with a small group of dedicated people, and America and the world are the better for it, even as the women's rights movement continues to work for *full* equality in the United States and recognition in those nations where women are still in slavery under religious law or male-dominated dictatorships.

OTHER HUMAN RIGHTS MOVEMENTS

As Martin Luther King and Mohandas Gandhi well understood, changing laws is a process that requires enormous and broad grassroots support. Recent events have shocked and awakened many of the people of the world, and expressions of a desire for change—from riots at WTO meetings to tectonic shifts in the politics of nations—are increasingly obvious.

But many of these efforts to protest globalization or poverty or corporate crimes are less than effective because they attack the symptoms of the problem rather than its cause. The new feudalism is not the result of bad people or even of bad corporations. It's the result of a structure that's broken down; a system of laws put in place in the United States and other nations in the late 1700s and early 1800s that had controlled the size, power, and political influence of the newly emerging business corporations were thrown aside by the pen of J. C. Bancroft Davis in 1886. At its core, it's the result of a dysfunctional cultural story—that corporations are persons—and that is the level at which it must be healed.

Our best hope for changing the current situation of the world is in restoring the story and vision of Jefferson and Madison—that corporations (and governments and *all* institutions) are subservient to the will of "we, the people." Restoring the control mechanism for this—effectively struck down in the *Santa Clara* ruling—means changing our laws and, ultimately, probably will require amending our Constitution.

THEN THE BIG WORK BEGINS

Once corporations are again under the authority of "we, the people" who sanctioned their formation, the real work begins as a whole realm of issues will become truly open for honest and vigorous debate.

The entire spectrum of human issues that humans should discuss with the governments they have empowered to represent them will once again be open for debate: This is the really vital work that must be done, but cannot be freely done until *Santa Clara* is reversed, whether by Supreme Court decree or by citizens joining together to replace the word "persons" in the Fourteenth Amendment with the phrase "natural persons." Because *Santa Clara* and its derivatives have been with us for over a century, correcting it won't instantly change common and case law, but it will provide a basis for us to begin making the changes that could re-invigorate both democracy and free enterprise. And not just in the United States, but across the world in the many nations where democracies thrive.

HEALING THE WORLD

As America goes, to a large extent so goes the world, and it's been that way ever since France followed the American colonists by just 6 years in revolting against royal institutions that denied human rights to all individuals and reserved them for the rich and powerful.

Alastair McIntosh, a Fellow of Edinburgh, Scotland's, Centre for Human Ecology, points out on his Web site that a multinational corporation recently demanded protection from Scotland's Court of Session (the Scottish Supreme Court), claiming Article 6 of the European Convention of Human Rights.

"Mammon [material wealth] got up in court and claimed human attributes," McIntosh writes. "It makes instant mockery of our new human rights protection." He points out that the trend of corporations claiming human rights "can be traced across the Atlantic to the case of *Santa Clara County v. Southern Pacific Railroad, 1886.*"

While the exact language of the laws proposed at the end of this book may not be applicable in all nations that claim democratic principles, similar ones can be passed. It is my hope that this book will inspire people across the world to come up with their own, appropriate language and begin the process of local and national legislative reform in their own nations.

As with the Twenty-Sixth Amendment (giving 18-year-olds the right to vote), we may get lucky. It could be that so many people are motivated to restore the balance to public discourse that change will happen quickly.

FEW QUICK FIXES

On the other hand, the process will most likely take time, and be fraught with dispute and unintended consequences. Who could have guessed, for example, that a constitutional amendment to free the slaves would end up empowering corporations?

When I was very young, I first discovered the writings of Thomas Jefferson. It was about the same time I was reading Henry David Thoreau and Ralph Waldo Emerson, and entranced with the thoughts of the Transcendentalist movement in early America. I was touched by Thoreau's vision of the natural world, Emerson's notions about an understanding of the eternal, and Jefferson's romance with the idealisms of his Saxon ancestors; the idealism of all three seemed made of the same cloth.

As Emerson said in 1842, "The light is always identical in its composition, but it falls on a great variety of objects, and by so falling is first revealed to us, not in its own form, for it is formless, but in theirs; in like manner, thought only appears in the objects it classifies."

LET US BEGIN . . .

I'm convinced that the light of idealism and hope is within all of us. In some, it shines as the noble desire to build institutions that may both help humanity and enrich the helpers; a desire that, it seems, sometimes extends beyond prudence. In others, it shines as the light of a passion to protect loved ones or the natural world of which we are a part.

Addressing the conflict between these two, Emerson added, "Amidst the downward tendency and proneness of things, when every voice is raised for a new road or another statute, or a subscription of stock, for an improvement in dress, or in dentistry, for a new house or a larger business, for a political party, or the division of an estate,—will you not tolerate one or two solitary voices in the land, speaking for thoughts and principles not marketable or perishable?"

As Delphin M. Delmas reminds us in his impassioned 1901 defense of the California redwoods, and Gilgamesh's 6,000-year-old ghost tells us in his tale of weather changes and the destruction of a civilization by commercial practices, this is not a new debate. These are, to again quote Emerson, "but the very oldest of thoughts cast into the mould of these new times."

Rescinding corporate personhood is the first step toward a larger vision of reclaiming and reinvigorating democracy around the world. It is a noble effort, but not the only effort. It is a start, not an end. And if we are to respond usefully to its challenges and to its perhaps unintended consequences, we must do so in the context of the larger vision of egalitarian society and the principles upon which the first democratic republics were founded.

As John F. Kennedy said about the ambitious goals he set for his new administration, "All this will not be finished in the first 100 days. Nor will it be finished in the first 1,000 days, nor in the life of this Administration, nor even perhaps in our lifetime on this planet. But let us begin."

POSTSCRIPT: A MESSAGE FROM A PRESIDENT OF THE UNITED STATES

"That very word freedom, in itself and of necessity, suggests freedom from some restraining power. In 1776 we sought freedom from the tyranny of a political autocracy—from the eighteenth-century royalists who held special privileges from the crown. It was to perpetuate their privilege that they governed without the consent of the governed; that they denied the right of free assembly and free speech; that they restricted the worship of God; that they put the average man's property and the average man's life in pawn to the mercenaries of dynastic power; that they regimented the people.

"And so it was to win freedom from the tyranny of political autocracy that the American Revolution was fought. That victory gave the business of governing into the hands of the average man, who won the right with his neighbors to make and order his own destiny through his own government. Political tyranny was wiped out at Philadelphia on July 4, 1776.

"Since that struggle, however, man's inventive genius released new forces in our land which reordered the lives of our people. The age of machinery, of railroads; of steam and electricity; the telegraph and the radio; mass production, mass distribution—all of these combined to bring forward a new civilization and with it a new problem for those who sought to remain free.

"For out of this modern civilization economic royalists carved new dynasties. New kingdoms were built upon concentration of control over material things. Through new uses of corporations, banks and securities, new machinery of industry and agriculture, of labor and capital—all undreamed of by the Fathers—the whole structure of modern life was impressed into this royal service.

"There was no place among this royalty for our many thousands of small-businessmen and merchants who sought to make a worthy use of the American system of initiative and profit. They were no more free than the worker or the farmer. Even honest and progressive-minded men of wealth, aware of their obligation to their generation, could never know just where they fitted into this dynastic scheme of things.

"It was natural and perhaps human that the privileged princes of these new economic dynasties, thirsting for power, reached out for control over government itself. They created a new despotism and wrapped it in the robes of legal sanction. In its service new mercenaries sought to regiment the people, their labor, and their property. And as a result the average man once more confronts the problem that faced the Minute Man.

"The hours men and women worked, the wages they received, the conditions of their labor—these had passed beyond the control of the people, and were imposed by this new industrial dictatorship. The savings of the average family, the capital of the small-businessmen, the investments set aside for old age—other people's money—these were tools which the new economic royalty used to dig itself in.

"Those who tilled the soil no longer reaped the rewards which were their right. The small measure of their gains was decreed by men in distant cities.

"Throughout the nation, opportunity was limited by monopoly. Individual initiative was crushed in the cogs of a great machine. The field open for free business was more and more restricted. Private enterprise, indeed, became too private. It became privileged enterprise, not free enterprise.

"An old English judge once said: 'Necessitous men are not free men.' Liberty requires opportunity to make a living—a living decent according to the standard of the time, a living which gives man not only enough to live by, but something to live for.

"For too many of us the political equality we once had won was meaningless in the face of economic inequality. A small group had concentrated into their own hands an almost complete control over other people's property, other people's money, other people's labor—other people's lives. For too many of us life was no longer free; liberty no longer real; men could no longer follow the pursuit of happiness.

"Against economic tyranny such as this, the American citizen could appeal only to the organized power of government. The collapse of 1929 showed up the despotism for what it was. The election of 1932 was the people's mandate to end it. Under that mandate it is being ended.

"The royalists of the economic order have conceded that political freedom was the business of the government, but they have maintained that economic slavery was nobody's business. They granted that the government could protect the citizen in his right to vote, but they denied that the government could do anything to protect the citizen in his right to work and his right to live.

"Today we stand committed to the proposition that freedom is no half-and-half affair. If the average citizen is guaranteed equal opportunity in the polling place, he must have equal opportunity in the market place.

"These economic royalists complain that we seek to overthrow the institutions of America. What they really complain of is that we seek to take away their power. Our allegiance to American institutions requires the overthrow of this kind of power. In vain they seek to hide behind the flag and the Constitution. In their blindness they forget what the flag and the Constitution stand for. Now, as always, they stand for democracy, not tyranny; for freedom, not subjection; and against a dictatorship by mob rule and the over-privileged alike.

"The brave and clear platform adopted by this convention, to which I heartily subscribe, sets forth that government in a modern civilization has certain inescapable obligations to its citizens, among which are protection of the family and the home, the establishment of a democracy of opportunity, and aid to those overtaken by disaster.

"But the resolute enemy within our gates is ever ready to beat down our words unless in greater courage we will fight for them.

"For more than three years we have fought for them. This convention, in every word and deed, has pledged that the fight will go on.

"The defeats and victories of these years have given to us as a people a new understanding of our government and of ourselves. Never since the early days of the New England town meeting have the affairs of government been so widely discussed and so clearly appreciated. It has been brought home to us that the only effective guide for the safety of this most worldly of worlds, the greatest guide of all, is moral principle.

"We do not see faith, hope, and charity as unattainable ideals, but we use them as stout supports of a nation fighting the fight for freedom in a modern civilization.

"Faith—in the soundness of democracy in the midst of dictatorships.

"Hope—renewed because we know so well the progress we have made.

"Charity—in the true spirit of that grand old word. For charity literally translated from the original means love, the love that understands, that does not merely share the wealth of the giver, but in true sympathy and wisdom helps men to help themselves.

"We seek not merely to make government a mechanical implement, but to give it the vibrant personal character that is the very embodiment of human charity.

"We are poor indeed if this nation cannot afford to lift from every recess of American life the dread fear of the unemployed that they are not needed in the world. We cannot afford to accumulate a deficit in the books of human fortitude.

"In the place of the palace of privilege we seek to build a temple out of faith and hope and charity.

"It is a sobering thing, my friends, to be a servant of this great cause. We try in our daily work to remember that the cause belongs not to us, but to the people. The standard is not in the hands of you and me alone. It is carried by America. We seek daily to profit from experience, to learn to do better as our task proceeds.

"Governments can err, presidents do make mistakes, but the immortal Dante tells us that Divine justice weighs the sins of the cold-blooded and the sins of the warm-hearted on different scales.

"Better the occasional faults of a government that lives in a spirit of charity than the consistent omissions of a government frozen in the ice of its own indifference.

"There is a mysterious cycle in human events. To some generations much is given. Of other generations much is expected. This generation of Americans has a rendezvous with destiny.

"In this world of ours in other lands, there are some people, who, in times past, have lived and fought for freedom, and seem to have grown too weary to carry on the fight. They have sold their heritage of freedom for the illusion of a living. They have yielded their democracy.

"I believe in my heart that only our success can stir their ancient hope. They begin to know that here in America we are waging a great and successful war. It is not alone a war against want and destitution and economic demoralization. It is more than that; it is a war for the survival of democracy.

We are fighting to save a great and precious form of government for ourselves and for the world.

"I accept the commission you have tendered me. I join with you. I am enlisted for the duration of the war."

—Franklin Delano Roosevelt
Acceptance speech for the Democratic nomination for President
Philadelphia—June 27, 1936

PASSING A RESOLUTION TO EDUCATE YOUR COMMUNITY ABOUT CORPORATE PERSONHOOD

While passing a law to ban corporate personhood may seem the most direct way to take on the issue, it may not be the most rapid or the best for your community, at least in the beginning. First, it's necessary to educate a community, and passing a non-binding resolution (instead of a binding law/ordinance) can do just that. Although it won't have the force of law, it begins the process of change because proposing and campaigning for it will educate the voters in your community. The other benefit of passing a resolution is that it won't draw legal fire from corporations, who can challenge an ordinance and engage a community in costly litigation.

Beginning with a resolution as an educational effort is important because change movements always work from the bottom up, not the top down. Leaders and elected officials usually don't just wake up one day and change: Citizens push them to do so. This is how it worked with the abolition and suffrage movements, among others: Books, articles, and editorials were written; citizens' groups formed; political parties eventually staked out positions; communities passed resolutions and laws, and worked for constitutional amendments; and court cases wound their way to the Supreme Court.

Thus, if the United States is to end corporate rule and move toward a modern version of the republican democracy envisioned by the Founders, the process will almost certainly flow from the bottom up. As the issue becomes more and more visible, eventually either the Supreme Court will reverse their clerk's error of 1886—the way in 1954 and 1973 they reversed their errors of 1896 and 1873, finally declaring that freed slaves and women are now "persons" under the law—or the States or Congress will take up the issue.

Whichever way the process of returning corporations to their former status ultimately happens, it'll only come about when a critical mass of the electorate realizes it's an issue.

To that end, an example of one of the most effective tools for educating people is what the town of Point Arena, California, did in the year 2000. Instead of passing an ordinance or law, the city council passed a resolution declaring that the City of Point Arena didn't think corporations were persons. The process took well over a year and was hotly debated in the town; as a result, today there is a high level of awareness about the corporate personhood issue in this part of northern California. Even though the resolution didn't have the force of law, it was a tremendously successful educational process, and, thus, may represent the best place for a local community to start.

Here's the text of the final draft of the resolution passed on a 4-to-1 vote by Point Arena's City Council on April 25, 2000:

Resolution on Corporate Personhood in the City of Point Arena, California

Whereas,

- *Citizens of the City of Point Arena hope to nurture and expand democracy in our community and our nation.*
- *Democracy means governance by the people. Only natural persons should be able to participate in the democratic process.*
- *Interference in the democratic process by corporations frequently usurps the rights of citizens to govern.*
- *Corporations are artificial entities separate and apart from natural persons. Corporations are not naturally endowed with consciousness or the rights of natural persons. Corporations are creations of law and are only permitted to do what is authorized under law.*
- *Rejecting the concept of corporate personhood will advance meaningful campaign finance reform.*

Therefore be it hereby resolved that:

The City of Point Arena agrees with Supreme Court Justice Hugo Black in his 1938 opinion in which he stated, "I do not believe the word 'person' in the 14th Amendment includes corporations."

Be it further resolved that:

The City of Point Arena shall encourage public discussion on the role of corporations in public life and urge other cities to foster similar public discussion.

The original resolution proposed to the city council was much longer and had some great language about democracy and corporate rule, but was eventually pared down to the lean version you see above. (The original is online at www.iiipublishing.com/alliance.htm) It's a marvelous template for something you may want to propose or pass in your community.

MODEL ORDINANCES TO RESCIND CORPORATE PERSONHOOD

Attorneys Daniel Brannen and Thomas Linzey drafted the following model ordinance for this book, and directions for its use. It's customized to one particular township, so you can see where and how to fill in the bolded text ordinance with your local information.

In our correspondence, Brannen noted, "You asked how a municipality can overrule the Supreme Court. Municipalities are not going to be overruling the Supreme Court with this ordinance. Rather, they are going to be giving the Supreme Court an opportunity to correct a legally incorrect ruling *(Santa Clara)*. That's the way constitutional jurisprudence develops. For a long time, the Supreme Court sanctioned the concept of separate but equal facilities. Eventually the Supreme Court overruled this concept, but it took local action to get a case before the Court to give it a chance to correct itself."

An ordinance by the Supervisors of Haines Township, Centre County, Pennsylvania eliminating constitutional privileges from corporations doing business within the Township

Section 1. Name. The name of this Ordinance shall be the "Corporate Privilege Elimination and Democracy Protection Ordinance."

Section 2. Authority. This Ordinance is adopted and enacted pursuant to the authority granted to the Township by all relevant state and federal laws, including, but not limited to, the following:

The general authority granted by the Constitution of **Pennsylvania** and the **Second Class Township Code** to make and adopt all such ordinances, bylaws, rules, and regulations as may be deemed expedient or necessary for the proper management, care, and control of the Township and its finances and the maintenance of the health, safety, peace, good government, and welfare of the Township.

The Constitution of Pennsylvania, Art. 1, § 2, which provides that all power is inherent in the people, and that all free governments are founded on their authority and instituted for their peace, safety, and happiness.

The Constitution of Pennsylvania, Art. 9, § 2, which provides that a municipality that has a home rule charter may exercise any power or perform any function not denied by the Constitution, charter, or General Assembly.

The Pennsylvania Statutes, Tit. 53, Municipal and Quasi-Municipal Corporations, § 66506, which empowers the board of supervisors of second class townships to make and adopt any ordinances, bylaws, rules, and regulations necessary for the proper management, care, and control of the township and its finances and the maintenance of peace, good government, health, and welfare of the township and its citizens.

Section 3. General Purpose. The general purpose of this Ordinance is to recognize that:

(1) A corporation is a legal fiction that is created by the express permission of the people of this Township as citizens of this Commonwealth;

(2) Interpretation of the U. S. Constitution by Supreme Court justices to include corporations in the term "persons" has long wrought havoc with our democratic process by endowing corporations with constitutional privileges originally intended solely to protect the citizens of the United States;

(3) This judicial bestowal of civil and political rights upon corporations interferes with the administration of laws within this Township and usurps basic human and constitutional rights exercised by citizens of this Township;

(4) The judicial designation of corporations as "persons" grants corporations the power to sue municipal governments for adopting laws that violate the claimed constitutional rights of corporations;

(5) The judicial designation of corporations as "persons" requires that municipal governments recognize the corporation as a legitimate participant in public hearings, zoning hearing board appeals, and other governmental matters before the municipality;

(6) The judicial designation of corporations as "persons" grants corporations unfettered access to local elections and First Amendment rights that

enable corporations to control public debate on and discussion about important issues;

(7) By virtue of the wealth possessed by corporations, buttressed by these protections of law, corporations enjoy constitutional privileges to an extent beyond the reach of most citizens;

(8) When the **Pennsylvania** legislature knowingly authorizes corporations to do business in this Commonwealth under the current framework of legal protections, the legislature enables corporations to wield their constitutional privileges to interfere with democratic governance within this Township;

(9) Democracy means government by the people. Only citizens of this Township should be able to participate in the democratic process in the Township and enjoy a republican form of government;

(10) Interference by corporations in the democratic process usurps the rights of citizens to participate in the democratic process in the Township and enjoy a republican form of government;

(11) The ability of citizens of this Township to establish rules to protect the health, safety, and welfare of Township residents has been diminished by the exercise of constitutional privileges by corporations.

Section 4. Specific Purpose. The specific purpose of this Ordinance is to eliminate the purported constitutional rights of corporations in order to remedy the harms that corporations cause to the citizens of the Township by exercise of such rights.

Section 5. Statement of Law. Corporations shall not be considered to be "persons" protected by the Constitution of the United States or the Constitution of the **Commonwealth of Pennsylvania** within the Township of **Haines.**

Section 6. Severability. The provisions of this Ordinance are severable. If any section, clause, sentence, part, or provision of the Ordinance shall be held illegal, invalid, or unconstitutional by any court of competent jurisdiction, such decision of the court shall not affect, impair, or invalidate any of the remaining sections, clauses, sentences, parts, or provisions of this Ordinance. It is hereby declared to be the intent of the Supervisors that this Ordinance would have been adopted if such illegal, invalid, or unconstitutional section, clause, sentence, part, or provision had not been included herein.

Section 7. Effective Date. This Ordinance shall be effective immediately upon passage or as soon thereafter as permitted by law.

GUIDANCE FOR CUSTOMIZING THE "CORPORATE PRIVILEGE ELIMINATION AND DEMOCRACY PROTECTION ORDINANCE" BY DANIEL J. BRANNEN JR.

This sample ordinance is one tool for taking democracy away from Corporate America and giving it to the people, who are its founders and rightful keepers. Yet it is only one tool. A single law will not reclaim democracy, as tempting as it is to believe that can be so. Reclaiming democracy requires a long process of education, grassroots organization and activism, and eventually stark change in the way government operates at all levels, local, state, and national. In the end, then, this ordinance is most valuable as a tool to begin that education in your community.

People who want to present this ordinance to their local government can use the table starting on page 299 to customize it. The author of this ordinance and these instructions (attorney Dan Brannen Jr., Of Counsel, Community Environmental Legal Defense Fund) has researched the municipal codes of all 50 states and the District of Columbia to allow customization at the municipal level that will allow greatest coverage. Where possible, this means the table allows customization for adoption at the county level of government. Simply find your state and insert the information pertaining to it into the bolded spots in the sample ordinance. For instance, the information from the second column of the table, Municipality, replaces the word "Township" in the sample. The information from the third column, Code Title, goes in Section 2 to replace the phrase "Second Class Township Code." Finally, the information below the columns, Code Sections, replaces the bolded, indented paragraphs in Section 2 of the sample ordinance. If you live in a state instead of a commonwealth, please change the language in the ordinance to reflect that. Likewise, please change the ordinance if your local municipal officials are called Commissioners, Councilpeople, or some title other than Supervisors.

For the most part, the authority to adopt this ordinance comes from some form of what's called the police power, which is a state's broad authority to legislate for the health, safety, and general welfare of its people. This power comes from the sovereignty of the people and their states as reserved by the Ninth and Tenth Amendments of the U. S. Constitution. In some states, the constitution or the legislature has delegated the police power to counties. Absent a specific delegation of authority to regulate corporations, the police power is the greatest potential source of authority for local government to adopt the ordinance.

In many states, counties have power to act only in specifically delegated areas, such as prison administration, operation of boards of health, and adoption of comprehensive plans. Most of those states have granted the general police power to municipal levels below the county, such as city and township government. For those states, the table usually contains information for customizing the ordinance at the city, town, or township level. Finally, a small number of states seem to have tried to reserve all police power to themselves without delegating any to the municipal levels of government. Adoption of this ordinance in local governments in those states may be the most challenging task of all.

Readers should keep in mind that this table contains the most likely source of power for enacting the corporate personhood ordinance based upon review of the constitution and municipal code of each state. Identifying the source of that power with certainty requires the assistance of an attorney familiar with the constitutional, municipal, and general laws of the state as interpreted by case law. Sometimes, for example, exercise of police powers by a municipality depends upon whether it has adopted what is called a home rule charter. Municipalities that have not adopted such a charter may lack the power listed. Also, municipal law sometimes provides that ordinances adopted by counties do not apply to smaller municipalities therein, or may be superseded by legislation concerning the same subject matter in a smaller municipality. In crafting this sample ordinance, the author has been unable to account for such specifics of local law. Finally, the author and publisher make no representation as to the constitutionality or other legality of this sample ordinance or the customizations below. While the Community Environmental Legal Defense Fund is preparing a model brief for defending the ordinance, there is no guarantee that the brief will succeed in our current systems of government. The ordinance is primarily a tool for beginning the process of education that must fuel the reclamation of democracy in America.

Finally, readers should be aware that the Community Environmental Legal Defense Fund (CELDF) owns the copyright to the sample ordinance on page 294. CELDF hereby waives the copyright only for people who want to copy and circulate the ordinance without financial gain. Readers who want to speak with an attorney about the ordinance may contact Dan Brannen Jr., Of Counsel, CELDF, P. O. Box 345, Aaronsburg, PA 16820. Those who want more information about CELDF may visit its Web site at www.celdf.org.

STATE	MUNICIPALITY	CODE TITLE
Alabama	City or Town	County and Municipal Corporations Code

The Constitution of Alabama of 1901, Article I, § 35, which provides that the sole object and only legitimate end of government is to protect the citizen in the enjoyment of life, liberty, and property.

The Code of Alabama, Section 11-47-117, which gives cities and towns the power to prevent injury or annoyances from anything dangerous or offensive or unwholesome.

The Code of Alabama, Section 11-47-130, which gives cities and towns the power to maintain the health and cleanliness of the city or town within its limits and within the police jurisdiction thereof.

Alaska	First Class Borough	Municipal Government Code

The Constitution of Alaska, Article I, § 2, which provides that all government originates with the people, is founded upon their will only, and is instituted solely for the good of the people as a whole.

Alaska Statutes Tit. 29, Municipal Government, § 29.35.200, which gives first class boroughs the authority to exercise by ordinance on a nonareawide basis any power not otherwise prohibited by law.

Arizona	County	Counties Code

The Constitution of Arizona, Art. 2, § 2, which provides that all political power is inherent in the people, and governments derive their just powers from the consent of the governed, and are established to protect and maintain individual rights.

The Constitution of Arizona, Art. 12, § 6, which provides that charter counties may exercise, if provided by the charter, all powers over local concerns of the county consistent with, and subject to, the constitution and the laws of Arizona.

Arizona Revised Statutes, Tit. 11, § 11-251(17), (21), and (31), which empowers county boards of supervisors to: (1) adopt provisions necessary to preserve the health of the county; (2) make and enforce rules and regulations for the government of its body, the preservation of order, and the transaction of business; and (3) make and enforce all local, police, sanitary and other regulations not in conflict with general law.

Arkansas	City or Town	Local Government Code

The Constitution of Arkansas, Art. 2, § 1, which provides that all political power is inherent in the people and government is instituted for their protection, security, and benefit.

The Arkansas Code of 1987, Tit. 14, Local Government, § 14-54-103(1), which empowers cities and incorporated towns to prevent injury or annoyance within the limits of the municipal corporation from anything dangerous, offensive, or unhealthy.

The Arkansas Code of 1987, Tit. 14, § 14-55-102, which empowers municipal corporations to make bylaws and ordinances, not inconsistent with the laws of Arkansas, that seem necessary to provide for the safety, preserve the health, promote the prosperity, and improve the morals, order, comfort, and convenience of such corporations and the inhabitants thereof.

STATE	MUNICIPALITY	CODE TITLE
California	County or City	Government Code

The Constitution of California, Art. IX, § 2(c)(ii), which provides that every local government shall have power to adopt and amend local laws relating to the government, protection, order, conduct, safety, health, and well-being of persons and property therein.

Colorado	City or Town	Government—Municipal Code

The Colorado Constitution, Art. 2, § 1, which provides that all political power is vested in and derived from the people, and that all government, of right, originates from the people, is founded upon their will only, and is instituted solely for the good of the whole.

Colorado Revised Statutes, Tit. 31, Government—Municipal, § 31-15-103, which empowers municipalities to make ordinances that are necessary and proper to provide for the safety, preserve the health, promote the prosperity, and improve the morals, order, comfort, and convenience of such municipality and the inhabitants thereof.

Colorado Revised Statutes, Tit. 31, Government—Municipal, § 31-15-401(a), (b), (c), which empowers municipalities to pass and enforce all necessary police ordinances, make all regulations which may be necessary or expedient for the promotion of health, and declare what is a nuisance and abate the same.

Colorado Revised Statutes, Tit. 31, Government—Municipal, § 31-15-501(a) and (c), which empowers municipalities to prohibit the carrying on of any business or establishment in an offensive and unwholesome manner and to regulate any business place.

Connecticut	Town, City, or Borough	Municipalities Code

The Constitution of Connecticut of 1965, Art. 1, § 2, which provides that all political power is inherent in the people, and all free governments are founded on their authority, and instituted for their benefit.

Connecticut General Statutes, Tit. 7, Municipalities, § 7-148(c)(7)(E), which empowers all municipalities to define, prohibit, and abate within the municipality all nuisances and causes thereof, and all things detrimental to the health, morals, safety, convenience, and welfare of its inhabitants.

Connecticut General Statutes, Tit. 7, Municipalities, § 7-148(c)(7)(H)(ii), which empowers all municipalities to regulate and prohibit the carrying on within the municipality of any trade, manufacture, business, or profession that is, or may be, so carried on as to become prejudicial to public health, conducive to fraud or cheating, or dangerous to, or constituting an unreasonable annoyance to, those living or owning property in the vicinity.

Connecticut General Statutes, Tit. 7, Municipalities, § 7-148(c)(7)(H)(viii), which empowers all municipalities to preserve the public peace and good order.

Connecticut General Statutes, Tit. 7, Municipalities, § 7-148(c)(7)(H)(xi), which empowers all municipalities to provide for the health of the inhabitants of the municipality and do all things necessary or desirable to secure and promote the public health.

Connecticut General Statutes, Tit. 7, Municipalities, § 7-148(c)(7)(H)(xiii), which empowers all municipalities to protect or promote the peace, safety, good government, and welfare of the municipality and its inhabitants.

Connecticut General Statutes, Tit. 7, Municipalities, § 7-148(c)(8), which empowers all municipalities to provide for the protection and improvement of the environment.

STATE	MUNICIPALITY	CODE TITLE
Delaware	County	Counties Code

Delaware Code, Tit. 9, Counties, §§ 1101, 4110, and 7001, which give New Castle, Kent, and Sussex counties all powers that the General Assembly constitutionally could grant to them and that are not denied by statute.

District of Columbia	District of Columbia	Government Organization Code

District of Columbia Official Code, Tit. 1, Government Organization, §§ 1-102, 1-203.02, and 1-204.04, which empowers the government of the District of Columbia to exercise all powers of a municipal corporation and all legislative power not inconsistent with the Constitution and laws of the United States of America and the provisions of the District of Columbia Official Code.

Florida	County	County Organization Code

The Florida Constitution—1968 Revision, Art. 1, § 1, which provides that all political power is inherent in the people.

The Florida Constitution—1968 Revision, Art. 8, § 1, which provides that counties have all powers of local self-government allowed by law.

Florida Statutes, Tit. XI, County Organization and Intergovernmental Relations, § 125.01(1)(h), which empowers counties to establish, coordinate, and enforce such business regulations as are necessary for the protection of the public.

Florida Statutes, Tit. XI, County Organization and Intergovernmental Relations, § 125.01(1)(w), which empowers counties to do anything not inconsistent with law that is in the common interest of the people of the county.

Georgia	County	Local Government Code

The Georgia Constitution, Art. 1, § 2, ∂ 1, which provides that all government, of right, originates with the people, is founded upon their will only, and is instituted solely for the good of the whole.

The Georgia Constitution, Art. 1, § 2, ∂ 2, which provides that government is instituted for the protection, security, and benefit of the people.

The Georgia Constitution, Art. 9, § 1, ∂ 1, which provides that each county shall be a body corporate and politic with such governing authority and with such powers as are provided in the Constitution and laws of Georgia.

The Georgia Constitution, Art. 9, § 2, ∂ 1, which provides that the governing authority of each county shall have legislative power to adopt clearly reasonable ordinances relating to its affairs and local government.

STATE	MUNICIPALITY	CODE TITLE
Hawaii	County	County Organization Code

The Hawaii Constitution, Art. I, § 1, which provides that all political power of the State of Hawaii is inherent in the people and all government is founded on this authority.

Hawaii's Revised Statutes, Tit. 6, County Organization and Administration, § 46-1.5, which empowers counties to enact ordinances deemed necessary to promote health, life, and property, and to preserve the order and security of the county and its inhabitants on any subject or matter not inconsistent with the intentions of state law.

Idaho	County	Counties and County Law Code

The Constitution of the State of Idaho, Art. I, § 2, which provides that all political power is inherent in the people and that government is instituted for their protection and benefit.

The Idaho Code, Tit. 32, Counties and County Law, § 31-714, which empowers boards of county commissioners to pass all ordinances and rules and make all regulations necessary or proper to provide for the safety, promote the health and prosperity, improve the morals, peace, good order, comfort, and convenience of the county and its inhabitants and for the protection of property therein.

Illinois	County	Counties Code

The Constitution of the State of Illinois of 1970, Art. 7, § 6, which empowers counties that are home rule units to exercise any power and perform any function pertaining to its government and affairs, including, but not limited to, the power to regulate for the protection of the public health, safety, morals, and welfare.

Indiana	County	Local Government Code

The Constitution of the State of Indiana, Art. 1, § 1, which provides that all free governments are founded on the authority of the people and are instituted for their peace, safety, and well-being.

The Indiana Code, Tit. 36, Local Government, §§ 36-1-3-2 and 36-1-3-4, which gives counties all powers that they need for the effective operation of government as to local affairs and all powers necessary or desirable in the conduct of their affairs.

Iowa	County	Local Government Code

The Iowa Constitution, Art. 1, § 2, which provides that all political power is inherent in the people and government is instituted for their protection, security, and benefit.

The Iowa Code, Tit. IX, Local Government, § 331.301, which provides that counties may exercise any power and perform any function it deems appropriate to protect and preserve the rights, privileges, and property of the county or of its residents and to preserve and improve the peace, safety, health, welfare, comfort, and convenience of its residents.

STATE	MUNICIPALITY	CODE TITLE
Kansas	County	Counties and County Officers Code

The Constitution of the State of Kansas, Bill of Rights, § 2, which provides that all political power is inherent in the people and all free governments are founded on their authority and are instituted for their protection and benefit.

The Kansas Statutes, Ch. 19, Counties and County Officers, § 19-101, which empowers counties to do all acts in relation to the concerns of the county necessary to the exercise of its corporate and administrative powers.

The Kansas Statutes, Ch. 19, Counties and County Officers, § 19-101a, which empowers counties to perform all powers of local legislation it deems appropriate.

The Kansas Statutes, Ch. 19, Counties and County Officers, § 19-101c, which provides that the powers granted to counties shall be liberally construed for the purpose of giving to counties the largest measure of self-government.

Kentucky	County	County Government Code

The Constitution of Kentucky, Bill of Rights, § 4, which provides that all power is inherent in the people and that all free governments are founded on their authority and instituted for their peace, safety, happiness, and the protection of property.

The Kentucky Revised Statutes, Tit. IX, Counties, Cities, and Other Local Units, § 67.083(3)(a), which empowers counties to enact ordinances to control and abate public nuisances.

The Kentucky Revised Statutes, Tit. IX, Counties, Cities, and Other Local Units, § 67.083(3)(m), which empowers counties to enact ordinance to regulate commerce for the protection and convenience of the public.

Louisiana	Parish	Municipalities and Parishes Code

The Constitution of the State of Louisiana, Art. 1, § 1, which provides that all government, of right, is instituted to protect the rights of the individual and the good of the whole, and that government's only legitimate ends are to secure justice for all, preserve peace, and protect the rights and promote the happiness and general welfare of the people.

The Constitution of the State of Louisiana, Art. 6, § 5, which provides that parishes may, in their home rule charters, provide for the exercise of any power and performance of any function necessary, requisite, or proper for the management of its affairs.

Maine	City or Town	Municipalities and Counties Code

The Constitution of Maine, Art. 1, § 2, which provides that all power is inherent in the people and all free governments are founded in their authority and instituted for their benefit.

The Constitution of Maine, Art. VIII, Pt. 2, § 1, which provides that the people of all municipalities have the power to alter and amend their charters on all matters not prohibited by the Constitution or general law that are local and municipal in character.

STATE	MUNICIPALITY	CODE TITLE
Maine—cont.		

The Maine Revised Statutes, Tit. 30-A, Municipalities and Counties, § 3001, which empowers all municipalities to adopt ordinances to exercise any power or function that the Legislature has power to confer upon the municipality.

Maryland	Town, Village, or other Municipality	Corporations—Municipal Code

The Constitution of Maryland, Declaration of Rights, Art. 1, which provides that all government of right originates from the people and is instituted solely for the good of the whole.

The Code of the Public General Laws of Maryland, Art. 23A, § 2, which gives incorporated municipalities general power to pass such ordinances as they deem necessary in order to assure the good government of the municipality, to protect and preserve the municipality's rights, property, and privileges, to preserve peace and good order, to secure persons and property from danger and destruction, and to protect the health, comfort, and convenience of the citizens of the municipality.

Massachusetts	City or Town	Cities, Towns, and Districts Code

The Constitution of the Commonwealth of Massachusetts, Pt. 1, Art. 1, which provides that government is instituted for the common good, for the protection, safety, prosperity, and happiness of the people, and not for the profit, honor, or private interest of any one man, family, or class of men.

The Constitution of the Commonwealth of Massachusetts, Amend. Art. 2, § 6, which empowers cities and towns to adopt local ordinances and exercise any power and function that the general court has power to confer upon it.

Massachusetts General Laws, Tit. VI, Counties and County Officers, Ch. 34A, § 16, which provides that cities and towns are the broad repository of local police power in terms of the right and power to legislate for the general health, safety, and welfare of their residents.

Michigan	Township	Townships Code

The Michigan Constitution of 1963, Art. 1, § 1, which provides that all political power is inherent in the people and that government is instituted for their equal benefit, security, and protection.

The Michigan Compiled Laws, Ch. 41, Townships, § 41.181, which empowers townships to adopt ordinances regulating the public health, safety, and general welfare.

Minnesota	City or Town	Cities Code or Town General Law Code

The Constitution of Minnesota, Art. 1, § 1, which provides that government is instituted for the security, benefit, and protection of the people, in whom all political power is inherent.

The Minnesota Statutes, Ch. 412, Statutory Cities, § 412.221, which empowers cities to

STATE	MUNICIPALITY	CODE TITLE
Minnesota—cont.		

provide by ordinance as they deem expedient for the government and good order of the city, the suppression of vice and immorality, the prevention of crime, the protection of public and private property, the benefit of residence, trade, and commerce, and the promotion of health, safety, order, convenience, and the general welfare.

The Minnesota Statutes, Ch. 365, Town General Law, § 365.10, which empowers electors to give town boards the authority to provide by ordinance for the government and good order of the town, the suppression of vice and immorality, the prevention of crime, the protection of public and private property, the benefit of residence, trade, and commerce, and the promotion of health, safety, order, convenience, and the general welfare.

Mississippi	City, Town, or Village	Municipalities Code

The Constitution of Mississippi, Art. 3, § 5, which provides that all political power is vested in and derived from the people, and that all government of right originates with the people, is founded upon their will only, and is instituted solely for the good of the whole.

The Mississippi Code 1972, Tit. 21, Municipalities, § 21-17-5, which empowers all municipalities to adopt any ordinances concerning their affairs.

The Mississippi Code 1972, Tit. 21, Municipalities, § 21-19-1, which empowers all municipalities to make regulations concerning the general health of the municipality.

The Mississippi Code 1972, Tit. 21, Municipalities, § 21-19-15, which empowers all municipalities to make all needful police regulations necessary for the preservation of good order and peace of the municipality and to prevent injury to, destruction of, or interference with public or private property.

Missouri	Town or Village	Cities, Towns, and Villages Code

The Constitution of 1945 of the State of Missouri, Art. 1, § 1, which provides that all political power is vested in and derived from the people, and that all government originates from the people, is founded upon their will only, and is instituted solely for the good of the whole.

The Constitution of 1945 of the State of Missouri, Art. 1, § 2, which provides that all constitutional government is intended to promote the general welfare of the people.

The Missouri Statutes, Tit. VII, Cities, Towns, and Villages, § 80.090(40), which empowers towns and villages to pass any ordinance for the regulation and police of the town and village as they shall deem necessary.

Montana	County	Local Government Code

The Constitution of Montana, Art. II, § 1, which provides that all political power is vested in and derived from the people, and that all government of right originates with the people, is founded upon their will only, and is instituted solely for the good of the whole.

STATE	MUNICIPALITY	CODE TITLE
Montana—cont.		

The Constitution of Montana, Art. XI, § 6, which provides that a local government unit adopting a self-government charter may exercise any power not prohibited by the constitution, law, or charter.

The Montana Code, Tit. 7, Local Government, Ch. 7, § 7-1-101, which repeats the constitutional provision that all local governments with the power of self-government may exercise any power not prohibited by the constitution, law, or charter.

Nebraska	City or Village	Cities and Villages Code

The Constitution of Nebraska, Art. I, § 1, which provides that governments are instituted among people, deriving their just powers from the consent of the governed, to secure the people's inherent and inalienable rights and to protect their property.

The Revised Statutes of Nebraska, Ch. 18, Cities and Villages, § 18-1720, which empowers all cities and villages to define, regulate, suppress, and prevent nuisances, and to declare what shall constitute a nuisance, and to abate and remove the same.

Nevada	County	Counties and Townships Code

The Constitution of Nevada, Art. 1, § 2, which provides that all political power is inherent in the people, and that government is instituted for the protection, security, and benefit of the people.

The Nevada Revised Statutes, Tit. 20, Counties and Townships, Ch. 244, § 244.357, which empowers each board of county commissioners to enact such local police ordinances as are not in conflict with the general laws and regulations of the State.

The Nevada Revised Statutes, Tit. 20, Counties and Townships, Ch. 244, § 244.335, which empowers boards of county commissioners to regulate all character of lawful trades, callings, industries, occupations, professions, and businesses conducted inside its county outside of the limits of incorporated towns and cities.

New Hampshire	City	Towns, Cities, Village Districts, and Unincorporated Places Code

The Constitution of New Hampshire, Pt. 1, Art. 1, which provides that all government, of right, originates from the people, is founded in consent, and instituted for the general good.

The Constitution of New Hampshire, Pt. 1, Art. 10, which provides that government is instituted for the common benefit, protection, and security of the whole community, and not for the private interest or emolument of any one man, family, or class of men.

The New Hampshire Revised Statutes, Tit. 3, Towns, Cities, Villages, and Unincorporated Places, Ch. 47, § 47:17(XV), which empowers cities to make any by-laws and regulations that seem for the well-being of the city.

STATE	MUNICIPALITY	CODE TITLE
New Jersey	City, Town, Township, Village, or Borough	Municipalities and Counties Code

The Constitution of New Jersey, Art. 1, ∂ 2, which provides that all political power is inherent in the people, and that government is instituted for the protection, security, and benefit of the people.

The New Jersey Statutes, Tit. 40, Municipalities and Counties, § 40:41A-28, which provides that municipalities are the broad repository of local police power in terms of the right and power to legislate for the general health, safety, and welfare of their residents.

The New Jersey Statutes, Tit. 40, Municipalities and Counties, § 40:42-4, which gives municipalities the fullest and most complete powers possible over the internal affairs of such municipalities for local self-government.

The New Jersey Statutes, Tit. 40, Municipalities and Counties, § 40:48-2, which empowers all municipalities to make any ordinances as it may deem necessary and proper for the good government, order and protection of persons and property, and for the preservation of the public health, safety, and welfare of the municipality and its inhabitants.

New Mexico	County	Counties Code

The Constitution of New Mexico, Art. II, § 2, which provides that all political power is vested in and derived from the people, and that all government of right originates with the people, is founded upon their will, and is instituted solely for their good.

The Constitution of New Mexico, Art. X, § 6, which provides that any municipality that adopts a charter may exercise all legislative powers and perform all functions not expressly denied by general law or charter.

The Constitution of New Mexico, Art. XI, § 14, which provides that the police power of the state is supreme over all corporations as well as individuals.

The New Mexico Statutes, Ch. 4, Counties, § 4-37-1, which provides that all counties are granted the same powers that are granted municipalities, including those powers necessary and proper to provide for the safety, preserve the health, promote the prosperity, and improve the morals, order, comfort, and convenience of the county or its inhabitants.

New York	All local government	Municipal Home Rule Law

The Constitution of the State of New York, Art. 9, § 2(c)(ii)(10), which provides that every local government shall have power to adopt and amend local laws relating to the government, protection, order, conduct, safety, health, and well-being of persons or property therein.

The Consolidated Laws of New York, Ch. 36-a, Municipal Home Rule Law, § 10.1(ii)(a)(12), which provides that every local government shall have power to adopt and amend local laws relating to the government, protection, order, conduct, safety, health, and well-being of persons or property therein, including, without limitation, the power to adopt local laws providing for the regulation of businesses.

STATE	MUNICIPALITY	CODE TITLE
North Carolina	County	Counties Code

The Constitution of North Carolina, Art. I, § 2, which provides that all political power is vested in and derived from the people, and that all government of right originates from the people, is founded upon their will only, and is instituted solely for the good of the whole.

The General Statutes of North Carolina, Ch. 153A, Art. 6, § 153A-121, which empowers counties, by ordinance, to define, regulate, prohibit, or abate acts, omissions, or conditions detrimental to health, safety, or welfare of its citizens and the peace and dignity of the county, and to define and abate nuisances.

The General Statutes of North Carolina, Ch. 153A, Art. 6, § 153A-134, which empowers counties, by ordinance, to regulate occupations, businesses, trades, and professions, and to prohibit those that may be inimical to the public health, welfare, safety, order, or convenience.

North Dakota	County	Counties Code

The Constitution of North Dakota, Art. I, § 2, which provides that all political power is inherent in the people, and that government is instituted for the protection, security, and benefit of the people.

The Constitution of North Dakota, Art. VII, § 1, which says that the purpose of this section is to provide for maximum local self-government by all political subdivisions.

The Constitution of North Dakota, Art. VII, § 6, which requires the legislative assembly to provide by law for the establishment and exercise of home rule in counties and cities.

The North Dakota Century Code, Tit. 11, Counties, § 11-09.1-05(5), which empowers home rule counties to adopt ordinances to provide for the public health, safety, morals, and welfare.

Ohio	City or Village	Municipal Corporations Code

The Constitution of Ohio, Art. I, § 2, which provides that all political power is inherent in the people, and that government is instituted for their equal protection and benefit.

The Constitution of Ohio, Art. XVIII, § 3, which provides that municipalities shall have authority to exercise all powers of local self-government and to adopt and enforce within their limits such police, sanitary, and other similar regulations, as are not in conflict with general laws.

The Ohio Revised Code, Tit. VII, Municipal Corporations, § 715.49, which empowers municipalities to preserve the peace and good order and protect the property of the municipal corporation and its inhabitants.

Oklahoma	City and Town	Cities and Towns Code

The Constitution of Oklahoma, Art. 2, § 1, which provides that all political power is inherent in the people, and that government is instituted for their protection, security, and benefit, and to promote their general welfare.

The Oklahoma Statutes, Tit. 11, Cities and Towns, § 14-101, which empowers the mu-

STATE	MUNICIPALITY	CODE TITLE
Oklahoma—cont.		

nicipal governing body to enact ordinances, rules, and regulations for carrying out municipal functions.

The Oklahoma Statutes, Tit. 11, Cities and Towns, § 22-101, which empowers incorporated municipalities to do all acts in relation to the affairs of the municipality necessary to the good government of the municipality.

The Oklahoma Statutes, Tit. 11, Cities and Towns, § 22-121, which empowers the municipal governing body to declare what shall constitute a nuisance and provide for the prevention, removal, and abatement of nuisances.

Oregon	County	Counties and County Officers Code

The Constitution of Oregon, Art. I, § 1, which provides that all power is inherent in the people, and all free governments are founded on their authority, and instituted for their peace, safety, and happiness.

The Oregon Revised Statutes, Tit. 20, Counties and County Officers, § 203.035, which empowers a county, by ordinance, to exercise authority within the county over matters of county concern to the fullest extent allowed by Constitutions and laws of the United States and Oregon, as fully as if each particular power comprised in that general authority were specifically listed in the County and County Officers Code.

Pennsylvania	Second Class Township	Second Class Township Code

The Constitution of Pennsylvania, Art. 1, § 2, which provides that all power is inherent in the people, and that all free governments are founded on their authority and instituted for their peace, safety, and happiness.

The Constitution of Pennsylvania, Art. 9, § 2, which provides that a municipality that has a home rule charter may exercise any power or perform any function not denied by the Constitution, charter, or General Assembly.

The Pennsylvania Statutes, Tit. 53, Municipal and Quasi-Municipal Corporations, § 66506, which empowers the board of supervisors of second class townships to make and adopt any ordinances, bylaws, rules, and regulations necessary for the proper management, care, and control of the township and its finances and the maintenance of peace, good government, health, and welfare of the township and its citizens.

Rhode Island	City or Town	Towns and Cities Code

The Constitution of Rhode Island, Art. I, § 2, which provides that all free governments are instituted for the protection, safety, and happiness of the people, and all laws should be made for the good of the whole.

The Constitution of Rhode Island, Art. XIII, § 1, which provides that it is the intention of Article 13 of the Constitution to grant and confirm to the people of every city and town in Rhode Island the right of self government in all local matters.

The Constitution of Rhode Island, Art. XIII, § 2, which provides that every city and

STATE	MUNICIPALITY	CODE TITLE
Rhode Island—cont.		

town shall have the power at any time to adopt a charter, amend its charter, and enact and amend local laws relating to its affairs and government not inconsistent with the Constitution and laws enacted by the general assembly in conformity with the powers reserved to the general assembly.

The General Laws of Rhode Island, Tit. 45, Towns and Cities, § 45-6-1, which empowers town and city councils to make and ordain all ordinances and regulations for their respective towns and cities, not repugnant to law, for the well ordering, managing, and directing of the prudential affairs and police of their respective towns and cities.

South Carolina	Township, City, or Town	Municipal Corporations Code

The Constitution of South Carolina, Art. I, § 1, which provides that all political power is vested in and derived from the people only.

The Constitution of South Carolina, Art. XII, § 1, which provides that the health, welfare, and safety of the lives and property of the people of South Carolina and the conservation of its natural resources are matters of public concern.

The Code of Laws of South Carolina, Tit. 5, Municipal Corporations, § 5-7-30, which empowers all municipalities to enact regulations, resolutions, and ordinances respecting any subject as shall appear to them necessary and proper for the security, general welfare, and convenience of such municipalities, or for preserving health, peace, order, and good government therein.

South Dakota	Township	Townships Code

The Constitution of South Dakota, Art. VI, § 26, which provides that all political power is inherent in the people, and that all free government is founded on their authority, and is instituted for their equal protection and benefit.

The Constitution of South Dakota, Art. IX, § 2, which provides that a chartered governmental unit may exercise any legislative power or perform any function not denied by its charter, the Constitution, or the general laws of the state, and that powers and functions of home rule units shall be construed liberally.

The Constitution of South Dakota, Art. XVII, § 4, which provides that the police power of the state shall never be abridged or so construed as to permit corporations to conduct their business in such manner as to infringe the equal rights of individuals or the general well-being of the state.

The South Dakota Codified Laws, Tit. 8, Townships, § 8-2-1, which empowers townships to pass bylaws and ordinances for the government of such township and for the protection of the lives and property of its inhabitants.

Tennessee	City or Town	Cities and Towns Code

The Constitution of Tennessee, Art. I, § 1, which provides that all power is inherent in the people, and that all free governments are founded on their authority, and instituted for their peace, safety, and happiness.

STATE	MUNICIPALITY	CODE TITLE
Tennessee—cont.		

The Constitution of Tennessee, Art. I, § 2, which provides that as government is instituted for the common benefit, the doctrine of non-resistance against arbitrary power and oppression is absurd, slavish, and destructive of the good and happiness of mankind.

The Tennessee Code, Tit. 6, Cities and Towns, § 6-2-201(20) (for Mayor-Aldermanic chartered municipalities), § 6-19-101(20) (for City Manager-Commission chartered municipalities), and § 6-33-101(a) (for Modified Manager-Council chartered municipalities), which empowers all such municipalities to regulate all persons, firms, corporations, companies, and associations engaged in any business, occupation, calling, profession, or trade not prohibited by law.

The Tennessee Code, Tit. 6, Cities and Towns, § 6-2-201(22) (for Mayor-Aldermanic chartered municipalities), § 6-19-101(222) (for City Manager-Commission chartered municipalities), and § 6-33-101(a) (for Modified Manager-Council chartered municipalities), which empowers all such municipalities to define, prohibit, abate, suppress, prevent, and regulate all acts, practices, conduct, businesses, occupations, callings, trades, uses of property, and all other things whatsoever detrimental, or liable to be detrimental, to the health, morals, comfort, safety, convenience, or welfare of the inhabitants of the municipality, and to exercise general police powers.

The Tennessee Code, Tit. 6, Cities and Towns, § 6-2-201(23) (for Mayor-Aldermanic chartered municipalities), § 6-19-101(23) (for City Manager-Commission chartered municipalities), and § 6-33-101(a) (for Modified Manager-Council chartered municipalities), which empowers all such municipalities to prescribe limits within which business occupations and practices liable to be nuisances or detrimental to the health, morals, security, or general welfare of the people may lawfully be established, conducted, or maintained.

The Tennessee Code, Tit. 6, Cities and Towns, § 6-2-201(32) (for Mayor-Aldermanic chartered municipalities), § 6-19-101(33) (for City Manager-Commission chartered municipalities), and § 6-33-101(a) (for Modified Manager-Council chartered municipalities), which empowers all such municipalities to have and exercise all powers that it would be competent for the Cities and Towns code specifically to enumerate, as fully and completely as though such powers were specifically enumerated in the Cities and Towns Code.

Texas	City, Town, or Village	Local Government Code

The Constitution of Texas, Art. 1, § 2, which provides that all political power is inherent in the people, and that all free governments are founded on their authority, and instituted for their benefit.

The Texas Codes, Local Government Code, Tit. 2, Organization of Municipal Government, § 51.001, which empowers the governing body of a municipality to adopt an ordinance, rule, or police regulation that is for the good government, peace, or order of the municipality.

The Texas Codes, Local Government Code, Tit. 2, Organization of Municipal Government, § 51.012, which empowers municipalities to adopt an ordinance that is necessary for the government, interest, welfare, or good order of the municipality as a body politic.

STATE	MUNICIPALITY	CODE TITLE
Utah	City	Utah Municipal Code

The Constitution of Utah, Art. I, § 2, which provides that all political power is inherent in the people, and that all free governments are founded on their authority for their equal protection and benefit.

The Constitution of Utah, Art. XI, § 5, which provides that each city and town forming its charter under this section of the Constitution shall have and is hereby granted the authority to exercise all powers relating to municipal affairs, and to adopt and enforce within its limits, local police, sanitary, and similar regulations not in conflict with general law.

The Utah Code, Tit. 10, Utah Municipal Code, § 10-8-84, which empowers all cities to pass all ordinances as are necessary and proper to provide for the safety and preserve the health, and promote the prosperity, improve the morals, peace, and good order, comfort, and convenience of the city and its inhabitants.

Vermont	City, Town, or Village	Municipal and County Government Code

The Constitution of Vermont, Ch. I, Art. 5, which provides that the people of Vermont by their legal representatives have the sole, inherent, and exclusive right of governing and regulating the internal police of the same.

The Constitution of Vermont, Ch I, Art. 7, which provides that government is instituted for the common benefit, protection, and security of the people, and not for the particular emolument or advantage of a single person, family, or set of persons.

The Vermont Statutes, Tit. 24, Municipal and County Government, Ch. 61, Regulatory Provisions; Police Power of Municipalities, § 2291(14), which provides that for the purpose of promoting the public health, safety, welfare, and convenience, a town, city, or incorporated village shall have the power to define what constitutes a public nuisance and to provide procedures and take action for its abatement or removal as the public health, safety, or welfare may require.

Virginia	County	Counties, Cities, and Towns Code

The Constitution of Virginia, Art. I, § 2, which provides that all power is vested in, and consequently derived from, the people.

The Constitution of Virginia, Art. I, § 3, which provides that government is instituted for the common benefit, protection, and security of the people, and that of all the various modes and forms of government, that is best which is capable of producing the greatest degree of happiness and safety, and is most effectually secured against the danger of maladministration.

The Code of Virginia, Tit. 15.2, Counties, Cities, and Towns, § 15.2-1200, which empowers a county to adopt such measures as it deems expedient to secure and promote the health, safety, and general welfare of its inhabitants.

The Code of Virginia, Tit. 15.2, Counties, Cities, and Towns, § 15.2-1700, which empowers any locality to provide for the protection of its inhabitants and property and for the preservation of peace and good order therein.

STATE	MUNICIPALITY	CODE TITLE
Washington	County	Counties Code

The Constitution of Washington, Art. 1, § 1, which provides that all political power is inherent in the people, and governments derive their just powers from the consent of the governed, and are established to protect and maintain individual rights.

The Constitution of Washington, Art. 11, § 11, which provides that any county, city, town, or township may make and enforce within its limits all such local police, sanitary, and other regulations as are not in conflict with general laws.

The Revised Code of Washington, Tit. 36, Counties, § 36.32.120(7), which provides that legislative authorities of the several counties shall make and enforce, by appropriate resolutions or ordinances, all such police and sanitary regulations as are not in conflict with state law.

West Virginia	County	County Commissions and Officers Code

The Constitution of West Virginia, Art. I, § 2, which provides that among the powers reserved to the states is the exclusive regulation of their own internal government and police, and that it is the high and solemn duty of the several departments of government created by the Constitution to guard and protect the people of West Virginia from all encroachments upon the rights so reserved.

The Constitution of West Virginia, Art. II, § 2, which provides that the powers of government reside in all the citizens of the State and can be rightfully exercised only in accordance with their will and appointment.

The Constitution of West Virginia, Art. III, § 3, which provides that government is instituted for the common benefit, protection, and security of the people, and that of all its various forms, that is the best which is capable of producing the greatest degree of happiness and safety, and is most effectually secured against the danger of maladministration.

The Constitution of West Virginia, Art. IX, § 11, which provides that county commissions shall, under such regulations as may be prescribed by law, have the superintendence and administration of the internal police and fiscal affairs of their counties.

The West Virginia Code, Ch. 7, County Commissions and Officers, § 7-1-3, which provides that county commissions shall, under rules prescribed by law, have the superintendence and administration of the internal police and fiscal affairs of their counties.

Wisconsin	County	Counties Code

The Constitution of Wisconsin, Art. 1, § 1, which provides that governments are instituted to serve the inherent rights of people born equally free and independent, and derive their just powers from the consent of the governed.

The Wisconsin Statutes, Ch. 59, Counties, § 59.03, which provides that every county may exercise any organizational or administrative power, subject only to the constitution and to any enactment of the legislature that is of statewide concern and that uniformly affects every county.

The Wisconsin Statutes, Ch. 59, Counties, § 59.04, which provides that to give counties the largest measure of self-government under the administrative home rule authority granted to counties in § 59.03(1), this chapter shall be liberally construed in favor of the

STATE	MUNICIPALITY	CODE TITLE
Wisconsin—cont.		

rights, powers, and privileges of counties to exercise any organizational or administrative power.

The Wisconsin Statutes, Ch. 59, Counties, § 59.51, which provides that the board of each county shall have the authority to exercise any organizational or administrative power without limitation because of enumeration, and that these powers shall be broadly and liberally construed and limited only by express language.

The Wisconsin Statutes, Ch. 59, Counties, § 59.54(6), which provides that county boards may enact and enforce ordinances to preserve public peace and good order within the county.

Wyoming	City or Town	Cities and Towns Code

The Constitution of Wyoming, Art. 1, § 1, which provides that all power is inherent in the people, and all free governments are founded on their authority, and instituted for their peace, safety, and happiness.

The Wyoming Statutes, Tit. 15, Cities and Towns, § 15-1-103(a)(xviii), which empowers the governing bodies of all cities and towns to regulate, prevent, or suppress any conduct that disturbs or jeopardizes the public health, safety, peace, or morality in any public or private place.

The Wyoming Statutes, Tit. 15, Cities and Towns, § 15-1-103(a)(xix), which empowers the governing bodies of all cities and towns to declare and abate nuisances.

The Wyoming Statutes, Tit. 15, Cities and Towns, § 15-1-103(a)(xli), which empowers the governing bodies of all cities and towns to adopt ordinances, resolutions, and regulations necessary for the health, safety, and welfare of the city or town.

CONSTITUTIONAL AMENDMENTS FOR EACH STATE

Attorney Daniel Brannen has drafted the following commentary and constitutional amendments for this book:

The rhetorical context in which the word "person" appears in the Fourteenth Amendment reflects that it means "natural person." Section 1 begins: "All persons born or naturalized in the United States, and subject to the jurisdiction thereof, are citizens of the United States and of the State wherein they reside." This sentence clearly defines which subset of natural persons are citizens of the United States. Thus, it is reasonable to assume that later references to "persons" mean natural persons. From this rhetorical context and the even more compelling social context of the Thirteenth, Fourteenth, and Fifteenth Amendments, it is clear that America adopted them to protect the civil liberties of newly freed slaves and all human beings, not of artificial corporations.

The Supreme Court, however, has since ruled that this language in the Constitution means that corporations are persons the same as natural persons.

One way to correct this is to change the language of the federal and state constitutions to refer to "natural persons" in the due process and equal protection sections. The following table contains proposed amendatory language. When a section contains many provisions in addition to the due process or equal protection clauses, the entry below indicates that it covers only a portion of the section by using the parenthetical indication "(in part)."

Keep in mind that changing the language in the equal protection and due process clauses in state constitutions may only be part of what is required to strip corporations of those protections. There are a number of reasons for this. First, many state constitutions, in addition to due process and equal protection clauses, contain separate sections that list the inherent or inalienable rights of "persons." Second, state constitutions often have separate sections concerning the rights of "persons" or "the accused" in criminal or civil trials or investigations. Third, state constitutions often identify other civil and political rights of "persons." Changing the due process and equal protection provisions to read "natural persons" while leaving these other sections intact may lead courts to interpret the unchanged sections to apply to corporations. Finally, many state constitutions have entire articles devoted to corporations, and many of these contain sections to the effect that corporations may sue, and are subject to being sued, in court in like cases as natural persons. Whether any of these articles or sections will have to be amended to strip corporations of due process and equal protection rights depends on the constitutional law of the individual states.

CONSTITUTION DUE PROCESS PROVISIONS

Federal

U.S. Const. Amend. XIV, § 1. All natural persons born or naturalized in the United States, and subject to the jurisdiction thereof, are citizens of the United States and of the State wherein they reside. No State shall make or enforce any law that shall abridge the privileges or immunities of citizens of the United States; nor shall any State deprive any natural person of life, liberty, or property, without due process of law; nor deny to any natural person within its jurisdiction the equal protection of the laws.

Alabama

Art. I, § 1. That all natural persons are equally free and independent; that they are endowed by their Creator with certain inalienable rights; that among these are life, liberty and the pursuit of happiness.
Art. I, § 6 (in part). Rights of accused: no natural person shall be compelled to give evidence against himself, nor be deprived of life, liberty, or property, except by due process of law.

Alaska

Art. I, § 1. Inherent Rights. This constitution is dedicated to the principles that all natural persons have a natural right to life, liberty, the pursuit of happiness, and the enjoyment of the rewards of their own industry; that all natural persons are equal and entitled to equal rights, opportunities, and protection under the law; and that all natural persons have corresponding obligations to the natural people and to the State.
Art I, § 7. Due Process. No natural person shall be deprived of life, liberty, or property, without due process of law. The right of all natural persons to fair and just treatment in the course of legislative and executive investigations shall not be infringed.

Arizona

Art. II, § 2. Political power; purpose of government. All political power is inherent in natural persons, and governments derive their just powers from the consent of the governed, and are established to protect and maintain the rights of natural persons.
Art. II, § 4. Due Process of Law. No natural person shall be deprived of life, liberty, or property without due process of law.

CONSTITUTION DUE PROCESS PROVISIONS

Arkansas

Art. 2, § 3. Equality Before the Law. The equality of all natural persons before the law is recognized, and shall ever remain inviolate; nor shall any citizen ever be deprived of any right, privilege, or immunity, nor exempted from any burden or duty, on account of race, color, or previous condition.

Art. 2, § 8 (in part). Criminal Charges—Self-Incrimination—Due Process—Double Jeopardy—Bail: nor shall any natural person be compelled, in any criminal case, to be a witness against himself; nor be deprived of life, liberty, or property, without due process of law.

Art. 2, § 21. Life, Liberty, and Property—Banishment Prohibited. No natural person shall be taken or imprisoned, or disseized of his estate, freehold, liberties, or privileges; or outlawed, or in any manner destroyed or deprived of his life, liberty, or property, except by the judgment of his peers or the law of the land; nor shall any natural person, under any circumstances, be exiled from the State.

California

Art. I, § 7(a) (in part). A natural person may not be deprived of life, liberty, or property without due process of law or denied equal protection of the laws; provided, that nothing contained herein or elsewhere in this Constitution imposes upon the State of California or any public entity, board, or official any obligations or responsibilities which exceed those imposed by the Equal Protection Clause of the 14th Amendment to the United States Constitution with respect to the use of pupil school assignment or pupil transportation.

Art. I, § 15 (in part). Natural persons may not twice be put in jeopardy for the same offense, be compelled in a criminal cause to be a witness against themselves, or be deprived of life, liberty, or property without due process of law.

Colorado

Art. II, § 3. Inalienable rights. All natural persons have certain natural, essential, and inalienable rights, among which may be reckoned the right of enjoying and defending their lives and liberties; of acquiring, possessing, and protecting property; and of seeking and obtaining their safety and happiness.

Art. II, § 25. Due process of law. No natural person shall be deprived of life, liberty, or property, without due process of law.

Connecticut

Art. I, § 8(a) (in part). No natural person shall be compelled to give evidence against himself, nor be deprived of life, liberty, or property without due process of law, nor shall excessive bail be required nor excessive fines imposed.

Art. I, § 20. No natural person shall be denied the equal protection of the law nor be subjected to segregation or discrimination in the exercise or enjoyment of his or her civil or political rights because of religion, race, color, ancestry, national origin, or sex.

Delaware

In theory, the Preamble to the Delaware Constitution already provides equal protection only to "men."

Art. I, § 7 (in part). Procedural rights in criminal prosecutions; jury trial; self-incrimination; deprivation of life, liberty, or property: no natural person shall be compelled to give evidence against himself, nor shall he be deprived of life, liberty, or property, unless by the judgment of his peers or by the law of the land.

CONSTITUTION DUE PROCESS PROVISIONS

District of Columbia (proposed)

Art. 1, § 3 (in part). Freedom from Discrimination. Every natural person shall have a fundamental right to the equal protection of the law and to be free from historic group discrimination, public or private, based on race, color, religion, creed, citizenship, national origin, sex, sexual orientation, poverty, or parentage.

Art. 1, § 5. Due Process. The State shall not deprive any natural person of life, liberty, or property without due process of law. The right of all persons to fair and just treatment in the course of legislative and executive investigations shall not be abridged.

Florida

The Florida Constitution already provides equal protection to "natural persons" in Article I, § 2.

Art. I, § 9. Due Process.—No natural person shall be deprived of life, liberty, or property without due process of law, or be twice put in jeopardy for the same offense, or be compelled in any criminal matter to be a witness against oneself.

Georgia

Art. I, § I, ∂ I. Life, liberty, and property. No natural person shall be deprived of life, liberty, or property except by due process of law.

Art. I, § I, ∂ 2. Protection to person and property; equal protection. Protection to natural persons and property is the paramount duty of government and shall be impartial and complete. No natural person shall be denied the equal protection of the laws.

Hawaii

Art I., § 5. Due Process and Equal Protection. No natural person shall be deprived of life, liberty, or property without due process of law, nor be denied the equal protection of the laws, nor be denied the enjoyment of the person's civil rights or be discriminated against in the exercise thereof because of race, religion, sex, or ancestry.

Idaho

Art. I, § 2. Political Power Inherent in the People. All political power is inherent in the natural people. Government is instituted for their equal protection and benefit, and they have the right to alter, reform, or abolish the same whenever they may deem it necessary; and no special privileges or immunities shall ever be granted that may not be altered, revoked, or repealed by the legislature.

Art. I, § 13 (in part). No natural person shall be twice put in jeopardy for the same offense; nor be compelled in any criminal case to be a witness against himself; nor be deprived of life, liberty, or property without due process of law.

Illinois

Art I, § 2. Due Process and Equal Protection. No natural person shall be deprived of life, liberty, or property without due process of law nor be denied the equal protection of the laws.

CONSTITUTION DUE PROCESS PROVISIONS

Indiana

Art. 1, § 1 (in part). Inherent and inalienable rights. WE DECLARE, That all natural people are created equal; that they are endowed by their CREATOR with certain inalienable rights; that among these are life, liberty, and the pursuit of happiness;

Iowa

Art. I, § 2. Political power. All political power is inherent in the natural people. Government is instituted for the equal protection, security, and benefit of the natural people, and they have the right, at all times, to alter or reform the same, whenever the public good may require it.

Art. I, § 9. Right of trial by jury—due process of law. The right of trial by jury shall remain inviolate; but the general assembly may authorize trial by a jury of a less number than twelve natural persons in inferior courts; but no natural person shall be deprived of life, liberty, or property, without due process of law.

Kansas

Bill of Rights, § 1. Equal Rights. All natural persons are possessed of equal and inalienable natural rights, among which are life, liberty, and the pursuit of happiness.

Kentucky

The Constitution of Kentucky already provides that all "men" are equal.

Bill of Rights, § 11 (in part). Rights of accused in criminal prosecution; change of venue. No natural person can be compelled to give evidence against himself, nor can he be deprived of his life, liberty, or property, unless by the judgment of his peers or the law of the land.

Louisiana

Art. I, § 2. Due Process of Law. No natural person shall be deprived of life, liberty, or property, except by due process of law.

Art. I, § 3. Right to Individual Dignity. No natural person shall be denied the equal protection of the laws. No law shall discriminate against a natural person because of race or religious ideas, beliefs, or affiliations. No law shall arbitrarily, capriciously, or unreasonably discriminate against a natural person because of birth, age, sex, culture, physical condition, or political ideas or affiliations. Slavery and involuntary servitude are prohibited, except in the latter case as punishment for crime.

Maine

Art. I, § 6 (in part). Rights of persons accused. No natural person shall be compelled to furnish or give evidence against himself or herself, nor be deprived of life, liberty, property, or privileges, but by judgment of that person's peers or the law of the land.

Art. I, § 6-A. Discrimination against natural persons prohibited. No natural person shall be deprived of life, liberty, or property without due process of law, nor be denied the equal protection of the laws, nor be denied the enjoyment of that person's civil rights or be discriminated against in the exercise thereof.

CONSTITUTION DUE PROCESS PROVISIONS

Maryland

Declaration of Rights, Art. 24. That no natural person ought to be taken or imprisoned or disseized of his freehold, liberties, or privileges, or outlawed, or exiled, or, in any manner, destroyed, or deprived of his life, liberty, or property, but by the judgment of his peers, or by the law of the land.

Massachusetts

Pt. 1, Art. X (in part). Each natural person of the society has a right to be protected by it in the enjoyment of his life, liberty, and property, according to standing laws.
Pt. I, Art. XII (in part). No natural person shall be arrested, imprisoned, despoiled, or deprived of his property, immunities, or privileges, put out of the protection of the law, exiled, or deprived of his life, liberty, or estate, but by the judgment of his peers, or the law of the land.

Michigan

Art. I, § 2. Equal Protection; discrimination. No natural person shall be denied the equal protection of the laws, nor shall any natural person be denied the enjoyment of his civil or political rights or be discriminated against in the exercise thereof because of religion, race, color, or national origin. The legislature shall implement this section by appropriate legislation.
Art. I, § 17. Self-incrimination; due process of law; fair treatment at investigations. No natural person shall be compelled in any criminal case to be a witness against himself, nor be deprived of life, liberty, or property, without due process of law. The right of all individuals, firms, corporations, and voluntary associations to fair and just treatment in the course of legislative and executive investigations and hearings shall not be infringed.

Minnesota

Art. I, § 1. Object of Government. Government is instituted for the security, benefit, and protection of the natural people, in whom all political power is inherent, together with the right to alter, modify, or reform government whenever required by the public good.
Art. I, § 7 (in part). Due Process; Prosecutions; Double Jeopardy; Self-Incrimination; Bail; Habeas Corpus. No natural person shall be held to answer for a criminal offense without due process of law, and no natural person shall be put twice in jeopardy of punishment for the same offense, nor be compelled in any criminal case to be a witness against himself, nor be deprived of life, liberty, or property without due process of law.

Mississippi

Art. 3, § 5. All political power is vested in, and derived from, the natural people; all government of right originates with the natural people, is founded upon their will only, and is instituted solely for the good of the whole.
Art. 3, § 14. No natural person shall be deprived of life, liberty, or property except by due process of law.

CONSTITUTION DUE PROCESS PROVISIONS

Missouri

Art. I, § 2. Promotion of general welfare—natural rights of persons—equality under law—purpose of government.—That all constitutional government is intended to promote the general welfare of the natural people; that all natural persons have a natural right to life, liberty, the pursuit of happiness, and the enjoyment of the gains of their own industry; that all natural persons are created equal and are entitled to equal rights and opportunity under the law; that to give security to these things is the principal office of government, and that when government does not confer this security, it fails in is chief design.

Art. I, § 10. Due process of law.—That no natural person shall be deprived of life, liberty, or property without due process of law.

Montana

Art. II, § 4. Individual dignity. The dignity of the human being is inviolable. No natural person shall be denied the equal protection of the laws. Neither the state nor any person, firm, corporation, or institution shall discriminate against any natural person in the exercise of his civil or political rights on account of race, color, sex, culture, social origin or condition, or political or religious ideas.

Art. II, § 17. Due process of law. No natural person shall be deprived of life, liberty, or property without due process of law.

Nebraska

Art. 1, § 1. All natural persons are by nature free and independent, and have certain inherent and inalienable rights; among these are life, liberty, the pursuit of happiness, and the right to keep and bear arms for security or defense of self, family, home, and others, and for lawful common defense, hunting, recreational use, and all other lawful purposes, and such rights shall not be denied or infringed by the state or any subdivision thereof. To secure these rights, and the protection of property, governments are instituted among natural people, deriving their just powers from the consent of the governed.

Art. 1, § 3. No natural person shall be deprived of life, liberty, or property, without due process of law.

Nevada

Art. 1, § 1. Inalienable rights. All natural persons are by Nature free and equal and have certain inalienable rights among which are those of enjoying and defending life and liberty; acquiring, possessing, and protecting property; and pursuing and obtaining safety and happiness.

Art. 1, § 2 (in part). Purpose of government; paramount allegiance to United States. All political power is inherent in the natural people. Government is instituted for the equal protection, security, and benefit of the natural people; and they have the right to alter or reform the same whenever the public good may require it.

Art.1, § 8.5. No natural person shall be deprived of life, liberty, or property, without due process of law.

CONSTITUTION DUE PROCESS PROVISIONS

New Hampshire

Pt. 1, Art. 1. Equality of Natural People; Origin and Object of Government. All natural people are born equally free and independent: Therefore, all government, of right, originates from the natural people, is founded in consent, and instituted for general good.
Pt. 1, Art. 2. Natural Rights. All natural persons have certain natural, essential, and inherent rights—among which are, the enjoying and defending life and liberty; acquiring, possessing, and protecting property; and, in a word, of seeking and obtaining happiness. Equality of rights of natural people under the law shall not be denied or abridged by this state on account of race, creed, color, sex, or national origin.
Pt. 1, Art, 15 (in part). Right of Accused. No natural person shall be arrested, imprisoned, despoiled, or deprived of his property, immunities, or privileges, put out of the protection of the law, exiled, or deprived of his life, liberty, or estate, but by the judgment of his peers, or the law of the land.

New Jersey

Art. I, § 1. All natural persons are by nature free and independent, and have certain natural and unalienable rights, among which are those of enjoying and defending life and liberty, of acquiring, possessing, and protecting property, and of pursuing and obtaining safety and happiness.
Art. I, § 5. No natural person shall be denied the enjoyment of any civil or military right, nor be discriminated against in the exercise of any civil or military right, nor be segregated in the militia or in the public schools, because of religious principles, race, color, ancestry, or national origin.

New Mexico

Art. II, § 18. Due process; equal protection; sex discrimination. No natural person shall be deprived of life, liberty, or property without due process of law; nor shall any natural person be denied equal protection of the laws. Equality of rights under law shall not be denied on account of the sex of any natural person.

New York

Art. I, § 6 (in part). No natural person shall be deprived of life, liberty, or property without due process of law.
Art. I, § 11. No natural person shall be denied the equal protection of the laws of this state or any subdivision thereof. No natural person shall, because of race, color, creed, or religion, be subjected to any discrimination in his civil rights by any other natural person or by any firm, corporation, or institution, or by the state or any agency or subdivision of the state.

North Carolina

Art. I, § 19. Law of the land; equal protection of the laws. No natural person shall be taken, imprisoned, or disseized of his freehold, liberties, or privileges, or outlawed, or exiled, or in any manner deprived of his life, liberty, or property, but by the law of the land. No natural person shall be denied the equal protection of the laws; nor shall any natural person be subjected to discrimination by the State because of race, color, religion, or national origin.

CONSTITUTION DUE PROCESS PROVISIONS

North Dakota

Art. I, § 2. All political power is inherent in the natural people. Government is instituted for the equal protection, security, and benefit of the natural people, and they have a right to alter or reform the same whenever the public good may require.
Art. I, § 12 (in part). No natural person shall be twice put in jeopardy for the same offense, nor be compelled in any criminal case to be a witness against himself, nor be deprived of life, liberty, or property without due process of law.

Ohio

Art. I, § 1. All natural persons are, by nature, free and independent, and have certain inalienable rights, among which are those of enjoying and defending life and liberty, acquiring, possessing, and protecting property, and seeking and obtaining happiness and safety.
Art. I, § 2. All political power is inherent in the natural people. Government is instituted for their equal protection and benefit, and they have the right to alter, reform, or abolish he same, whenever they may deem it necessary; and no special privileges or immunities shall ever be granted, that may not be altered, revoked, or repealed by the general assembly.

Oklahoma

Art. II, § 1. Political power—Purpose of government—Alteration or reformation. All political power is inherent in the natural people; and government is instituted for their equal protection, security, and benefit, and to promote their general welfare; and they have the right to alter for reform the same whenever the public good may require it: Provided, such change be not repugnant to the Constitution of the United States.
Art. II, § 7. Due process of law. No natural person shall be deprived of life, liberty, or property, without due process of law.

Oregon

Art. I, § 1. Natural rights inherent in people. We declare that all natural persons, when they form a social compact are equal in right: that all power is inherent in the natural people, and all free governments are founded on their authority, and instituted for their peace, safety, and happiness; and they have at all times a right to alter, reform, or abolish the government in such manner as they may think proper.

Pennsylvania

Art. I, § 9 (in part). Rights of Accused in Criminal Prosecutions: no natural person can be compelled to give evidence against himself, nor can he be deprived of his life, liberty, or property, unless by the judgment of his peers or the law of the land.
Art. I, § 26. No Discrimination by Commonwealth and Its Political Subdivisions. Neither the Commonwealth nor any political subdivision thereof shall deny to any natural person the enjoyment of any civil right, nor discriminate against any natural person in the exercise of any civil right.

CONSTITUTION DUE PROCESS PROVISIONS

Rhode Island

Art. I, § 2. All free governments are instituted for the protection, safety, and happiness of the people. All laws, therefore, should be made for the good of the whole; and the burdens of the state ought to be fairly distributed among its citizens. No natural person shall be deprived of life, liberty, or property without due process of law, nor shall any natural person be denied equal protection of the laws. No otherwise qualified natural person shall, solely by reason of race, gender, or handicap, be subject to discrimination by the state, its agents, or any person or entity doing business with the state. Nothing in this section shall be construed to grant or secure any right relating to abortion or the funding thereof.

Art. I, § 10 (in part). Nor shall any natural person be deprived of life, liberty, or property, unless by the judgment of their peers, or the law of the land.

South Carolina

Art. I, § 3. Privileges and Immunities; Due process; Equal protection of laws. The privileges and immunities of citizens of this State and of the United States under this Constitution shall not be abridged; nor shall any natural person be deprived of life, liberty, or property without due process of law, nor shall any natural person be denied the equal protection of the laws.

South Dakota

Art. VI, § 2. Due process—Right to work. No natural person shall be deprived of life, liberty, or property without due process of law. The right of persons to work shall not be denied or abridged on account of membership or nonmembership in any labor union or labor organization.

Art. VI, § 26. Power inherent in natural people—Alteration in form of government—Inseparable part of Union. All political power is inherent in the natural people, and all free government is founded on their authority, and is instituted for their equal protection and benefit, and they have the right in lawful and constituted methods to alter or reform their forms of government in such manner as they may think proper. And the state of South Dakota is an inseparable part of the American Union and the Constitution of the United States is the supreme law of the land.

Tennessee

Art. I, § 1. That all power is inherent in the natural people, and all free governments are founded on their authority, and instituted for their peace, safety, happiness, and equal protection; for the advancement of those ends they have at all times, an unalienable and indefeasible right to alter, reform, or abolish the government in such manner as they may think proper.

Art. I, § 8. That no natural person shall be taken or imprisoned, or disseized of his freehold, liberties, or privileges, or outlawed, or exiled, or in any manner destroyed or deprived of his life, liberty, or property, but by the judgment of his peers, or the law of the land.

Texas

The Texas Constitution already restricts the application of equal protection to "men" and the right of due process to "citizens." If courts pervert these words to mean corporations, then it would be necessary to rewrite Art. 1, §§ 3, 4, and 19 to apply to natural persons.

CONSTITUTION DUE PROCESS PROVISIONS

Utah

Art. I, § 2. All political power is inherent in the natural people; and all free governments are founded on their authority and for their equal protection and benefit, and they have the right to alter or reform their government as the public welfare may require.
Art. I, § 7. No natural person shall be deprived of life, liberty, or property, without due process of law.

Vermont

Ch. 1, Art. 7. Government for the Natural People; They May Change It. That government is, or ought to be, instituted for the common benefit, protection, and security of the natural people, nation, or community, and not for the particular emolument or advantage of any single person, family, or set of persons, who are a part only of that community; and that the community hath an indubitable, unalienable, and indefeasible right, to reform or alter government, in such manner as shall be, by that community, judged most conducive to the public weal.
Ch. 1, Art. 10 (in part). Rights of Persons Accused of Crime; Personal Liberty; Waiver of Jury Trial: nor can any natural person be justly deprived of liberty, except by the laws of the land, or the judgment of the natural person's peers.

Virginia

Art. I, § 3 (in part). Government instituted for common benefit. That government is, or ought to be, instituted for the common benefit of the natural people, nation, or community.
Art. I, § 8 (in part). Criminal prosecutions. No natural person shall be deprived of life or liberty, except by the law of the land or the judgment of his peers, nor be compelled in any criminal proceeding to give evidence against himself, nor be put twice in jeopardy for the same offense.
Art I, § 11 (in part). Due process of law; obligation of contracts; taking of private property; prohibited discrimination; jury trial in civil cases. That no natural person shall be deprived of life, liberty, or property without due process of law.

Washington

Art. I, § 1. Political Power. All political power is inherent in the natural people, and governments derive their just powers from the consent of the governed, and are established to protect and maintain the individual rights of natural people.
Art. I, § 3. Personal Rights. No natural person shall be deprived of life, liberty, or property, without due process of law.

West Virginia

Art. III, § 3-3 (in part). Rights reserved to people. Government is instituted for the common benefit, protection, and security of the natural people, nation, or community.
Art. III, § 3-10. Safeguards for life, liberty, and property. No natural person shall be deprived of life, liberty, or property, without due process of law, and the judgment of his peers.

CONSTITUTION DUE PROCESS PROVISIONS

Wisconsin

Art. I, § 1. Equality; inherent rights. All natural people are born equally free and independent, and have certain inherent rights; among these are life, liberty, and the pursuit of happiness; to secure these rights, governments are instituted, deriving their just powers from the consent of the governed.

Art. I, § 8(1) (in part). No natural person may be held to answer for a criminal offense without due process of law, and no natural person for the same offense may be put twice in jeopardy of punishment, nor may be compelled in any criminal case to be a witness against himself or herself.

Wyoming

In the Constitution of Wyoming, the equal protection provisions already apply only to humans and to citizens. Art. I, §§ 2 and 3.

Art. I, § 6. Due process of law.—No natural person shall be deprived of life, liberty, or property without due process of law.

ENDNOTES

INTRODUCTION

P. 2: www.genome.uci.edu.

CHAPTER 1: THE VALUES WE CHOOSE TO LIVE BY

P. 12: www.ecotrust.org/publications/farmed_salmon_steak.html.

P. 12: "Many of World's Lakes Face Death, Expert Warns," Reuters, 12 November 2001.

P. 13: Mary Pemberton, The Associated Press, "Wildlife Biologists Fret as Alaska Otters Dwindle" and John Heilprin, The Associated Press, "Overreporting Masks Drop in Fish Catch," *Burlington Free Press*, 29 November 2001.

P. 13: www.rain-tree.com.

P. 14: Address before the California Legislature by Delphin M. Delmas, Sacramento, 18 February 1901. D. M. Delmas, *Speeches and Addresses* (San Francisco: A. M. Robertson, 1901).

P. 15: Ibid.

P. 15: Ibid.

P. 16: Thanks to Jeff Gates, author of *Democracy at Risk*, for pointing this out to me.

P. 17: 22 July 1966 Internal Chrysler memo file number 118-H-00.

P. 18: Human rights groups such as Amnesty International (www.amnesty.org) and Project Underground (www.moles.org) do an excellent job of documenting it.

P. 18: I recount the story in my book *The Prophet's Way*.

P. 21: Ken Saro-Wiwa's brother, Owens Saro-Wiwa, M. D., testified before the U. S. Congress about this issue. His testimony is at www.sierraclub.ca.

P. 21: www.shellnigeria.com.

CHAPTER 2: BANDING TOGETHER FOR THE COMMON GOOD: CORPORATIONS, GOVERNMENT, AND "THE COMMONS"

P. 28: L. L. Blake, *The Young People's Book of the Constitution* (England: Sherwood Press, 1987).

P. 32: Worldwatch Institute's 2000 report "Overfed and Underfed: The Global Epidemic of Malnutrition" cites U. N. figures that at least 1.1 billion humans suffer from an outright "deficiency of calories and protein" (starvation or hunger) and another 2 to 3.5 billion suffer from a "deficiency of vitamins and minerals" (malnutrition).

P. 33: Robin Dunbar, *Grooming, Gossip, and the Evolution of Language* (Cambridge: Harvard University Press, 1996).

P. 37: Statistics cited by Verne Harnish in *Mastering the Rockefeller Habits* (New York: SelectBooks, 2002).

P. 37: Jeff Gates, *Democracy at Risk* (Cambridge: Perseus Books, 2000).

P. 38: www.epa.gov.

P. 40: www.federalreserve.gov.

P. 41: Thanks to Jock Gill for this data.

P. 41: An excellent resource of information on the topic of water privatization is: www.transnationale.org.

CHAPTER 3: THE BOSTON TEA PARTY REVEALED

P. 46: Albert J. Beveridge, *Abraham Lincoln* (Riverside Press, 1928). From the introduction by his wife, quoting him at an earlier date.

P. 47: Buckminister Fuller, *The Grunch of Giants* (also noted in other sources). Internet: www.bfi.org.

P. 47: Ibid.

P. 49: Another corporation to claim America during that time was the Massachusetts Bay Colony. They weren't quite as successful, however, as the East India Company, and when the corporation wasn't performing up to the measure of King James, he threatened to revoke their charter. One of the documents in the possession of the University of Virginia, compiled as "Thomas Jefferson, Notes on the State of Virginia, Chapter 23" contains Jefferson's note to himself of his possessing, "An order of council for issuing a quo warranto against the charter of the colony of the Massachuset's [sic] bay in New-England, with his majesty's declaration that in case the said corporation of Masschuset's [sic] bay shall before prosecution had upon the same quo warranto make a full submission and entire resignation to his royal pleasure, he will then regulate their charter in such a manner as shall be for his service and the good of that colony. 1683, July 26. 35. Car. 2." Much of America was then considered plantation land for British corporations. Another of Jefferson's documents in the same collection is titled: "A proclamation for prohibiting the importation of commodities of Europe into any of his majesty's plantations in Africa, Asia, or America, which were not laden in England: and for putting all other laws relating to the trade of the plantations in effectual execution. 1675, Oct. 1. 27. Car. 2." The most powerful of the British corporations of the time, though, was the East India Company.

P. 49: The East India Company designed their flag with 13 red and white bars long before there were 13 states. Many historians believe it was because most of the stockholders in the East India Company were initiates in the Masonic Order, and the Masons considered 13 to be a metaphysically powerful number. Virtually every signer of the Constitution was also a Mason, which may be why they chose to limit the original colonies to thirteen. But that's all speculation: Nobody knows for sure, or if they do, they're not telling.

P. 50: www.theeastindiacompany.com.

P. 51: The law was explicit about its purpose and the death penalty for operating without a license. It read, in part: ". . . it shall be felony for any Person, which now doth, or within four Years last past heretofore hath or here after shall Inhabit or belong to this Island, to serve in America in an hostile manner, under any Foreign Prince, state or Potentate in Amity with his Majesty of Great Britain, without special License for so doing, under the hand and seal of the Governour or Commander in chief of this Island for the time being, and that all and every such offender or offenders contrary to the true intent of this Act being thereof duly convicted in his Majesties supreme Court of Judicature within this Island to which court authority is hereby given to hear and to determine the same as other cases of Felony, shall suffer pains of Death without the benefit of Clergy.

"Be it further Enacted by the Authority aforesaid, that all and every Person or Persons that shall any way knowingly Entertain, Harbour, Conceal, Trade or hold any correspondence by Letter or otherwise with any Person or Persons, that shall be deemed or adjudged to be Privateers, Pirates or other offenders within the construction of this Act, and that shall not readily endeavour to the best of his or their Power to apprehend or cause to be apprehended, such Offender or Offenders, shall be liable to be prosecuted as accessories and Confederates, and to suffer such pains and penalties as in such case by law is Provided."

P. 52: From Encyclopedia Britannica at www.britannica.com.

P. 52: See note to page 50.

P. 53: Esther Forbes, *Paul Revere and the World He Lived In* (Houghton Mifflin Company, 1942).

P. 55: *Retrospect of the Boston Tea Party with a Memoir of George R.T. Hewes, a Survivor of the Little Band of Patriots Who Drowned the Tea in Boston Harbor in 1773*, (New York: S. S. Bliss, 1834).

P. 56: A slang term of the time for "peasant," based on the 1577 "Rusticus in Gallia" drawing of a French peasant from *Habitus*, a book on the dress of the nations of Europe by Hans Weigel.

P. 57: Hewes refers to the local East India Company employees who doubled as agents of Britain as the "ministers" and their local claim at governance in cooperation with and to the profit of the East India Company as the "ministerial enterprises."

P. 59: Presumably Hewes is referring to himself in the third person, a form considered good manners in the 18th century, or this is the voice of the narrator who interviewed him.

P. 59: *Retrospect*, 154–55.

P. 63: www.ilovefreedom.com.

CHAPTER 4: JEFFERSON'S DREAM: THE BILL OF RIGHTS

P. 67: A statement by Albert Gallatin, who later became Secretary of the Treasury after the Federalists lost power.

P. 69: The First Amendment protected citizens from the predations of churches by guaranteeing freedom of religion in a new nation that still had states and cities that demanded obedience to and weekly participation in state-recognized churches or religious doctrine. The Ninth Amendment was a direct and clear acknowledgement of Jefferson's concept of the natural right of humans to hold all personal powers that they haven't specifically and intentionally given to their government of their own free will. It reads, in its entirety, "The enumeration in the Constitution, of certain rights, shall not be construed to deny or disparage others retained by the people."

CHAPTER 5: THE EARLY ROLE OF CORPORATIONS IN AMERICA

P. 74: Jane Anne Morris is also a brilliant researcher, and I gratefully owe much of the Wisconsin-related content of this chapter to her work, and thank her for her generous permission to share it with you.

P. 75: Alfons J. Beitzinger and Edward G. Ryan, *Lion of the Law* (Madison: The State Historical Society of Wisconsin, 1960), 115–16. From an 1873 address to the graduating class of the University of Wisconsin Law School.

P. 75: See the "reserved power" clause.

P. 75: Wis. AG. Op. (1913), Vol. 2, 169.

P. 75: Act of August 21, 1848, Wis. Laws, p. 148 (Gen. Incorp. for Plank Roads).

P. 75: State ex rel. *Kropf v. Gilbert*, 251 N. W. 478 (1934).

P. 75: Dudley O. McGovney, "A Supreme Court Fiction: Corporations in the Diverse Citizenship Jurisdiction of the Federal Courts," *Harvard Law Review* 16 (May 1943): 853–98, 1090–1124, 1225–60.

P. 75: Wis. R. S. 1878, Sec. 1776; Wis. Stat. 1931, 180.13.

P. 75: Wis. G. L 1864, Ch. 166, Sec. 9.

P. 75: Wis. G. L 1864, Ch. 166, Secs. 4, 33.

P. 75: Wis. R. S. 1878, Sec. 1775.

P. 75: Wis. R. S. 1849, Ch. 54 Sec. 7; Wis. G. L 1864, Ch. 166, Secs. 6, 15.

P. 75: And it was a felony to do so. Wis. State 1953, Ch. 346.12–346.15.

P. 75: For example, Wis. G. L 1864, Ch. 166, Sec. 7.

P. 76: *Stone v. State of Wisconsin*, 94 U. S. 181 (1876).

P. 76: Wis. R. S. 1849, Ch. 54, Sec. 22.

P. 77: Charles & Mary Beard, *The Rise of American Civilization* (Macmillan, 1927).

P. 77: Many states had laws on the books similar to this old Wisconsin statute:

Political contributions by corporations.lv No corporation doing business in this state shall pay or contribute, or offer consent or agree to pay or contribute, directly or indirectly, any money, property, free service of its officers or employees or thing of value to any political party, organization, committee or individual for any political purpose whatsoever, or for the purpose of influencing legislation of any kind, or to promote or defeat the candidacy of any person for nomination, appointment or election to any political office.

Penalty.lvi Any *officer, employee, agent or attorney or other representative* of any corporation, acting for and in behalf of such corporation, who shall violate this act, shall be punished upon conviction by a fine of not less than one hundred nor more than five thousand dollars, or by *imprisonment* in the state prison for a period of not less than one nor more than five years, or by both such fine and imprisonment in the discretion of the court or judge before whom such conviction is had and if the corporation shall be subject to a penalty then by forfeiture in double the amount of any fine and *if a domestic corporation it may be dissolved*, if after a proper proceeding upon quo warranto, in either the circuit or supreme court of the state to be prosecuted by the attorney general of the state, the court shall find and give judgment that section 1 of this act has been violated as charged, and if a foreign or non-resident corporation *its right to do business in this state may be declared forfeited*. [Emphasis added.]

P. 78: Ibid.

P. 80: Ibid.

P. 81: Most of the information in this and the preceding paragraph are derived from the pamphlet *Taking Care of Business: Citizenship and the Charter of Incorporation* by Richard L. Grossman and Frank T. Adams, published by Charter, Ink, 1999, and available from POCLAD.

P. 82: Thomas Hobbes, *Leviathan* (chapter 29). Here's the quote in context: "Another infirmity of a Commonwealth is the immoderate greatness of a town, when it is able to furnish out of its own circuit the number and expense of a great army; as also the great number of corporations, which are as it were many lesser Commonwealths in the bowels of a greater, like worms in the entrails of a natural man. To may be added, liberty of disputing against absolute power by pretenders to political prudence; which though bred for the most part in the lees of the people, yet animated by false doctrines are perpetually meddling with the fundamental laws, to the molestation of the Commonwealth, like the little worms which physicians call ascarides."

P. 85: 17 Ill. 291–7.

P. 86: Charles L. Capen to John G. Drennan, 6 April 1906, MSS. Files Legal Dept. I.C.R.R.Co.

P. 86: Adlai E. Stevenson's statement, 6 April 1906, MSS. Files Legal Dept. I.C.R.R.Co.

P. 86: I.C.R.R.Co. notice published in the New York papers and signed by the railroad's Treasurer, J. N. Perkins.

P. 86: *Central Illinois Gazette*, 14 April 1858.

P. 87: Albert J. Beveridge, *Abraham Lincoln* (Riverside Press, 1928). Notes Whitney to Herndon, August 27, 1887.

P. 87: Ibid.

P. 87: Ibid.

P. 87: John F. Stover, *History of the Illinois Central Railroad* (New York: Macmillan, 1976).

P. 88: Carl Sandburg, *Abraham Lincoln* (Harcourt, Brace, and World, 1926).

P. 89: The most wealthy and powerful of the railroad barons were famous names in the 19th century: Leland Stanford, Colis Huntington, Jay Gould, and James J. Hill.

P. 90: This usage began in 16th-century England when lawyers for the East India Company argued that their corporation could not be convicted of a crime because the corporation was not a person and English laws regulating criminal behavior always began with, "No person shall . . ." In response to this, legislators from that time on began passing laws to specifically regulate the "artificial persons" of corporations. While they wanted to regulate corporations, they also wanted to acknowledge that corporations shared some things with humans: They were taxed, were subject to laws, and could be parties to lawsuits.

P. 91: Emanuel Hertz, *Abraham Lincoln, A New Portrait* (Horace Liveright, 1931), Vol. 2, 954. In my 1931 first-edition copy of this book, this note by Lincoln is not addressed and unsigned, and Elkins is not mentioned (although he is referenced in many other later sources). Dale Carnegie tells a famous story, in his book *How to Win Friends and Influence People* about how Lincoln would often write letters to others or even to himself expressing his greatest concerns, and then hide them away, often to be later destroyed. It's my guess that this letter was one of those, later found by Hertz as he collected Lincoln's personal effects in the early decades after Lincoln's death. From its order in Hertz's book, this letter sits between a signed and dated letter to Secretary Stanton on 10 November 1864 and a signed note about Colonel Lamon dated 29 November 1854. Hertz certifies it is in Lincoln's hand, but gives us no clues as to whom he wrote the note or how he planned to send or dispose of it before his death.

P. 91: Howard Zinn, *A People's History of the United Sates: 1492-Present* (New York: Harper-Perennial, 2001).

P. 92: 83 U. S. 36, 81 (1873).

P. 92: The cases are: 94 U. S. 155, 94 U. S. 164, 94 U. S. 179, and 94 U. S. 180, all in 1877.

CHAPTER 6: THE DECIDING MOMENT

P. 95: *Proceedings and Debaters of the Constitutional Convention of the State of Ohio*, 1912, Vol. 1, 667–69.

P. 97: Description of Delmas by Charles Samuels, *The Girl in the Red Velvet Swing* (Aeonian Press, reprinted in limited edition of 300 copies in 1953).

P. 100: www.tourolaw.edu.

P. 101: Blackstone, Book I, 123 (reference from Delmas). *Blackstone's Commentaries to the Constitution and Laws of the Federal Government of the United States* (Philadelphia: Birch and Small, 1803). At the time of this pleading, it was considered the preeminent commentary on American law.

P. 105: *Connecticut General Life Insurance Company v. Johnson* [303 U. S. 77 (1938)].

P. 106: You can find the entire text of the decision at http://caselaw.lp.findlaw.com.

P. 111: Quoted by Howard Jay Graham, *Everyman's Constitution* (Madison: Wisconsin Historical Society Press, 1968).

P. 113: "The Waite Court and the Fourteenth Amendment," *Vanderbilt Law Review* 17 (March 1964).

P. 113: Ibid.

P. 113: C. Peter Magrath, *Morrison R. Waite: Triumph of Character* (New York: Macmillan, 1963).

P. 114: Field's letter to Pomeroy, 28 July 1884, cited in *Everyman's Constitution*.

P. 114: See note to page 106.

P. 115: Excerpted from the *Santa Clara County v. Union Pacific Railroad* decision. Even more interesting reading is found in Field's original opinion in the Ninth Circuit Court, when he ruled that corporations were persons and thus sent the case to the Supreme Court.

CHAPTER 7 : THE CORPORATE CONQUEST OF AMERICA

P. 120: *First National Bank of Boston v. Bellotti* [435 U. S. 765 (1978)].

P. 121: *Marshall v. Barlow's, Inc.* [436 U. S. 307 (1978)].

P. 121: *Liggett v. Lee* [288 U. S. 517 (1933)].

P. 125: 163 U. S. 537 (1896).

P. 126: *By What Authority*, Summer 2001, Program on Corporations, Law, and Democracy.

P. 127: See second note to page 91.

P. 128: Ibid.

P. 128: Report of the Committee on General Laws on the Investigation Relative to Trusts, 6 March 1888.

P. 129: House Trust Investigation, 1888, 316, 317.

P. 132: Ohio Committee on Corporations, Law, and Democracy, *Citizens over Corporations: A Brief History of Democracy in Ohio and Challenges to Freedom in the Future* (1999).

P. 132: The Federal Trade Commission defines price discrimination as, "A seller charging competing buyers different prices for the same 'commodity' or discriminating in the provision of 'allowances'—compensation for advertising and other services—may be violating the Robinson-Patman Act. This kind of price discrimination may hurt competition by giving favored customers an edge in the market that has nothing to do with the superior efficiency of those customers. . . . Price discrimination also might be used as a predatory pricing tactic—setting prices below cost to certain customers—to harm competition at the supplier's level." Internet: www.ftc.gov.

P. 134: James Willard Hurst, *The Legitimacy of the Business Corporation in the Law of the United States, 1780-1970* (Charlottesville: University Press of Virginia, 1970).

P. 134: State of Delaware Web site at www.state.de.us.

P. 135: Ralph Nader, Mark Green, and Joel Seligman, *Corporate Power in America* (Norton, 1976).

CHAPTER 8: TRANSNATIONAL CORPORATIONS: THE GHOST OF THE EAST INDIA COMPANY RISES AGAIN

P. 137: Raymond F. Mikesell, *The Bretton Woods Debates: A Memoir* (Princeton: International Finance Section, Department of Economics, Princeton University, 1994).

P. 138: The Smith Act of 1940 made it a criminal offense for anyone to knowingly or willfully advocate, abet, advise, or teach the duty, necessity, desirability, or propriety of overthrowing the Government of the United States or of any State by force or violence, or for anyone to organize any association which teaches, advises, or encourages such an overthrow, or for anyone to become a member of or to affiliate with any such association. From http://caselaw.lp.findlaw.com.

P. 139: Ibid.

P. 140: George Gilder, *Wealth and Poverty* (Institute for Contemporary Studies, 1993).

P. 142: See note to page 135.

P. 143: Noreena Hertz, Ph.D., *The Silent Takeover: Global Capitalism and the Death of Democracy* (London: Heinemann, 2001). As of this writing, this edition of the book is available only through www.amazon.com.co.uk.

P. 143: www.lights.com summarizes an analysis of NAFTA's impact by Public Citizen's Global Tradewatch and the Institute for Policy Studies. Interestingly, in 1996, the U. S. government stopped including "inputs of imported goods and services" in its calculations of "U. S. Jobs

Supported by Goods and Services Exports." See John R. MacArthur, *The Selling of Free Trade* (Hill & Wang, 2000).

P. 144: Gannett, a $6 billion corporation, also owns *USA Today* as well as 97 newspapers and 22 television stations across the United States and the United Kingdom as of this writing.

P. 144: Bernie Sanders, "'Fast Track' Hurts Here and Abroad," *Burlington Free Press*, 14 December 2001.

P. 145: Paul Geitner, The Associated Press, "WTO Rules Against U. S. Law on Tax Breaks," *Burlington Free Press* 15 January 2002.

P. 147: Just a week after Canada paid $10 million to the American corporation for lost revenues during that ban, another American company slapped Canada with a similar lawsuit under NAFTA's MAI provision, which allows corporations to sue sovereign states. That case is pending as of this writing.

P. 147: www.epa.gov.

P. 148: The World Bank provides NAFTA with a private court system called the International Center for Settlement of Investment Disputes.

P. 148: www.aidc.org.za.

P. 149: Private correspondence with the author, January 2002.

P. 149: In a speech given at the Ohio Constitutional Convention, February 1912.

CHAPTER 9: UNEQUAL USES FOR THE BILL OF RIGHTS

P. 158: "Children, Adolescents, and Advertising," *Pediatrics* 95, (1995): 295–97.

P. 158: *Pacific Gas & Electric Co. v. Public Utility Commission of California* [475 U. S. 1 (1986)].

P. 158: Ralph Nader and Carl J. Mayer, "Corporations Are Not Persons," *New York Times*, 9 April 1988.

P. 159: *Marshall v. Barlow's, Inc.* [436 U. S. 307 (1978)] and *See v. City of Seattle* [387 U. S. 541 (1967)].

P. 159: *Hale v. Henkel* [201 U. S. 43 (1906)].

P. 159: cited by Ralph Nader in the *New York Times*.

P. 159: *Dow Chemical v. The United States* [476 U. S. 227 (1986)].

P. 159: See second note to page 158.

P. 160: Declaration of Independence of the United States of America.

CHAPTER 10: UNEQUAL REGULATION

P. 162: Robert Monks and Nell Minow, *Power and Accountability* (New York: Harper Collins, 1991). Currently out of print and unavailable.

P. 162: Kurt Eichenwald, "Redesigning Nature: Hard Lessons Learned," *New York Times*, 25 January 2001.

P. 162: Ibid.

P. 163: Ibid.

P. 163: Marian Burros, "Shoppers Unaware of Gene Changes," *New York Times*, 20 July 1998.

P. 163: www.commondreams.org.

P. 163: Even Ben & Jerry's must, by law, say something nice about the outcome of this incident on their labels, although you can read the entire story on the wall of their Waterbury, Vermont, manufacturing facility, as Vermont has not yet passed a law making it illegal to question the safety of the American food supply.

P. 163: See second note to page 163.

P. 164: Anne Platt McGinn, "Detoxifying Terrorism," Worldwatch Institute, 16 November 2001.

P. 164: Interview with Thomas Linzey, Esq., and POCLAD published in *Defying Corporations, Defining Democracy*, ed. Dean Ritz (New York: Apex Press, 2001).

P. 164: Julie Brussell, "Our Family Farms: A Final Requiem or a Route to Recovery?" *Conscious Choice*, May 2001.

P. 164: Ibid.

P. 164: See second note to page 163.

CHAPTER 11: UNEQUAL PROTECTION FROM RISK

P. 165: Buckminster Fuller, *Grunch of Giants*. Internet: www.bfi.org.

P. 167: *Terry v. Little* [101 U. S. 216, 217, 25 L.Ed. 864 (1879)].

P. 167: Joel Seligman, "A Brief History of Delaware's General Corporation Law of 1899," 1 Del. J. Corp. L. 249, 255–56 (1976).

P. 168: *Fields v. Synthetic Ropes, Inc.* 215 A.2d 427, 433 (Del. 1965).

P. 170: *Cape Cod Times*, 27 March 1999.

P. 170: www.environmentaldefense.org.

P. 170: From a Bill Moyers documentary on the chemical industry titled "Trade Secrets." A transcript is available at www.pbs.org.

P. 171: Bryan A. Garner, ed., *Black's Law Dictionary*, 7th ed., (St. Paul: West Group, 1999), 1393.

CHAPTER 12: UNEQUAL TAXES

P. 174: www.newportmansions.org.

P. 174: www.about-new-york-city.com.

P. 175: Annie S. Daniel, "The Wreck of the American Home: How Wearing Apparel Is Fashioned in Tenements" *Charities* 14, No. 1 (April 1905), 624–29.

P. 175: www.aflcio.org.

P. 176: www.taxfoundation.org.

P. 176: See second note to page 175.

P. 176: David C. Korten, *When Corporations Rule the World* (Bloomfield: Kumarian Press, 2001).

P. 176: www.commoncause.org.

P. 176: The Institute on Taxation and Economic Policy 2001 report at www.auschron.com.

P. 176: Richard Cohen, "Enron: No Taxes," *Washington Post*, 22 January 2002.

P. 176: 1995 GAO study commissioned by Senator Byron Dorgan of North Dakota.

P. 176: Ibid.

P. 177: See second note to page 175.

P. 177: www.house.gov.

P. 177: The Economic Recovery Tax Act of 2001.

P. 177: Paul A. Gusmorino III, "Main Causes of the Great Depression," *Gusmorino World*, 13 May 1996. Internet: www.escape.com.

P. 177: Ibid.

P. 177: Ibid.

P. 178: www.fair.org.

P. 178: Paul Vitello, *Newsday* 24 May 2001.

P. 178: (202) 622-1680 is the phone number for the Public Liaison Office of the Secretary of the Treasury.

P. 179: When working on his article "Natural Capitalism" for *Mother Jones* magazine. It was later expanded to a book of the same name.

P. 179: David Barboza, "Chicago, Offering Big Incentives, Will Be Boeing's New Home" *New York Times*, 11 May 2001.

P. 179: Stephen Moore and Dean Stansel, "How Corporate Welfare Won," Cato Institute, 1996.

P. 179: David C. Korten, *The Post-Corporate World* (San Francisco: Berrett-Koehler, 1999).

P. 179: Borden Chemicals, noted by Noreena Hertz, Ph.D., in *The Silent Takeover* (London: Heinemann, 2001).

P. 179: Hertz notes in *The Silent Takeover* that, "Beneficiaries of Ohio's 'corporate welfare' included Spiegel, Wal-Mart, and Consolidated Stores Corporation, all of which were absolved from property taxes. . . . As one school treasurer put it, 'Kids get hurt and stockholders get rich.'"

P. 179: *New York Times*, 21 September 1995.

P. 179: Ibid.

P. 180: David E. Buchholz, Ph.D., "Mercedes-Benz: The Deal of the Century" (Washington, D. C.: Business Incentive Reform Clearinghouse, Coalition for Enterprise Development). Internet: www.cfed.org.

P. 180: Donald L. Barlett and James B. Steele, "Corporate Welfare," *Time*, 9 November 1998.

P. 180: Office of Technology Assessment report cited in "Local Governments on Safari for Big Game" by Geoffrey Anderson at www.smartgrowth.org.

P. 180: Charles V. Bagli, "Companies Get Second Helping of Tax Breaks," *New York Times*, 17 October 1997.

P. 180: See note to page 50.

P. 180: Greg LeRoy, "No More Candy Store: States and Cities Making Job Subsidies Accountable," Federation for Industrial Retention and Renewal, and Grassroots Policy Project, 1994.

P. 180: Ibid.

P. 180: Ibid.

P. 180: Michael LaFaive, "MEGA Program Shifts Jobs to Where They Are Needed Least," Mackinac Center for Public Policy, 7 April 1999. Internet: www.mackinac.org.

P. 180: See note to page 55.

P. 181: "Political Donors Profiteering in the Name of Economic Stimulus: Stimulus Legislation Is Lobbying Opportunity of a Lifetime, Says Common Cause," 25 October 2001 news release.

P. 181: Ibid.

P. 181: Ibid.

P. 181: Ibid.

P. 181: Ibid.

P. 181: Ibid.

P. 181: Ibid.

P. 181: Ibid.

P. 181: Ibid.

P. 181: See fourth note to page 176.

P. 181: Sarah Anderson and John Cavanagh, "Top 200: The Rise of Corporate Global Power," The Institute for Policy Studies. Internet: www.ips-dc.org.

P. 182: Editorial, "Another Casualty of the Left," *Washington Post*, 15 March 1999.

P. 182: Julian Borger, "For Sale: The Race for the White House," *The Guardian*, London, 7 January 2000.

P. 182: Charles Lewis, *The Buying of the President* (New York: Avon Books, 2000).

CHAPTER 13: UNEQUAL RESPONSIBILITY FOR CRIME

P. 184: *Rachel's Hazardous Waste News* #309, 28 October 1992.

P. 185: Russell Mokhiber and Robert Weissman, "Ball Park Franks Fiasco: 21 Dead, $200,000 Fine," 26 July 2001 for Common Dreams News Center at www.commondreams.org.

P. 186: Ibid.

CHAPTER 14: UNEQUAL PRIVACY

P. 188: http://computer.idg.net.

P. 189: See last note to page 181.

P. 189: Ibid.

P. 189: Ibid.

P. 189: Ibid.

CHAPTER 15: UNEQUAL CITIZENSHIP AND ACCESS TO THE COMMONS

P. 191: www.cdc.gov.

P. 191: U. S. Census Bureau.

P. 191: www.ilo.org.

P. 191: World Health Organization Web site, June 2001.

P. 192: Ken Belson, "Themes of Gloom and Doom Fill Japanese Bookstores," *New York Times*, 19 November 2001.

P. 192: Thomas Bonczar and Lauren Glaze, U. S. Department of Justice, Bureau of Justice Statistics, Probation and Parole in the United States (Washington, D. C.: U. S. Department of Justice, August 1999), 1.

P. 192: Allen J. Beck, Ph.D., and Paige M. Harrison, U. S. Department of Justice, Bureau of Justice Statistics, Prisoners in 2000 (Washington, D. C.: U. S. Department of Justice, August 2001), 2.

P. 193: U. S. Department of Justice, Bureau of Justice Statistics, Prisoners in 1996 (Washington, D. C.: U. S. Department of Justice, 1997).

P. 193: U. S. Department of Justice, Bureau of Justice Statistics, Sourcebook of Criminal Justice Statistics 1996 (Washington, D. C.: U. S. Department of Justice, 1997), 20; Executive Office of the President, Budget of the United States Government, Fiscal Year 2002 (Washington, D. C.: U. S. Government Printing Office, 2001), 134.

P. 193: Stephen Nathan, "The Prison Industry Goes Global," *Yes!*, Fall 2000.

P. 193: www.doc.state.or.us; www.cdc.gov.

P. 193: February 8, 2002 news release issued by Wackenhut Corporation.

P. 194: Michael Grunwald, "How Enron Sought to Tap the Everglades," *Washington Post*, 8 February 2002.

P. 194: James Flanigan, "Enron Is Blazing New Business Trail," *Houston Chronicle*, 26 January 2001.

P. 194: Ibid.

P. 197: David C. Korten, "Money Versus Wealth," *Yes!*, Spring 1997.

P. 197: Ibid.

P. 198: Maggie McDonald, "International Piracy Rights," review of *Protect or Plunder? Understanding Intellectual Property Rights* by Vandana Shiva, *New Scientist*, 12 January 2002, 23.

P. 198: Ibid.

P. 198: "Patently Rewarding Work," *New Scientist*, 12 January 2002, 50.

P. 198: Ibid, 51.

P. 198: Karen Hoggan, "Neem Tree Patent Revoked," BBC Web site, 11 May 2000. Internet: http://news.bbc.co.uk.

P. 199: www.globalissues.org.

P. 199: David Cay Johnson, "U. S. Companies File in Bermuda to Slash Tax Bills," *New York Times*, 18 February 2002.

P. 200: David Cay Johnston, "Enron's Collapse: The Havens; Enron Avoided Income Taxes in 4 of 5 Years," *New York Times*, 17 January 2002.

P. 200: See note to page 28.

CHAPTER 16: UNEQUAL WEALTH

P. 201: Many of the statistics in this chapter are from Jeff Gates in various sources. Jeff is president of the Shared Capitalism Institute and author of numerous books and articles, all of which I strongly recommend. His Web site is www.sharedcapitalism.org.

P. 202: Harold James, *The End of Globalization: Lessons from the Great Depression* (Harvard University Press, 2001).

P. 202: Robert A. G. Monks and Nell Minow, *Corporate Governance* (Malden: Blackwell Publishers, [1995], 1999) 267.

P. 202: From the map titled "Big Loop" at www.theyrule.net.

P. 204: See last note to page 181.

P. 204: United Nations Conference on Trade and Development report, "Foreign Direct Investment Soars," 18 September 2001.

P. 204: Ibid.

P. 204: See note to page 14.

P. 204: Ibid.

P. 204: Ibid.

P. 204: Ibid.

P. 205: "Working America: The Current Economic Situation" by the AFL-CIO. Internet: www.aflcio.org.

P. 205: Ibid.

P. 205: See second note to page 37.

P. 205: Ibid.

P. 205: "Human Development Report 2000," United Nations Development Program at www.undp.org.

P. 206: Oswald Spengler, *The Decline of the West* (Oxford University Press).

P. 206: George Soros, *The Crisis of Global Capitalism* (PublicAffairs Publishers, 1998).

P. 206: See first note to page 143.

P. 206: Sharon Beder, *Global Spin: The Corporate Assault on Environmentalism* (Slow Food, 2002); David Helvarg, *The War Against the Greens: The 'Wise Use' Movement, the New Right, and Anti-Environmental Violence* (San Francisco: Sierra Club Books, 1997); Marshall Clinard, *Corporate Corruption: The Abuse of Power* (Westport: Praeger Publishers, 1990); and Robert W. McChesney, *Rich Media, Poor Democracy: Communication Politics in Dubious Times* (Champaign: University of Illinois Press, 1999).

P. 206: Sir James Goldsmith, *The Trap* (New York: Carroll & Graf, 1994).

P. 207: Marc Bloch, trans. L. A. Manyon, *Feudal Society* (Chicago: University of Chicago Press, 1961).

P. 207: Ibid.

P. 208: Ibid.

P. 209: Statistics from the AFL-CIO Web site: www.aflcio.org.

P. 209: Ibid.

P. 209: "Estimates of Federal Tax Liabilities for Individuals and Families," Congressional Budget Office Memorandum, May 1998, cited by Jeff Gates, *Democracy at Risk* (Cambridge: Perseus Books, 2000).

P. 209: See first note to page 209.

P. 210: National Constitution Center at www.constitutioncenter.org.

P. 210: Ibid.

P. 210: Ibid.

CHAPTER 17: UNEQUAL TRADE

P. 212: Sir James Goldsmith in an interview with Yves Messarovitch, published as *The Trap* (New York: Carroll & Graf, 1994).

P. 215: A more detailed explanation of the concepts in these points are found in *The Trap*.

P. 217: The collapse of "the Asian tigers" also had much to do with IMF structural adjustment programs, according to many commentators.

P. 218: "An Ecological-Economic Assessment of Deregulation of International Commerce under GATT" by Herman Daly and Robert Goodland, World Bank, Washington, D. C., 1992, quoted in *The Trap* by Sir James Goldsmith.

P. 220: www.aflcio.org.

CHAPTER 18: UNEQUAL MEDIA

P. 225: Many sources say the correct quote is, "Freedom of the press is guaranteed only to those who own one," but the point is the same either way.

P. 226: Maureen Dowd, "The Axis of No Access" *New York Times*, 13 February 2002.

P. 226: Ben H. Bagdikian, *The Media Monopoly* (Beacon Press, 1997, 2000).

P. 226: Ibid, 2000 edition.

P. 227: Ibid, 2000 edition.

P. 227: www.motherjones.com.

P. 227: Ibid.

P. 227: www.jmm.com.

P. 227: This issue of giant ISPs selling speed of access to commercial sites and its consequences for the "commons of ideas" represented by the Internet is well-discussed by Lawrence Lessig, *The Future of Ideas* (Random House, 2002).

P. 228: From an e-mail received by the author.

P. 229: See first note to page 13.

P. 229: www.fair.org.

P. 229: http://people-press.org.

P. 230: http://fecweb1.fec.gov.

P. 230: www.michaelmoore.com.

P. 233: From a position paper by the National Nutritional Foods Association at www.nnfa.org.

P. 233: The history of the event is on the Web at www.foxBGHsuit.com.

P. 233: *Adbusters*, 14 November 1996.

P. 234: www.adbusters.org.

P. 234: www.ejnet.org.

P. 235: Neil Hickey, "Unshackling Big Media," *Columbia Journalism Review*, May/June 2001.

P. 235: Kathleen Abernathy, "a longtime Telco lobbyist" according to *Broadcast and Cable* magazine, 21 May 2001; and Michael Copps, a former lobbyist for a trade group and a Fortune 500 plastics company.

P. 235: Marsha Macbride.

P. 235: Susan Eid is a former lobbyist for MediaOne Group.

P. 235: Tom Wolzien of Sanford C. Bernstein and Co., quoted in "More Media Freedoms Seen Under New FCC Chairman" by Tim Jones, Tribune Media Writer, *Chicago Tribune*, 24 January 2001.

P. 235: Janine Jackson, "Their Man in Washington," FAIR Extra!, October 2001 at www.fair.org.

P. 235: Ibid.

P. 236: David Wessel, "U. S. Stock Holdings Rose 20 Percent in 1998," *Wall Street Journal*, 15 March 1999.

P. 236: See first note to page 13.

P. 236: Ibid.

P. 236: See note to page 49.

P. 237: Anne E. Becker, M.D.; Rebecca A. Burwell, M.Phil.; Stephen Gilman, B.A.; David B. Herzog, M.D.; and Paul Hamburg, M.D., "The Impact of Television on Disordered Eating in Fiji," a paper presented at the 2000 meeting of the International Conference on Eating Disorders in New York by Anne E. Becker, M.D., Ph.D.

CHAPTER 19: UNEQUAL INFLUENCE

P. 238: *Federal Election Commission v. Massachusetts Citizens for Life, Inc.* [479 U. S. 238 (1986)].

P. 238: Michael T. McMenamin and Walter McNamara, *Milking the Public* (Nelson Hall, 1980).

P. 238: Ibid.

P. 239: www.notmilk.com.

P. 239: Thom Hartmann, *Thom Hartmann's Complete Guide to ADHD* (Underwood Books, 2001).

P. 239: "CRS Report for Congress," Order Code RL30942, by Wayne Clifton Riddle, Specialist in Education Finance, Domestic Social Policy Division.

P. 242: From an interview with the author, 18 February 2002.

P. 242: Ibid.

P. 242: www.txpeer.org.

P. 243: www.mapcruzin.com.

P. 243: Ibid.

CHAPTER 20: CAPITALISTS AND AMERICANS SPEAK OUT FOR COMMUNITY

P. 245: George Soros, "The Capitalist Threat," *The Atlantic Monthly*, February 1997.

P. 245: George Soros, "The Free Market for Hope," *Newsweek*, October 2001. The text of the article can be found at www.soros.org.

P. 246: Joseph Stiglitz, "Thanks For Nothing," *The Atlantic Monthly*, October 2001.

CHAPTER 21: END CORPORATE PERSONHOOD

P. 251: Arizona Statute, I-29 (definitions).

P. 251: *Frontier Pacific Insurance Company v. Federal Trade Commission*, 1998.

P. 254: Comments by Thomas Linzey, published as "Turning the Tables on Pennsylvania Agri-Corporations" in *Defying Corporations, Defining Democracy*, ed. Dean Ritz, published by POCLAD (Apex Press, 2001).

CHAPTER 22: A NEW ENTREPRENEURIAL BOOM

P. 263: Statistics for 1998, the most recent year available in early 2002. From "The State of Small Business: A Report by the President," published in 1999 by the U. S. Government Printing Office.

P. 264: Taitlin Quistgaard, "The New Economy: Microlending in Bangladesh," *Wired News*, 19 February 1998.

P. 264: E. N. Wolff, "Recent Trends in Wealth Ownership" (New York: New York University, a paper for the conference "Benefits and Mechanisms for Spreading Asset Ownership in the United States," 10–12 December 1998).

P. 264: "Estimates of Federal Tax Liabilities for Individuals and Families by Income Category and Family Type for 1995 and 1999" (Washington, D. C.: Congressional Budget Office Memorandum, May 1998).

P. 264: www.census.gov ("income" at Table H-2).

P. 264: Reported in *The Economist*, 16–22 June 2001.

P. 264: "Executive Pay Special Report," *Business Week*, 9 April 2001, cited by Jeff Gates in the January 2002 issue of *Tikkun* magazine.

P. 264: S. Claessens, S. Djankov, and L. H. P. Lang, "Who Controls East Asian Corporations?" (Washington, D. C.: The World Bank, 1999).

P. 265: United Nations Human Development Report 1998, 2.

P. 265: L. Brown et.al., "State of the World 2001" (Washington, D. C.: Worldwatch Institute, 2001).

P. 266: Organization for Economic Cooperation and Development.

P. 266: W. Bello, "The WTO: Serving the Wealthy, Not the Poor," in *Does Globalization Help the Poor?* (Washington, D. C.: International Forum on Globalization, 2001), 27.

P. 266: The IMF estimates that the amount in offshore tax havens grew from $3.5 trillion in 1992 to $4.8 trillion in 1997. Other estimates, also badly dated, put the amount as high as $13.7 trillion. See D. Farah, "A New Wave of Island Investing," *Washington Post National Weekly Review* (18 October 1999): 15; and A. Cowell and E. L. Andrews, "Undercurrents at a Safe Harbor," *New York Times* (24 September 1999): C1.

P. 266: "Small Business and the Corporation," U. S. Department of State, International Information Programs.

P. 266: Ibid.

P. 267: Ibid.

P. 267: Ibid.

P. 267: From "The State of Small Business: A Report by the President," published in 1999 by the U. S. Government Printing Office.

P. 267: Cited from the U. S. Small Business Administration's Web site, www.sba.gov.

P. 267: www.bls.gov.

P. 267: "Annual Report on Small Business and Competition," U. S. Small Business Administration, most current document in 2002 written in 1998, Government Printing Office.

P. 267: Ibid.

P. 267: Ibid.

CHAPTER 23: A DEMOCRATIC MARKETPLACE

P. 269: US Supreme Court Justice Brandeis in his dissenting opinion on the 1933 *Liggett v. Lee* case that—based on the *Santa Clara* headnotes—gave chain stores equal tax rights under the Fourteenth Amendment to "compete" against small, locally owned retailers, and led in part to the loss by local communities of their abilities and rights to regulate chain stores and to have a say in the size of businesses operating in their communities.

P. 271: Paul Hawken, *The Ecology of Commerce* (HarperCollins, 1994).

P. 272: Wisconsin Law, Section 4489a. [Sec. 1, ch. 492, 1905].

P. 273: Jerry Brown, *Dialogues* (Berkeley Hills Books, 1998).

P. 273: Letter from Thomas Jefferson to Dr. Walter Jones, written at Monticello, 2 January 1814.

CHAPTER 25: OUR FIRST STEPS FORWARD

P. 280: Lawrence Mitchell, in a discussion with the author, February 2002.

P. 280: Lawrence Mitchell, quoted in *Corporate Crime Reporter*, 3 December 2001.

P. 280: Richard Cohen, "Enron: No Taxes . . ." *Washington Post*, 21 January 2002.

P. 280: Quoting a national radio talk-show host I heard in autumn 2001.

P. 280: John C. Stauber and Sheldon Rampton, *Toxic Sludge is Good for You* (Common Courage Press, 1995). This is an excellent book about the chemical industry's P. R. machine.

P. 280: Abraham Lincoln, in a speech given on February 22, 1861 in Independence Hall while traveling to his first inauguration as President.

P. 281: *Amending America* by Richard B. Bernstein is a brilliant book on the process.

P. 283: www.alastairmcintosh.com.

P. 284: From a lecture he read at the Masonic Temple, Boston, January 1842.

P. 285: Ibid.

P. 285: President John F. Kennedy, Inaugural Address, 20 January 1961.

RESOURCES

Here are a few organizations involved in working to redefine corporate personhood and encourage a revitalization or renewal of democracy. You can find many, many more on the links page for this book from www.thomhartmann.com or www.unequalprotection.com.

Adbusters
www.adbusters.org

Common Dreams
www.commondreams.org

Community Environmental Legal Defense Fund (CELDF)
2859 Scotland Road
Chambersburg, PA 17201
(717) 709-0457
www.celdf.org
info@celdf.org

Program on Corporations, Law and Democracy (POCLAD)
P. O. Box 246
South Yarmouth, MA 02664
(508) 398-1145
www.poclad.org

Public Citizen
1600 20th St. NW
Washington, DC 20009
(202) 588-1000
www.citizen.org

Public Information Network
www.endgame.org

The Tikkun Community
2107 Van Ness Avenue
San Francisco, CA 94104
(415) 575-1200
www.tikkun.org

They Rule
www.theyrule.net

Women's International League for Peace and Freedom
Campaign to Challenge Corporate Power
1213 Race Street
Philadelphia, PA 19107
(215) 563-7110
www.wilpf.org

ACKNOWLEDGMENTS

I am deeply indebted to a number of people for their help in the creation of this book. Those who particularly helped form and organize my thinking on the subject include David Korten, Richard Grossman of POCLAD, and Thomas Linzey of CELDF. Richard B. Bernstein provided me with many excellent leads, and I was challenged to dig deeper and deeper by our correspondences. Dave deBronkart, who has helped edit several of my books, helped this one into its final form, and Neil Wertheimer helped give it birth and structure.

So many writers I know these days complain that their editors no longer edit, but that was not my experience, for which I'm very grateful to Rodale and to their and my editor, Troy Juliar. Stephanie Tade, Tom Mulderick, Kelly Schmidt, Leslie Schneider, Dana Bacher, and Cindy Ratzlaff of Rodale helped move this book along as well—thanks!

Paul Hannam, Tim King, Michael Pottinger, and Rob Kall provided particularly valuable input and suggestions. Thanks to Jayne Kennedy for her research work, to Paul Donovan and Marge Zunder for helping me track down arcane documents in the library in the Vermont Supreme Court building, and to Jane Anne Morris for sharing her illuminating documentation of former laws in the state of Wisconsin.

Daniel Brannen of CELDF spent many long hours with law books from every state in the union in putting together the proposed ordinances and constitutional amendments in this book, for which I am very grateful. My agent, Bill Gladstone, helped move this project along and provided valuable input. Special thanks to Michael Kinder, who waded through piles of 19th-century documents in the Library of Congress to find the personal correspondences of Morrison R. Waite and J. C. Bancroft Davis that were pivotal to a chapter of this book, to Paula Bennet, who provided valuable insights into the women's suffrage movement, and to Kathy Roeder of the AFL-CIO, who took the time to track down details for me and return my calls.

I'm very grateful to Jock Gill, Jack Rieley, and Jaye Mueller, who often pointed me in the right directions and kept me focused on track and on issue, and to Judy Kahrl, who brought to my attention the important difference between citizenship and personhood in relation to the Fourteenth Amendment. William Meyers has done us all a great service by writing and publishing in the public domain his paper "Santa Clara Blues" on the Internet at www.iiipublishing.com, and I gratefully thank him for the added permission to reprint. Jeff Gates also gave me the valuable gift of allowing republication of more than just a "fair use" portion of his words, and I both thank him and recommend to you his several books and his Web site at www.sharedcapitalism.org.

Chanin Rotz sent articles from the *Fulton County News*, Roger C. Parker gave valuable editorial suggestions and encouragement, and Scott Berg and Bob Koski were particularly important sources of information and reference. Thanks to Booth Gunter and Shannon Little of Public Citizen, and B. J. Kinkade for sharing her story with me. And the folks at Bear Pond Books and Montpelier's Kellogg-Hubbard Library were very helpful in my early research efforts. Thank you all.

Throughout the research and writing of this book, I've tried to be as clear and accurate as possible. No doubt there are errors in a work of this size, and the responsibility for them is mine, and not that of the people I thanked above.

INDEX

Boldface page references indicate quotations used as an introduction at the beginning of each part or chapter.

H

T

Y